A Feminist Companion to the Acts of the Apostles

A Feminist Companion to the Acts of the Apostles

edited by
Amy-Jill Levine
with Marianne Blickenstaff

THE
PILGRIM
PRESS
Cleveland

BS
2625.52
.F46
2004

Published in the USA and Canada (only) by
The Pilgrim Press
700 Prospect Avenue East, Cleveland, Ohio 44115-1100, USA
www.thepilgrimpress.com

© T&T Clark International, 2004

This edition of this work is published by arrangement with T&T Clark International, an imprint of Continuum. All rights reserved. No part of this publication may be reproduced, stored in a retrieval system, or transmitted in any form or by any means, electronic, mechanical, photocopying, recording or otherwise, without prior permission of the publisher.

The Pilgrim Press edition published 2004. All rights reserved.

Printed in Great Britain by MPG Books Ltd

ISBN 0-8298-1657-7

CONTENTS

Preface   vii
Acknowledgments   viii
Abbreviations   ix
List of Contributors   xii

AMY-JILL LEVINE
   Introduction   1

JANICE CAPEL ANDERSON
   Reading Tabitha: A Feminist Reception History   22

BEVERLY ROBERTS GAVENTA
   What Ever Happened to Those Prophesying Daughters?   49

MUSIMBI KANYORO
   Thinking Mission in Africa   61

BARBARA E. REID, OP
   The Power of the Widows and How to Suppress It (Acts 6.1–7)   71

KATHY CHAMBERS
   'Knock, Knock—Who's There?' Acts 12.6–17 as a Comedy of Errors   89

ROBERT M. PRICE
   Rhoda and Penelope: Two More Cases of Luke's Suppression of Women   98

DENNIS R. MACDONALD
   Lydia and her Sisters as Lukan Fictions   105

SHELLY MATTHEWS
   Elite Women, Public Religion, and Christian Propaganda in Acts 16 111

F. SCOTT SPENCER
   Women of 'the Cloth' in Acts: Sewing the Word   134

JAMES M. ARLANDSON
   Lifestyles of the Rich and Christian: Women, Wealth, and Social Freedom   155

VIRGINIA BURRUS and KAREN TORJESEN
   Afterword to 'Household Management and Women's Authority'   171

JEFFREY L. STALEY
  Changing Woman: Toward a Postcolonial Postfeminist Interpretation of
  Acts 16.6–40   177

TODD PENNER and CAROLINE VANDER STICHELE
  Gendering Violence: Patterns of Power and Constructs of Masculinity in
  the Acts of the Apostles   193

Bibliography   210
Index of References   232
Index of Authors   238

Preface

A Feminist Companion to the Acts of the Apostles is the ninth volume in a new series with excellent precedent. These volumes on the texts and history of Christian origins adopt the model established by Athalya Brenner, editor of the enormously successful Feminist Companion to the Bible series. This sister series to the FCB, originally published by Sheffield Academic Press, marks an important new dimension in T&T Clark International's list of titles in the areas of feminist hermeneutics and theology, and its contents underline the extent to which feminist critique is established as a core discipline of biblical, historical, and theological research.

In addition to publishing 'classics' in feminist analysis (primarily from sources either out of print or difficult to find), the series invited authors of such works to reconsider their views, make alterations where required, and track how their feminist sensibilities had developed. The series also sought contributions from biblical scholars not known for feminist interests or even, in some cases, sympathies: write a 'feminist' piece, they were exhorted; when a few demurred ('I don't "do" feminist critique'; 'I don't know what feminist critique is'), the response was to the effect of, 'You should find out about it; you should engage it; if you don't like it, explain why; if you do, use it and, better, assign it to your classes.' This process also yielded a number of contributors.

Letters of invitation to contribute to this series went well beyond the scholars known from explicitly feminist or women-identified collections or from books and articles with 'feminist' in the title. Authors already established as having feminist interests were asked to suggest names of newer voices, and so interpreters at the beginning of their academic careers joined their senior colleagues in the pages of the volumes. Invitations went beyond North America and Western Europe to East and South Asia, Africa, Eastern Europe, Central and South America, and Australia/New Zealand. For either new or previously published work not in English, Vanderbilt Divinity School/The Carpenter Program in Religion, Gender, and Sexuality provided funds for translation.

ACKNOWLEDGMENTS

The editors and publisher are grateful to Sheffield Academic Press (an imprint of Continuum) for 'Reading Tabitha: A Feminist Reception History', by Janice Capel Anderson, from E.S. Malbon and E.V. McKnight (eds.), *The New Literary Criticism and the New Testament* (1994); Stanford University Press for 'Elite Women, Public Religion, and Christian Propaganda in Acts 16', by Shelly Matthews, in *First Converts: Rich Pagan Women and the Rhetoric of Mission in Early Judaism and Christianity* (2001); and *International Review of Mission* for 'Thinking Mission in Africa', by Musimbi Kanyoro (1998).

ABBREVIATIONS

AB	Anchor Bible
ABD	David Noel Freedman (ed.), *The Anchor Bible Dictionary* (6 vols.; New York: Doubleday, 1992)
AJP	*American Journal of Philology*
ATR	*Anglican Theological Review*
BAG	Walter Bauer, William F. Arndt, and F. William Gingrich, *A Greek–English Lexicon of the New Testament and Other Early Christian Literature* (Chicago: University of Chicago Press, 1957)
BAGD	Walter Bauer, William F. Arndt, F. William Gingrich, and Frederick W. Danker, *A Greek–English Lexicon of the New Testament and Other Early Christian Literature* (Chicago: University of Chicago Press, 2nd edn, 1979)
BDAG	Walter Bauer, Frederick W. Danker, William F. Arndt, and F. William Gingrich, *A Greek–English Lexicon of the New Testament and Other Early Christian Literature* (Chicago: University of Chicago Press, 3rd edn, 2000)
BDF	F. Blass, A. DeBrunner, and Robert W. Funk, *A Greek Grammar of the New Testament and Other Early Christian Literature* (Chicago: University of Chicago Press, 1961)
BibInt	*Biblical Interpretation*
BJS	Brown Judaic Studies
BR	*Bible Review*
BS	The Biblical Seminar
BTB	*Biblical Theology Bulletin*
BTC	Bible in the Twenty-first Century
BZNW	Beihefte zur *Zeitschrift für die neutestamentliche Wissenschaft*
CBQ	*Catholic Biblical Quarterly*
CIL	*Corpus inscriptionum latinarum*
ConB	Coniectanea biblica
ConBNT	Coniectanea biblica, New Testament
CP	*Classical Philology*
EDNT	*Exegetical Dictionary of the New Testament*
EH	Europäische Hochschulschriften
ESEC	Emory Studies in Early Christianity
ETL	*Ephemerides theologicae lovanienses*
FCNT	Feminist Companion to the New Testament and Early Christian Writings
FRLANT	Forschungen zur Religion und Literatur des Alten und Neuen Testaments
HDR	Harvard Dissertations in Religion
HSCP	*Harvard Studies in Classical Philology*

HTKNT	Herders theologischer Kommentar zum Neuen Testament
HTR	*Harvard Theological Review*
HTS	Harvard Theological Studies
IBC	Interpretation Bible Commentary
ICC	International Critical Commentary
ILS	H. Dessau, *Inscriptiones latinae selectae* (Berlin, 1892–1916)
Int	*Interpretation*
JBL	*Journal of Biblical Literature*
JFSR	*Journal of Feminist Studies in Religion*
JJS	*Journal of Jewish Studies*
JSNT	*Journal for the Study of the New Testament*
JSNTSup	*Journal for the Study of the New Testament*, Supplement Series
JSOT	*Journal for the Study of the Old Testament*
JSOTSup	*Journal for the Study of the Old Testament,* Supplement Series
JTS	*Journal of Theological Studies*
KJV	King James Version
LCL	Loeb Classical Library
LS	*Louvain Studies*
LSJ	H. G. Liddell and R. Scott, *A Greek-English Lexicon* (rev. edn.) ed. H. Jones and R. McKenzie, 1968
LXX	Septuagint
MELUS	*Multi-Ethnic Literature of the United States*
NIB	*New International Bible*
NovT	*Novum Testamentum*
NovTSup	Novum Testamentum Supplement Series
NRSV	New Revised Standard Version
NTS	*New Testament Studies*
OBT	Overtures to Biblical Theology
PW	A. Pauly - G. Wissowa *Real Encyclopädie der classischen Altertumswissenschaft* (49 vols.; Stuttgart: J. B. Metzler, 1894–1978)
RB	*Revue biblique*
SBL	Society of Biblical Literature
SBLDS	SBL Dissertation Series
SBLEJL	SBL Early Judaism and its Literature
SBLMS	SBL Monograph Series
SBLSP	SBL Seminar Papers
SBLSS	SBL Semeia Studies
SBLSyms	SBL Symposium Series
SCJ	Studies in Christianity and Judaism
SNTSMS	Society for New Testament Studies Monograph Series
SJT	*Scottish Journal of Theology*
TBT	*The Bible Today*, Collegeville, MN
TDNT	Gerhard Kittel and Gerhard Friedrich (eds.), *Theological Dictionary of the New Testament* (trans. Geoffrey W. Bromiley; 10 vols.; Grand Rapids: Eerdmans, 1964–)
THKNT	Theologischer Handkommentar zum Neuen Testament
VCSup	Vigiliae christianae Supplement

WBC	Word Biblical Commentary
WUNT	Wissenschaftliche Untersuchungen zum Neuen Testament
ZNW	*Zeitschrift für die neutestamentliche Wissenschaft*

LIST OF CONTRIBUTORS

Janice Capel Anderson, University of Idaho, Moscow, ID, USA
James M. Arlandson, Southern California College, Costa Mesa, CA, USA
Virginia Burrus, Drew University, Madison, NJ, USA
Kathy Chambers, Vanderbilt University, Nashville, TN, USA
Beverly Roberts Gaventa, Princeton Theological Seminary, Princeton, NJ, USA
Musimbi Kanyoro, World YWCA, Ancienne, Switzerland
Dennis R. MacDonald, Claremont School of Theology, Claremont, CA, USA
Shelly Matthews, Furman University, Greenville, SC, USA
Todd C. Penner, Austin College, Sherman, TX, USA
Robert M. Price, Drew University, Madison, NJ, USA
Barbara E. Reid, OP, Catholic Theological Union, Chicago, IL, USA
F. Scott Spencer, Baptist Theological Seminary, Richmond, VA, USA
Jeffrey L. Staley, Pacific Lutheran University, Tacoma, WA, USA
Karen Torjesen, Claremont Graduate University, Claremont, CA, USA
Caroline Vander Stichele, University of Amsterdam, Amsterdam, the Netherlands

INTRODUCTION

AMY-JILL LEVINE

Like the Gospel of Luke, the Acts of the Apostles has its feminist advocates and its feminist detractors. Acts can be read as promoting women's discipleship (indeed, the only woman explicitly called a 'disciple', Tabitha, appears in this volume), leadership roles in the nascent church, prophetic voice, and public spirit. The text opens with Joel's exultant message of prophesying women; the mother of John Mark emerges as the leader of a house-church; Rhoda the slave calls prevailing social norms into question by recognizing a truth her masters fail to see; Tabitha promotes a community of self-sufficient women; Lydia prevails upon Paul to remain with her and so facilitates the conversion of Europe; Philip's virgin daughters are recognized as possessing prophetic voices; even Sapphira is recognized as having fiduciary responsibilities. Yet Acts can also be classified as a systemic dismantling of any authority women in the early church may have had: the prophesying daughters are silenced; widows become victims in need of rescue by the male leaders of the church; the mission and expansion of the church becomes the paradigm for colonialist practices; slaves—especially female slaves—are portrayed as annoying at best; the chain of command is restricted to men.

Complicating any assessment of Acts is the question of approach: how much of the work is reporting of history and how much based on classical templates from Homer or the *Bacchae* or Menander? Is women's public participation in religious activities shameful or commendable, or a bit of both? Is Acts to be assessed according to interpretations of distinct pericopae or through a thorough reading that begins at Lk. 1.1 and continues through Paul's Roman mission? Presuppositions and experiences also impact understanding of the Acts of the Apostles: is the volume a promotion of empire, or is it counter to it? Does it promote Christian hegemony, or does its mention of numerous ethnic groups and nations add a multicultural voice to early Christianity?

As with the Gospel of Luke, so with Acts, a 'double message'[1] emerges: the volume both liberates and constrains, both inspires and disturbs. What one reader will find to be historically credible another will regard as a fictionalized trope or the airy stuff of legend. While it is evident that Acts has been used to promote harmful agendas, be they sexist or anti-Jewish or colonialist, readers will continue to debate whether the cues for such conclusions are embedded in the text or spring from the minds and experiences of the interpreters.

The articles in this volume, as with all the Feminist Companions to the New Testament and Early Christian Writings, range from explicitly feminist approaches to studies that, while not 'feminist' as many might define the term, offer materials

---

1 Turid Karlsen Seim, *The Double Message: Patterns of Gender in Luke–Acts* (Studies of the New Testament and its World; Edinburgh: T. & T. Clark, 1994).

readers interested in feminist analysis have considered and should continue to consider. The opening essay is a reprint of the first major explicitly feminist study of Acts; several of the contributions represent work developed during the writing of dissertations; others are reconsiderations of or addenda to earlier studies. Some proceed from historical questions of sources, templates, tropes, and conventions; others draw upon personal experience and select intertexts; some focus on a specific incident or character, others find categories, such as widows, 'women of the cloth', and slaves, helpful heuristics for understanding Luke's construction of gender. Recent PhDs and graduate students and scholars whose publications are primarily outside the West or the English-speaking academy join together with established faculty to display the complex and often contradictory messages that Acts conveys and readers receive.

Janice Capel Anderson begins both her 1994 'feminist reader-response' to Acts 9.36–42 and so this volume by identifying elements that by the mid-1990s came to epitomize feminist concerns and by explaining how such elements serve liberative purposes. First, the author's identification by 'social location' defined according to categories of ethnicity/race, age, class, sexual orientation, religion/denomination, gender, and profession (today, physical condition is sometimes included) precludes any claims to 'true' readings based on objectivity and thus prevents both hegemonic interpretations and the foreclosure of new voices. Second, all forms of social inequity, themselves typically seen as having a gendered component such as Capel Anderson's 'male domination' along with 'patriarchal', 'kyriarchal', and 'phallic' elements, embraces and even commends the reader's necessary subjectivity as well as resistance to codes not her own. Third, recognition of reading as a political and therefore subversive act (readers are presumed to know what the systemic and pervasive structures of inequity are) moves biblical studies from the 'what' to the 'so what'. Finally, Judith Fetterley's description of 'immasculation'—the process by which women identify with select male characters in patriarchal texts despite often being co-opted into rejecting the texts' depictions of women characters—becomes the site of protest. Readers can become adept at recognizing narrative strategies that promote particular values and so consciously choose to accept or deny them; the choices will vary both among readers and even in relation to a single text. Anderson thus offers a 'dual hermeneutic' that names the text's complicity with systems of oppression even as it locates within the text alternative possibilities.

These programmatic considerations apply to all forms of analysis, as Anderson demonstrates by her feminist take on what might seem a quite old-fashioned way of proceeding, namely, through a 'reception history'. But instead of tracing the history of interpretation via the male line (mostly nineteenth- and twentieth-century German scholars along with the church 'fathers', Luther, and Calvin), Anderson opens her study to nineteenth-century women as well as to contemporary feminist-identified readers. Along the way, she notes a number of specific observations feminists have productively employed: querying a pericope's name;[2] remarking how certain words trigger inter- and intra-textual forays; observing how autobiographical

---

[2] See Barbara Reid's '"Do You See this Woman?": A Liberative Look at Luke 7.36–50 and Strategies for Reading Other Lukan Stories against the Grain', in A.-J. Levine (ed.), *A Feminist Companion to Luke* (FCNTECW, 3; London: Sheffield Academic Press, 2002), pp. 206–20.

elements in an exegesis can enhance the understanding of a text and how generic classification and method impact interpretive focus; discussing the role of voice and agency; attending to the 'effect' of a narrative on readers and the implications of one's scholarly community (with notices of connections among feminist commentators); acknowledging the problem of feminist anti-Judaism along with the debits as well as possible benefits of essentialist readings; recovering women interpreters from the past; even delineating problems feminist interpreters may face in the tenure process.

I suspect a number of readers today might be less sanguine about the application of each interpretive move, although the moves themselves remain in the feminist thesaurus. For example, an autobiographical approach or emphasis on personal identification can serve to preclude critique: while feminist readers frequently note the failings of earlier studies, and while feminist biblical interpretation is now sufficiently healthy that a party line or group solidarity among all feminist readers is not needed to impact the guild, counters to readings offered by voices previously unheard remain problematic. Next, a feminist reader might claim that all readings derive from social location and therefore all readings are correct; they are what the interpreter has found and so are true to her experience. Such an approach risks devolving into solipsism, and solipsism is no way either to build community or to change normative interpretive patterns. Third, the problem with 'male-stream' or 'patriarchal' or even 'kyriarchal' labels is that a negative male element—the gender is variously constructed, but the connotations of 'male' as opposed to 'female' and so, for many readers, of 'what men do' as opposed to 'what women do'—remains. Thus, the labels reinforce, especially for the neophyte and especially in these days of feminist backlash, the view that 'feminist' means 'hatred or at least distrust of' men even as they risk minimizing or ignoring the experience of non-powerful men.

Even notices of social location can misdirect or frustrate. The categories typically listed are often arbitrary and indistinct (why not mention whether the interpreter has had children, enjoys sex, believes in the divine inspiration of the Scripture, has had a conversion experience, likes weaving, or has ever prepared a dead body for burial?). They are also not usually brought into conversation with the results: how does one's being heterosexual, or middle-class, specifically prompt a question or conclusion? Since readers must therefore make the connections, we are forced into applying the very stereotypes feminist criticism seeks to break ('middle-class, white, Protestant women find important ...') even as we wind up emphasizing the interpreter's background over and against her individual contributions. Complicating these observations are the writings of the contemporary 'feminists' identified by Anderson. The article marvelously summarizes the contributions of, and scholarly dependence among, numerous interpreters, but we are not told their denominations, marital status, or race (in part because some of these women do not provide such information).

In like manner, while Anderson, appropriately concerned not to elide differences among interpreters, acknowledges that one author should be located within 'a nineteenth-century African American AME female evangelistic/sanctification reading community', for white women she is content with the label 'middle-class American Protestant'. When she cannot find specific commentary on her pericope from groups underrepresented (or ignored) by the academic mainstream, she moves to one representative voice's general views on Acts (these views take up more space than the comments on Acts 12 by anyone else cited). 'Difference' remains a political issue, and certain voices not merely become heard in the study but receive a pride of place and even a particularly gentle handling. Why one set of voices is recorded and another not (where are the diverse voices of Asian Evangelicals? Today's 'women's Bible reading' groups? Those who self-identify as widows? Anyone past the time of Luther and Calvin for whom English is not the preferred or native language?) remains another unarticulated concern. Whether this approach is paternalistic (yes, a male-coded term) or, if it is, if it is nevertheless good, remains unacknowledged, let alone explored.

In her concluding paragraphs, Anderson turns to the 'multiple emphases occurring within feminist readings'; her observations not only remain correct but in fact appear prescient. New voices continue to appear as more and more interpreters are drawn to 'feminist' readings, defined in various ways. The so-called 'male-stream' scholars now address feminist concerns; readings from postcolonial perspectives enrich Anderson's points concerning the impact of social location on interpretation; new interests (e.g. medical texts, cultural anthropology, comedic conventions, Homeric models) add new insight. While the story of Tabitha will never—can never—be told in all its possible interpretations, Anderson provides the map to past readings as well as the interpretive keys by which that map can be followed. In so doing, she provides a compass by which future readers can forge their own paths.

Acts would initially seem a welcoming location for such exploration. The work opens with what might be seen as an eschatological-feminist manifesto: sons and daughters, young and old, free and slave, male and female, will all receive the divine Spirit and will all prophesy; that the Gospel of Luke starts with similar promise, as Elizabeth and Mary both appear as Spirit-filled visionaries, heightens the anticipation for gender equity. The problem, for both volumes, is what happens after ch. 2 or, as Beverly Roberts Gaventa phrases the matter, 'What Ever Happened to Those Prophesying Daughters?' The first woman to speak in Acts is Sapphira; her words are lies, and she drops dead. Rhoda proclaims the truth of Peter's release; she is ridiculed. The mantic slavegirl correctly identifies Paul and Silas as 'servants of the Most High God'; she is deemed, at best, as 'annoying'. Prophesying daughters do appear, as Joel 3 and Acts 2 anticipate, in Acts 21, but Luke gives them nothing to say. For Gaventa, this less-than-encouraging list prompts questions not just of Acts' eschatological vision narrowly defined, but more generally of Acts' presentation of women.

Gaventa begins with the 'conventional wisdom', that is, the responses to her question ranging from Eusebius, who reports on the burials of Philip's prophesying virgin daughters, to von Harnack, who combined Acts, the Pauline Epistles and later church tradition to conclude that Philip and his daughters were one of Luke's major sources (he similarly identified Priscilla as a candidate for the author of the Epistle to the Hebrews). Imagination unites with chauvinism as von Harnack goes on to state that Philip's daughters were, although 'altogether wanting in sober-mindedness and credibility' (whether because they were ecstatics, or women, or both), the source of Luke's concern with 'the feminine'. In turn, von Harnack is the source of the convention, still asserted by interpreters of the Third Gospel and Acts, that Luke emphasized Jesus' love for the 'despised'—sinners, Samaritans, and women. Why 'women' should be placed in the category of 'despised' and why Luke's readers would despise Samaritans are questions rarely asked.

The break in such positive and positivistic reading Gaventa traces to the publication of Elisabeth Schüssler Fiorenza's (1983) *In Memory of Her*, and its argument that Luke obscures women's actual roles as church apostles, missionaries, and preachers. Gaventa then details the major feminist studies on Acts, including Mary Rose D'Angelo's thesis, informed by Roman imperial values, that Luke removed reference to women's prophecy and leadership to silence critics of the church and to instruct Christian women as to the boundaries of their roles; Turid Karlsen Seim's delineation of Luke's 'double message' that both grants women independence and relegates them to domestic settings; Ivoni Richter Reimer's more sanguine notices of independent women in Acts who head house-churches and are involved in mission. Gaventa also references the important works of James Arlandson on women, class, and society in Luke–Acts, Robert Price on the widow traditions, and Scott Spencer on widows and working women.[3] The section concludes with the different readings of Jane Schaberg and Gail O'Day. In *The Women's Bible Commentary* entry on 'Gospel of Luke', Schaberg classifies the text as 'perhaps the most dangerous in the Bible' as it excludes women from power and responsibility; in the same volume's entry on 'Acts of the Apostles', O'Day remarks on the central roles women play in Luke's second narrative. There is thus no consensus on the question of Acts and women, and even von Harnack's blithe reconstruction still informs scholarship.

By inquiring into the presentations of women in literature contemporary with Acts, of men in Acts itself, and of women and men together in the larger narrative, Gaventa seeks answers the positivistic historiography associated with von Harnack could not yield. For her first inquiry, Gaventa turns to the *Roman Antiquities* of Dionysius of Halicarnassus and Chariton's novel *Callirhoe*. In the former, women function primarily as wives and daughters; their sexuality is commodified; rarely do they engage in direct discourse; the murderous Tullia and the noble Veturia do issue lengthy remarks, but their casting is stereotypical. Conversely, Callirhoe, who is drop-dead (literally) gorgeous as well as virtuous, is at the center of Chariton's plot. The women in Acts conform to neither pattern: they do not issue speeches; their sexuality is of limited concern save for Luke's interest in categories of virgin and widow; their physical attributes and even their virtues are of no concern. Most notable: many act independently of male characters.

With regard to the presentation of male characters, Gaventa recognizes the fluidity in antiquity of 'gender' categorization; slippage from the 'male' virtues of reason and self-control effeminates the male character, but no such effemination marks Acts' Peter, who boldly proclaims his message and unhesitatingly leads the early church. Conversely, the Third Gospel's Peter is by no means a paragon of self-mastery: he denies Jesus three times despite earlier protestations of loyalty, and Luke never provides him a scene of repentance. Gaventa next finds the Ethiopian eunuch

---

3 That Acts has prompted the greatest number of sustained, explicitly feminist and feminist-informed work by men has various explanations, including the utilitarian point that Acts has lots of stories about women that have not received much critical attention and so are open to creative work, and the possible factor that Acts—like Revelation (which in the 1970s received a disproportionate amount of sustained attention from feminist readers)—is 'less important' to the church and scholarship than, say, the Pauline Epistles or the Gospels.

outside gender norms and does remark that in antiquity eunuchs were regarded with ridicule. Yet this eunuch may be an exception via his exotic markers: he is an officer of a queen (another bending of gender), well-off, literate, with freedom of travel and the means to engage it, and from Ethiopia (i.e., a 'foreign' land but one nevertheless associated with power, as the military campaign planned by Nero against Meroe indicates). No disempowered man, the Ethiopian holds the subject position in relation to Philip and, given Isaiah's fulfillment citation, he is again accorded a position of honor. Paul of Acts starts out as ruled by passions, but with conversion comes a virtuous, self-controlled demeanor. Nor, finally, are the men in Acts independent: they are rather, like the women, slaves of God. As Gaventa concludes, 'Luke treats all human characters in relation to that primary agent.'

This primary relation to divinity then explains, at least in part, Luke's lack of attention to those prophesying daughters. Luke does discuss some women who help to fulfill Joel's prediction—the women are not the possessions of men; they are not classified according to physical appearance; they display the virtues of generosity and loyalty; they offer instruction and possess prophetic gifts. They are not deliberately removed from the narrative because Luke is a misogynist or fears repercussions from a more conservative pagan environment. They are simply of no more concern to him than the fate of Matthias or the Hellenists appointed to wait tables. For Gaventa, the news is ultimately good: because the divine promises are continually being fulfilled, those in Joel will eventually find their turn as well.

The Pentecost scene that sparked Gaventa's question inspires the next essay, Musimbi Kanyoro's 'Thinking Mission in Africa'. In an effort to supply the Feminist Companion series with pluriform perspectives, letters of invitation were by no means limited to contributors known from explicitly feminist or women-identified collections, such as the two volumes of *Searching the Scriptures*[4] and the *Women's Bible Commentary*,[5] or from writings with 'feminist' in the title. As the preface notes, established authors were asked to suggest names of newer voices and those more familiar to theological or evangelical rather than biblical studies. The series deliberately sought contributions from men not known for feminist interests or even, in some cases, sympathies: write a 'feminist' piece, they were exhorted; when a few demurred ('I don't "do" feminist critique'; 'I don't know what feminist critique is'), the response was to the effect of, 'You should find out about it; you should engage it; if you don't like it, explain why; if you do, use it and, better, assign it to your classes.' For either new or previously published work not in English, Vanderbilt Divinity School/The Carpenter Program in Religion, Gender, and Sexuality provided funds for translation. Finally, the series deliberately sought voices from East and South Asia, Africa, Eastern Europe, Central and South America, and Australia/New Zealand.

Although Musimbi Kanyoro was unable to write a new piece for the series, she did offer the text of a lecture, which appears here in edited form. Focusing on women's missionary roles in African contexts, Kanyoro bridges numerous communities: the Netherlands Reformed Church and the African mission, Nairobi

---

4 E. Schüssler Fiorenza (ed.), *Searching the Scriptures*. I. *A Feminist Introduction* (New York: Crossroad, 1993); II. *A Feminist Commentary* (New York: Crossroad, 1994).

5 C.A. Newsom and S.H. Ringe (eds.), *The Women's Bible Commentary* (Louisville, KY: Westminster/John Knox Press, 1992; expanded edn, 1998).

and Geneva, Jerusalem and Rome. Taking neither a sentimental nor a cynical view of mission—postcolonial insight eliminates the former, personal experience the latter—Kanyoro reveals the complications inherent both in the term 'mission' and in evangelizing practices. She rejects the common understandings that mission requires traveling to 'other' places and witnessing to 'other' people and that it positions individuals in mutually exclusive roles of giver (of good news, of medicine, of money) and receiver (seen as ignorant, sick, and poor). Instead, she begins her understanding with the more complex, interrelated picture she finds in Acts, a picture that insists, 'every believer is obligated to share'.

Kanyoro moves between historical-critical data, such as how Acts can be understood in light of Rome's imperial power and the destruction of the Jerusalem Temple, to pastoral interests such as the necessity of trust, hope, and patience, self-examination and repentance, and the need to carve out space and time for the entry of the Spirit. Her experiences with the communication difficulties created by Africa's numerous languages, difficulties exacerbated by tribalism and nationalism, gloss the Pentecost scene in a profound way: whereas the West might want to celebrate diversity, Kanyoro recognizes the need for unity or at least a bridge that connects those of different ages, genders, ethnicities, and classes. Given the AIDS epidemic on the continent, increasing debt-based economies, illiteracy and poverty, civil wars and genocides, such bridges are essential. For Kanyoro, the bridge is the Gospel message that, as Acts demonstrates, crosses all divisions.

This is no naïve vision. Kanyoro insists that the church not merely tend the wounded but stop the war, and that can only be done by speaking up and acting—at the risk of one's own life. Testimony must be made before 'governors and kings' (Acts 25.1–12; 26); martyrdom remains a real possibility (Acts 7) as does persecution of the church (Acts 8.1–3). Personal security must be sacrificed for the sake of social change, for only by acting does the church gain credibility. For Kanyoro, African women are 'the foundation of hope in church and society' although cultural customs both indigenous and colonial create another gap, this one between the promise of the church and its treatment of its women members. Ecclesial and political leaders do not address crimes committed against women, lack of maternal health care, the destructiveness of cliterodectomies, the treating of women as slaves, the denial of women's constitutional rights ... even as they keep women out of decision-making roles in church and society. As she succintly states, 'When we ask for partnership, we get paternalism.' This situation does not, however, prompt Kanyoro to cast women solely as victims. To the contrary, she notes their control of non-monetary transactions and participation in informal cash-economy sectors, their contribution of 80 per cent of the continent's food production, along with their typically unacknowledged work on the domestic scene: child care, health care, home care. These women find their foresisters in Acts: Lydia, who prevails upon Paul; Priscilla, who instructs Apollos; daughters who prophesy; women who risk persecution and even death to preach and act upon their faith. The Board of Mission of the Netherlands Reformed Church, to whom Kanyoro's speech was originally given, should recognize in her voice the fulfillment of Joel's prediction, and will aid her in her goals. Readers of this volume should do the same.

Barbara Reid, like Kanyoro, focuses on the locus of power, its relationship to concern for the poor, and Scripture's potentials for overcoming 'cultural, theological, and social conflict' both in Acts and in the church today. Approaching these matters through a detailed analysis of Acts 6, Reid locates both 'the power of widows' and 'how to suppress it'. Reid, like several of the other contributors to this volume, chooses not to isolate a select pericope; instead, her interest in the widows of Acts 6 leads her to find within Luke–Acts a larger literary pattern concerning women's discipleship, namely, that the seven passages in the Gospel and the two in Acts that recount stories of widows attest to increasing conflict over women's ministry, and Luke takes the side of those who would suppress it in favor of women's more domestic, more traditional roles.

The widows in the Gospel, so Reid argues, do not always correspond to the classic image of the widow as poor, helpless, and lacking social status; they are not linked—as they are frequently in the Pentateuch and Prophetic literature—with orphans or foreigners. The two who fit this picture—the widows of Zarephath and Nain—may even hold some agency: although granting that Luke sees these women as politically nonthreatening, Reid compares them to the Madres de la Plaza de Mayo. By their presence, they call men with power to action. The other widows in the Gospel are less conventional. The first, Anna, models the fasting and prayer that will be practiced by Jesus' own disciples; she functions as a temple prophet, and Reid notes the 'kind of power it takes for a young widow to decide to exercise a countercultural ministry and then to remain faithful to this for 84 years'. But, as Gaventa's article suggests, in contrast to Simeon and Agabus and numerous other male prophets throughout the two volumes, Anna is accorded no direct discourse, audience, or response. The 'widow pursuing justice' (Lk. 18.1–8) is neither passive nor incapable: like Ruth and Tamar, she does what is necessary for her own salvation. Reid goes so far as to compare her to Jesus, whose 'seeming helplessness' is 'the very embodiment' of divine power. Conversely, it could be argued that the widow is comparable to the dishonest steward: we have no reason, other than our stereotypes, even to believe that her cause is just, but she nevertheless prevails. Yet whether her goal is true justice or self-service, Luke reins in her agency with the parable's introduction: the widow, for Luke, is simply the model of ceaseless prayer.

The case of the Levirate widow who dies childless, presented in completely androcentric terms, may represent for Jesus' audience a source of resistance: in the kingdom now breaking in, 'different arrangements from patriarchal marriages' can be envisioned. Jesus' denunciation of the scribes who 'devour the houses of widows' shows that alternatives to present economic structures are possible. From this denunciation, Reid takes her cue for interpreting the 'widow who gives her life' (Lk. 21.1–4). Rather than see her as (just) the epitome of generosity, Reid proposes two additional interpretations. The widow first prefigures Jesus, who also 'put in all the life' he had on behalf of others, but—seeing this widow in relation to those whose homes are devoured—Reid also takes her example as a cautionary tale: perhaps Jesus is lamenting 'the religious system that takes advantage of her'. Yet the converse of this reading is also possible: as Reid notes, Anna and the poor widow frame the Gospel narrative; each finds a laudable place in the Temple, and thus that same institution can be seen as a force that empowers women to use the gifts they have in service to others. Such a reading counters the anti-Temple polemic (which threatens to bleed into anti-Judaism) found in Luke–Acts and its interpreters.

Having located two strands of tradition in Luke—one that repeats the stereotype of the helpless widow and one that subverts it—Reid returns to Acts 6. She speculates, based on the several connotations of the term διακονία, that the widows may not be overlooked in terms of food but rather in terms of the distribution of service such as eucharistic table ministry; nothing, she observes, states that the Hellenist widows were either poor or needy. 'The Hellenist women, more accustomed to participating in symposia and festive dinners, probably took for granted their participation in eucharistic meals in the Christian house churches, whereas such a practice would have been more problematic for the Hebrews.' Then again, Jerusalem itself was highly Hellenized, so culturally the Hebrew–Hellenist divide is complicated. Further, the Hellenists likely originated in various parts of the Empire, with the Greek East being more concerned with gender segregation than the Roman West, so division could also exist among the Hellenists. Finally, to presume that the Hebrews would have found women's ministry problematic from a cultural perspective calls into question both Jesus' own table practice among the Hebrews and the diverse roles of Jewish women. Reid also offers the suggestion that the Hellenist widows were being overlooked in financial administration, but then the distinction from the Hebrew widows becomes even less clear. Whatever the explanation, Luke resolves the problem by putting the church firmly under the direction of men. Left unspoken is whether the widows were among those 'pleased' by this solution (Acts 6.5) or even whether the overlooking of the Hellenist widows was resolved.

Finally, Luke presents the widows who weep at Tabitha's death. If the story does reflect the role of independent women who ran house-churches (cf. 1 Tim. 5.16), then Luke has again disempowered women. Although a 'disciple' (μαθήτρια), Tabitha functions primarily as a corpse whom Peter raises. The real power is invested in the male apostle. Yet Reid ends on a note of hope, for within these various accounts are indications of women's authority and autonomy. 'The power given to women by the Spirit for ministry, exemplified by Luke's widows, cannot ultimately be squelched.'

To speak out in protest, as Kanyoro does, is one strategy for achieving liberation, voice, and agency; to locate authority behind an androcentric agenda, as Gaventa and Reid do, is another; a third approach is to recover women's history, as Anderson demonstrates. But there is a fourth pathway, most often used internally by those engaged in such struggle: humor. Whether as satire, irony, slapstick, or pun, comedy has long been a component in the arsenal of self-determination and resistance. To 'make fun' of someone or something carries a subversive element, and as anyone whose protest received the response 'it's only a joke' well knows, jokes can harm, and jokers always hold power.[6] Moreover, humor's pedagogical aspects were well known, as Horace's instructions concerning 'profit with delight' demonstrate.[7] By staging the book of Acts in the lights of comedic conventions and feminist analysis, Kathy Chambers reveals a production ranging from the sobering to the celebratory.

---

6 See discussion in Amy-Jill Levine, 'Women's Humour and Other Creative Juices', in Athalya Brenner (ed.), *Are We Amused? Humour about Women in the Biblical Worlds* (London: T. & T. Clark, 2003), pp. 120–26.

7 Richard I. Pervo, *Profit with Delight: The Literary Genre of the Acts of the Apostles* (Philadelphia: Fortress Press, 1987).

Reading the account of the slavegirl (παιδίσκη) Rhoda of Acts 12 in light of comedic conventions,[8] Kathy Chambers locates tentative challenges to church leadership, gender constructions, and social class. Although comedy in antiquity ultimately serves to reinforce the status quo, its elements do offer alternatives to social norms, and its representatives—who are frequently those outside the male citizenship group, who are frequently women and slaves—do emerge at least temporarily to voice valid critique.

Recovering the slave is already an overdue exegetical move; some commentaries all but ignore Rhoda and, as Chambers points out, when she is noticed, she is dismissed as 'flighty' or 'having lost her wits'. Yet Rhoda may be the most aware person in Acts 12. The chapter's first pericope, the narrative of Peter's prison-escape, sets up the narrative of Rhoda's recognizing Peter at the gate, her failure to admit him, and the failure of the prayerful gathered in the home of Mary, the mother of John Mark, to believe Rhoda's words. Whereas Peter, with angelic help, miraculously slips out of his chains and exits numerous gates, he cannot gain entrance to the house-church. Whereas Peter is aided by an angel, whom he fails to recognize, Mary and her companions respond to Rhoda's insistence upon Peter's presence with, 'it is his angel'. Whereas neither Peter nor the house-church recognizes at first the true nature of the events surrounding them—Peter more or less sleeps through his escape; the house-church, although likely praying for Peter's release, cannot imagine that their prayers are answered—Rhoda understands that Peter has escaped and conveys the correct message. Given Luke's earlier report that the women who testified to Jesus' resurrection were also not believed (Luke 24 also offers angel-like messengers [24.4] and a potentially confused Peter [24.12]), Rhoda appears not as flighty slave but as apostle herself.

But Luke is, as Chambers remarks, 'no social revolutionary'. Rhoda is dismissed at the end of the story: the truth of her message is not acknowledged as such, and her failure to grant Peter entry is sealed by Peter himself, who refuses the offer given by the free members of the church. Nor does Luke even make clear that Rhoda is a member of the believing community; given the comedic convention of the *servus currans*, the 'running slave', identified by J. Albert Harrill and elaborated upon by Chambers, Rhoda's 'joy' at Peter's arrival may have more to do with her expectation of a reward than with any concern for Peter himself or the church. Thus Rhoda, like Peter, remains an outsider.

Matters are no better with Mary, the mother of John Mark. Already we might query what a member of the Way is doing owning slaves—so much for Jesus' concerns about serving two masters (Lk. 16.3)—but even if we grant that slave-owning is considered 'natural' in Luke's culture, Mary still emerges as a negative model. She is clearly an elite woman, as Arlandson notes, for only the elite could afford homes in Jerusalem, and her presumed relationship to Barnabas, the property-owning Levite, confirms that the family is socially well placed. She is not, as

---

8. A fourth παιδίσκη who participates in humorous scenes and whose understanding surpasses the leaders of both Israel and the invading empire appears in Jdt. 8.10, as Arlandson notes. See Amy-Jill Levine, 'Sacrifice and Salvation: Otherness and Domestication in the Book of Judith', in James C. VanderKam (ed.), *'No One Spoke Ill of Her': Essays on Judith* (Early Judaism and its Literature, 2; Atlanta: Scholars Press, 1992), pp. 17–30.

Arlandson also observes, condemned for her wealth, but she is depicted as foolish: even her slave is more aware than she. The humor in Acts 12 occurs at the expense of Peter, Rhoda, and the members of the house-church, but only Peter is rehabilitated. Peter, who leaves the scene for some vaguely identified 'other place', returns to seriousness with his raising of Tabitha, his conversion of Cornelius, and his speech at the Jerusalem council. For Peter, who has already had one difficult encounter with a truth-telling female slave (Lk. 22.56), any place is better than the home of Mary and Rhoda; for Paul (so Acts 16), any repeated assertion by a female slave, no matter how true, is at best an annoyance. Nevertheless, Rhoda the female slave momentarily stops the action, just as the exorcism of the mantic slave girl lands Paul and Silas in prison. Neither Peter, nor even an angel, gets by the door Rhoda bars; neither her owner, nor even the entire house-church, can stifle her claims to the truth. As Chambers correctly states, 'As warnings to the elite of any system, be it religious, political, or economic, the voices of the slave girl in the high priest's court, the slave girl in the Jerusalem church, and the slave girl in Philippi—all of whom insisted on the truth even when it was denied—echo still.'

Robert Price also turns to classical literature in order to understand Rhoda, and his conclusion is hardly humorous. In his 1997 *The Widow Traditions in Luke–Acts*,[9] Price argued that in both the Third Gospel and Acts Luke edited a number of pericopae that originated among celibate Christian groups in order to suppress women characters. The present essay develops this thesis, as Price explores 'Two More Cases of Luke's Suppression of Women'. Price's first example, drawn from the Gospel's parable of the prodigal son, advances Dennis R. MacDonald's suggestion of classical, especially Homeric, influence on the evangelists (as it anticipates MacDonald's contribution in this volume); his second test-case, from Acts, complements Chambers's reading of Rhoda in light of New Comedic conventions by finding her antecedents not in Plautus and Menander, but in the women who report the empty tomb and are not believed.

Given Price's analysis, Luke's parable of the prodigal son could aptly be retitled the parable of the absent mother. Price begins by noting connections between the prodigal and Odysseus; then, adducing actantial forms, Bettelheim's *Uses of Enchantment*, diverse philosophical views of Odysseus, and an occasional connection between Luke's prodigal and his Hebrew antecedents, he weaves a more complete tapestry of connections. The metaphor is not accidental, for the actual weaver in this scene of the *Odyssey*, Penelope, is dropped from Luke's creation. Whereas, for Homer, the loving wife and mother offers compassionate reconciliation, Luke offers only the father figure. Whether Luke constructed the parable with the *Odyssey* in mind or not, or indeed whether the parable came from Jesus himself, the intertextual reading forces forward the mother's absence.

Yet had a mother announced the return of the prodigal, would any have believed her? The male disciples did not believe the women who had visited the tomb, and the members of the house-church did not believe the woman who reported Peter's release from his own tomb-like prison. Price finds in Rhoda not only a parallel to Mary Magdalene and the other women of Luke 24 but also a possible rewriting of

---

9 Robert M. Price, *The Widow Traditions in Luke–Acts: A Feminist-Critical Scrutiny* (SBLDS, 155; Atlanta: Scholars Press, 1997).

the account of the women witnesses: 'Luke knew good and well that the female disciples of Jesus were supposed to have seen the Risen Christ himself, such an account underlying his story of Rhoda and Peter, but when he wrote his Jesus version, he eliminated this element, purposely excising any possible basis for women's appeal to the empty tomb story as a precedent for their own apostolic ministry.'

Once intratextual connections are in play, Price's approach opens up additional areas of inquiry. For example, threads drawn between the women at the tomb and Rhoda continue forward to the mantic slave girl even as they find a possible origin in Lk. 8.1-3, the notice that Mary Magdalene and the other women were healed of infirmities, including Mary's seven demons. Both Mary and the slave girl are exorcised (surely Apollo, who possesses the slave girl, has the power of seven demons), and both are ignored. Both provide funds to their 'masters', although Mary does so voluntarily 'out of her means' while the slave girl is a commodity. While Mary Magdalene may be seen as finding a new community among Jesus and his male and female followers, the threads together create a much more problematic picture: slaves are still ignored, not all exorcised women are welcomed into the new community, women are appreciated especially for their advancing men's financial well-being. Or, for another connection, Price's notice of the absent mother might cause readers to take notice of mothers where they are mentioned or implied: the ineffectual mother of John Mark, who is never shown in a maternal role; Timothy's absent Jewish mother and grandmother; the numerous widows who appear to have no children to support them; Philip's absent wife and mother of his four virgin daughters; the mother of Paul's nephew ... Through this lens, Acts not only resonates with Homer, it begins to look, with its marginalization of mothers, like a Disney movie.

Acts 16, the accounts of Lydia and the mantic slave girl—accounts in the earlier literature described as 'Paul's mission to Europe' or 'Paul's second missionary journey'—provides the focus of the next six articles. The first, by Dennis R. MacDonald, argues that Euripides' *Bacchae* provided the model not only for the reference to the women at the 'prayer [place]' (προσευχή) but also for the characters of Lydia, the women worshiping with her, and even the mantic slave girl. Their function for Luke was to encourage readers to compare Paul's arrival in Europe with that of Dionysius, a missionary god known for his appeal to women. Once again women, or at least female characters, serve a male agenda: Jesus is better than Dionysius and Paul is stronger than Apollo. Whereas Dionysius drove women mad, Paul exorcises a possessed girl. Not to be outdone, the women in the church are certainly to be preferred over the women who follow those Greek gods: Lydia, calmly worshiping at a place of prayer rather than ripping up animals—let alone her own children—on the hillside, is the sort of woman any *ekklesia* would be happy to claim. MacDonald offers no naïve comparison; nor does his contribution rest solely on a narrowly circumscribed intertextual focus. He grounds his reading of ch. 16 with other scenes in Acts that reveal traces of Euripides' influence, from importing to the resurrected Jesus a quotation from Dionysius, to imprisonment because of contact with raving women, to earthquake-induced jail-breaks.

Interest in Lydia appears to have come full circle: from a focus on Paul, to early feminist attempts at locating 'real' women in the early church, to a recognition that the women some feminist historians have worked so assiduously to recover were never present in the first place. In MacDonald's reading, gone is the place of prayer frequented only by women; the scene is not history but an appeal to Euripides' wild women; gone is Lydia, whose name functions not to identify a historical figure but to draw immediate connections to the cult center of Dionysius; gone are her fellow worshipers, who serve as Luke's Greek chorus (and, for Luke, they are silent). Even Lydia's purple cloth serves to connect her to Dionysius, whose purple cloak, along with his entourage of women, was one of his signatures. As MacDonald concludes, 'every detail about Lydia in Acts points to her as a Christian Maenad'.

Some readers will conclude that MacDonald has gone too far: while his numerous correspondences between Acts and the *Bacchae* may be seen as legitimate, they do not obviate a historical core. The costuming of the figures may be from the Greek tragedies, but the existence of upper-class or at least fiscally independent women who provided support to Paul is confirmed by Paul's own letters. Further, historical work is not and cannot be dismissed from the feminist study of Acts; not only MacDonald but the other authors interested in Lydia offer cautious moves toward reconstructing at least some religious options open to women, how Luke perceived those roles, and, perhaps, even actual activities to which Luke was responding.

Also drawing upon the *Bacchae*, but working independently of MacDonald's study, Shelly Matthews agrees that Lydia and her sister are, in effect, modeled on Euripides' women, but her explication for their function concentrates less on the bad Dionysius/good Jesus argument than on the implications of the connection for understanding Luke's portrayal of elite women. She discovers a convention of sorts, utilized not only by Euripides and Luke but also by Josephus (*Ant.* 18), in which elite women serve as mediators between new religious movements and the wider culture. Bringing into conversation Jewish, Christian, and pagan writings, Matthews finds a common core: the women who affiliate with the new group are respectable; those whose morality is questionable and class status comparably lower remain on the outside as negative exemplars. Thus, as Matthews notes, the only inspired woman's speech in Acts is that of the slave who stands outside the church and whose words are said to be mantic rather than prophetic. Jesus' female prophets are, as far as Luke–Acts evinces, not slave girls but 'virgins and educated women'.

Connections among the three texts also prompt Matthews to consider how gender functions in relation to Dionysiac propaganda, pro and con. First, Matthews observes that ecstatic, female-identified rites yielded historically to male-oriented sobriety. Concurrently, however, elitist (male) writers continued to regard 'foreign rites' as marked by women, sexual immorality, and subversion of the state. Euripides himself introduces the conjunction, albeit on the lips of a man undone by Dionysius, Pentheus. Livy follows suit, as do Cicero and Tacitus. Conversely, throughout the Greek and Roman periods Matthews also locates positive assessments of women's Bacchic involement. In Euripides' play, Pentheus's suspicions of women's orgiastic excess are proven false several times, the *Senatus consultum de Bacchanalibus* permits women, but not men, to become priests of Bacchus, and even Cicero acknowledges that women's participation in foreign rites was accepted by many in his cultural cohort. The list of approval for women's participation in Bacchic or Bacchic-like rites continues. Philo's Therapeutrides engage in what sounds like Bacchic worship: nocturnal vigils, dancing, the mixing of men and women, and 'most honorable drunkenness' (this metaphoric only), and Plutarch's *Mulierum virtutes* is dedicated to Clea, 'a leader of the Delphic maenads'. This evidence leads Matthews to conclude that Josephus and Luke both make positive Dionysiac connections to converts to, respectively, Judaism and Christianity. The Bacchic connection has an apologetic caché.

Matthews's next step is to investigate the intersections of women's activities, religion, and public life. Homer, Euripides, Virgil, and others both present religion as the proper concern of women and find that such participation redounds positively to the state. Next, she explains how narratives in which elite women provide new religions their initial receptions serve ultimately to resolve the conflict between local male elites and the male missionary/god. These conventions then serve tentatively to resolve the question of Lydia's class: responding to liberationist claims in which Lydia epitomizes the 'last who became first' and therefore heads a 'contrast society' consistent with Luke's attention to the poor, Matthews argues that Acts shifts the focus from economic to social 'outsiders': an Ethiopian officer, a Roman centurion, a proconsul, gentile men and women of high standing. On the outside remain the slave girl in Philippi, along with the other prisoners in the Philippian jail (and, perhaps to be added, all Jews who refuse the Christian message). 'Elites' like Lydia are, while well-to-do, not of the high class represented by Pliny or Cicero or even Philo; nor is Paul among patrician ranks. Luke's 'elites' in Matthews's construction resemble the sponsors, the patrons, of Luke's own community.

The final component of this detailed article concerns the Philippian church, for there are numerous early Christian sources in addition to Acts that suggest women's prominence there. Cautiously concluding that Lydia is a fictional character, Matthews nonetheless proposes that Luke may have known of women like her, patrons and congregational leaders (such as Euodia and Syntyche, mentioned in Phil. 4.2-3). Perhaps Luke has substituted the story of an accommodating woman for the received tradition of church conflict. Finally, perhaps Luke has used the story of the mantic slave girl to deflect the fact that lower-class women as well as slaves did join the church in significant numbers. Luke offers no slaves, and certainly no female slaves, as church leaders, but Luke's contemporary, Pliny, certainly knew of slave women leading Christian groups in Bythinia. Lydia and the slave girl thus, by their presumed fictional nature, point to the alternative *realia* of Christian women's lives.

F. Scott Spencer weaves gender studies, postmodern literary theory, a historical investigation of attitudes toward women's textile production, and references from Homer, Ovid, and the Septuagint into 'Women of "the Cloth" in Acts: Sewing the Word'. As Spencer's three 'women of the cloth'—Tabitha the tunic-sewer, Lydia the fabric-dyer, and Priscilla the tent-maker—knit together, respectively, Peter to the Joppan church, Paul to Philippi, and, in Priscilla's case, both Paul to Ephesus and Apollos to orthodoxy, they recollect not only Kanyoro's remarks on African women's economic contributions on the domestic and local levels but also the concerns expressed by many in Anderson's survey for locating women's 'proper' place in the family, society, and church. Given that Tabitha, Lydia, and Priscilla promote the growth of the church and the well-being of its members, it would not be unwarranted to note that, for Acts, the *Basileia* might be compared to a sewer who went out to sew.

Rejecting the optimistic theses that Tabitha's being a 'disciple' (μαθήτρια) makes her a leader equal to Peter (Peter talks and raises the dead; Tabitha, ever-silent, dies and is raised), that she is a wealthy patron with a support staff (that she 'makes' [ἐποίει] the clothes may suggest a less elite status), and even that she is a widow (Luke never calls her a 'widow' [χήρα]) or a resident of the house in which her corpse lies ('upper rooms' are common Christian gathering places), Spencer locates the significance of Tabitha's work in its 'religious' dimension: clothing the naked, sharing one's garments, caring for widows. Yet Spencer also rejects the thesis that Luke has necessarily denigrated Tabitha's contributions by calling them merely 'good works' (ἔργον ἀγαθόν) rather than 'service' or 'ministry' (διακονία). Jesus, he notes, is also presented as doing good (εὐεργετῶν), and Tabitha's charitable works (ἐλεημοσύναι) are matched by both Cornelius and Paul. Citing Anderson's work on Tabitha, he advances discussion of her story through close reading of the Greek text in conversation not only with biblical and classical intertexts but also with textile-manufacturing references in American women's writing.

Spencer and Anderson both comment on the name 'Tabitha', Aramaic for 'gazelle' or 'antelope': Luke highlights the name by providing its Greek translation, 'Dorcas'. Chrysostom describes Tabitha as 'active and wakeful as an antelope'; Calvin offers the less appealing 'wild she-goat'. I wonder if the name could be seen as amusing: 'Gazelle' is a tad ironic for a character whose main action is to be a corpse. The name is, in effect, 'out of place'; the same point can be made for Lydia, who is 'out of place' in her Philippian setting, for 'Lydia' is the name for the region of Western Asia Minor that includes Thyatira, our protagonist's hometown. As Spencer also observes, Lydia is also the home of the perpetually spinning Arachne, the mortal weaver who challenged Athena with a tapestry depicting the gods' sexual exploitations of women. It may hang by a weak thread, but the picture of Lydia 'compelling' Paul into her web even as she challenges the gods of the state, does have a certain appeal.

Lydia is further 'out of place' by her location outside the city gates (16.13). Although, like Tabitha, she is frequently classified as 'wealthy' or 'high standing' or even as a first-century version of, as Spencer archly puts it, a top-line Avon Lady or Mary Kay representative, her location outside the gates—where purple-dyeing, a task requiring, as even Plutarch noted, the use of animal urine—all but eliminates this possibility. It might be more accurate to see Tabitha as clothing widows but not one herself, just as to see Lydia as providing purple clothes to the wealthy (hardly a 'charitable' venture, cf. Lk. 16.19-31), but not being one herself. The distinction is that Tabitha's work has religious and charitable import; Lydia's business venture is fully commercial. Appropriately, Spencer connects Lydia not only to other women 'of the cloth' but also to Simon the tanner, with whom Peter stays (Acts 10).

Spencer's final 'woman of the cloth' is Priscilla the tent-maker. Although identified as the wife of Apollos, a Jew from Pontus, Priscilla's name is, like that of Tabitha and Lydia, over-determined. On the one hand, it is twice cited before that of her husband (18.18, 26; cf. Rom. 16.3; 2 Tim. 4.1) and it recollects the venerable *gens Prisca* family; on the other, it appears in the diminutive—the formal name is Prisca—and Priscilla's own familial identification is omitted. Whether coded as elite because of her possible patrician background (unlikely, given Luke's lack of hesitation in identifying patrician women's support for the church) or categorized as among the working poor, Priscilla does hold religious authority. Acts might even be seen as promoting the roles of textile-working women in the Christian mission.

Tabitha is a domestically situated Jewish woman whose good works support a community of widows; Lydia is a godfearer (perhaps a convert to Judaism) who leads a heterogeneous gathering that meets both outdoors and in; Priscilla may well be a gentile (only Aquila is called a 'Jew') who travels in spreading the gospel, who not only provides Paul lodging but also employment, and who preserves the correct gospel by correcting the eloquent but insufficiently informed Apollos.

James M. Arlandson's 'Lifestyles of the Rich and Christian: Women, Wealth, and Social Freedom' confirms Spencer's reluctance to locate the women of the cloth in the upper echelon. Tabitha, Lydia, and Priscilla are not among the 'leading' (literally, 'first'; πρώτη) women of Acts 17.4 or the 'prominent' (εὐσχήμονων) women of 17.12 or even on a par with the slave-owning Mary, the landowner of Acts 12.12–17. Attending to these wealthy women first by determining their class and then their relative social and economic freedom in the late-first–early-second-century Mediterranean context, Arlandson offers insight into Luke's—and perhaps our—attitude toward the intersection of wealth, public presence, and gender.

Using not only Josephus and Strabo but also Chariton's *Chaereas and Callirhoe* (a particularly good choice given generic connections between Acts and the Hellenistic novel and helpful as well in providing additional insight into Gaventa's use of this work), Arlandson demonstrates how the designation 'first man' (πρῶτος), an expression appearing also in Acts 28.7 in reference to Publius of Malta, indicates political control along with wealth and prestige. Inscriptional evidence supports the connotation of political authority and adds to it the application of related terms ('first honors'; 'of the first family') to women who supported the public good through offering sacrifices, supplying oil to athletes, holding banquets, and serving as priestesses. Given that Acts 13.50 pairs 'prominent women' (γυναῖκας τὰς εὐσχήνομας) with 'first men', the former group must be seen as holding the same elite social class (cf. Mk 15.43, where 'prominent' describes Joseph of Arimathea). Again, external sources confirm the class categorization. Plutarch, for example, mentions Tarpeia, one of the 'prominent virgins' accused of offering a bribe (social prominence and wealth are not equivalent to moral rectitude); a second-century CE inscription links the term 'prominent' to the ruling class via other designations, such as *Stephanophori*, priests, and *archons*.

Luke signifies with these adjectives that the female converts in Thessalonica and Berea were politically and socially elite. From external sources as well as Acts itself, Arlandson demonstrates with numerous examples that such women, even if they were married, had financial independence, could contribute lavishly to the public good, and could be awarded political as well as religious office. Moreover, their public roles did not provoke accusations of shameful behavior or immodesty: they did what would be expected of anyone, male or female, of their class. Given this social setting, Arlandson argues against one popular feminist reading of Acts, namely, that Luke's silence about women's prominence in the church signals restriction. To the contrary, the titles Luke accords the women necessarily indicate their prestige. Moreover, here recalling Gaventa's argument, he finds that Luke does not detail the contributions to the church of Bartholomew or Matthias whereas Tabitha, Lydia, and Priscilla do receive attention, so the presumed 'silence' concerning the prominent women need not indicate a negative. Indeed, as Arlandson suggests, given the freedom such women had, Luke's silence about their roles might be seen as an acceptance of them. For Arlandson, it would also be overreading in seeing Luke as condemning wealthy women for their wealth. While the Gospel does insist that one 'cannot serve God and wealth' (Lk. 16.13), both the women of Luke 8 and the women of Acts 17 (and elsewhere) manage to retain their wealth while serving the church. Like the author of 1 Timothy, Luke does not find wealth itself an evil; the problem is the 'love of money'.

Given that, as Arlandson puts it, 'the almost exclusive source of wealth was land', we should therefore expect to find wealthy women as landowners. Luke does not disappoint. Mary the mother of John Mark (Acts 12.12–17) owns a house in Jerusalem large enough to serve as the church's gathering point (12.12; later tradition suggests the house was also the location of the 'Last Supper' and the Pentecost event). Perhaps Mary should be seen as of the same class as Barnabas: Col. 4.10 identifies her son John Mark as Barnabas's cousin, and Barnabas too owned land, likely within Jerusalem's walls (Acts 4.37). Perhaps Martha (Luke 10), who owns a home, might also fit into this category.

Arlandson's final examples of women with independent funds are drawn from the retainer class, and it is here he locates Joanna (Lk. 8.1–3), the wife of Herod's estate manager (ἐπίτροπος). Although such managers could be slaves, they nevertheless had extensive latitude in regard to their employer's funds. As he observes, the contributions of Joanna and her fellow female travelers 'out of their resources' matches the language found in the Babatha papyri as well as a number of inscriptions concerning women donors, and Arlandson speculates that 'a woman like Joanna could have her own wealth and contribute it in any way she wished without incurring the least bit of social stigma or patriarchal opposition; that Luke does not comment on it proves that he does not find these actions unusual or inappropriate for a woman'.

Like Arlandson, Virginia Burrus and Karen Torjesen draw upon rigorous historical investigation in order to understand Luke's presentation of women. As early as the mid-1980s, they recognized the incontrovertible evidence for Mediterranean women's roles as householders and patrons and so concluded that such roles should be the presupposition for understanding early Christian groups. Thus women's absence from the literature, or accentuations of their submissiveness, should be held suspect. Close to two decades later, as Burrus and Torjesen revisit this subject area, they are even more aware of the difficulties of moving from representation to 'social reality'; nevertheless, as they so correctly ask, 'are we not in danger of overshooting our goal, if feminist critique results in the loss of all purchase on female subjectivity in ancient texts and the bracketing of women's agency in the making of history?'

Their 'Afterword' to the prior study looks to both the Third Gospel and Acts: under the speculum fall the ministering women of Lk. 8.1–3, presented in terms of lack (no longer are they afflicted with disease), what they receive (healing), and what they are in the process of divesting (their resources, used for the support of the twelve).[10] They connect Joanna, the wife of Herod's steward, with both the 'devout women of high standing' (Acts 13.50) who reject Paul and Barnabas and the several 'Greek women of high standing' who accept Paul and Silas's message in Acts 17.

---

10 And perhaps of other women. See Esther A. deBoer, 'The Lukan Mary Magdalene and the Other Women Following Jesus', in Levine (ed.), *Feminist Companion to Luke*, pp. 140–60.

Others in the category of women householders and benefactors include Martha (Luke 10), Sapphira (Acts 5), Tabitha (Acts 9), Mary the mother of John Mark (Acts 12), Lydia (Acts 16), and Priscilla (Acts 18).

Whether these women all represent 'elite patronage' and so 'symbolic capital', or whether Luke portrays women's support across the economic spectrum will remain matters of debate, and the debate itself will prompt questions of what is the 'good news', at least in feminist perspective. If the women are all seen as elite, we have on the one hand recognition of actual social roles and, by extenuation, of women's influence on church activity. On the other hand, we return to the sad news that Luke is interested in women as long as they are, like Mary the sister of Martha, or Sapphira, or even the woman who anoints Jesus in Luke 7, silent and at the feet of the community's male leader. If we accept the upper-class construct, we risk imposing our own limited understanding of history on the ancient texts, for at least some of these women could have been among the working poor (as were Jesus and the twelve). We might celebrate their benefaction because that is precisely what patrons do; we might, less charitably, condemn it because, at least as Luke presents it, the benefaction is done in gratitude for healing, it leads to no explicit recognition of the women's actual interests, and the overall impression may be that women are an exploited group whose responsibility is to support the agenda, and the person, of the male leader.

Turning finally to one of Luke's famous gendered pairs, Cornelius and Lydia, Burrus and Torjesen recover for Lydia, *in light of this comparison*, her role as householder and patron. True, Lydia is not shown in a leadership capacity; but neither is Cornelius. Citing Staley's work, the article then adduces the next Lukan double, that of Lydia and the slave girl—and again the results are ambiguous: Paul may be seen as freeing the slave from demonic possession and economic exploitation (a good thing), or as robbing her of her power, let alone of her connection to her god (a bad thing—at least in today's interfaith context). Continuing the connection, then, they wonder if Paul has robbed Lydia of her leadership, or even exploited her hospitality; but perhaps he brings new honor to her household, even as he provides her the only means of salvation. Moreover, it is Lydia who prevails upon Paul: is she subjective agent or is she Luke's model of appropriate behavior for women in the church? Should she be hailed as the patron of a house-church, or condemned for owning slaves whom she forces to participate in her new-found religion?

Luke offers today's readers both good news and bad, both liberation and exploitations. As Torjesen and Burrus so aptly conclude, 'We should not defend Luke from well-deserved feminist critique. We should, however, do our best to exploit the resources of his double messages in such a way as to acknowledge the necessarily ambiguous power of "some women", as well as the complexity of both domination and resistance.'

Burrus and Torjesen anticipate Jeffrey Staley's article by their reference to his refusal to separate Lydia from the slave girl, but this helpful reading strategy is only one of the numerous suggestive moves that Staley makes. Informed like Kanyoro by both autobiographical reflection and awareness of the effects of 'colonialist missionary movements', Staley's postcolonial, postfeminist reading focuses on the 'good' Lydia and the 'bad' possessed slave girl of Acts 16. Staley recognizes that Luke's doubling of the women deflects attention from Paul himself and so his colonizing message: readers are forced to choose either Lydia's humble acceptance of Paul's message and consequent opening of her house to him or the slave girl's challenge sparked by the spirit of Apollo. Complexity is foreclosed; the indigenous tradition will be colonized in any case, either by denial (Lydia) or destruction (the slave girl). But decolonizing strategies are available. Invoking Slim Girl of Oliver La Farge's *Laughing Boy*, the Spider Woman of Leslie Marmon Silko's *Ceremony*, and the story of his childhood friend, Sarah Tsosie, dead from alcohol and abuse, Staley shows how these three Native American women either replicate or challenge Luke's dualistic structure.

Staley's inquiry begins with a sharp critique of biblical commentators who, despite their assertion that Acts' first major plot shift occurs in either chs. 13–14 (Paul's proclamation to gentiles) or ch. 15 (the Jerusalem council), nevertheless classify the second missionary journey, the entry of Christianity into Europe, as marking a substantially new movement in the plot. In Staley's terms, the designation of Macedonia as 'the European continent legitimizes the missionizing agendas of modern colonial empires'. Staley then turns, fittingly in the essay's second part, to his own 'colonialist meta-autobiography'. Geography changes from Lydia in Macedonia to the Navajo Reservation in northern Arizona; style changes from academic analysis to visceral images; the topic changes from 'the scholars' and 'Luke' to 'all of us'. Recollections of Sarah Tsosie merge with 'Slim Girl' as well as Native American border women like Pocahontas and Malinche. It was, as Staley comes to realize, 'colonialist ideology' that created not only the independent godfearer and the abject slave of Acts 16, but also these other border women who 'embody' the ambiguous relationship of colonized to colonizers.

Part three returns the reader to Luke's construction of Macedonia as place and concept. The construction begins with Paul's vision of the 'man from Macedonia': the angel of the region has summoned and thereby authorized him. In Staley's analysis (following both Origen and Walter Wink), this man of Macedonia is the region's 'angel' or 'prince'; no wonder one of Paul's first acts upon arriving is to perform an exorcism: he expels the reigning system—of Greek culture, of Apollo, of Delphi—in favor of his own. The distinction between Paul and his missionary targets is reinforced by ch. 16's introduction of the 'we' passages, even as the distinction between Paul's Jewish/Christian identity and the power of Rome is reinforced by the second journey's intensified use of Roman territorial and politically charged vocabulary. The war between 'us' (Paul, the gospel) and 'them' (Apollo, Rome) is engaged; women mark the battlefield.

For Acts, the conquest of Macedonia (Europe) is facilitated not by the conventional single woman but by two women. Lydia functions as the 'good girl', the humble patron; the pythonic slave is the 'bad girl' who, as one commentator describes, 'prostituted her divine capacity' (the sense that she had a choice is all the more remarkable). Like La Farge's Slim Girl, Lydia uses her wealth to adapt to the colonizers' values and desires to learn from their male representative the true teachings. Concurrently, like Slim Girl, the slave girl 'represents all things new and evil' and the adaptation of both Slim Girl and slave girl to the colonizers' culture destroys them as it destroyed Sarah Tsosie. Yet Silko's fluid blue markers of the Spider Woman of Pueblo mythology (Changing Woman in Navajo mythology), markers that mutate from the blue satin dress of a Mexican prostitute to the blue swimsuit of a calendar model to the blue of a medicine man's shirt, provide the alternative response: the empowerment of the colonized, the refusal of imposed or static identity, the ability to draw what is needed from both tradition and imposed/appropriated stories. Redemptory voices for Staley are not heard in Acts 16; they echo rather in the intertextual challenge issued by our own informed ethical commitments and ideological awareness.

Todd Penner and Caroline Vander Stichele, like Staley, also attend to the intersections of geography, violence, alternative readings, and intertextual conversation, and their focus on the role of violence as both 'Lukan theme and narrative strategy' and the attendant constructions of masculinity reinforces the sense of imperial discourse Staley locates within Acts 16. For Penner and Vander Stichele, Luke's insistence on Christian victimhood (and, necessarily, the depiction of the non-Christian as perpetrator) as well as the narrative justification of the violence must be interrogated rather than, as is typical, blithely accepted as objective fact and, with more harmful potential, celebrated. Making Luke's writing even more potentially lethal is its affirmation of violence perpetrated by insiders, whether through divine agency (Ananias and Sapphira, Herod Agrippa I), or by ecclesial agents via dualistic and condemnatory rhetoric (what might be called 'fighting words'), as exemplified in the speeches, or by physical mutilation as exemplified by Elymas's blinding. As Penner and Vander Stichele conclude, 'when "we" do it, it is "justice"; when "they" do it, it is "violence"'.

The essay's introduction is already replete with issues on the feminist radar: discussions of so-called 'justified' suffering, the dangers of dualism, the questioning of objectivity, the threats of cooptation, the need to hear through other sets of ears as well as recognize one's own ideological groundedness. Penner and Vander Stichele then conjoin these matters with exploration of how Luke's narrative strategies concerning the role of violence are also gender-coded. Following the work of Mary Rose D'Angelo, they acknowledge gender's function within imperial discourse: women, and especially women's bodies, are the site in which the Empire inscribes its power (the same point, *mutatis mutandis*, is found in Staley's discussion of Slim Girl and Sarah Tsosie). More, they propose that 'violence in the narrative of Acts arises from the same discursive structures that also underlie the narrative's display of women'. Violence is gendered.

Penner and Vander Stichele's next step is to demonstrate how gender and violence, already intertwined, are also related to geography and narrative voice. For Acts, women's domestication complements men's public exhibition of power attested either as sufferer or as perpetrator, but the location of the violence also conveys a dualizing message. There is no violence in Athens or Rome, the respective centers of Greek and Roman life. Violence occurs rather in Jerusalem, the (destroyed, at least in Luke's own time) center of Jewish life, and in the Empire's colonies. Cities marked by violence are not merely ignoble or even out of control, they are implicitly effeminized. Nor, however, is Rome fully exculpated: its ability to maintain order is destabilized, in Luke's narrative especially by the Jews, and its *imperium* and *virtus* are embodied not by emperor or state, but by Paul and church and, perhaps, by Luke the author.

For Penner and Vander Stichele, Acts' paired stories of women confirm its acceptance of normative gender roles. Lydia, for example, is fully domesticated; she demonstrates domestic virtues such as hospitality and recognition of male superiority even as her moves outside the home are fully female-identified (i.e., a prayer gathering of women). Conversely, the unnamed slave girl is fully in the public sphere, where her body—she herself, as individual, Luke finds irrelevant—is the site of battle between Paul and her (male) owners. For Luke, elite women subject themselves to male (and usually Christian) authority; lower-class women are, so Acts 16, at best an 'annoyance'; but men who challenge Paul's authority lose not only status, but honor and, occasionally, health or even life. Humiliated, impotent, and so emasculated, they become even lower than the slave girl.

The so-called message of peace is thus promulgated in imperial language and imposed by imperial tools: violence is sanctioned if perpetrated by insiders; suffering is sanctioned if the victims are insiders; men find their role in the public forum while women are either tucked away as silent hostesses, silent corpses, slain villains, or ignored slaves. Vander Stichele and Penner warn that unless feminist readers critically engage matters of violence and gender in Acts, they risk reinscribing the very oppressive structures they oppose. I want to applaud everything they say, but I do so with hesitance, for their values are my values: they condemn what I would condemn, they find a reinforcing of status-quo gender roles (as do I) where other readers, such as Kanyoro, find not silent domestication but calls for resistance. Luke's rhetorical brilliance must be acknowledged, but we cannot afford to forget that scholarly commentary has always had—depending upon the status of the commentator—similar persuasive rhetoric. For any feminist reader, and for any text under discussion, Penner and Vander Stichele's warning should remain paramount.

The conclusion to the book of Acts is open-ended. Paul is in chains, in Rome, but his death is not recorded. Nor does Luke record the eventual success of the Christian mission. So too the feminist analysis is open-ended. Acts can be read with the image of Paul in chains: a message of liberation hampered by imperial and colonial agendas. Whether the story ends with Paul's death or with the birth of the church universal, let alone which would be the 'happier' ending, remains for the reader to decide.

Reading Tabitha: A Feminist Reception History*

Janice Capel Anderson

Introduction

In this essay I explore how a number of readers have read Acts 9.36–42. In doing so, I consciously write in the tradition of feminist reader-response criticism. I will begin with a brief review of feminist reader-response criticism. This will be followed by an interpretative reception history. Finally, I will consider a number of insights this reception history offers from the perspective of a feminist critic. All that I write is itself a reading of an Anglo-American, middle-aged, middle-class, heterosexual, Protestant feminist biblical scholar. I ally myself with other feminists who define feminism with bell hooks as 'common resistance to all the different forms of male domination'[1] and with Linda Alcoff as 'the affirmation ... of our right and our ability to construct, and take responsibility for, our gendered identity, our politics and our choices'.[2] Chandra Talpade Mohanty's description of Third World Feminism as 'imagined communities of women with divergent histories and social locations, woven together by the *political* threads of opposition to forms of domination that are not only pervasive but also systemic'[3] is a definition that, provided various social locations are remembered, could well serve as a definition embracing all feminisms.

Feminist Reader-Response Criticism

Reader-response criticism has been one of the most important approaches to the Gospels and Acts in the 1980s and 1990s. Today most New Testament scholars have some notion of the 'reader' as developed in literary studies—whether they are most interested in actual or hypothetical, internal or external, first-time or ideal readers.[4] Less attention has been paid to the social locations, to the gender, race, class and

---

* Originally published in E.S. Malbon and E.V. McKnight (eds.), *The New Literary Criticism and the New Testament* (JSNTSup, 109; Sheffield: Sheffield Academic Press, 1994; Valley Forge, PA: Trinity Press International, 1994), pp. 108–44. Reprinted by permission.

1 Sandra Harding, 'Conclusion: Epistemological Questions', in S. Harding (ed.), *Feminism and Methodology* (Bloomington: Indiana University Press, 1987), pp. 181–90 (188), describing the views of bell hooks in *Feminist Theory from Margin to Center* (Boston: South End Press, 1983).

2 Linda Alcoff, 'Cultural Feminism versus Post-Structuralism: The Identity Crisis in Feminist Theory', *Signs* 13 (1988), pp. 405–36 (432).

3 Chandra Talpade Mohanty, 'Cartographies of Struggle: Third World Women and the Politics of Feminism', in C. Talpade Mohanty, A. Russo, and L. Torres (eds.), *Third World Women and the Politics of Feminism* (Bloomington: Indiana University Press, 1991), pp. 1–47 (4).

4 Robert M. Fowler, *Let the Reader Understand: Reader-Response Criticism and the Gospel of Mark* (Minneapolis: Fortress Press, 1991); Elizabeth Struthers Malbon and Janice Capel Anderson, 'Literary-Critical Methods', in E. Schüssler Fiorenza (ed.), *Searching the Scriptures* (2 vols.; New York: Crossroad, 1993), I, pp. 241–54.

other particularities of actual readers and reader constructs. Feminist literary critics in English and biblical studies have raised these issues in very fruitful ways.[5] These critics have raised these issues because they have seen very clearly how social location affects interpretation—what, how, and why one reads. Some of them emphasize the power of the text over the reader, others the power of the reader over the text. All of them explore what it means to read as a woman or a feminist, constructing what it means to be a woman or a feminist as they proceed. The difficulties in such a task can be glimpsed if one asks how a Guatemalan female peasant leader belonging to a base community, a white female middle-class urban German Lutheran biblical scholar, and a black female Holiness preacher in the rural southern United States might read the Lukan birth story even if they all embraced a general understanding of feminism. There are differences between them, and even a single one of them belongs to multiple interpretative communities operating with different reading conventions and goals.

As females reading an androcentric and patriarchal text they may also be engaged in a process Judith Fetterley calls *immasculation*. Immasculation is the process of a woman reading and identifying as a male when reading an androcentric and patriarchal text such as *Rip Van Winkle*. Fetterley writes,

> While the desire to avoid work, escape authority and sleep through the major decisions of one's life is obviously applicable to both men and women, in Irving's story this 'universal' desire is made specifically male. Work, authority, and decision-making are symbolized by Dame van Winkle, and the longing for flight is defined against her. She is what one must escape from, and the 'one' is necessarily male ... In such fictions the female reader is co-opted into participation in an experience from which she is explicitly excluded; she is asked to identify with a selfhood that defines itself in opposition to her; she is required to identify against herself.[6]

In many cases, as Renita Weems points out, a text or a dominant reading practice may call for females to read not only as males but also 'like a certain kind of man',[7]

---

5 See Judith Fetterley, *The Resisting Reader: A Feminist Approach to American Fiction* (Bloomington: Indiana University Press, 1978); Mary McClintock Fulkerson, 'Contesting Feminist Canons: Discourse and the Problem of Sexist Texts', *JFSR* 7 (1991), pp. 53–74; Diana Fuss, 'Reading Like a Feminist', *Differences* 1 (1989), pp. 77–92; Malbon and Anderson, 'Literary-Critical Methods'; Clarice Martin, 'A Chamberlain's Journey and the Challenge of Interpretation for Liberation', *Semeia* 47 (1989), pp. 105–36; *idem*, 'The *Haustafeln* (Household Codes) in African American Biblical Interpretation: "Free Slaves" and "Subordinate Women"', in Cain Hope Felder (ed.), *Stony the Road We Trod: African American Biblical Interpretation* (Minneapolis: Fortress Press, 1991), pp. 206–31; Alicia Suskin Ostriker, *Feminist Revision and the Bible* (Bucknell Lectures in Literary History; Oxford: Basil Blackwell, 1993), pp. 206–31; Patrocino P. Schweickart, 'Reading Ourselves: Toward a Feminist Theory of Reading', in Elizabeth A. Flynn and Patrocino P. Schweickart (eds.), *Gender and Reading: Essays on Readers, Texts, and Contexts* (Baltimore: Johns Hopkins University Press, 1986), pp. 31–62; Elaine Showalter, 'Critical Cross-Dressing: Male Feminists and the Woman of the Year', *Raritan* 2 (1983), pp. 130–49; Mary Ann Tolbert, 'Protestant Feminists and the Bible: On the Horns of a Dilemma', in A. Bach (ed.), *The Pleasure of her Text: Feminist Readings of Biblical and Historical Texts* (Philadelphia: Trinity Press International, 1990), pp. 5–23; Renita J. Weems, 'Reading *Her Way* through the Struggle: African American Women and the Bible', in Felder (ed.), *Stony the Road We Trod*, pp. 57–80.

6 Fetterley, *Resisting Reader*, p. xii.

7 Weems, 'Reading *Her Way*', p. 67.

an upper-class white Anglo male, for example. Once a reader recognizes this process, however, she can read self-consciously as a member of one or more resistant interpretative communities. As she reads she can recognize the process of immasculation and particular male reading strategies she uses. She can also recognize what the text excludes or tensions within it. She recognizes that she can affirm or resist, read with or against the text. She can read it with the interpretative conventions operative in liberative reading communities. She can ask what interests the text serves or may serve in particular social and historical circumstances. For biblical texts, many women readers have found that the texts can be both oppressive and liberative, depending upon the context in which they are read. Feminist reader-response critics struggle with how to read androcentric and patriarchal texts that nonetheless have evoked positive as well as negative responses. Schweickart writes,

> My point is that *certain* (not all) male texts merit a dual hermeneutic: a negative hermeneutic that discloses their complicity with patriarchal ideology, and a positive hermeneutic that recuperates the utopian moment—the authentic kernel—from which they draw a significant portion of their emotional power.[8]

Within feminist biblical scholarship Schüssler Fiorenza, Tolbert and Weems have all—each from her own particular perspective—stressed the importance of this dual hermeneutic when dealing with the Scriptures. Schüssler Fiorenza has written of a hermeneutics of suspicion and a hermeneutics of re-vision.[9] A literary critic, the poet Alicia Suskin Ostriker, has written of a tri-partite hermeneutic for biblical texts. Taking a cue from feminist biblical critics and theologians, she speaks of a hermeneutics of suspicion, but she adds to this a hermeneutics of desire in which 'the reader finds in the text what she wants it to say' and a hermeneutics of indeterminacy that emphasizes the 'necessity for plural readings which won't cancel each other out'.[10] Ostriker approvingly cites Mieke Bal, who says in *Lethal Love,* 'Texts trigger readings; that is what they are; the occasion of a reaction ... Every reading is different from, and in contact with, the text.'[11]

Reception History

As a practical matter the situated reading strategies and interests of readers can be seen in the reception history of particular texts. Below I will show how various readers have read Tabitha. First I will indicate the points of departure for differing interpretations in Acts 9.36–42. Then I will look at how modern male biblical scholars, key male interpreters of the past, several nineteenth-century women, and contemporary feminist scholars have read the text. I begin with modern biblical

---

8 Schweickart, 'Reading Ourselves', pp. 43–44.
9 Elisabeth Schüssler Fiorenza, 'Introduction: Transforming the Legacy of the *Women's Bible*', in *idem* (ed.), *Searching the Scriptures*, I. pp. 1–28 (11). Schüssler Fiorenza has also multiplied these categories, writing of a hermeneutics of suspicion, imagination, remembrance, proclamation and a hermeneutics of liberative vision and imagination in *idem*, *But She Said: Feminist Practices of Biblical Interpretation* (Boston: Beacon Press, 1992), pp. 52–55.
10 Ostriker, *Feminist Revision*, pp. 57, 121–22.
11 Ostriker, *Feminist Revision*, p. 122.

scholarship because most of the readers of this essay are members of that interpretative community, although they belong to others as well. I want to emphasize those reading conventions and then to show others by contrast. Those in the biblical guild may say that they have always known that the questions one poses determine the kinds of answers one receives. I want to go beyond this to indicate that one's social and historical location determine the questions one asks and the kind of answers one constructs. Feminist reception history shows that the 'context of discovery' as well as the 'context of justification' reflects individual and communal perspectives.[12]

Jumping Off Points
As we read, certain features of a text stand out and others recede in importance. Our own experiences, questions, and interests as well as shared reading conventions shape which aspects of a text are central and which peripheral, which are puzzling and which are obvious, which are noticed and which ignored. They also influence connections we draw between the text we are reading and other texts we have heard or read. The case is no different with the story of Tabitha. The setting in Joppa is read as significant by some interpreters and ignored by others. Some interpreters focus on the meaning of the name Tabitha and its translation into Greek as Dorcas. Interpreters of the past often use it to characterize Tabitha; modern interpreters do not. Some interpreters place a great deal of significance on the use of the term μαθήτρια (female disciple) to describe Tabitha; others downplay or ignore it. Many interpreters focus on the meaning of the description of Tabitha as someone who does 'good works and almsdeeds' (9.36, KJV). The giving of alms is an indication of Tabitha's social status as a wealthy independent woman for some. Various readers have puzzled over questions that the text raises for them: Why is Tabitha's corpse washed and placed in an upper room? Why do the disciples at Joppa wait until Tabitha is dead to send for Peter? Why does Peter heal Tabitha in private? Readers have made intertextual connections to various other texts and used them to interpret this one. Some readers pair Tabitha's story with the preceding healing of Aeneas. Some readers connect the story to the healing of Jairus's daughter found in Mk 5.21–43 = Mt. 9.18–26 = Lk. 8.40–56. 'Tabitha, rise' reminds some of 'Talitha cum' ('Little girl, rise', Aramaic) in the Markan version, Talitha and Tabitha differing by only one letter. Some connect the Tabitha story to miracles Elijah and Elisha perform in 1 and 2 Kings. Those who look within Acts for parallels see a parallel between Peter's raising of Tabitha and Paul's healing/raising of Eutychus in Acts 20.7–12. The references to widows in vv. 39 and 41 set off other bells. Some readers think of Acts 6, some of 1 Timothy, where widows are mentioned. The mention of the widows also causes some interpreters to read Tabitha as a widow, although the text never directly refers to her as such. One of the biggest differences between various readings is whether the interpreter focuses primarily on Peter or Tabitha as the main character or divides his or her attention roughly equally. Finally, one major difference between readers of Acts is the degree to which they attend to the story of Tabitha, if they attend to the story at all. For many modern biblical scholars the story has little or no significance for the overall interpretation of Acts or for the reconstruction of early church history.

---

12 My point here rests on one made about science by b. hooks, 'Conclusion: Epistemological Questions', pp. 181–90 (183–84).

Modern Male Biblical Scholarship
The reading conventions of modern biblical scholarship primarily arise out of historical-critical scholarship. In recent years Acts has been read predominantly in terms of the redactor's shaping and interpretation of previous traditions. Questions about the author's theology and the community he addresses are central. Usually, Luke and Acts are studied in the light of one another as parts of a two-volume work (although questions about this practice have been raised recently).[13] Discussion of Tabitha's story rarely occurs in scholarly monographs on Luke–Acts.[14] The story fares better in scholarly commentaries, which must find something to say about each pericope. For the most part when traditional biblical scholarship reads Tabitha's story it reads it as the story of Peter. A brief review of titles for the section in which it is included is telling: '9.32–43 Peter's Journey to Lydda and Joppa';[15] 'Peter's Pastoral Visit to Lydda and Joppa';[16] 'Peter Continues the Prophetic Ministry of Healing (Acts 9.32–43)';[17] 'Acts 9.32–43 Peter Heals Aeneas and Raises Tabitha';[18] 'Petrus als Wundertäter in Lod [Lydda] und Jafo [Joppa]: 9.32–43';[19] and 'Peter's General Tour through Lydda to Joppa'.[20] The focus on Peter may in part stem from the fact that most biblical scholars are male, but it also comes from looking for ways to connect various pericopes in Acts to one another or to other biblical texts.

Redaction critics look for connections between pericopes in which a single character appears or connections between characters who appear frequently. They also look for geographical, theological, or thematic threads to tie Acts together and to link it to other texts. Most scholars tie the healing of Aeneas in 9.32–35 to that of Tabitha. Both stories demonstrate Peter's miraculous actions as preparation for the healing of Cornelius in Acts 10. These acts continue the spread of the gospel. The references to Lydda and Joppa in the two stories also enable a geographical and

---

13 See Mikeal C. Parsons and Richard I. Pervo, *Rethinking the Unity of Luke and Acts* (Minneapolis: Fortress Press, 1993).

14 Exceptions are Martin Dibelius ('Style Criticism of the Book of Acts', in Martin Dibelius *Studies in the Acts of the Apostles* [ed. H. Greeven; trans. M. Ling; London: SCM Press; New York: Charles Scribner's Sons, 1956]) and Richard I. Pervo (*Profit with Delight: The Literary Genre of the Acts of the Apostles* [Philadelphia: Fortress Press, 1987]), although their discussions are not lengthy. Jacob Jervell barely mentions Tabitha in his collection of essays titled *The Unknown Paul*, but he does devote a whole chapter to a discussion of women in Acts ('The Daughters of Abraham: Women in Acts', in Jacob Jervell, *The Unknown Paul: Essays on Luke–Acts and Early Christian History* [Minneapolis: Augsburg, 1984], pp. 146–57, 186–90).

15 Sherman E. Johnson (annotator), 'Acts', in Herbert G. May and Bruce M. Metzger (eds.), *The New Oxford Annotated Bible, Revised Standard Version* (New York: Oxford University Press, 1977), pp. 1319–60 (1332).

16 Johannes Munck, *The Acts of the Apostles* (AB, 31; Garden City, NY: Doubleday, 1967), p. 87.

17 Robert C. Tannehill, *The Narrative Unity of Luke–Acts: A Literary Interpretation*, (Minneapolis: Fortress Press, 1986), II, p. 125.

18 Ernst Haenchen, *The Acts of the Apostles: A Commentary* (trans. B. Noble and G. Shinn; rev. R.M. Wilson; Philadelphia: Westminster Press, 1971), p. 337; Hans Conzelmann, *Acts of the Apostles: A Commentary on the Acts of the Apostles* (ed. E.J. Epp and C.R. Matthews; trans. J. Limburg, A.T. Kraabel, and D.H. Juel; Hermeneia; Philadelphia: Fortress Press, 1987), p. 76.

19 Gerhard Schneider, *Die Apostelgeschichte. II. Kommentar zu Kap. 9,1–28,31* (HTKNT, 5; Freiburg: Herder, 1982), p. 46.

20 J.W. Packer, *The Acts of the Apostles* (The Cambridge Bible Commentary on the New English Bible; Cambridge: Cambridge University Press, 1966), p. 76.

theological movement from Judea, Samaria, and Galilee to Caesarea where Peter will baptize Cornelius, often viewed as the first Gentile convert in Acts.[21] The connection to the Holy Spirit, which is important in Acts, is preserved by Peter's prayer for Tabitha, which parallels his statement to Aeneas, 'Jesus Christ, he heals you'.[22] Scholars find parallels between the story and the healing of Jairus's daughter (Lk. 8.40–46 = Mk 5.21–43 = Mt. 9.18–26), Elijah's healing of the widow's son (1 Kgs 18.17–24) and Elisha's healing of the Shunammite's son (2 Kgs 4.32–37). Peter's command, 'Tabitha, rise', in v. 40 sounds like, and has an effect similar to, Jesus' command, 'Talitha cum', in Mk 5.41 (although the Aramaic is not used in Luke). Thus scholars read the story as authorizing Peter as a type of the ancient prophets and of Jesus. Haenchen, citing Loisy, notes, however, that 'it is out of the question for Peter to proceed with a woman as Elijah and Elisha with a dead boy'.[23] Haenchen expresses some delicacy about physical connections between male and female. Comparisons sometimes are also drawn between Peter's raising of Tabitha and Paul's raising of Eutychus in 20.9–12.[24] These readers read the story in the context of Acts as the parallel story of the missions of Peter and Paul. It is quite natural for scholarly readers who spend their time teaching and writing about *biblical* studies to make (or find) biblical parallels.

Apart from noting parallels to other similar biblical healings, modern scholars are not particularly concerned with details of the story, such as the washing of the corpse, which Conzelmann informs us was a common ancient custom,[25] or the removal of the body to the upper room. Nor do they focus particular attention on the garments that the widows show to Peter.

Incidental curiosity does arise from the references to the widows who weep over Tabitha and to whom she is restored as a benefactor. Again, intertextual biblical bells go off. Since widows are mentioned in Acts 6.1–6 and in 1 Tim. 5.3–16, commentators sometimes feel compelled to discuss whether Tabitha's story should be read in the light of these passages. There is a dispute among interpreters over whether the widows in Acts 6 represent an official group with an official role. Most modern scholars read 1 Timothy as at least indicating an incipient church order of widows. In terms of Tabitha's story some simply announce that the widows are not members of an official group with a specific office.[26] Haenchen, citing Wellhausen, writes that 'in v. 39 the χήραι (widows) appear only as a knot of women mourners, but in v. 41 they represent a social class in their own right'.[27] He gives no reason for this distinction. Perhaps the grounds for it are the same as those that lead Stählin to suggest that the widows may represent a special class for whom Tabitha is raised. He takes the presence of the phrase 'saints and widows' in v. 41 to refer to two distinct groups.[28]

---

21 Haenchen, *Acts of the Apostles*, pp. 341–42.
22 Tannehill, *Narrative Unity*, p. 126.
23 Haenchen, *Acts of the Apostles*, p. 339.
24 W. Ward Gasque, *A History of the Interpretation of the Acts of the Apostles* (Peabody, MA: Hendrickson Publishers, 1989), p. 34.
25 Conzelmann, *Acts of the Apostles*, p. 77.
26 Conzelmann, *Acts of the Apostles*, p. 77, and Frederick F. Bruce, *Commentary on the Book of the Acts* (New ICC; Grand Rapids: Eerdmans, rev. edn, 1992), p. 199, nn. 83 and 85.
27 Haenchen, *Acts of the Apostles*, p. 341.
28 Gustav Stählin, 'χήρα', *TDNT*, IX, pp. 440–65 (452).

Stählin also conjectures that Tabitha is a widow, since no husband is mentioned, and that she may have been commissioned by the church at Joppa to care for the other widows.[29]

Form-critical and narrative-critical approaches have somewhat different reading conventions. Form criticism's focus on the individual units of the tradition and the focus of both form criticism and narrative criticism on style produce slightly different readings of Tabitha's story. Dibelius classifies the Tabitha pericope as a legend coming from an independent tradition that the author had available. He argues that the story is told in an edifying style, like a gospel paradigm, but it is a legend because it has a personal interest in Peter and Tabitha.[30] He notes an 'abundance of personal details: Tabitha's name is given, her character is described, the garments she made for widows are mentioned as evidence of her beneficence, and perhaps some reference to her appearance is implied by the particular mention of the care of the corpse'.[31] Pervo, noting Dibelius's comments, highlights the details as producing pathos, something the sentimental readers of ancient romance novels would appreciate.[32] Tannehill, responsive to verbal and thematic connections, finds ties between Tabitha's concern for the poor and similar concerns in the rest of Acts. He also notes that Tabitha's practice of charity provides a 'bridge' to the charity of Cornelius in the next pericope,[33] a point also noted by Schneider.[34] Tannehill writes with more sensitivity to passages that concern wealth and ethnicity or feature female characters or males such as the Ethiopian eunuch and Cornelius. His use of narrative criticism and his theological/ideological concerns are all marks of more recent exegetical practice in the biblical guild. Reading Tabitha's story with a focus on the entire book of Acts or of Luke–Acts as a two-volume work, as redaction critics do, or in the context of the entire sweep of early Christian history, as many historical critics do, tends to eclipse Tabitha. One can easily see this in the comment of Johannes Munck: 'While the preceding and the following passages deal with decisive events, Paul's call and Peter's baptism of the first Gentile, this short passage (Acts 9.31–43) forms a pause in the account of the great climaxes'.[35] Form criticism's focus on individual pericopes tends to bring Tabitha more into focus. Narrative criticism, like redaction criticism, reading either the narrative of Acts or Luke–Acts as a whole, tends to downplay Tabitha. However, narrative criticism's focus on characters may foreground 'minor' characters as well as major ones. In this respect form-critical and narrative-critical readings may have more in common with readings from the past, which focused on individual pericopes and on moral character for the purposes of preaching and edification.

---

29 Stählin, 'χήρα', p. 452.
30 Dibelius, 'Style Criticism', pp. 12–13.
31 Dibelius, 'Style Criticism', p. 13.
32 Pervo, *Profit with Delight*, pp. 66–67.
33 Tannehill, *Narrative Unity*, p. 127.
34 Schneider, *Die Apostelgeschichte*, II, p. 49.
35 Munck, *Acts of the Apostles*, p. 89.

Male Readings from Church History

Chrysostom: Tabitha 'as active and wakeful as an antelope'. Chrysostom (c. 347–407), given the appellation 'golden-mouthed' in recognition of his preaching prowess, became Bishop of Constantinople in 398. He was soon embroiled in controversy, however, and ended his life in exile.[36] Chrysostom was known for his homilies and his literalist method of interpretation.[37] He reads Tabitha's story for what it might teach his listeners about how to behave rather than for any esoteric spiritual meaning. He reads the characters as models or types, which was a common practice in the ancient world. While his reading might be considered too fanciful or personal by the modem biblical guild, he notes the similarity between this story and that of Jairus's daughter (as modern biblical scholars are wont to do).

Chrysostom's reading begins with the sensible question: Why do the disciples wait until Tabitha is dead to send for Peter? His answer is that the disciples at Joppa did not want to trouble the disciples (Peter), 'about such matters, and to take them away from their preaching: as indeed this is why it mentions that the place was near, seeing they asked this as a thing beside his mark, and not now in the regular course'.[38]

Apparently, they did not want to interrupt Peter's preaching with concern about a sick person (woman?) unless she was dead and he happened to be nearby. Chrysostom's original question seems like a good one to me, but I am not so sure about his answer. The mid-nineteenth-century translators and editors of the homily think his answer makes perfect sense from Chrysostom's perspective. In a note they write, 'This is a hint to the hearers that they should show like forbearance and discretion, in not giving their Bishop unnecessary trouble.'[39] Chrysostom indicates that the disciples ask Peter not to delay because Tabitha is a disciple (μαθήτρια). The weeping of the widows and the showing of garments, Chrysostom interprets as a 'cheering inducement to alms'.[40] In contrast to the widows' weeping, Peter, he notes, took the circumstances calmly. Chrysostom then engages in an excursus on why the author 'informs us of the woman's name'.[41] Her name matches her character, 'as active and wakeful was she as an antelope'.[42] He notes she was full of good works as well as giving alms, making clothes with great humility along with the others. Returning to his recounting of the miracle, Chrysostom asks why Peter puts the widows out of the room. His answer is so that Peter is neither 'confused nor disturbed by their weeping'.[43] Chrysostom notes that Peter reaches out his hand to Tabitha as Christ did to Jairus's daughter. Peter presents Tabitha alive to the saints

---

36 F.L. Cross and E.A. Livingstone (eds.), *Oxford Dictionary of the Christian Church* (Oxford: Oxford University Press, 2nd edn, 1983), pp. 285–286.

37 Robert M. Grant, *A Short History of the Interpretation of the Bible* (Philadelphia: Fortress Press, 2nd edn, 1984), pp. 68–69.

38 J. Chrysostom, *Homilies on the Acts of the Apostles and the Epistle to the Romans* (Nicene and Post-Nicene Fathers, 11; ed. Philip Schaff; trans. J. Walker, J. Sheppard, and H. Browne; Grand Rapids: Eerdmans, 1956), p. 137.

39 Chrysostom, *Homilies on the Acts of the* Apostles, p. 137 n. 1.

40 Chrysostom, *Homilies on the Acts of the Apostles*, p. 137.

41 Chrysostom, *Homilies on the Acts of the Apostles*, p. 137.

42 Chrysostom, *Homilies on the Acts of the Apostles*, p. 137.

43 Chrysostom, *Homilies on the Acts of the Apostles*, p. 137.

and widows, 'to some for comfort, because they received back their sister, and because they saw the miracle, and for kindly support to others'.[44] Chrysostom praises Peter's humility in that he stays in the home of a tanner, rather than with 'this lady', that is, Tabitha, 'or some other person of distinction ... by all his acts leading men to humility, neither suffering the mean to be ashamed, nor the great to be elated!'[45]

Thus Chrysostom regards Peter as an important figure engaged in important work. Peter is a model. He is calm and collected, as well as attractively unassuming. Tabitha, who receives as much space in Chrysostom's reading as Peter, is also held up as a model. A disciple, she is active and wakeful as an antelope, full of good works as well as alms, and even though a person of distinction, suitably humble, working in company with the widows and saints. The widows come off as somewhat overly emotional, but as those to whom Peter shows compassion. In Chrysostom's homiletic reading, both Peter and Tabitha serve as edifying models for listeners. Peter, of course, is the one who is engaged in the important work of preaching and who shows compassion on the widows, healing Tabitha.

St Basil the Great: 'The example of Dorcas'. Basil the Great was one of the Cappadocian fathers of the church. He was the brother of St Gregory of Nyssa and St Macrina.[46] Early in his career he was a hermit. Later he became Bishop of Caesarea and vigorously opposed Arianism.[47] Eastern Orthodoxy groups Basil with Gregory of Nazianzus and Chrysostom as one of the three hierarchs.[48] Like Chrysostom, Basil is concerned with community behavior. He reads Scripture to find examples.

In *The Morals* Basil sets forth a series of rules, each followed by scriptural supports. Rule 74 states, 'A widow who enjoys sufficiently robust health should spend her life in works of zeal and solicitude, keeping in mind the words of the Apostle and the example of Dorcas.'[49] Basil supports this rule by references to Acts 9.36, recounting that Tabitha/Dorcas was 'full of good works and alms deeds', and to Acts 9.39, which refers to the coats and garments she made for the widows. He follows this with a reference to 1 Tim. 5.9–10 that lists the requirements for a true widow: chosen by the church for service and good works. Thus Basil reads Tabitha as a widow who serves widows and as a good example for widows to follow. A true widow perseveres 'day and night in prayer and supplication, with fasting'.[50] The rules that precede and follow rule 74 concern the prohibition of divorce unless one of the partners commits adultery or is a hindrance to the other in the service of God (rule 73) and the requirements that bondservants obey their masters (rule 75). In elaborating the prohibition of divorce Basil cites biblical passages enjoining that women be subject to their husbands, refrain from adornment for the sake of beauty, and keep silent in church. Thus Basil is concerned, much in the mold of 1 Timothy

---

44 Chrysostom, *Homilies on the Acts of the Apostles*, p. 137.
45 Chrysostom, *Homilies on the Acts of the Apostles*, p. 137.
46 Cross and Livingstone (eds.), *Oxford Dictionary of the Christian Church*, p. 857.
47 Cross and Livingstone (eds.), *Oxford Dictionary of the Christian Church*, pp. 139–40.
48 Frederick W. Norris, 'Basil of Caesrea', in Everett Ferguson (ed.), *Encyclopedia of Early Christianity* (New York: Garland, 1990), p. 141.
49 Basil, St, *Saint Basil: Ascetical Works* (Fathers of the Church: A New Translation, 9; trans. M. Monica Wagner; New York: Fathers of the Church, Inc., 1950), p. 191.
50 Basil, *Saint Basil: Ascetical Works*, p. 192.

and the New Testament household codes, with the 'proper' roles for Christian women. Tabitha/Dorcas is read as an example of the proper widow.

Calvin: The author 'applies the same word to a woman'. Calvin (1509–64) was a prolific exegete, writing commentaries on most of the canonical books of the Bible. He sought to make clear the literal sense of the text in its original historical and literary context. He used the editions of the Bible and scholarly techniques available at the time. Theologically, the three Reformation principles of *sola scriptura* (Scripture alone), *sola fide* (faith alone, rather than works) and *solo Christo* ('Christ alone is the source of salvation') guided his interpretation.[51] The words of the Bible only become the Word of God for readers or hearers by the power of the Holy Spirit.[52]

Calvin comments extensively on the story of Tabitha. While he notes such things as a possible parallel between Peter and Elisha (also seen by many modern biblical scholars), he sees the story as a powerful example of Christ's power. Calvin focuses on God's actions and purposes rather than upon Peter. He commends both Tabitha and Peter for their faithfulness to God, describing both as instruments of God. Calvin highlights the description of Tabitha as a disciple:

> Several times already he [the author of Acts] has used the word *disciple* for a Christian man, and in case we might think that it is suitable for men only, he applies the same word to a woman. But this title warns us that Christianity does not exist without teaching, and that the learning prescribed is of such a kind that the same Christ may be the only Teacher for all. This is the highest commendation, this is the basis of a holy life, this is the root of all virtues, to have learned from the Son of God what is the way to live, and what true life is.[53]

He then argues that Tabitha's good works and almsgiving spring from her faith as a disciple, taking the opportunity in good Reformation fashion to stress faith before works and the equality before God of all believers. As with the term 'disciple', Calvin notes the translation of Tabitha's name into Greek as Dorcas, a point often made by interpreters of all periods and schools. He, however, offers a unique interpretation. He translates Dorcas as a wild she-goat, a name he views as 'far from complimentary'.[54] But, he says, 'the sanctity of her life easily wiped out the stigma of a rather unbecoming name'.[55] Calvin explains that the washing of Tabitha's body and the placing of the body in the upper room are proof that Tabitha was dead, although the placing of it in the upper room rather than in a tomb shows that the faithful had 'some hope of restoring her to life'.[56] The washing of the body produces a long excursus on washing and burial practices on Calvin's part. It culminates in a condemnation of the washing and anointing practices of 'monks', that is, Roman Catholics. Calvin reads with an eye

---

51 C. Schwöbel, 'Calvin', in R.J. Coggins and J.L. Houlden (eds.), *A Dictionary of Biblical Interpretation* (Philadelphia: Trinity Press International; London: SCM Press, 1990), pp. 98–101 (98–99).
52 Schwöbel, p. 99
53 John Calvin, *The Acts of the Apostles* (Calvin's New Testament Commentaries; trans. John W. Fraser and W.J.G. McDonald; Grand Rapids: Eerdmans, 1965), I, p. 278.
54 Calvin, *The Acts of the Apostles*, p. 278.
55 Calvin, *The Acts of the Apostles*, p. 278.
56 Calvin, *The Acts of the Apostles*, p. 278.

on how other readers may read the passage. As for the weeping widows and the poor distressed at Tabitha's death, Calvin argues that God had pity on their needs and also uses the miracle to strengthen their faith. The Spirit of God directs Peter's role in the whole affair. When Peter puts others out of the upper room in which Tabitha's body lies, he does so 'so that no one may ascribe to his power a work of God, of which he is only the agent',[57] not, as Chrysostom argues, in order to avoid distraction.

Calvin also responds to a charge, apparently made by some other readers, that the story of Tabitha proves that after death the soul is but a breath until the Resurrection Day. Otherwise, they ask, what good does it do Tabitha to be restored to bodily life, a prison house of suffering? Calvin again stresses God, arguing that God was 'more concerned about his own glory than about Tabitha herself', although since 'the advantage of the faithful is always connected to the glory of God, it was a greater blessing to her to be restored to life, in order to be a more illustrious instrument of the divine goodness and power'.[58]

Thus, because Calvin's reading lens is theocentric and christocentric, Tabitha and her role as an agent receive more attention than in many modern scholarly readings. Both Peter and Tabitha are subordinated to God and God's purposes. Although one certainly could not call Calvin a feminist, Calvin is more open to accepting God's use of women than many of his male contemporaries.[59]

Matthew Henry's Commentary: 'Tabitha was a great doer, no great talker'. Matthew Henry (1662–1714) was a non-conformist, or dissenting, English minister. For several centuries English-speaking Protestant ministers used his *Commentary on the Bible*. The *Commentary* is still popular among conservative Protestants today, often in its abridged version. Like Chrysostom, also a homilist, Henry focuses on Peter and Tabitha as models for believers to emulate. Tabitha is 'a disciple, eminent above many for works of charity'.[60] Like Calvin, Henry notes that her faith is shown by her works. Like a tree full of fruit, she is full of good works: 'Many are full of good words, who are empty and barren in good work; but Tabitha was a great doer, no great talker.'[61] Henry commends Tabitha at some length for her clothing of the needy. The widows are also praised for their gratitude to Tabitha for her charity and industry. They also do a good work in commending the dead, 'modestly, soberly, and without flattery'.[62] They repeat Tabitha's virtues 'not in word, but in deed' by showing the clothes she had made.[63] They weep to induce Peter to have compassion upon them, to restore Tabitha, who had likewise had compassion upon them. Although Henry devotes less space to Peter, Peter is praised because of his compassion and humility.

---

57 Calvin, *The Acts of the Apostles*, p. 281.
58 Calvin, *The Acts of the Apostles*, p. 282.
59 For a discussion of Calvin's views on women, see Jane Dempsey Douglass, *Women, Freedom, and Calvin* (Philadelphia: Westminster Press, 1985). Douglass argues that Calvin in his biblical interpretation evidences 'little explicit positive support for the traditional general subordination of women' (*Women*, p. 62). Calvin, for example, understands the command for women to keep silence in the church as human governance that can change, not eternal law (*Women*, p. 62).
60 Matthew Henry, *Matthew Henry's Commentary in One Volume* (ed. L.F. Church; Grand Rapids: Zondervan, 1961), p. 1673.
61 Henry, *Matthew Henry's Commentary*, p. 1673.
62 Henry, *Matthew Henry's Commentary*, p. 1673.
63 Henry, *Matthew Henry's Commentary*, p. 1673.

Peter comes when called for help, even though he is a great apostle, and he raises Tabitha privately to avoid 'vainglory'.[64] Thus Henry solves one of the puzzles Chrysostom and Calvin also see in the passage: Why does Peter heal Tabitha in private? Henry's interpretation is similar to Calvin's, emphasizing Peter's humility.

Although Henry disagrees with Chrysostom on this point, Chrysostom and Henry, two preachers seeking to edify their hearers, have much in common. The praise of Tabitha is very welcome to my feminist ears, but there is a disturbing undertone. Tabitha is a great doer, but no great talker. From the perspective of putting her faith into practice rather than just being full of empty talk, this sounds good. From the perspective that a lot of men in Acts do a lot of talking and preaching, and women seem limited to good works and bankrolling the male talking, Henry's interpretation has a dark side.

Three Late Nineteenth-Century/Early Twentieth-Century Women's Readings: Stanton, Sangster, and Foote

Speaking very generally, two currents played important roles in the nineteenth- and early twentieth-century 'woman suffrage movement' in the United States. Liberal feminism emphasized the rationality and equal natural rights of women as individuals. Liberal feminists argued that women should have public-sphere legal rights to property, custody of children, control of inheritance, and the right to sue as well as the vote. Examples of nineteenth-century thinkers often classified as liberal feminists include Elizabeth Cady Stanton, Sarah Grimké, Sojourner Truth, and Frances Wright. At the same time there was a great surge of what Josephine Donovan labels cultural feminism. A central thesis of cultural feminism was that women were different from men, and were in many ways, especially morally, superior. Motherhood and 'female' values were celebrated. This position was largely, but not entirely, a white middle- and upper-class phenomenon. It was associated in some ways with the cult of True Womanhood. Donovan's examples of cultural feminists include thinkers such as Margaret Fuller, Charlotte Perkins Gilman, Jane Addams, and, in some respects, Anna Julia Cooper and Elizabeth Cady Stanton, one of the most powerful figures in the 'woman suffrage movement'.[65] Although a gross oversimplification, in some ways one could say that

---

64 Henry, *Matthew Henry's Commentary*, p. 1673.
65 Josephine Donovan, *Feminist Theory: The Intellectual Traditions of American Feminism* (New York: F. Ungar, 1985; New York: Continuum, paperback, 1990). Chapter Two focuses on cultural feminism. How to view Cooper and Stanton in terms of liberal and cultural feminism is a matter of some controversy. For discussions of the ambiguities in Cooper's position see b. hooks, *Ain't I A Woman: Black Women and Feminism*, (Boston: South End Press, 1981), pp. 166–68, and M.H. Washington, 'Introduction to *A Voice from the South* by Anna Julia Cooper', in H.L. Gates (ed.), *Spiritual Narratives: M.W. Stewart; J. Lee; J.A.J. Foote; V.W. Broughton* (The Schomburg Library of Nineteenth-Centry Black Women Writers; New York: Oxford University Press, 1988; facsimile of 1886 edn), pp. xlii–li. For Stanton see the debate between Karen Offen, 'Defining Feminism: A Comparative Historical Approach', *Signs* 14 (1988), pp. 119–57 and Ellen Carol DuBois, 'Comment on Karen Offen's "Defining Feminism: A Comparative Historical Approach"', *Signs* 15 (1989), pp. 195–97. My own view is that there are elements of individualist/equality feminism as well as elements of relational/cultural feminism in both Stanton and Cooper, probably with equality feminism dominating. Both were products of the nineteenth century with its emphasis on the positive moral contribution of women. Stanton's *The Women's Bible* project, with its focus on passages concerning women, tends in many places toward a cultural feminism.

cultural feminists took the binary oppositions that devalued women, such as reason–passion, aggression–peacefulness, public–domestic, and reversed the value polarity. In their particular historical circumstances, emphasizing female moral superiority was an effective tool to argue for women's suffrage and education. A negative and destructive use of this view occurred when it was tied to attempts to argue for women's suffrage as a way of countering the black male vote. Liberal feminists opposed this view because they had striven long and hard to establish that the rationality and agency of women were equal to those of men. This was the basis for their argument that women possessed the same natural rights as men. Many thinkers, such as Anna Julia Cooper and Elizabeth Cady Stanton, combined various elements of liberal and cultural feminism.

Elizabeth Cady Stanton: 'What men teach in their high places, such women as Dorcas illustrate in their lives'. Toward the end of her life Stanton (1815–1902) edited and wrote most of a commentary on the Bible designed to counter what she saw as reactionary elements in organized religion. In *The Woman's Bible* (1898) Stanton comments briefly on the Tabitha story:

> Tabitha was called by this name among the Jews; but she was known to the Greeks as Dorcas. She was considered an ornament to her Christian profession; for she so abounded in good works and alms-deeds that her whole life was devoted to the wants and the needs of the poor. She not only gave away her substance, but she employed her time and her skill in laboring constantly for the poor and the unfortunate. Her death was looked upon as a public calamity. This is the first instance of any Apostle performing a miracle of this kind. There was no witness to this miracle. What men teach in their high places, such women as Dorcas illustrate in their lives.[66]

Stanton pictures Tabitha as a woman devoted to the cause of the poor, a living example. Echoing in some respects Henry's comment about those who 'talk the talk but do not walk the walk', she sees Tabitha as the type of woman who practices what men merely teach. Her praise also raises the question of why there are no women teaching in high places.

Margaret E. Sangster: 'Their names are inscribed in no Hall of Fame, but they are written in the Book of Life'. Like Stanton, Margaret E. Sangster (1838–1912) produced a book on biblical texts concerned with women, including Tabitha. Sangster, a prolific popular author and editor, was much less radical than Stanton. Nevertheless, she wrote in favor of equal educational opportunity for women as well as advancing many tenets of cultural feminism.[67] The tenor of her writing can be seen in the conclusion to her book *The Women of the Bible* (1911):

---

66 Elizabeth Cady Stanton, *The Woman's Bible* (Salem, NH: The Ayer Company; repr. edn from Part II [1898]; New York: European Publishing Company, 1988), p. 146.

67 For more information on Sangster, see Margaret E. Sangster, *From My Youth Up* (Signal Lives: Autobiographies of American Women; New York: Arno Press, 1980; repr. of the 1909 edn [New York: Revell Company under the title *An Autobiography: From My Youth Up: Personal Reminiscences*]) and Frances E. Willard and Mary Livermore, 'Mrs Margaret Elizabeth Sangster', in *idem, A Woman of the Century* (Detroit: Gale Research, 1967; repr. of the orig. edn [Buffalo: C.W. Moulton, 1893]), p. 632, and Margaret E. Sangster, *The Women of the Bible: A Portrait Gallery* (New York: The Christian Herald, 1911).

The portrait gallery of women, beginning with Eve in the Garden of Eden, shows us woman in every age essentially the same. The woman soul leads on. For good or for ill, for weal or for woe, woman influences man and, to a great extent, controls his destiny... Woman holds in her hand at this hour a great moral responsibility. If she choose to throw her influence in the scale in favor of peace, the knell of war will be sounded. If she awaken to the shame and infamy of child labor that the greed of Mammon may be satisfied, the children will cease to be enslaved before they have had time to play. Woman owes so much to Christ that it behooves her in a Christian land to remember the women in lands that are still in the shadow of death. The work of woman for woman and the work of woman for Christ should go hand in hand in this wonderful century in which we live.[68]

Sangster's discussion of Tabitha is entitled 'The Raising of Dorcas'. The discussion is much in the spirit of a cultural feminism that saw Woman as a moral model who from the domestic sphere fights for justice and cares for the poor. She also makes a point similar to that of Stanton that women doers are often unsung heroines. She begins the chapter with a comparison between Tabitha's work in the days of the early church and the work of providing clothes for needy women and support for the mission field in her own day. This is work women did 'conspicuously' in Tabitha's day and 'have been doing all along the line ever since'.[69] The needle is their weapon of choice. Sangster sees Dorcas as a model that women can and have followed: 'In the course of my life I have known not a few women who wrought for Jesus Christ after her pattern. Their names are inscribed in no Hall of Fame, but they are written in the Book of Life.'[70] To Sangster's mind Dorcas fits the picture of gentle and caring womanhood. She imagines Dorcas as 'gentle, tender, comforting and, I think, beautiful'.[71] As for Peter, Sangster humanizes him. She begins by recalling examples of Peter's lack of faith from the Gospels. The Peter that prays for and offers his hand to Dorcas, she writes, is not the Peter who walked on the water and sank or who denied the Lord three times. It is the Peter whom the Lord asks, 'Lovest thou Me?' and the Peter who heals the cripple at the Beautiful Gate.[72] Jesus, says Sangster, calls all disciples to humble care for his lambs, men and women alike. She concludes with the remark that the church in Joppa had a 'revival of dead souls that day, when the living soul came back to Dorcas by the grace of Jesus Christ at the summons of his servant'.[73] As with Calvin, the emphasis is on Christ's action rather than Peter's power.

Sangster, however, operates with little hermeneutics of suspicion—or at least not openly. She does not ask why women are wielding the needle rather than ascending the pulpit stairs. Or why their names are not inscribed in a Hall of Fame. On the other hand, she celebrates the work of the little people who do the nitty-gritty work of caring for those in need in a way that makes it clear that that work is indispensable and might not get done otherwise. Her picture of Tabitha as a model woman is essentialist, describing woman as a gentle caregiver and moral beacon. It never poses a direct threat to a patriarchal social order. It certainly would permit men to continue

---

68 Sangster, *The Women of the Bible*, pp. 361–62.
69 Sangster, *The Women of the Bible*, p. 326.
70 Sangster, *The Women of the Bible*, p. 327.
71 Sangster, *The Women of the Bible*, p. 327.
72 Sangster, *The Women of the Bible*, p. 328.
73 Sangster, *The Women of the Bible*, p. 329.

to view women as those whose job it is to care for others and to protect moral values while the men handle the public sphere. The subject position that Sangster holds up as a model—'Woman works in fairs and bazaars, she sends boxes and barrels to missionary stations near and far, she clothes the orphans and cheers the destitute'[74] —is one that would most easily be filled by middle-class American Protestant women in her day. She does not write from the position of the destitute or of those to whom the missionaries go. At the same time, her description of unsung women church workers might be recognized with modifications for their own situations by many differently situated women. Her women may wield the needle rather than the sword or pen, but they are agents nonetheless.

Julia A.J. Foote: 'God is no respecter of persons'. If we do look to nineteenth- and early twentieth-century American women differently situated from the white middle-class Stanton and Sangster, it is difficult to find records of their interpretation of Tabitha. One middle-class, educated, African American evangelist, Virginia W. Broughton, provides very brief topical outlines of several of her sermons. In one on the biblical authority for women's work she cites Acts 9.39 and Rom. 16.1 as examples of women as missionaries.[75] In a sermon on Christian work she offers Peter, Paul, Mary, Dorcas (Tabitha), and Lydia as illustrations that one's work is 'indicated by one's natural gifts and adaptability'.[76] Unfortunately, how Broughton developed these examples is not preserved. It seems safe to say that she was justifying women's work in fields traditionally understood as male.

If it is difficult to find examples of interpretations of Tabitha, it is not difficult to find examples of African American women's use of Acts.[77] A particularly striking example is found in the autobiography of Julia A.J. Foote (1823–1900), an African Methodist Episcopal female evangelist. Foote focuses not on female characters, but on males such as the Ethiopian eunuch of Acts 8 and the Roman centurion Cornelius in Acts 10. She also finds great inspiration as many feminists have done in Acts 2.16-21, which announces that the spirit of prophecy is poured out on daughters as

74 Sangster, *The Women of the Bible*, p. 326.
75 Virginia W. Broughton, 'Twenty Years Experience of a Missionary', in H.L. Gates (ed.), *Spiritual Narratives* (Chicago: The Pony Press, 1907), pp. 1–140 (130).
76 Broughton, 'Twenty Year's Experience', p. 132.
77 African American women interpreters of Acts include Jarena Lee, Anna Julia Cooper, and Zilpha Elaw. The epigraph of Jarena Lee's autobiography, *The Life and Religious Experience of Jarena Lee*, is Joel 2.28, which is quoted in Acts 2: 'And it shall come to pass ... that I will pour out my Spirit upon all flesh, and your sons, and your *daughters* shall prophecy [prophesy]' (italics in original) in W.L. Andrews (ed.), *Sisters of the Spirit: Three Black Women's Autobiographies of the Nineteenth Century* (Bloomington: Indiana University Press, 1986), p. 27. Anna Julia Cooper makes use of the Cornelius episode. She considers Acts 10.34 (God is no respecter of persons) to be one of the Scripture passages that is key to the Christian message (Karen Baker-Fletcher, 'Anna Julia Cooper and Sojourner Truth: Two Nineteenth-Century Black Feminist Interpreters of Scripture', in Schüssler Fiorenza [ed.], *Searching the Scriptures*, I, pp. 41–51 [45]). Zilpha Elaw, after recounting a vision of Jesus guaranteeing the forgiveness of her sins, compares herself to the Ethiopian eunuch of Acts 8 (Andrews, *Sisters of the Spirit*, p. 57). Nineteenth-century English Methodist women preachers also found Joel 2.28 = Acts 2.17-21 especially empowering (Christine Krueger, *The Reader's Repentance: Women Preachers, Women Writers, and Nineteenth-Century Social Discourse* [Chicago: University of Chicago Press, 1992], pp. 63–64), as did Katherine Zell during the Reformation in Strasbourg (Douglass, *Women*, pp. 92–93).

well as sons. Foote's reading strategies illumine and enrich our understanding of possible approaches to texts like Acts. Foote reads from a very particular social and historical location but finds in that particularity universal implications. She intertwines her autobiography with, and sees parallels between her life and, these texts in Acts. She reads one in the light of the other. This practice, according to Renita Weems, is characteristic of the African American female interpretative community's hermeneutics. These readers, according to Weems, 'measure what they have been told about God, reality, and themselves against what they have experienced of God and reality and what they think of themselves as it has been mediated to them by the primary community with which they identify'.[78]

As Julia Foote describes her spiritual journey, a sense of sin and something missing troubled her as a young girl. She believed that if she was educated God would help her understand what she needed. Troubled by a lack of education and hampered by lack of educational opportunity for 'colored' children, the young Foote was forced to become self-taught after but a few weeks of school. She carefully studied the Bible. After a time she met an older man and woman who testified about their previous troubles overcoming sin and their experience of joy after sanctification. She interpreted herself as the Ethiopian eunuch and the older couple as Philip: 'I at once understood what I needed. Though I had read in my Bible many things they told me, I had never understood what I read. I needed a Philip to teach me.'[79] The female saint of the couple read and explained many passages of Scripture to Foote, and shortly after Foote felt herself sanctified.[80] Neither Foote's parents nor her minister were much taken with her keeping company with the elderly saints, her adoption of the doctrine of sanctification, or her belief that she had been sanctified. Her minister was particularly unhappy when she joyfully shared her beliefs with others. He argued that she was too young 'to read and dictate to persons older than yourself'.[81] But Julia Foote was not deterred 'by what man might think or say'.[82] Neither age nor sex were barriers to the one who was no respecter of persons (Acts 10.34):

> Bless the Lord, O my soul, for this wonderful salvation, that snatched me as a brand from the burning, even me, a poor, ignorant girl! And will he not do for all what he did for me? Yes, yes; God is no respecter of persons.[83]

Acts 2.16–21, where Peter quotes Joel 2.28–29, is also significant for Foote. She strongly felt her commission to preach came from the Holy Spirit. The minister of the AME Zion church in Boston opposed her efforts to preach sanctification and had her

---

78 Weems, 'Reading *Her Way*', p. 66. Weems is careful to note that her strategic use of the term African American women can obscure differences between African American women ('Reading *Her Way*', p. 59 n. 4). My placing Foote within the African American women's reading community can also elide differences. It would be more accurate to classify Foote as a member of a nineteenth-century African American AME female evangelistic/sanctification reading community.

79 Julia A.J. Foote, 'A Brand Plucked from the Fire: An Autobiographical Sketch by Mrs Julia A.J. Foote', in Andrews (ed.), *Sisters of the Spirit*, pp. 161–234 (185) (originally published privately in 1879).

80 Foote, 'A Brand Plucked from the Fire', pp. 186–87.

81 Foote, 'A Brand Plucked from the Fire', p. 188.

82 Foote, 'A Brand Plucked from the Fire', p. 189.

83 Foote, 'A Brand Plucked from the Fire', p. 189.

excommunicated. She made an appeal to a higher level in the AME Zion church. Her appeal was ignored, she argued, on the basis of her sex. In writing of this experience she said that 'there was no justice meted out to women in those days. Even ministers of Christ did not feel that women had any rights which they were bound to respect.'[84] As William Andrews points out, these words were a clear echo of the Supreme Court's words in the Dred Scott decision, which held that black Americans 'had no rights which the white man was bound to respect' (*Dred Scott v. Sanford*, 19 Howard 393).[85] Thus Foote tied together unjust racism and sexism.[86] Immediately following her discussion of her rejection she offers an entire chapter entitled 'Women in the Gospel'. There she writes of the authorization of Acts 2 for her preaching:

> I could not believe that it was a short-lived impulse or spasmodic influence that impelled me to preach. I read that on the day of Pentecost was the Scripture fulfilled as found in Joel ii. 28, 29; and it certainly will not be denied that women as well as men were at that time filled with the Holy Ghost, because it is expressly stated that women were among those who continued in prayer and supplication, waiting for the fulfillment of the promise. Women and men are classed together, and if the power to preach the Gospel is short-lived and spasmodic in the case of women, it must be equally so in that of men; and if women have lost the gift of prophecy, so have men.[87]

Many black Americans have been drawn to the Ethiopian eunuch as a 'culturally affirming and empowering tradition'.[88] It may very well be that Foote found the story of an African Christian illuminating for that reason as well. At the same time Foote did not feel that she could not identify with the eunuch because he was male, or because he was a high official. She explicitly states that she identified with his need for inspired interpretative guidance. This reading did not mean that she assumed a position of racial or sexual subordination, however. The persons she saw in the role of Philip were an elderly African American couple, especially the female saint. At the same time as Foote looked to the Ethiopian eunuch, she turned to other passages in Acts where she read the Holy Spirit's authorization of women's preaching and teaching activities. While the story of Cornelius in Acts 10 (as well as the story of the Ethiopian eunuch in Acts 8.26–40)[89] marks the inclusion of Gentiles as previously excluded from Christianity, Foote reads the passage in the light of the exclusion of young girls who advocate sanctification. Her minister cannot exclude what God includes, whether pious Roman centurions or Julia Foote herself. According to Vincent Wimbush, Acts 2 and Acts 10, especially 10.34–35, were passages frequently used in African American biblical interpretation to argue for universal salvation, especially in relation to the racial situation in the United States.[90] Foote's use of the passages marks her as a member of an African American reading community in the African American churches, particularly the AME churches.

---

84 Foote, 'A Brand Plucked from the Fire', p. 207.
85 Quoted in Andrews (ed.), *Sisters of the Spirit*, p. 20.
86 Andrews (ed.), *Sisters of the Spirit*, p. 20.
87 Foote, 'A Brand Plucked from the Fire', p. 208.
88 Martin, 'A Chamberlain's Journey', pp. 105–36 (125).
89 See Martin, 'A Chamberlain's Journey', and Tannehill, *Narrative Unity*, pp. 107–12.
90 Vincent L. Wimbush, 'Reading Texts through Worlds, Worlds through Texts', *Semeia* 62 (1993), pp. 129–39 (132).

However, Foote extends the use of the passages to the impartiality of God in areas of gender as well as race. Her double perspective as an African American female enriches her reading. As Foote read the biblical text, she read it with a dual hermeneutic of suspicion and re-vision. She recognized and experienced biblical passages being used against her. She also found within Scripture what Schweickart[91] calls utopian moments, for her the truer meanings vouchsafed by the Holy Spirit. Like the Ethiopian eunuch she had read many passages but only understood them after her eyes were opened by the elderly couple who served as her Philip. For Foote the gospel message of Acts spoke to her particular situation as an African American woman evangelist, but it did so because its message properly understood was universal. Universality did not mask a hidden male face, black or white, nor did it deny her particularity.

Modern Feminist Scholars' Readings
The most recent resurgence of readings of the New Testament by those who identified themselves as part of the women's movement or feminists began in the late 1960s and early 1970s. Many of these interpreters argued for an equal role in the churches for women. Often ordination and more power for women as well as combat against misogynism were goals. One of the most widely read works that contained interpretations of Luke–Acts, and Tabitha in particular, was Constance Parvey's essay, 'The Theology and Leadership of Women in the New Testament'.[92] In the 1980s, feminist interpretation of the New Testament blossomed. Historical-critical, literary and social context methods were all employed. Bonnie Bowman Thurston's work, *The Widows: A Women's Ministry in the Early Church*, arose out of the contrast she saw between the triple marginality of elderly poor women and the important role these women play in the service and support of churches today.[93] She found that 'If women were marginal in church history, widows were invisible!'[94] Thus Thurston (citing Parvey) sought to recover the history of widows from the time of Jesus to 325 CE. The early 1990s saw the publication of Mary Rose D'Angelo's 'Women in Luke–Acts: A Redactional View' in the flagship journal of the American biblical guild, the *Journal of Biblical Literature*,[95] and Gail R. O'Day's commentary on Acts in *The Women's Bible Commentary*;[96] both discuss Tabitha. D'Angelo, using redaction criticism, a well-accepted method in the guild, refers to Parvey's earlier work. She notes that Parvey and others have celebrated the significance of the role given to women in Luke–Acts. She also calls attention to subsequent feminist work that argues Luke–Acts 'appears to take a more conventional view of the role of

---

91 Schweickart, 'Reading Ourselves'.
92 Constance F. Parvey, 'The Theology and Leadership of Women in the New Testament', in Rosemary Radford Ruether (ed.), *Religion and Sexism: Images of Woman in the Jewish and Christian Traditions* (New York: Simon & Schuster, 1974), pp. 117–49.
93 Bonnie Bowman Thurston, *The Widows: A Women's Ministry in the Early Church* (Minneapolis: Fortress Press, 1989).
94 Thurston, *The Widows*, p. 7.
95 Mary Rose D'Angelo, 'Women in Luke–Acts: A Redactional View', *JBL* 109 (1990), pp. 441–61.
96 Gail R. O'Day, 'Acts', in C.A. Newsom and S.H. Ringe (eds.), *The Women's Bible Commentary* (Louisville, KY: Westminster/John Knox Press, 1992), pp. 305–12.

women than do the other gospels'[97] and downplays women's leadership in the early church. D'Angelo wants to 'give a rationale for different feminist perceptions'[98] of Luke–Acts. O'Day, writing the commentary on Acts in *The Women's Bible Commentary*, continues a chain of feminist interpretation begun by Parvey, listing D'Angelo in her bibliography and depending on her for some of her arguments. In line with the pattern of the volume, she comments directly on women who appear in the narrative, including Tabitha. She notes the overall '*de facto* silencing' of women in Luke–Acts but also the subversive glimpses of women's experience and universal theology of Acts.[99]

Constance Parvey: Women in the New Testament. Parvey notes the number of stories about women in Luke–Acts, highlighting the pairing of male and female illustrations. She argues that this served a pedagogical purpose, making 'the message clearly understandable to different groups—the female and the male listeners'.[100] Here we have a hallmark of feminist readings, a concern for the effects upon hearers/readers, especially women. She interprets the story of Mary and Martha as a 'keystone': 'While previously the learning of scriptures was limited to men, now it is opened to women. The story of Mary and Martha allowed women to choose.'[101] Parvey argues that the traditional role of a woman as a domestic servant is challenged when Mary is allowed to sit at the feet of a rabbi. Parvey notes what she sees as the more liberal educational policies of Christianity in contrast to those of rabbinic Judaism, a scape-goating and ill-informed move typical of many Christian feminists in the 1970s and one that Plaskow[102] and Brooten[103] have soundly criticized. Still, Parvey does note that 'cultural, religious, and legal impediments' are part of Christianity as well as part of Judaism.[104] Parvey sees Acts as evidence for the prominent and active role of women in the early church. Parvey identifies Tabitha as a woman with a special status as a 'disciple'. She notes that, like Paul and Barnabas, Tabitha is never named as one of the Twelve, but 'unlike them, her designation as "disciple" has been minimized by the Church'.[105] Whether Tabitha is 'merely a follower' or one of a 'small elite group' of Jesus' adherents, Parvey argues, she is clearly important. Parvey reads Tabitha as 'a Jewish woman of independent means', well known for her charity, craftsmanship (Parvey, like Sangster, has an appreciation for Tabitha's needle), and 'graceful manner', since 'Tabitha' means 'gazelle'. Parvey reads the widows' weeping and Peter's swift arrival as evidence of Tabitha's importance:

97 D'Angelo, 'Women in Luke–Acts', p. 442.
98 D'Angelo, 'Women in Luke–Acts', p. 442.
99 O'Day, 'Acts', p. 312.
100 Parvey, 'The Theology and Leadership of Women', pp. 117–49 (139).
101 Parvey, 'The Theology and Leadership of Women', p. 141.
102 Judith Plaskow, 'Christian Feminism and Anti-Judaism', *Crosscurrents* 28 (1978), pp. 306–309, and *idem*, 'Anti-Judaism in Feminist Christian Interpretation', in Schüssler Fiorenza (ed.), *Searching the Scriptures*, I, pp. 117–29.
103 Bernadette Brooten, 'Early Christian Women and their Cultural Context: Issues of Method in Historical Reconstruction', in Adela Yarbro Collins (ed.), *Feminist Perspectives on Biblical Scholarship* (SBL Biblical Scholarship in North America, 10; Chico, CA: Scholars Press, 1985), pp. 65–92.
104 Parvey, 'The Theology and Leadership of Women', p. 142.
105 Parvey, 'The Theology and Leadership of Women', p. 145.

To be recorded as raised from the dead, and to be the focus of the first such miracle by a fellow disciple, she must have been considered indispensable to the congregation. Her exact status remains unknown, but that she was much more than merely one of the many followers is clear from the story about her.[106]

This is quite a different reading of the story than that of modern scholars who see Tabitha as the incidental, if somewhat colorfully described, object of a miracle that demonstrates Peter's status as a prophet like Jesus, Elijah, and Elisha. Parvey concludes her discussion of women in Acts by noting that women of all social levels participated: 'In worship, teaching, institutional and missionary life, the Spirit, indeed, was poured out on both "sons and daughters".'[107]

Parvey's summary, concluding her entire article on women in the New Testament, restates the view seen in the section on Acts. Women, she argues, had prominent leadership roles in the early church, although not without the subordination coming from the Jewish cast of its cultural milieu. She also reiterates her interpretation of Paul as one who had preached a theology of equivalence in Christ. She sees the later church as struggling with a dualism of other-worldly spiritual equality and practical this-worldly subordination. The result has been that

> One might on rare occasion become a saint, but certainly not a priest; one might become a teacher, but certainly not a theologian or bishop. The consequence of this distorted spirituality and skewed social reality has been that women have been precluded from receiving or ever developing fully responsible and equal roles in the Church's spiritual, theological and institutional life.[108]

Bonnie Bowman Thurston: The Widows in the New Testament. Thurston begins her discussion of Acts with a statement typical of much feminist New Testament scholarship. She reiterates the 'interestedness' of the New Testament: 'the writings of the early church were shaped in part by a struggle among opposing groups over the equality of women and therefore cannot be taken as an objective record of the actual condition of women in the early church'.[109] With many other interpreters Thurston notes that the Tabitha story carries forward a favorite Lukan theme—paralleling apostles with Jesus—although with Parvey and Stanton she remarks that this is the first time an apostle raises someone from the dead. Her reading of Tabitha's story, however, centers, as does Parvey's, on the foci of the *hapax legomenon* of Tabitha as μαθήτρια and on the status of the term 'widow'. She notes the ambiguity of the term 'disciple' in the early church but points out that it may indicate a special status as one of Jesus' early key followers, reading Peter's swift arrival and later use of the term μαθήτρια in gnostic works as possible evidence of this. Thurston notes that the references to widows in Acts 9 as well as in Acts 4 and 6 may be read as referring simply to women whose husbands have died *or* as referring to a special group among these set aside for a special role in the church. Thurston takes issue with the interpretation of Foakes Jackson and Lake that it is unlikely that the widows in Acts 9

---

106 Parvey, 'The Theology and Leadership of Women', p. 145.
107 Parvey, 'The Theology and Leadership of Women', p. 146.
108 Parvey, 'The Theology and Leadership of Women', p. 147.
109 Thurston, *The Widows*, p. 28.

represent an order that dispenses as well as one that receives charity.[110] Thurston, along with Stählin[111] and Swidler,[112] reads the reference to 'saints and widows' in v. 41 as evidence for a distinction between the widows and the rest of the members of the early church. For Thurston, this suggests the possibility that a society of widows existed outside of Jerusalem as early as 43 CE. Thurston reads Tabitha herself as a woman of independent means, a caretaker of the group of widows. Since no husband is mentioned, Tabitha may herself be a widow, with the responsibility to care for the widows as a 'recognizable group'[113] as enjoined in 1 Tim. 5.16 and mentioned in later Christian writings. Thus Thurston is recovering the important role in New Testament history of older women, a role she sees modern women playing as well. She makes one of the classic moves of feminist historians, rendering visible women's agency in history. But this move is not simply compensatory, it is a rewriting of the history of the early church. Because Acts is a source for reconstructing women's agency, it can serve a liberatory function.

Mary Rose D'Angelo: Women in Luke–Acts. D'Angelo's study of the 'Women in Luke–Acts' is primarily redactional, focusing on the ideology, theology, and community concerns of the editor—unlike Parvey's and Thurston's readings, which are primarily, although not exclusively, oriented to the reconstruction of early Christian history. As I noted above, D'Angelo announces that the goal of the essay is to give account of differences in feminist perceptions of Luke–Acts as liberatory or restrictive. Her thesis is captured in the following statement:

> On the one hand, the author of Luke does increase the number of stories about women in the Gospel, and the increase is a deliberate choice on the part of the author. On the other, the roles in which women appear are more restricted by what is acceptable to the convention of the imperial world than are the roles of women in Mark or John. It [the essay] will argue that the ambiguity results from the tension between the necessity of catechizing women converts who are still of real political importance to the church of Luke's day and the anxiety that an expanded role for women may cause Christians to be seen as practitioners of 'un-Roman activities'. Thus the Gospel offers to its women readers a wide variety of female role models who are the means at once of edification and of control.[114]

Again we see the concern for effects on women readers, as well as an interest in the Lukan redactional purpose. D'Angelo agrees with Parvey that Luke–Acts shows a special concern for female illustrations and that these serve an educational purpose for women converts. However, these roles are rather conventional. Taking her cue from Schüssler Fiorenza's interpretation of the Mary and Martha episode[115] as a story that criticizes Martha's active ministry as διάκονος in favor of Mary's passive

---

110 F.J. Foakes Jackson and Kirsopp Lake, *The Acts of the Apostles*, IV. (The Beginnings of Christianity, Part I; ed. Henry J. Cadbury and Kirsopp Lake; London: Macmillan, 1933).
111 Stählin, 'χήρα', p. 452.
112 Leonard Swidler, *Biblical Affirmations of Women* (Philadelphia: Westminster Press, 1979), p. 305.
113 Thurston, *The Widows*, p. 34.
114 D'Angelo, 'Women in Luke–Acts', pp. 442–43.
115 E. Schüssler Fiorenza, 'A Feminist Critical Interpretation for Liberation: Martha and Mary (Luke 10.38–42)', *Religion and Intellectual Life* 3 (1986), pp. 16–36; and see also now *idem*, *But She Said*, pp. 51–76.

listening role, D'Angelo reads Tabitha's story as another example where 'women's ministry is not denied or forbidden, but rather avoided'.[116] Although Tabitha is depicted as administering charity, it is from her own funds rather than the church's. 'Despite the manifest importance of Tabitha[,] the μαθήτρια to her community, her work is described as making garments for widows (the ultimate in economic and matronal virtue, 9.36).'[117] D'Angelo sees the playing down of heroic roles for women in Acts as part of Luke's concern to show the safety of Christianity in a world where the prominent roles of women in oriental religions were viewed as a threat. But Luke's goal is not only to represent the role of women in Christianity as safe, it is to educate women to restricted roles. Luke's portrayals of women, however, have 'subversive potential', at times having 'given a message against his intention'.[118]

Gail R. O'Day: Women in Acts. O'Day begins her reading of the story of Tabitha by noting its pairing with the shorter story of the healing of a man in 9.32–33. She identifies the function of both stories in Acts as the same: 'to portray Peter as a miracle worker in the line of Elijah and Elisha and Jesus and to win converts to Christianity (9.35, 42)'.[119] Thus O'Day situates the stories in Acts much as any contemporary scholarly reader would. She goes on to highlight Tabitha's importance, reading the sending of two disciples to fetch Peter and the identification of Tabitha by the μαθήτρια as evidence. She also emphasizes Tabitha's good works and her acts of charity, the latter being the giving of alms. She emphasizes the importance of this female character. From this, however, she turns to the androcentrism of the text, exercising what Schüssler Fiorenza calls a hermeneutics of suspicion. She notes that the author does not use the term διακονία (ministry) to describe Tabitha's care for the widows, whereas he does so for men's care of widows in Acts 6.1, 4. This point echoes Schüssler Fiorenza's interpretation of the Mary and Martha story in Luke noted above. O'Day suggests that 'when Luke's description of Tabitha is read carefully, it becomes clear that Tabitha is valued as a philanthropist'.[120] Tabitha, who may be a widow herself, takes care of the widows out of her own pocket. While these actions are praiseworthy and make Tabitha a valuable model of discipleship, Luke's description of Tabitha, O'Day implies, is not exactly revolutionary. Echoing D'Angelo, O'Day describes Tabitha as 'the proper society matron, doing works of charity and sewing clothes for the less fortunate'.[121] Thus, O'Day agrees with D'Angelo's assessment that Acts portrays women in roles—including that of wealthy patronesses—that would be acceptable to a patriarchal Greco-Roman world view. Luke conducts a 'silencing' of the actual roles of women in the early church. 'One has to wonder, however,' O'Day writes, 'why when men take care of widows, Luke calls it "ministry" (6.4) but when Tabitha performs the

---

116 D'Angelo, 'Women in Luke–Acts', p. 455.
117 D'Angelo, 'Women in Luke–Acts', p. 455.
118 D'Angelo, 'Women in Luke–Acts', p. 461; Jane Schaberg, 'Luke', in Newsom and Ringe (eds.), *The Women's Bible Commentary*, pp. 275–92, focusing on the Gospel of Luke, advocates a similar interpretation of Luke–Acts. If anything, she stresses the negative aspects of Luke more than D'Angelo.
119 O'Day, 'Acts', p. 309.
120 O'Day, 'Acts', p. 309.
121 O'Day, 'Acts', pp. 309–10.

same services Luke calls it "good works" '.[122] But, for O'Day, the limitation of women's roles, including that of Tabitha in Acts, is not the whole story. The 'heart of Acts' theology, the universal appeal of the gospel and its spread to the Gentiles', subverts Luke's attempt to control women.[123] She writes of the Cornelius episode:

> The dissolution of cultic distinctions between clean and unclean refers to [Christian] Jews and Gentiles, but the implications are farther reaching. When Luke's theology is played out in a different context, this dissolution of cultic distinctions provides the theological grounds for removing cultic classifications of women as unclean or impure. Women and men can stand as equals before the impartial God of Acts.[124]

O'Day's reading of the Cornelius episode is very similar to Foote's. For both women Cornelius represents the excluded female. Provided that we do not read the opening of Christianity to all nations and to all genders in an anti-Jewish fashion, both readings make a powerful feminist point. The danger in reading the Roman centurion as an unclean female Other is that Judaism may be cast as exclusive-misogynist, Christianity as inclusive-feminist. If we remember that Peter is a Jewish Christian, that it was Jewish conversion of Gentiles that created proselytes and God-fearers, and that Jonah and Ruth as well as Ezra–Nehemiah are part of Hebrew Scripture, this pitfall may be avoided.

Learning from Reception History

As one reviews the history of the reception of Tabitha's story it is clear that readers' interpretative conventions, ideological commitments, and historical contexts shape their responses. Text and readers are partners in the dance of interpretation. One distinction between modern male-stream scholarship on the one hand and pastoral males, Stanton and Sangster, and recent feminists on the other is concern for pragmatic effects on hearers or readers. Reading the passage as exemplary literature shifts the emphasis from Peter to Tabitha. So does reading it to reconstruct the roles of women in early church history. Reading the story as exemplary literature is a practice scholars usually reject as leading to an ahistorical dogmatic interpretation. Oddly enough, however, this may actually provide a reading closer to the reading conventions of many first-century readers, who were taught to read characters as types.

Another shift in interpretation occurs depending on whether the reader reads the story in the context of Acts or Luke–Acts as a whole or independently. Reading the story independently, at least for a moment, before reinserting it, brings out a focus on Tabitha. Within the story itself Tabitha and Peter are dual centers of attention. Within the context of Acts, and even more so of Luke–Acts read as a two-volume work, Tabitha recedes in importance. Because the Gospels and Acts are androcentric and patriarchal and women appear only here and there, it is not surprising that feminists have concentrated on the passages in which women appear. For historical critics these passages then become the basis for constructing a more accurate picture of Jesus' ministry, early Christian history in general, or even an evangelist's community. For

---

122 O'Day, 'Acts', p. 310.
123 O'Day, 'Acts', p. 312.
124 O'Day, 'Acts', p. 312.

literary critics the passages become occasions to reflect on women characters or ideological representation. For social context critics the passages become sociohistorical data or elements that contribute to the development of social models. For devotional readers these passages speak to experiences of oppression and liberation.

Reception history also reveals a contrast between reading Tabitha as a general model of discipleship and reading her as similar to or in contrast to Peter. The latter tends to keep her within the bounds of patriarchal subordination. Her service is not quite the same as Peter's preaching and healing power—after all, she, initially her inert body, is the object of Peter's healing action. The former highlights Tabitha's own actions, the power of her almsdeeds, oversight of others, and her needle. Reading and identifying with Peter involves immasculation.

Another point that reception history brings out is that discipleship and widowhood are contested categories. Tabitha as μαθήτρια means different things to different readers. To Calvin it can be used against Rome to establish Christ as the only Teacher and the equal discipleship of all believers. Despite the fact that μαθήτρια is a *hapax legomenon*, a phenomenon on which biblical scholars love to dwell, most male-stream biblical scholars tend to pass over it, assuming women did not play prominent roles in the early church. Like the designation of Junia as a female apostle in Rom. 16.7,[125] the designation of Tabitha as a μαθήτρια and its dismissal as a title of significance without much consideration is an important example of androcentrism. The case of the widows who appear in Tabitha's story is similar. Whether the widows are read as a distinct order and whether Tabitha herself is read as a widow serve as signposts pointing to readers' interests and assumptions.

The Feminist Readings

An examination of the feminist readings of Tabitha is enlightening because it reveals a tradition of our own, oscillation between equality and difference,[126] and an emphasis on the multiplicity of texts and readers. Although more apparent in work on Pauline Epistles and the Gospels, an examination of the reception history of Tabitha's story shows that we now have a tradition of our own, a tradition of feminist New Testament scholarly interpretation. In our writing we can cite and respond to the work of other feminists. The chains of citations no longer carry only male names. In addition we are beginning to recover women's readings of the New Testament from various historical settings.[127] Although these readings are not necessarily feminist, predating the modern use of the term, women's interpretation history is becoming visible. On the one hand, feminists can celebrate this discovery because

---

125 See Bernadette Brooten, 'Junia ... Outstanding among the Apostles', in L. Swidler and A. Swidler (eds.), *Women Priests: A Catholic Commentary on the Vatican Declaration* (New York: Paulist Press, 1977), pp. 141–44.

126 Ann Snitow ('A Gender Diary', in Marianne Hirsch and Evelyn Fox Keller [eds.], *Conflicts in Feminism* [New York: Routledge and Kegan Paul, 1990], pp. 9–43), citing Joan Kelly and Denise Riley, uses the term 'oscillation' (p.13) to describe a shifting 'divide' (p. 9) in feminism.

127 See e.g. Baker-Fletcher, 'Anna Julia Cooper and Sojourner Truth', pp. 41–51; Carolyn De Swarte Gifford, 'American Women and the Bible: The Nature of Woman as a Hermeneutical Issue', in Collins (ed.), *Feminist Perspectives*, pp. 11–34; and Gerda Lerner, *The Creation of Feminist Consciousness: From the Middle Ages to Eighteen-Seventy* (Women and History, 2; New York: Oxford University Press, 1993).

we no longer 'have to reinvent the wheel',[128] unaware of what our predecessors have done.[129] We can build upon what our predecessors have done[130] as earlier women could not because the work of previous women interpreters was hidden in history.[131] We can fruitfully enter dialogue with differing perspectives. On the other hand, it is a source of difficulty, especially for new graduate students and young scholars. It is no longer possible to write the first contemporary feminist scholarly interpretation of most pericopes, let alone of a whole Gospel or letter of Paul. Within the scholarly community, jobs, tenure, and prestige are often based on innovation and sometimes on successfully savaging one's predecessors. As feminists become more prominent in the guild, we must now increasingly ensure that our criticism of other scholars, male and female, remains bold and also constructive.

Another enlightening aspect of the reception history of women's readings of Tabitha is how it highlights the alternation between the celebration and downplaying of female difference. One of the ongoing oscillations in feminist discourse in the United States has been between an emphasis on women's equality (in what respects and for what purposes) and the celebration of female difference (defined by whom, for what ends). It is an oscillation also related to oscillations between essentialism and anti-essentialism, 'American' and 'French' feminism, pro-sex and anti-pornography, and so on.[132] With Sangster we see a celebration of Tabitha's female virtue, often unsung, but especially worthy and powerful. Although this move was essentialist, in her cultural context this provided a way to claim moral authority and a degree of influence for women. With figures like Foote and Parvey, who justify the service of women in roles usually reserved for men, we see the press for equality. We see the celebration of leadership roles of women in the early church, including Tabitha's importance as a disciple. She is an eminent figure, the first to be raised from the dead by an apostle. As women pressed for more power, especially in the role of ordained ministers in the 1960s and 1970s, the argument that women in the earliest church were not excluded from important spiritual or institutional roles supported the argument that they should not be excluded today. Women were and are not limited to the role of domestic servant. Thurston also highlights Tabitha as disciple and Tabitha as leader of an order of widows. Tabitha is one of the examples showing that women and, especially important for Thurston, older women, likely had official status positions in the early church. The position of women like Tabitha provides a strong argument for an equal role for women in modern churches. Parvey and perhaps Thurston represent what D'Angelo perceives to be a positive feminist scholarly reading of Luke–Acts.

Beginning with D'Angelo and O'Day writing in the early 1990s we see a backing away from celebration of early egalitarianism to highlighting the text's (or redactor's) androcentrism and domestication of women under a patriarchal umbrella,

---

128 Schüssler Fiorenza, 'Introduction', p. 1.
129 Schüssler Fiorenza, 'Introduction'; Lerner, *The Creation of Feminist Consciousness*.
130 Lerner, *The Creation of Feminist Consciousness*.
131 Lerner, *The Creation of Feminist Consciousness*.
132 Alcoff, 'Cultural Feminism versus Post-Structuralism', pp. 405–36; Ann Snitow, 'A Gender Diary', in Marianne Hirsch and Evelyn Fox Keller (eds.), *Conflicts in Feminism* (New York: Routledge & Kegan Paul, 1990), pp. 9–43; Teresa de Lauretis, 'Upping the Anti in Feminist Theory', in Hirsch and Keller (eds.), *Conflicts*, pp. 255–70.

the re-patriarchalizing of what may have been more initial equality for women in the early church. There is a sarcasm about, rather than a celebration of, Tabitha's matronly (upper-class female) virtue. The emphasis is more on Luke's restriction of women.

So far in my reading I have emphasized the equality–difference oscillation, which interpreters often harden into a rigid dichotomy. Now I want to argue that my initial reading is complicated by multiple emphases occurring within feminist readings. Stanton, who emphasizes Tabitha's female virtue, also implicitly asks why there are no women teaching in high places. Even Sangster, who is most thoroughly a cultural feminist, emphasizes that males and females alike must feed Christ's lambs. Both see agency in 'female' tasks. The egalitarian Parvey, who approved of Mary as student over Martha as domestic servant, celebrates Tabitha's needlework and her gentle manner. D'Angelo and O'Day, who emphasize restriction rather than liberation in Luke–Acts, also recognize the text's subversive potential. They obviously are not keen on celebrating female virtues if this means a disallowing of women's non-traditional roles. At the same time they praise the importance of Tabitha's work on behalf of her community. This more complicated reading coheres with feminist reader-response criticism's hermeneutics of suspicion (its recognition of immasculation) and its hermeneutics of re-vision (its reading against the grain and/or reading for utopian moments).

The feminist readings are complex and multiplicative in other dimensions as well. Sangster and Stanton emphasize Tabitha's concern for the poor. Parvey notes that women of all social levels are empowered by the spirit in Acts. D'Angelo and O'Day also highlight class as an analytic category, noting Tabitha's position as a wealthy matron. They also read Acts recognizing the impact of the colonial context on the author and his desire to make Christianity acceptable to Roman imperial power. Thurston brings marital status and age to the fore. She emphasizes the position of widows, especially elderly widows, in the first-century Greco-Roman context as well as in contemporary society. Foote brings into clear focus the intersection of race and gender.

Reading the feminist reception history suggests that there is no first moment of naïve celebration of female characters to be superseded by the wise eye that sees through the patriarchal devices immasculating us. Nor need we read Tabitha as only heroine or victim. Nor is there an easy way to separate egalitarian readings from those that represent and celebrate difference. An emphasis on either or both may be important in specific situations. Recent feminist theorists such as Patricia Hill Collins[133] and in New Testament studies Elisabeth Schüssler Fiorenza[134] have emphasized that patriarchy involved and involves a pyramid of interlocking or multiplicative oppressions that takes different forms in different historical circumstances. With an awareness of this, feminists may choose to stress one or more of the following categories as they read Tabitha as female, a Jewish Christian, a person of wealth, and perhaps a widow. They also stress the importance of learning from a variety of readings from different particular social and historical locations. This is necessary for a hermeneutics of suspicion to locate exclusions and oppressive uses

---

133 Patricia Hill Collins, *Black Feminist Thought* (New York: Routledge & Kegan Paul, 1990).
134 Schüssler Fiorenza, *But She Said*.

of biblical texts as well as to open possibilities for a hermeneutics of re-vision. Feminist readings, like that of Foote, for example, urge us not to restrict ourselves to passages with female characters or passages that discuss the roles of women. We can exercise a hermeneutics of re-vision as well as suspicion on all texts. At the same time we must exercise a hermeneutics of suspicion with regard to our own readings. As we have seen, even the celebration of universality in Foote and O'Day's readings could be misused. If we are concerned about the pragmatic effects of interpretation on women, we must be concerned about the pragmatic effects of all sorts of interpretations on all sorts of women and men.

Conclusion

Biblical scholarship teaches scholarly readers to see how texts are multilayered, often reflecting multiple historical situations. A text from a Gospel, for example, may reflect a setting in life in the ministry of Jesus, in the oral tradition of the early church, and in the evangelist's community. Reception history shows us the multiplicity of readers. Textual multiplicity and the multiplicity of readers also help us see the importance of multiple feminist readings in the service of critique and revision. In the reception history we have examined, an emphasis on the power of God or the Holy Spirit rather than on human authority strengthens the utopian moment for women. This is what we see in Calvin and Foote, for example. It is compatible with a theological understanding that rests authority in the ἐκκλησία of women, as with Schüssler Fiorenza, or in a Protestant understanding of the text as the Word of God, provided we understand with Calvin that the words written on the page only become the Word of God when the Holy Spirit illuminates the reader. If we follow Foote, the Bible can become the Word of God anew in each new historical and social context of reading, as the Holy Spirit—rather than any oppressive human interpreter—leads. A single verse can be both oppressive and liberative. I may read Tabitha to commend the older women in my community who run the rummage sales, make baby clothes for those who need them, and are there with food when someone is too ill to cook. At the same time my celebration of caregiving may entail accepting the separation of public and private spheres, acquiescing in a limitation of women to the domestic sphere, to their 'proper' place. With Foote I may be bold to see myself as Cornelius, celebrating God as no respecter of persons, but when I do I read from a different position from Foote. I may also ignore the immasculation or apology for colonialism that Cornelius, the Roman centurion, might represent in certain circumstances. This is why it is important to examine readings from many different subject positions. For Christian feminist reader-response critics it is also why verse five of the hymn 'Holy is the Lamb' written by Julia Foote rings so true:

> Sometimes I read my Bible,
> It almost seems a task;
> Sometimes I find a blessing
> Wherever I do look.[135]

---

135 Gates (ed.), *Spiritual Narratives*, p. 123.

WHAT EVER HAPPENED TO THOSE PROPHESYING DAUGHTERS?*

BEVERLY ROBERTS GAVENTA

In the last days it will happen, God declares,
I will pour out my Spirit upon all flesh,
and your sons and your daughters shall prophesy,
and your young men shall see visions, and your old men shall dream dreams.
Even upon my male slaves and my female slaves, in those days
I will pour out my spirit; and they shall prophesy. (Author's trans.)

These dramatic words, modified only slightly from the Septuagint of Joel 3, stand near the beginning of Peter's programmatic address at Pentecost. Readers who have followed Luke's story from the beginning of the Gospel will surely associate Peter's words with the prominence Luke accords Elizabeth and Mary. Elizabeth is filled with the Holy Spirit when she cries out to Mary, 'Blessed are you among women'. Gabriel tells Mary that the Holy Spirit will come upon her, and Mary's 'Magnificat' celebrates God's intervention in her life and that of Israel. It may be Zechariah's house, but it is Elizabeth and Mary who do the talking.

Recalling not only Mary and Elizabeth but also the numerous women who appear in Luke's Gospel and alert for the voices of those sons and daughters, male and female slaves, the reader begins to make her way through Acts. There she will often encounter women. There are women who believe Christian preaching, women persecuted by Paul, and women who later join in the persecution of Paul. Tabitha, Mary (mother of John Mark), Lydia, and Damaris are among the believers who are mentioned by name. Luke also makes passing references to the Candace, the queen of the Ethiopians, Drusilla, and Bernice.

And there are women who speak: Sapphira speaks to Peter, a terminal lie, as it turns out. As Scott Spencer puts it: 'The famous—or rather infamous—first words from a woman in Acts are her last! This is scarcely an encouragement to women speakers'.[1] Rhoda tells the truth about Peter's presence outside the house of Mary, for which she is ridiculed. Another female slave speaks the truth about Paul and Silas, but only because she is the captive of a Pythian spirit. Knowing Luke's fondness for fulfilled prophecies, we read on, looking for those daughters who prophesy. Finally in ch. 21, we find them. They are Philip's four unmarried daughters and, although Luke tells us that they prophesy, he gives us not a word from their mouths. This silence prompts, of course, the title of this essay.

What ever happened to those prophesying daughters? Where did they go and why do we not hear them speak? My question serves to introduce not only this specific

---

* A version of this paper was delivered as the plenary address at the annual meeting of the Southeastern Commission on the Study of Religion (SECSOR), March 2002; the present version substantially retains the style of the oral delivery.

1 F. Scott Spencer, *Acts* (Readings: A New Bible Commentary; Sheffield: Sheffield Academic Press, 1997), p. 58.

prophecy and its apparent non-fulfillment but the general problem of the presentation of women in Luke's second volume.

The Old Conventional Wisdom: Von Harnack and Early Feminism

It should come as no surprise, I suppose, to recall that Eusebius knew the answer to my question (at least in its specific form—about the prophesying daughters). Eusebius reports that Philip and two of his daughters were buried in Hierapolis, adding that a third daughter was buried in Ephesus (*Ecc. Hist.* 3.31). Curiously, in the next passage Eusebius refers to the tombs in Hierapolis of Philip and all four prophesying daughters, introducing a small anomaly (which might not have been so small to that fourth daughter, who is omitted in the first comment). Eusebius further indicates that Papias met Philip's daughters and learned from them a wondrous story about someone who had been raised from the dead (*Ecc. Hist.* 3.31, 39).

Late in the nineteenth century Adolf von Harnack took that bit of tradition and wove from it an extensive theory according to which Philip and the daughters form one of Luke's primary sources. According to von Harnack, Luke not only met Philip and the daughters when he accompanied Paul during his stay in Caesarea (reported in one of the 'we' passages in Acts 21), but he must have met them later on in Asia as well. (Von Harnack's reasoning seems to have been as follows: if Papias met them, then Luke could have also.) Philip and the daughters become the source of those elements in Luke that are concerned with the Holy Spirit (since they were all ecstatics 'altogether wanting in sober-mindedness and credibility'[2]). They are also the reason for Luke's interest in Samaritans (given Philip's earlier mission in Samaria, recounted in Acts 8). And even more certainly, according to von Harnack, Philip's daughters are the source of Luke's concern with 'the feminine element'. As evidence of this 'feminine' element, von Harnack cites the numerous Lukan (i.e., Gospel) stories involving women. Elsewhere he elaborates on the place of women in Acts also, giving particular attention to Priscilla whom he identifies as a missionary and teacher (as well as perhaps the author of Hebrews).[3]

That set of observations seems to make its way into the secondary literature in the form of a general characterization of Luke as particularly interested in the place of women both in Jesus' ministry and in the early church. One measure of its near-canonical status may be taken from this line in Kümmel's introduction to the New Testament: 'according to Luke Jesus expressed ... God's love for the despised, both by his behavior and by his message: to sinners ... to Samaritans ... [and] to women'.[4] This conventional wisdom about Luke's concern for women gathered new energy in the early feminist exegetical work of the 1970s.

---

2 Adolf von Harnack, *Luke the Physician: The Author of the Third Gospel and the Acts of the Apostles* (trans. J.R.Wilkinson; London: Williams & Norgate; New York: G.P. Putnam, 2nd edn, 1909), p. 153.

3 A. von Harnack, *Luke the Physician,* pp. 125, 153–164; *idem, Mission and Expansion of Christianity in the First Three Centuries* (trans. and ed. James Moffatt; 2 vols.; London: Williams & Norgate; New York: G.P. Putnam's Sons; 2nd edn, enl. and rev., 1908), II, p. 68.

4 Werner George Kümmel, *Introduction to the New Testament* (trans. Howard Clark Kee; Nashville and New York: Abingdon Press, 17th edn, 1975), p. 139.

A New Conventional Wisdom

That conventional wisdom began to dissolve with the publication in 1983 of Elizabeth Schüssler Fiorenza's landmark study, *In Memory of Her*.[5] As she undertook to reconstruct the roles of women in early Christianity that remain hidden within patriarchal texts, Schüssler Fiorenza drew attention to the 'Lukan silence', that is, the absence of reference in Luke–Acts to women among the apostles, missionaries, or preachers. According to Schüssler Fiorenza, Luke presents women, especially those who are wealthy proselytes or god-fearers, as supporters or opponents of Paul's mission,[6] and Luke obscures the actual involvement of women in the origins of the Christian movement.[7]

A more extended challenge to the conventional wisdom comes with Mary Rose D'Angelo's 'Women in Luke–Acts: A Redactional View'.[8] Instead of reconstructing earliest Christianity, D'Angelo undertakes to explain a perceived ambiguity in Luke–Acts by reference to the situation of the Lukan community. Luke does 'increase the number of stories about women in the Gospel' and does so deliberately; however, more than in Mark or John, the roles women take in Luke conform to standards that would have been acceptable in the imperial world.[9] D'Angelo attributes this ambiguity to the tension Luke faces. On the one hand, female converts are 'of real political importance to the church of Luke's day' and they require instruction in the Christian faith. On the other, an enlarged role for women may prompt outsiders to view Christians as 'practitioners of "un-Roman activities"'.[10] D'Angelo regards as a primary goal of Luke–Acts to show the ἀσφάλεια (*asphaleia*; reliability) of the gospel, which she takes to include not only its reliability but also the safety or security of the Christian community within the Roman Empire. By removing women from prophecy and leadership, Luke addresses those critics who would interpret women's leadership as indicative of 'social disorder, of magic, of the Jewish and therefore oriental character of the new movement'.[11] And within the community, Luke hopes to instruct women as to the boundaries of their proper behavior.

The last decade has produced a spate of books and articles on the topic, of which I will mention only two. In *Women in the Acts of the Apostles*,[12] Ivoni Richter Reimer offers a somewhat more positive assessment than does D'Angelo. Despite the androcentric narrative, which focuses on the male personalities of Peter and Paul rather than on a coherent presentation of women's experience, readers may detect several things: Luke's female characters work independently of males, and some of them appear to live independently of males as well.[13] Women often appear in the story when there are conflicts (e.g. Sapphira, the Hellenist widows, the female slave with a Pythian spirit).

---

5 Elisabeth Schüssler Fiorenza, *In Memory of Her: A Feminist Theological Reconstruction of Christian Origins* (New York: Crossroad, 1983).
6 Schüssler Fiorenza, *In Memory of Her*, p. 161.
7 Schüssler Fiorenza, *In Memory of Her*, p. 167.
8 Mary Rose D'Angelo, 'Women in Luke–Acts: A Redactional View', *JBL* 109 (1990), pp. 441–61.
9 D'Angelo, 'Women in Luke–Acts', p. 442.
10 D'Angelo, 'Women in Luke–Acts', p. 443.
11 D'Angelo, 'Women in Luke–Acts', p. 461.
12 Ivoni Richter Reimer, *Women in the Acts of the Apostles: A Feminist Liberation Perspective* (trans. Linda M. Moloney; Minneapolis: Fortress Press, 1995).
13 Reimer, *Women in the Acts of the Apostles*, p. 260.

There are women who head house-churches (e.g. Mary, mother of John Mark, in Jerusalem; Lydia in Philippi). The believing community includes women involved in business, but also 'in the mission, in philosophy, and in prophecy'.[14] Richter Reimer appears to see these women as representing women in Luke's own community.

She concludes: 'The Acts of the Apostles reflects no particular tendency to keep women at home and subject them to men, i.e., to their own husbands. Even though it is silent about important women like Mary Magdalene, it is still far from what was written, at about the same time as its composition, in the Pastoral letters and similar works ... regarding the subordination of women and slaves.'[15] Richter Reimer sees in Sapphira in particular an example of how women should *not* function only as cooperators and co-conspirators, since Sapphira's punishment occurs precisely *because* she consents to her husband's proposal.[16]

If Richter Reimer's assessment is more positive, that of Turid Karlsen Seim is perhaps more cautious. In *The Double Message*,[17] Karlsen Seim offers a literary analysis of women's roles in Luke–Acts (with somewhat more emphasis on Luke than on Acts) and does not engage in the historical task of either Schüssler Fiorenza (i.e., reconstructing the place of women in actual early Christian communities) or of D'Angelo (i.e., reconstructing the intention of Luke with respect to his contemporaries). As her title indicates, she finds in Luke's work conflicting signals. On the one hand, Luke–Acts contains stories in which women play a significant role, as in the work of Lydia, and Luke can refer to groups of women on their own apart from their relationship to men. On the other hand, the text goes out of its way to specify that the leaders are males (in Acts 1, e.g., when Peter stipulates that Judas's successor must be an ἀνήρ, 'male'). In addition, women largely take private roles rather than public ones. They teach and work in the home rather than in the synagogue or marketplace. This results in a certain irony, a mixed message. I want to make clear that Seim does not carry this analysis into the life of the historical Lukan community itself; she leaves open the possibility that Luke himself is not even conscious of what he is doing, much less doing it in order to silence women. (Here there is a sharp contrast with Schüssler Fiorenza and D'Angelo.)

Books and articles on various aspects of this question continue to issue forth, including James Arlandson's *Women, Class, and Society in Early Christianity*,[18] Robert Price's *The Widow Traditions in Luke–Acts*,[19] and important essays by Scott Spencer on the widows in Acts 6 and the prophesying female slaves.[20] Consequently, to speak of a new conventional wisdom regarding women in Luke–Acts would be

---

14 Reimer, *Women in the Acts of the Apostles*, p. 260.
15 Reimer, *Women in the Acts of the Apostles*, p. 267.
16 Reimer, *Women in the Acts of the Apostles*, p. 267.
17 Turid Karlsen Seim, *The Double Message: Patterns of Gender in Luke–Acts* (Studies of the New Testament and its World; Edinburgh: T. & T. Clark, 1994).
18 James Arlandson, *Women, Class, and Society in Early Christianity: Models from Luke–Acts* (Peabody, MA: Hendrickson, 1996).
19 Robert Price, *The Widow Traditions in Luke–Acts: A Feminist-Critical Scrutiny* (SBLDS, 155; Atlanta, GA: Scholars Press, 1997).
20 F. Scott Spencer, 'Neglected Widows in Acts 6.1–7', *CBQ* 56 (1994), pp. 715–33 (728–31); and 'Out of Mind, Out of Voice: Slave Girls and Prophetic Daughters in Luke–Acts', *BibInt* 7 (1999), pp. 132–53.

premature. It is symptomatic of the state of the discussion that Jane Schaberg, in her *Women's Bible Commentary* treatment of Luke's Gospel, characterizes it as 'an extremely dangerous text, perhaps the most dangerous in the Bible', because it contains 'a great deal of material about women that is found nowhere else in the Gospels' but 'deftly portrays [women] as models of subordinate service, excluded from the power center of the movement and from significant responsibilities'.[21] Gail O'Day's discussion of Acts, in the same one-volume commentary, concedes the silencing of women, which she attributes to Luke's concern about propriety and decorum in the new movement.[22] Nevertheless, O'Day draws attention to the important roles women do play in Acts. Whatever the range of judgments on this question of Luke's treatment of female characters, I suspect that it would be difficult to find in recent work the glib assessments that characterize earlier generations of treatments of Luke and women. Von Harnack's blithe comment on the feminine in Luke–Acts is a thing of the past.

Questions Yet to Be Explored

My comments are not intended to evoke a new consensus on women in Luke's second volume. Instead, I want to complicate matters further by introducing some additional questions into the discussion of Luke's prophesying daughters. First, notice how work on this question has proceeded. Von Harnack engaged in historical reconstruction based on a combination of Acts, the Pauline letters, and later Christian tradition. More recent approaches have traced the appearances of women in Luke and Acts and analyzed their roles in the story. Occasionally, Luke's corpus is compared with the letters of Paul and the roles attributed to women there, with some attention to the social context. Yet there is still a need to contextualize Luke's women in a different way: first, by inquiring about the presentation of women in literature contemporary with Luke; second, by exploring the presentation of male characters in Lukan narrative; and third, by analyzing the place of both men and women in Luke's larger narrative program.

Luke's Literary Context
Much work in Lukan studies in recent decades has been devoted to comparing Luke–Acts, or elements of Luke–Acts, with literature contemporary with Luke, particularly historical writings and ancient novels. Yet I am not aware that that pursuit has had any significant impact on the way in which the question of Luke's presentation of women has been pursued. I do not have in mind now the historical question of the actual status of women in varying locations, a question that carries its own interpretive perils. Instead, I am asking specifically about the presentation of female characters and the comments about women that appear in ancient literature often adduced as in some sense comparable with Acts.

The question is vast, and I have no illusion that I can solve it here, but I do want to make some preliminary and admittedly partial comments about a few roughly

---

21 Jane Schaberg, 'Luke', in Carol A. Newsom and Sharon H. Ringe (eds.), *The Women's Bible Commentary* (Louisville, KY: Westminster/John Knox, expanded edn, 1998), pp. 363–80 (363).
22 Gail O'Day, 'Acts', in Newsom and Ringe (eds.), *Women's Bible Commentary*, pp. 394–402.

contemporaneous texts that surface prominently in the study of Acts. From the work of those engaged in comparative historiography, I have chosen the *Roman Antiquities* of Dionysius of Halicarnassus, since it often comes into the discussion of Luke–Acts (especially in the work of Plümacher and Balch[23]). And from the work of those interested especially in the ancient novel, features of which seem to be contained in Luke's own literary vocabulary, I have selected Chariton's *Callirhoe* as an excellent example of the ancient novel.[24]

The extensive *Roman Antiquities* of Dionysius of Halicarnassus (eleven books extant, extending to seven volumes in the Loeb edition) began to appear late in the first century BCE. As the title indicates, the *Antiquities* focus on the origins of Rome and its emergence as a power, with primary attention to rulers, their battles, and their successes and failures. Occasionally, Dionysius does venture into elements of what we might term cultural history, for example, religious practices, agriculture, and plagues, most often with a view to celebrating the outstanding character and accomplishments of Rome and its people. The *Antiquities* are often discussed by Lukan scholars because of the speeches contained therein.

In Dionysius's history, women figure almost entirely as the property of males, either as wives or as daughters. They come into the story largely when their sexual behavior is the commodity under discussion—either they are daughters being given away as wives, mothers producing offspring for their husbands, wives whose virtue is under assault, or, occasionally, they are Vestal virgins whose activity is severely monitored. The overwhelming majority of references to women are brief reports in which no speech is attributed to them and they engage in no independent action. There are exceptions, however. We hear at length from Tullia, the wicked daughter of King Tullius, who proposes a plan to her brother-in-law in which the two of them arrange the deaths of their inconvenient spouses, their subsequent marriage to one another, and then the murder of her father (4.29).

At the other extreme, we also hear at length from the noble Veturia, mother of Marcius Coriolanus, a woman who might have been dispatched by Central Casting to play the role of the Roman matron par excellence. Veturia first defends to other women her son's anger against the Romans who exiled him. Later, in an extended speech, she persuades her son to be reconciled with his country and its citizens. Veturia argues that even the anger of the gods can be appeased, so that Marcius's anger should be moderated accordingly. Then she asks Marcius either to comply with her wish or to commit matricide, and finally she pulls out every rhetorical stop by reciting all her labor on his behalf. As a widow, she claims:

> [I was] not only a mother to you, but also a father, a nurse, a sister, and everything that is dearest. When you reached manhood and it was in my power to be freed from these cares by marrying again, to rear other children, and lay up many hopes to support me in my old

---

23. See, for example, Eckhard Plümacher, 'The Mission Speeches in Acts and Dionysius of Halicarnassus', in David P. Moessner (ed.), *Jesus and the Heritage of Israel: Luke's Narrative Claim upon Israel's Legacy* (Philadelphia: Trinity Press International, 1999), pp. 251–66; and David L. Balch, 'ἀκριβῶς... γράψαι (Luke 1.3): To Write the *Full* History of God's Receiving All Nations', in Moessner (ed.), *Jesus and the Heritage of Israel*, pp. 229–50.

24. Chariton, 'Chaereas and Callirhoe', in B.P. Reardon (ed. and trans.), *Collected Ancient Greek Novels* (Los Angeles: University of California Press, 1989).

age, I would not do so, but remained at the same hearth and put up with the same kind of life, placing all my pleasures and all my advantages in you alone. Of these you have disappointed me, partly against your will and partly of your own accord, and have made me the most wretched of all mothers (8.51.4).

We may perhaps be forgiven for suspecting that Marcius accedes to her wishes largely in order to get her to stop talking. These two women demonstrate that Dionysius's female characters speak occasionally, but they do so in highly confined and rather predictable roles.

If women are present only in tiny segments of the *Roman Antiquities*, such a complaint can hardly be lodged against Chariton and his novel, *Callirhoe*. From the opening page until the final one, the beautiful Callirhoe is either present in the narrative or she is the object of seemingly endless plots revolving around her. When Callirhoe is introduced, she is described as:

a marvel of a girl and the idol of all Sicily. In fact her beauty was not so much human as divine... [that] of Aphrodite herself. Reports of this incredible vision spread far and wide: suitors came pouring into Syracuse, potentates and princes, not only from Sicily, but from Italy, the continent, and the peoples of the continent (1.2).

The plot will sound familiar to anyone who has glanced at the romance novels of antiquity: Callirhoe and Chaereas fall in love and are married, but her scorned suitors, acting out their envy, set in motion a complex plot involving pirates, apparent death, marriage to another man, and at long last the rescue and restoration of the young couple. What is of major interest to the characters about Callirhoe is that she is beautiful, although she is also virtuous in her faithfulness to Chaereas and her concern for Dionysius, whom she marries in order to rescue her child from slavery. Other women in the novel are minor characters, either assisting Callirhoe or occasionally reinforcing the theme of her beauty by their own jealousy. In other words, *eros* is the driving force in the book, and Callirhoe's beauty a major contributor to the force of *eros*.

Whether Luke is 'better' or 'worse' in his presentation of women than these contemporary sources is not the issue; rather, these other writings may make us more aware of certain features of Luke's presentation. For example, Luke never describes the beauty (or lack thereof) of a female character. Neither does Luke draw particular attention to a mother's devotion to her children or a wife's devotion to her husband. Even with Mary, the mother of Jesus, where we might anticipate some celebration of her virtues, Luke is restrained. Instead of a portrayal of Mary as a loving Roman matron, in the Magnificat Luke offers Mary's celebration of God's intervention in and reversal of the social order. Occasionally, scholars notice that Luke's women disproportionately are virgins or widows. When viewed in the context of either the *Roman Antiquities* or *Callirhoe*, however, Luke's women are noticeable for their relative independence. Many of the women who appear in Acts seem to act independently of male characters or in partnership with them rather than simply as their appendages (as Richter Reimer rightly points out). Nothing is said of a male relation for either Dorcas or Lydia, for example.Priscilla's teaching occurs alongside, rather than behind, that of her husband. Apart from passing references to the queen of

Ethiopia, Paul's sister, Bernice, and Drusilla, what Luke reports regarding women has entirely to do with them as believers or in opposition to believers.

Luke's Male Characters and Cultural Norms of Masculinity

Another way to contextualize Luke's treatment of female characters is by looking at the males in the narrative. My impression is that analysis of women's roles has largely been treated in isolation from those of men. In a sense that approach is understandable, since so much of exegetical history neglected to notice women in these stories, or noticed them in demeaning ways. Yet if we are to achieve a more well-rounded sense of Luke's treatment of women, we must look also more closely at the portrayal of male characters.

Recent work on gender construction articulates the assumption in Greco-Roman literature that there is a 'fundamental polarity between men and women' and that maleness is 'reversible'. In the language of John Winkler, men are 'always in peril of slipping into the servile or the feminine'.[25] Men are always in danger of 'going AWOL from [their] assigned place in the gender hierarchy'.[26] Included in this gender hierarchy is a hierarchy of virtue in which men are understood to be 'self-controlled, wise, just, and generous' while women are 'dissolute, foolish, capricious, and cowardly'.[27] In the words of Mathew Kuefler, 'Reason and rationality guided men; emotion and sentiment impelled women. Morally, women were but inverts, men turned inside out.'[28] That association of men with virtue, particularly with the virtues of reason, self-control, and wisdom, prompts the question of how Luke's characters rank on the scale of masculinity. How successfully do Luke's males defend their place in the gender hierarchy?

A few preliminary observations will have to suffice, beginning at the beginning, with Peter. Following Jesus' ascension, Peter emerges without explanation or challenge as the leading spokesperson for Jesus' followers. He announces the necessity of replacing Judas and proposes a method for doing so. When the Spirit's descent at Pentecost necessitates explanation ('No, we aren't drunk just yet'), Peter speaks, and he continues speaking over the next several chapters. Throughout chs. 1–5 and again from 9.32 until his deliverance from Herod in ch. 12, Peter is the most prominent among Jerusalem Christians, what we would refer to as their 'leader'. Surely he is a strong male character—one who speaks with boldness even in the presence of Jerusalem religious authorities (παρρησία, Acts 4.13).

Yet that characterization of Peter overlooks the ending of Luke's first volume. At the Passover meal, Peter first assures Jesus that he is ready to go with him to prison and even to death. Within the same night, of course, he lies three times about even knowing Jesus. The fact that the first denial comes in response to a mere servant girl further indicates Peter's shame. Again at the Passover meal, Jesus himself predicts this event: 'Satan has demanded to sift all of you like

---

25 John J. Winkler, *The Constraints of Desire: The Anthropology of Sex and Gender in Ancient Greece* (New Ancient World; New York: Routledge, 1990), p. 50.

26 Winkler, *Constraints of Desire*, p. 21. On this topic, see also Maud W. Gleason, *Making Men: Sophists and Self-Presentation in Ancient Rome* (Princeton, NJ: Princeton University Press, 1995).

27 Mathew Kuefler, *The Manly Eunuch: Masculinity, Gender Ambiguity, and Christian Identity in Late Antiquity* (Chicago: University of Chicago Press, 2001), p. 20.

28 Kuefler, *The Manly Eunuch*, p. 20.

wheat, but I have prayed for you that your own faith may not fail' (22.31). Although Peter next emerges as leader of the community, there is no turning point at which his character is salvaged. Nothing indicates that Peter has repented or been restored as a result of self-mastery. If anything, both the denial and the leadership of Peter indicate just how *little* Peter is in control of himself.

A second Lukan male, the Ethiopian eunuch, clearly stands outside the normal gender hierarchy. It is tempting to overlook this story, since the eunuch does not become a leader of the community or even continue in the story after ch. 8. On the other hand, his is the first of three developed stories of the conversions of individuals (the eunuch, Saul/Paul, and Cornelius), and he is in some sense an ideal convert: he seeks out the gospel, responds to it immediately, and goes on his way rejoicing. The eunuch is not a character over whom Luke would have lingered had he been seriously concerned about emphasizing the standing of his male characters. As is well known, Deut. 23.1 bans the participation of castrated males in Israel's assembly, and Isa. 56.3–5 anticipates their inclusion.[29] In a world that worried very much about preserving the male from any hint of effeminacy, eunuchs were regarded with great ridicule. Writing in the second century, Lucian reports on a competition between philosophers in which one is accused of being a eunuch: 'Such people ought to be excluded ... from temples and holy-water bowls and all the places of public assembly.' It is 'an ill-omened, ill-met sign if on first leaving home in the morning, one should set eyes on any such person ... observing that a eunuch was neither man nor woman but something composite, hybrid, and monstrous, alien to human nature' (*The Eunuch* 6). Given that attitude as reflective of a general cultural disposition, the eunuch is scarcely a character guaranteed to enhance the male stature of the community.[30]

Paul is surely the most complicated and important of Luke's male characters, entering as he does early in the book, with the martyrdom of Stephen, returning in ch. 9 and then again in ch. 11, finally becoming the chief witness for the gospel at 15.36 and continuing to occupy that role for the remainder of the book. John Lentz has argued that Luke presents Paul as a paragon of moral virtues: self-control, wisdom, righteousness, and bravery.[31] Lentz does not notice the gendered nature of these virtues, but the association is clear: it is men and not women who are understood to be holders of these virtues. Yet there are important ways in which Paul fails to live up to the male norm in Acts: notably his conversion, where he is portrayed as out of control both before ('breathing threats and murder', 9.1) and after (he is rendered helpless) his encounter. Lentz distinguishes between Paul's pre-history as persecutor and his later behavior as witness, but that Paul returns to his persecuting activity in two of the major defense speeches suggests that Paul's earlier history is part of what Luke wants us to know about him.

29 See also the discussion in Josephus, *Ant.* 4.40.
30 To be sure, the question of the character's standing is complicated by the high status of chamberlains/eunuchs in royal households, which also plays a role in Acts 8. See Beverly Roberts Gaventa, *From Darkness to Light: Aspects of Conversion in the New Testament* (OBT; Philadelphia: Fortress Press, 1986), pp. 98–107.
31 John Lentz, *Luke's Portrait of Paul* (SNTSMS, 77; Cambridge: Cambridge University Press, 1993).

More telling is the speech to the Ephesian elders in 20.18–38. Paul summarizes his work in Asia and perhaps the whole of his ministry, just before he returns to Jerusalem where he is arrested. Where we might expect Paul to speak of his accomplishments, his manly virtues, he does not. He makes no reference to miracles accomplished through him or to his defeat of magicians. Instead, he speaks of working with his own hands, of laboring in tears, and indeed of being a captive to the Spirit.

These observations about a few individuals, preliminary and fragmentary as they are, lead to a few tentative conclusions about the presentation of men in Acts. First, generally speaking, Luke's account does not emphasize men as having power over women. To be sure, the apostles are all male and they exercise leadership in the community, but Luke does not go out of his way to depict male power over females. There is one clear exception to that rule and one possible exception: Ananias and Sapphira may constitute an exception, since Ananias is apparently the one who plans to withhold money from the treasury and does so with Sapphira's knowledge (see Acts 5.1–2). The clear exception is with the female slave with the spirit of divination whose owners profit from her ability as a fortune-teller. Both of these Luke presents as disasters.

Second, although it might be argued that Luke depicts women as associated with private life and men with public life, much of the witnessing in Acts is neither public nor private, strictly speaking. Matthew Skinner's work on the captivity of Paul has underscored the liminality of this setting.[32] It is neither public nor private. Similarly, Seim notes that the book of Acts concludes with Paul engaging in witness from within his own lodging.[33] Here he is in a private setting where others must come to him.

Third, and most important, the men in Acts do not present themselves as independent. Unlike Epictetus, who claims to be his own king and master (*Discourse* 3.22.38–49) or Seneca, who declares himself not God's slave but God's follower (*On Providence* 5.4–7), in Luke the men who are portrayed favorably all understand themselves to be under God's direction. They are not only followers of the superior instruction offered by Jesus, but are themselves God's slaves (as in 2.18; 16.17).

Men and Women in Luke's Narrative Program
Scholars still remain deeply shaped by the notion that Acts intends to convey the history of the church, whether we mean by that the geographical spread of the witness, the history of Jesus' successors, or the history of the church as institution. The problem is that none of those approaches works as a *sustained* interpretation of the text.

First, Acts does depict the *spread* of the church's witness, but if that is the larger rubric under which we should read the whole story, why is it that we find Paul in Rome (finally!) and meeting believers there, without a word about how the gospel arrived in the city? Given Rome's central importance, it would seem obvious that a

---

32 Matthew Skinner, *Locating Paul: Places of Custody as Narrative Settings in Acts 21–28* (SBL Academia Biblica, 13; Atlanta: Society of Biblical Literature; Leiden: Brill Academic Publishers, 2003).

33 Seim, *Double Message*, p. 145.

chronicle devoted to recounting the geographical movement of the church should include that arrival. There are other instances in which Luke refers to places as having believers in them, but he never tells us how that happened. For example, on Paul's final journey to Jerusalem, he seeks out disciples in Tyre (21.14), although nothing has been said earlier of a mission in Tyre, and Luke does not present the story of the Canaanite (so Mt. 15) or Syrophoenician (so Mk 7) woman set in the region of Tyre and Sidon.[34]

Second, the notion that Acts is the story of *Jesus' successors* is also problematic. It works, perhaps, for the account of the appointment of a successor for Judas, since there Peter takes initiative and it seems important to identify a replacement. But the successor himself, Matthias, plays no further role. This way of reading becomes even more problematic later on. For example, after Peter's angelic rescue from death in Herod's prison (ch. 12), Peter goes to greet fellow-believers; Luke then comments that Peter 'went to another place'; no reference is given to where or why. Peter makes a cameo appearance at the Jerusalem Council in Acts 15, after which he vanishes from the narrative. Moreover, given Luke's extensive use of Scripture, he surely knew succession stories on which he might have drawn to show the mantle of leadership passed, but he has not employed them.[35]

Third, concerning institutional history, there are places where that too might seem an adequate way of putting the story, especially in the portrayals of the gathered community in Jerusalem and the selection of the individuals for the distributing of food to the widows. Yet Luke manifests a decided lack of interest in anything remotely like church order once the narrative moves beyond Judea and perhaps Samaria. For much of the last chapters of Acts Paul seems quite isolated from other believers, which is a strange way to convey institutional history.

The problem with all of these readings is that Acts is finally not a story about human beings—male or female—but about God. It is not enough to say that the 'plan of God' is a major Lukan theme, for God is the primary actor in Luke–Acts (I include the actions of the Holy Spirit and of the Risen Jesus, although it would require another essay to explain that claim). Luke treats all human characters in relation to that primary agent. Either they rightly perceive God's plan and align themselves with it (as in the case of Mary, Paul, and the unnamed women and men who become believers), or they resist God's plan (as in the case of Sapphira, Simon Magus, and a host of other women and men). Concerns that we today identify as important— independent agency, human leadership, public speech, decision-making—are simply not important in Luke's narrative world.

So: What Ever Happened to Those Prophesying Daughters?

This essay seeks to introduce some further questions and observations into the discussion of women in Luke's second volume. Inquiry into the presentation of female characters in literature contemporary with Luke, the Lukan presentation of male characters, and Luke's larger narrative program promotes a more

---

[34] Beverly Roberts Gaventa, *Acts* (Abingdon New Testament Commentaries; Nashville: Abingdon, 2003), p. 55.
[35] Gaventa, *Acts*, pp. 42–43.

comprehensive answer, beyond the simplistic and debatable 'Luke doesn't like women', to the question: What ever happened to those prophesying daughters?

The women in Acts, although for the most part they do not speak, are nevertheless present in the narrative and in ways that distinguish them at least from some of the literature in Luke's world. They do not exist in the story merely as the possession of men, nor are they depicted solely as mothers or described in terms of their physical appearance. Luke reports that they speak, although the predominant speaking parts are distributed to the other gender. When Luke introduces them, he does so in order to comment on them in relationship to the gospel. They are believers, or they are opponents. They act generously with respect to others, as in the case of Dorcas and Lydia. They offer instruction, as in the case of Priscilla, and possess prophetic gifts, as in the case of Philip's daughters, even if we never hear the content of their speech.

What to make of the silence? I cannot agree with those who argue that Luke deliberately silences the women and that he fears repercussion from outsiders who will associate female leadership with exotic cults from the East.[36] I suspect (and here I knowingly enter into the territory of speculation) that Luke is not even aware of it, just as he is not aware that Peter disappears from the story without comment or that five of the seven deacons disappear without a trace immediately after their commissioning. So intent is Luke on narrating God's history with these people, that his interest in the people as such is slight.

The prophecy of Acts 2 stands only partially fulfilled. As Scott Spencer has demonstrated, when the slave girl Rhoda does speak the truth, she is not believed.[37] And when the slave with the spirit of divination speaks the truth, she is silenced. Yet Luke has constructed a story in which God relentlessly fulfills God's promises, permitting the reader to conclude that these other prophecies will also be fulfilled.

---

36 On this question, see Shelly Matthews, *First Converts: Rich Pagan Women and the Rhetoric of Mission in Early Judaism and Christianity* (Contraversions: Jews and Other Differences; Stanford: Stanford University Press, 2001), esp. pp. 72–95, and her article in this volume 'Elite Women, Public Religion and Christian Propaganda in Acts 16', pp. 11–133.

37 Spencer, 'Out of Mind'.

Thinking Mission in Africa*

Musimbi Kanyoro

I am delighted to be invited to this Jubilee celebration commemorating two hundred years of mission work of the Board of Missions of the Netherlands Reformed Church. I am glad to be able to participate because my graduate scholarship was partially supported by the Reformed churches in this country through the Netherlands Bible Society. It is good to give back some of myself to the churches in this country who invested in me. Thank you for the invitation and for a chance to say thank you to the Christian community in this country.

I was asked to speak about the role of women and their contribution to the way in which churches understand their calling within the African community, including their conflicts. I decided to interpret this request for myself: I wish to share some of my own thought about the mission of the churches in Africa in general and in particular to focus on women in regard to mission.

Challenged to Do Mission

I often think that we in Africa have misunderstood our call to mission. The word 'mission' itself creates certain ambiguities in our understanding. Mention 'mission' and 'missionaries' and you think of all the foreign brothers and sisters living in our villages, working in hospitals, translating our Bibles, and teaching women hygiene and sewing. They bring themselves and their money that runs our churches. We therefore often understand mission as something that we *receive* but *not give*. We also often think mission is only possible when it involves movement to other places and witness to other people, that is, other than one's own. Thus mission among ourselves and for ourselves is not an issue that keeps us awake with concern.

It is not only Africans who interpret mission in this manner. Our Christian sisters and brothers who qualify to become missionaries in our lands even believe it more than we do ourselves. I am reminded with some concern of an incident that happened to us in Nairobi only recently. My family arrived in Nairobi from Geneva, and we went to a place that has apartments owned by a church in Kenya. We asked if there was room for us to stay, and we were turned away: not because there was no room, but because the apartments were reserved for missionaries—meaning for white people from Europe and America! Even though we saw ourselves as missionaries in our service abroad and at home, we could not qualify.

We as the people of God empowered by the Holy Spirit must get back to the Scriptures and strive to reclaim our rights and responsibilities as missionaries of

---

* A presentation to the 200 Years of Jubilee of the Board of Mission of the Netherlands Reformed Church, 22–23 November. Reprinted by permission from the *International Review of Mission*, 87, no 345 (April, 1998), pp. 221–31, with the title 'Mission at the Crossroads'. 1998.

God's work. We must indeed ask, 'Where is our Jerusalem? Where must we start our mission work before going to the ends of the world?'

Biblical Mission Mandate

In my adult life as a practicing Christian and theologian, my rereading of the Bible for myself has completely changed my understanding about mission. The apostolic mandate for mission found in the Gospel of Matthew (28.18–20) challenges all Christians to share the good news of Jesus with others both in their own 'homes' and beyond their geographical boundaries.

The book of Acts tells the beginning of that mission story. The scene in Acts is set with the ascension of Jesus and the beginning of the new era of the *Ekklesia*. In Acts, *Ekklesia* refers to a community of the Lord's people, men and women living with concrete hopes, undeniable anxieties, and, most of all, a willingness to be changed by God and to bring change to their community. In Acts, people share their learning, their belongings, their personal experiences of the good news. Their very actions define mission as the sharing of the good news both in proclamation of God's words as well as in material welfare. This has no limitation. Indeed, every believer is obligated to share.

I, and all Africans too, have a mandate to be missionaries, beginning in Jerusalem. Our localities in Africa are our Jerusalem; they are our home where our mission work must begin.

Hardly any other book gives such vivid description of this movement, not only by relating the numerous travels, but also by documenting the continual changes of the people and places that come in contact with its missionaries. This movement was to 'begin in Jerusalem and to continue to the ends of the earth' (Acts 1.8). The specification of place indicates more than that the story began there. Jerusalem was the indispensable city to the nation of the Jewish people. The beginning of Acts brings us right to the center of Judaism and as such to the center of the religion of Israel. Thus mission is centered where there is the greatest need and the greatest challenge.

Africa, my continent, is a place of mission. We have many needs and challenges.

But equally important is the fact that by the time Acts was written, the Temple no longer existed. It had been obliterated by the Roman legions. It is for this reason that the people ask whether the kingdom will be restored to Israel (Acts 1.6). The new movement was to begin in Jerusalem, where people needed their hope restored, but it had to spread to other parts. In spreading, a challenge was being put directly to the Roman Empire, and, as we know, the movement spread beyond what was considered the Roman Empire.

Africa, my continent, is a place of mission. Many of our people need their hope restored.

Luke hastens to show that the spread of this movement was made possible by the activity of the Holy Spirit. The centrality of the Holy Spirit is shown by the fact that believers were instructed *not* to begin their task of the witness alone: 'Do not leave Jerusalem, but wait for the gift I told you about; the gift my father promised' (Acts 1.4).

The Holy Spirit is given freely as a gift to enable the disciples to enter into a new life of intimacy with and obedience to God. Obedience in Acts begins with the helpless, waiting: the disciples are helpless in the sense that they were told that on their own, they have no power. They needed to be empowered for whatever service or call God would send them to do. The disciples were also being told that they did not have to perform any particular duties, nor did they need to win the Holy Spirit. Rather, their task was to wait in trust and hope. This is the hope which Christians continue to carry on at every Easter as we proclaim, 'Christ is risen. He is risen indeed.'

This waiting was a command to all the followers who had believed. The command is given to the apostles, to the men of Galilee, some women, Mary the mother of Jesus, his brothers, and, finally, 120 other persons (Acts 1.13–15). Yet all are addressed with the same words, and all are given the same promise without reference to status or any other distinctions imaginable. Every one of them was commanded by the risen Savior to wait for this gift from God the father!

The waiting for the Holy Spirit is not an event without aim or purpose. It is an event which invokes patience, hope, and trust. Waiting is the making of space and time for God. It is the prayer time, the self-examination and the willingness to turn away from that which obstructs the work of the Holy Spirit. Prayer is the heart of spirituality. All of us who are serious about wanting to experience the Holy Spirit's action in our lives must find ways to make space and time for God by waiting in prayer. There are no specifications for prayer. There are no set patterns, no perfect times or ideal places.

Africa my continent has learned to wait and to pray and to believe. That is why the church is growing on this continent with so many ambiguities.

The book of Acts tells us that waiting culminates in the receiving of the Holy Spirit: 'When the Spirit comes upon you, you will be filled with power and you will be witnesses for me in Jerusalem, in all Judea and Samaria and the end of the earth' (Acts 1.8).

The Pentecost outpouring of the Spirit is a new beginning. The prophet Joel had long foretold this event (Joel 2.28–32). It is, however, a new beginning in God's saving activity in human history: through this event, Pentecost ceased to be only a Jewish celebration and became a realization that God's salvation extends far and beyond the chosen people of Israel. Clearly there is scriptural emphasis for inclusivity in God's mission. All were to wait for the Holy Spirit (Acts 1.4). All had to be witnesses (Acts 1.8). All were filled with the Holy Spirit (Acts 2.4).

This emphasis on 'all' in the book of Acts is too conspicuous to be insignificant. The author must have wanted to communicate a message. This affirmation is recorded in the Scriptures: 'And it shall be that whoever calls on the name of the Lord will be saved' (Acts 2.21).

The drama of the Pentecost event becomes even more interesting when we see it in its totality. The apostles and disciples were gathered in prayer (Acts 1.12–14), and suddenly those present heard the sound of a mighty wind rush upon them. This sound filled the whole house where they were sitting (Acts 2.2). They saw tongues of fire resting on each one of them. They all acted by speaking words of prophecy in many languages. Each one heard the others as if they were all speaking the same language.

Why have I extensively used the book of Acts and so diverted from the focus on Africa? If I were preparing a presentation for the United Nations, my reference to the Bible would be minimal or altogether absent. I believe that as churches we must return to the Scriptures for the authority of what we do and say. In our times, scriptural illiteracy is a trend that we can only change by reverting back to the reading of the Bible. Without identifying the source of what we do as Christians, we endanger losing our role as *Ekklesia* and becoming simply a social organization. I believe when we do mission—whether it includes proclamation, advocacy, or *diakonia* (service)—we do so because our faith through our commitment to the gospel commands us.

The book of Acts presents to me many points of connection to the challenges facing us Africans. Think of the passage on Pentecost and think of my continent Africa and indeed many other parts of the world where the plurality of languages translates into difficulties; our barriers include but are not limited to physical boundaries, ethnic conflicts, and illiteracy. I wish that Pentecost would literally come to us. By this I mean, at least, the gift of speaking and understanding languages different from our own, so that we could at least communicate with one another. I think of the many wise people who, because of language barriers, are unable to share their testimonies beyond their borders. I think of how these language barriers become the causes of other tensions, how they lead to ethnic imprisonment or so called tribalism or nationalism. I think of how the knowledge of English, French, or Portuguese determines success on my continent. When I see how fragmented our continent is because of linguistic and cultural differences, I thirst for the oneness of the Pentecost event.

But I am also aware of the fact that the outpouring of the Holy Spirit indicates not just that people who spoke different languages could now understand each other. The real point of this outpouring is both that it makes a connection, a bridge, between Jesus and the believers and that it removes the barriers that separate the believers in terms of age, gender, ethnic identity, and class. The outpouring of the Spirit, not only at Pentecost but throughout the book of Acts, is a conspicuous event, visible with physical signs and realized by all: the apostles, men servants, maidservants, the youth, the old, the Jews and Gentiles. What other affirmation would be needed as evidence that, in the new order, all have value before God's eyes?

And so we come, perhaps, to the crux of the matter. What does it mean for us African Christians that we see ourselves as empowered by the Holy Spirit to be witnesses for Jesus? What tasks is the Spirit calling us to heed in regard to our continent and its many challenges? To what is the Holy Spirit calling us, as individual men and women, young and old, poor and rich, as faith communities or as members of the civil society at large? What is our witness in Africa and to the uttermost ends of the earth?

African Challenges in Mission

On our continent, every minute spells death. We are perpetually put down by malaria; our children die from mere dehydration. Today we have the extra burden of the deadly AIDS. Wars of various types are at our doorsteps. The economic situations of our countries do not provide even basic needs for a majority of the population. Every younger generation inherits an increasing national debt, while the accumulation of national wealth by a few knows no bounds. Frequently our eyes are clouded with tears as we experience sorrow after sorrow. In the village where I grew up, I remember vividly the sounds of the drum, announcing death: we always had to run quickly and say, 'Who is it today?' In this context, every day is clouded with the question: 'What does the Holy Spirit give us, the Christians in Africa, the power and the ability to do in our setting and time?'

Facing our Mission Challenges

When we look at our troubled Africa, imprisoned by wars, debts, famine, corruption, political irresponsibility, held to ransom by disease and poverty, blinded by elitism, tribalism, materialism, illiteracy, and the list has no end, perhaps we see no beginning or end to what our mission could be. We wonder how individual Christians and the church in Africa can or should witness the risen Jesus when so much effort is needed just to alleviate human suffering and to improve community life. How can we, as a church, be involved in programs which provide for the witness of the gospel not only by word but also by deed? Is it part of our mission as the church in Africa to respond to the socioeconomic needs of our communities, or to the human rights which are violated every day? Is our task mainly to preach the gospel in word?

The civil wars in Liberia, Somalia, and Rwanda–Burundi left us tonguetied and helpless at the atrocities inflicted upon human life. While celebrating the independence of South Africa from the structure of apartheid, we nevertheless cannot stop to hope for good to come out of the truth commission still going on. We on the continent must reflect on the question of accountability of our actions in both the past and the present. Without doing that we will be unable to leave any heritage for our country. One of our most urgent tasks is to remember the future. Do we care enough for our continent now so as to lay the foundation for the future?

To this question many of us will say that we are already involved in numerous good deeds. The churches have established community centers, kindergartens, schools, and hospitals. Eager to live in obedience to Christ and his life, we as churches continually throw ourselves into activities of loving service of others. We have gathered in the street children, fed the hungry, visited the lonely, given refuge to victims of war and other displaced people; we have tended the sick and dying. Our hearts ache for orphans from war, AIDS, and other calamities.

We have been busy binding wounds, but we have not stopped the war. We have prepared bodies for burial, but we have not stopped the killing. I dare ask, is our involvement a sufficient and efficient way of our mission? Do these efforts witness effectively to our being missionaries on our continent?

We should see these challenges as presenting exciting rather than depressing moments in our journey of faith. In the early church, the more the persecution and the conflict grew, the more the disciples made it a priority to proclaim the good news about Jesus. In the book of Acts, Luke paints a picture of rapid evangelistic growth. Three thousand persons were converted (Acts 2.41), then five thousand (Acts 4.4), etc. Converted disciples included religious leaders whom Luke describes as 'a great many priests' (Acts 6.7).

The disciples also testified before kings and governors even as Jesus had foretold (Lk. 12.12). Peter proclaimed the good news of salvation in Jesus Christ to the rulers, elders, and scribes gathered in Jerusalem (Acts 6.12–15). Paul testified before Festus (Acts 25.1–12) and before King Agrippa (Acts 26).

We know that Stephen was stoned to death. Stephen's death marked a decisive escalation of tension, conflict, and persecution for the church (Acts 8.1–3). But it also opened new evangelistic outreach within the church which spread to Judea and Samaria and to the uttermost parts of the earth (Acts 1.8); this included Africa, through the testimonies of a man from Ethiopia described as a eunuch (Acts 8). These stories of Acts are familiar to us. They are being re-enacted on our continent today.

I want to suggest that it does not matter how much material wealth the church has and devotes to our communities: we will not save Africa through providing bandages for the wounds our communities continue to receive. Our children will continue to die because of lack of sufficient medical help, while the resources of our countries are directed to military services and the benefit of the privileged few. Therefore, we bring no good news to the poor of our societies. Illiteracy will continue to haunt us. We need to reread our Scriptures with new eyes and see that God is calling us and empowering us to do the more difficult tasks of our mission, that is, to speak out for the truth. We must rethink our mission tasks as Africans in Africa.

This means daring to be a conscience and a stimulus for change in our own societies. Speaking up on issues that diminish life has been the most difficult part of our self-understanding as individuals and church. Speaking out is a prophetic task. It involves very serious risks. For our situation, where democracy is thought to be a luxury, speaking up involves foremost risking wrath from the powerful. This is the horrendous situation of Africa today.

Second, there is the risk of facing the different understandings of the witness of the church. We must come to accept that even within the church, opinions will differ.

Speaking up also calls for credibility. If the Christian community in Africa is to be credible in its witness, we must approach the complex situations before us with expertise. The churches have to open up more possibilities for the believers to hear the many points of view and to exercise the discipline needed to understand the complex forces at work in modern society.

Like the believers of the Acts, we too are called to discussion with our governments and communities. We must summon our respective governments to use the resources we have and which we borrow to meet the needs of the people. We also must show by our lives that the churches' resources are used to heal society. We as a community of empowered believers must be able to risk our own security by being open about getting to the roots of what is wrong in our society and how that wrong should be put right. Our witness of Jesus does not depend only on how we preach the gospel, but how we live the gospel. Yes, they will know we are Christians by our love, our love for truth, fairness, and justice.

Most important, as individuals we must be credible. With regard to this last issue I have so much concern.

The Acts of the Apostles give us more than an account of the beginning of the church of Jesus Christ. It is also the story of God's faithfulness in times of opposition, persecution, and trial. God, who took the initiative to send Jesus Christ to become an agent of blessing to the world, secures and preserves that blessing by protecting and delivering those who become witnesses to this good news. But as it was in the early church, even those who trust in God go through periods of temptation, failure, struggle, weakness, and conflict.

Such is the case for the Christian church in Africa today. The church in Africa is experiencing opposition and self-conflict in regard to other faiths, especially Islam; it faces conflict over ethical issues concerning sexual morality, cultural traditions and practices, power and leadership. We used to claim that our communitarian cultures helped us to be custodians of each other's morality. This claim is passé. We also know that the church is facing conflict with regard to the dichotomy between the authority and responsibility of church and state. Should the church speak out on the political and economic reforms being requested by the masses of African countries? Opinions are divided. Some feel the church has no business in state matters. Others feel the church is the conscience of society and must speak on every subject that affects God's creation: people, the land, and all that was created.

Thus we have conflicts even within ourselves as the church of Jesus Christ. We are struggling in the area not only of politics but also of identity: Should we be the church of Africa or an African church? Are we Christians in Africa or African Christians? Should we, or can we, retrieve some of our authentic spirituality?

For me, those who have dared to speak out despite all the risks involved are the missionaries that we need today. I think of individual clergy from both the Roman Catholic and Protestant churches in Zaire, Kenya, Malawi, South Africa, and so on. I think of the Councils of Churches on the continent. I think of others who have risked prison and detention in order to present the voices of the weak and the dying. These people model for me mission. They model mission which addresses our needs in our Jerusalem. They are our missionaries, our bearers of the good news. I think of women: women of Africa who are saying *no* to be being relegated to the back, women who are saying *no* to cultural practices which dehumanize them and prevent them from having life in abundance. Women are the prophets of Africa.

Mission to Women

One urgent issue that must receive attention is the status of women in African societies. African women, through their caretaking responsibilities, continue to be the foundation of hope in church and society. Within our present setup, African women have more to offer than they have opportunities. I can boldly say that women of Africa are the missionaries to our ailing society. Women of Africa celebrate their experiences and affirm their gifting through service and reading of the Scripture. They hear life-giving words about baptism, Pentecost, being created in the image of God, the priesthood of all believers.

Yet this is one area where the body of Christ is hurting. These same women find a gap between the words and the practice of the church! The same leaders who have wonderfully heeded the prophetic call by addressing other issues are often unprepared to take risk on issues concerning women. Many have marched for political issues, but one fails to hear of similar fires burning for the crimes committed against the women of Africa. How long must we wait? The rape cases in the war of the Great Lakes have received hardly any attention either locally or internationally. The daily deaths of women in childbirth have not made our governments change their policies to give priority to maternal health care. The frequent threats of and deaths from female circumcision have not made the church rise up in all its force to teach something new about culture and human dignity. African women are silenced daily by health issues, cultural prescriptions, illiteracy, and endless chores that make us old before our time.

Women may have constitutional rights which are often overlooked or remain unknown, and hence their talents are unused except as typists and telephone operators. Therefore, improving the status of women is the *key* to development in Africa. It is crucial for improving health status, slowing population growth, and achieving economic and social progress. Investing in women leads to more rewarding lives for the women themselves as well as their families, communities, and countries. Increasing the involvement of women at decision-making levels remains crucial to long-term success in improving their status. This is dependent upon women's having the knowledge and skills required for such roles. A mission to women must take care that they be equipped with education and health facilities and that they be given a voice in making decisions in our churches and societies.

Actions advocated by African women activists include working to reduce discrimination, providing educational and vocational opportunities, seeking mechanisms to increase women's capacity to cope with situations that threaten survival, transforming unequal relations in the family, community, workplace, and church, overhauling power-relations that hamper equitable development, improving women's access to support systems and resources, targeting women's programs based on available information concerning needs, employing a community-based approach to facilitate the empowerment of women, exploring new approaches to enhancing people-centered development, and creating an information-exchange network to enhance learning from the experiences of others.

Women Doing Mission

One must ask: So what about this litany of the sorry state of African women? Are the women of Africa just sitting there waiting for a handout? Far from being helpless victims of hunger, disease, and exploitation, as we are often portrayed, the women of Africa are a major resource in search of ways out of the circumstances in which we are entrapped.

Women are key actors in the economic system: they function as small-business entrepreneurs, often in inventive ways; they control the non-monetary economy (subsistence agriculture, bearing and rearing of children, domestic labor) and they comprise 60 per cent of those involved in informal-sector cash economy (informal trade and wage employment). Eighty per cent of economically active African women are in agriculture, and they produce over 80 per cent of the continent's food.

Women are the main health-care givers, in the home, community and even at the health facilities. Africa takes the brunt of the impact of disease and death, physically and emotionally, and yet we women who work to cure and to comfort are neither adequately recognized nor rewarded.

Speaking for Ourselves

To cope with the tensions and strains emanating from our subordinate positions and to help execute our many roles, African women have over the years developed various activist networks, groups, and movements. Through these movements, they struggle collectively to combat poverty, low social status, social alienation, backbreaking chores, and other socioeconomic and political vagaries. These movements share the common objective of improving the condition of women in society while varying in their strategies. Some make efforts to consciencitize not only their members but the society at large. Women in these movements are concerned about education, health care, adequate shelter, security, theology, and the quest for justice.

> Then justice will dwell in the wilderness, and righteousness abide in the fruitful field. And the fruit of righteousness will be peace and the result of righteousness, undisturbed security for ever (Isa. 32.15–17).

The key words in this prophetic vision for a new world order are righteousness, justice, peace, and security . A just society depends on just people. A just society is one where men and women are equally united in their struggle and in their reward (loss or gain; success or failure); it is a society of true partnership among men and women. Gender roles are neither unchangeable nor divine. They must change over time as contexts change over time. Recognition of this necessity will enhance women's participation not only in social and political development, it will also contribute to greater efficiency in the utilization of resources.

The notion of women as partners with men in church still frightens some in our communities. I remember a meeting I had with clergymen in Soweto, South Africa, in February 1993. These brothers had no problem with using 'partnership' in referring to marital relationships, but they found the terminology quite unacceptable in addressing the relationship of women and men in the church. Many women in Africa testify to the churches' fear of 'women's sexuality'. Sexuality is given as an excuse for denying ordination to women. Not only are women's bodies seen as symbols of sexuality, but also, and because of that, women are seen to be unacceptable for church leadership. It is interesting to me that African society, which is so hospitable to new life, has not provided a theology which affirms the woman through whom new life finds a possibility for growth.

In listening to many experiences of churchwomen in Africa, I feel that our cry for partnership in the church is loud and clear. When we are denied partnership, we are denied the opportunity to bring our gifts to the altar to offer to God. Our talents often remain unused for church growth. As women theologians, we may teach in scholastic institutions or work with secular and para-church organizations, but we are often not called upon to be coministers in the shaping of the theology and mission of the church. When we ask for partnership, we get paternalism.

The church leaders from our communities continually heap praises over us with words such as 'women are the backbone of the church'. Our paternalistic leaders desire to shield us from growing up. They encourage us to continue organizing our own forums, but they do not listen to the issues that concern us. They encourage us to be virtuous, to serve as volunteers for the church, and to accept and support the status quo! They encourage us to remain children in our understanding of ourselves and our call to participate in God's mission. They do not listen to our chorus of pain and contradictions. They do not hear the harmony of our lamentation. Our song asks our churches to empower us, to nurture us towards maturity, and finally to welcome us as partners in God's mission and ministry.

Partnership is rooted in the shared resources of the community. The ministry of the church in Africa today requires new, more collaborative strength. It is time that our male leaders let go the heroic image of owning the church. God does not assign talents according to sex but according to divine will. To ignore this and to continue business as usual at a time of crisis is to be a bad steward of God's resources.

African women in the church can no longer wait for things to take their natural course. The models of women in the Bible teach us that change comes when the personal is made political and when the political is made personal. How else could you read the story of Lydia (Acts 16.14–15), who practices her faith in public, and who prevails upon Paul? If we African women continue to separate our private lives from the public, we will continue to experience both cultural and domestic violence on our bodies. So today, we read the Bible and then, encouraged by women such as Lydia, or Priscilla (Acts 18), who insists on teaching the eloquent Apollos the true 'Way of God', we say 'No!' In the Bible, women who need help demonstrate a political and faith decision to act in a way in which they themselves cause help to come to them from a source beyond their immediate environment. This is what Joel said they would do: 'Your sons and your daughters shall prophesy!' (Acts 2.17).

We Christians of Africa are learning from the experiences of the Christian community recorded for us in the book of Acts. That community was empowered for discipleship amid struggles and suffering for the sake of the gospel. God through the Holy Spirit gives the church power to stand and endure. The church of God is made up of both men and women. God will definitely give the church in Africa the power to stand firm. The church in Africa has hope that through trusting and obedience, the promise given to us by the Holy Spirit is ours for claiming. Will you claim this promise with us? This is what we would ask of you on your Jubilee celebration.

THE POWER OF THE WIDOWS AND HOW TO SUPPRESS IT (ACTS 6.1–7)

BARBARA E. REID, OP

It seems a simple problem with a quick solution. Acts 6.1 relates that as the number of disciples was increasing the Hellenists lodged a complaint against the Hebrews because their widows were being neglected in the daily distribution (ἐν τῇ διακονίᾳ τῇ καθημερινῇ). So the twelve called together the whole community of disciples and declared that it was not right for them to neglect the word of God in order to wait on tables (διακονεῖν τραπέζαις, v. 2). Their solution was to have the community (ἀδελφοί) select seven men (ἄνδρας) of good standing (μαρτυρουμένους) whom they would appoint to this task (v. 3). They, meanwhile, would attend constantly (προσκαρτερήσομεν) to prayer and ministry of the word (διακονίᾳ τοῦ λόγου, v. 4). Luke narrates that this pleased (ἤρεσεν) the whole community and they chose Stephen, a man full of faith and of the Holy Spirit, together with Philip, Prochorus, Nicanor, Timon, Parmenas, and Nicolaus, a proselyte of Antioch (v. 5). They had these men stand before the apostles, who prayed and laid their hands on them (v. 6). The episode concludes with the assertion that the word of God continued to spread and the number of the disciples increased greatly in Jerusalem, and a great many priests became obedient to the faith (v. 7).

At first this seems to be simply one of several episodes in Acts that describe how the fledgling church acts when its peace and unity are threatened. As in the stories of Ananias and Sapphira (Acts 4.32–5.11), the arrest of the apostles (5.12–42), Simon Magus (8.6–13 and 8.14–25), the seven sons of Sceva (19.11–20), the episode about the Hellenist widows follows the same four-part pattern: (1) there is peace among the believers; (2) this peace is threatened; (3) a resolution is found; (4) harmony is restored.[1]

These stories serve to advance Luke's narrative of the steady growth of the church despite obstacles, and to affirm the leadership of the apostles as they are led by the Spirit. The particular function of Acts 6.1–7 is to trace the succession from the apostles to the post-apostolic leadership, and to introduce the extension of the mission outside Jerusalem.[2]

But this analysis overlooks a host of exegetical difficulties. What is the meaning of τῇ διακονίᾳ τῇ καθημερινῇ in v. 1? Who are the Hebrews and the Hellenists? What does Luke mean when he says the widows 'were overlooked' (παρεθεωροῦντο, v. 1)? How does the solution fit the problem? How is this passage

---

1 This pattern is identified by Joseph B. Tyson, 'Acts 6.1–7 and Dietary Regulations in Early Christianity', *Perspectives in Religious Studies* 10.2 (1983), pp. 145–61; *idem*, 'The Problem of Food in Acts: A Study of the Literary Patterns with Particular Reference to Acts 6.1–7', in Paul J. Achtemeier (ed.), *Society of Biblical Literature 1979 Seminar Papers* (Missoula, MT: Scholars Press, 1979), I, pp. 69–85.

2 Tyson, 'Dietary Regulations', p. 152; John B. Polhill, 'The Hellenist Breakthrough: Acts 6–12', *Review and Expositor* 71 (1974), pp. 475–86.

related to Luke's themes of table companionship and of concern for the poor? How does this episode address Luke's concern for universality and for the overcoming of cultural, theological, and social conflict? How does this pericope function in Luke's overall treatment of women?[3]

In this essay I will take up analysis of these various difficulties from a feminist perspective, posing yet another set of questions that are rarely addressed by others who have explored this passage. What does this pericope tell us about the power, or lack thereof, of women for decision-making in the early church? What was the social situation of ministering widows and how did their economic resources, or lack of them, affect their ability to exercise decision-making power? How did patriarchal leadership of the early church affect their ability to minister? What was the reaction of the widows to the solution provided by the twelve? Were they, indeed, 'pleased', as Luke asserts 'the whole community' was in v. 5? How does the way this decision was arrived at relate to the way the decisions about Gentiles were reached in Acts 15? How does this episode fit Luke's treatment of women overall? And finally, what does this passage offer to us today concerning decision-making power by women in the church?

In addressing these questions my approach is to examine Acts 6.1–7 not as an isolated pericope, but as part of a larger literary pattern in Luke–Acts concerning the discipleship of women.[4] I will argue that the pericopes involving widows reveal an

---

3 Not all of these questions are able to be adequately addressed in this essay. On the question of the identity of the Hebrews and the Hellenists, see Joseph A. Fitzmyer, *The Acts of the Apostles: A New Translation with Introduction and Commentary* (AB, 31; New York: Doubleday, 1998), pp. 347–48 and the references therein. I understand 'Hellenists' to be Jews and Jewish Christians who spoke primarily Greek; 'Hebrews' were those who spoke not only Greek, but also Hebrew or Aramaic. The former would pray and read their Scriptures in Greek, while the latter would use Aramaic or Hebrew. On the Lukan theme of possessions and the poor see: John Gillman, *Possessions and the Life of Faith: A Reading of Luke–Acts* (Zacchaeus Studies: New Testament; Collegeville, MN: Liturgical Press, 1991); Luke T. Johnson, *The Literary Function of Possessions in Luke–Acts* (SBLDS, 39; Chico, CA: Scholars Press, 1977); Philip Esler, *Community and Gospel in Luke–Acts* (SNTSMS, 57; Cambridge: Cambridge University Press, 1987), pp. 164–200. For further discussion of Lukan table sharing see: Esler, *Community and Gospel*, pp. 71–109; Eugene LaVerdiere, *Dining in the Kingdom of God: The Origins of the Eucharist according to Luke* (Chicago: LTP, 1994); Jerome Neyrey, 'Ceremonies in Luke–Acts: The Case of Meals and Table Fellowship', in *idem* (ed.), *The Social World of Luke–Acts* (Peabody, MA: Hendrickson, 1991), pp. 361–87. For fuller treatments of women in Luke and Acts, see Barbara E. Reid, *Choosing the Better Part? Women in the Gospel of Luke* (Collegeville, MN: Liturgical Press, 1996); Mary Rose D'Angelo, '(Re)Presentations of Women in the Gospel of Matthew and Luke–Acts', in Ross Shepard Kraemer and Mary Rose D'Angelo (eds.), *Women and Christian Origins* (Oxford: Oxford University Press, 1999), pp. 171–95; *idem*, 'Women in Luke–Acts: A Redactional View', *JBL* 109 (1990), pp. 441–61; Turid Karlsen Seim, *The Double Message: Patterns of Gender in Luke–Acts* (Studies of the New Testament and its World; Edinburgh: T. & T. Clarke, 1994); *idem*, 'The Gospel of Luke', in Elisabeth Schüssler Fiorenza (ed.), *Searching the Scriptures* (2 vols.; New York: Crossroad, 1994), II, pp. 728–62; Jane Schaberg, 'Luke', in Carol A. Newsom and Sharon H. Ringe (eds.), *The Women's Bible Commentary* (Louisville, KY: Westminster/John Knox, 2nd edn, 1998), pp. 363–80; James Arlandson, *Women, Class, and Society in Early Christianity: Models from Luke–Acts* (Peabody, MA: Hendrickson, 1997); Jacob Jervell, 'The Daughters of Abraham: Women in Acts', in *idem*, *The Unknown Paul: Essays on Luke–Acts and Early Christian History* (Minneapolis: Augsburg, 1984), pp. 146–57.

4 Because the term 'widow' was also used of some women who were virgins or women separated from still-living husbands, the episodes concerning widows are indicative of treatment of women in general. See further Bonnie Bowman Thurston, *The Widows: A Women's Ministry in the Early Church* (Minneapolis: Fortress Press, 1989).

increasing conflict in the early church over the ministry of widows and that part of Luke's aim is to squelch the controversies engendered by the widows' attempts to exercise their power.

There are seven passages in the Gospel of Luke that make explicit reference to widows and two in Acts of the Apostles.[5] Further, there are a number of passages in Luke and Acts that speak of women who may well have been widows, though that is not made explicit.[6] By comparison, Mark mentions widows in only three pericopae (12.18–27, 38–40, 41–44) and Matthew in one (22.23–33), all of which have Lukan parallels. In the remainder of the New Testament, Paul mentions widows at 1 Cor. 7.8, 25–40, where he advises them to stay unmarried so they can focus entirely on serving the Lord. In 1 Tim. 5.3–16 is a more extended treatise on qualifications for the ministry of widows. In Jas 1.27 there is an exhortation, much like the admonitions in the Old Testament, to care for widows along with orphans. And lastly, in the Book of Revelation, in a dirge about the fall of Babylon, she is said to have boasted 'I am no widow, and I will never know grief' (18.7). Clearly, Luke has the most interest in widows, as numerous references to them punctuate both the Gospel and Acts.

Mention widows in a biblical context and immediately what comes to the mind of most people is the classic image of poor, helpless women, without social status and with no resources of their own. In the Old Testament they typify those who are entirely dependent on mercy—God's mercy and the charity of the community. Usually they are linked with orphans and foreigners as the most vulnerable in the society (e.g. Deut. 14.19; 26.13; Jer 49.11). But widows as objects of charity are only one strand of the tradition visible in Luke and Acts; there is also a strand in which they are the ones doing the ministry. I will argue that Luke presents a mixed message about widows. While he is aware of the growing number of ministering widows in the early church and of the controversies surrounding their attempts at exercising their power, he is intent on taming them and presenting a traditional, respectable image of them.

In the first four scenes of the Gospel that involve widows, they are not so much the subject of the story as they are vehicles for advancing the theme of discipleship; they aim to provoke the reader to come to faith in Jesus. Signs involving widows are part of the larger agenda of the narrative that recounts the ingathering of the first disciples at the outset of the Jesus movement.

---

5 The seven in the Gospel are: Anna in the Temple (2.36–38), widows in Israel and the widow at Zarephath (4.25–26), the widow at Nain (7.11–17), a widow who confronts an unjust judge (18.1–8), a question about widows at the resurrection (20.27–40), widows whose houses are devoured by scribes (20.45–47), a widow who gives all her livelihood to the temple treasury (21.1–4). In Acts, in addition to the widows of the Hellenists and of the Hebrews (6.1–7), there are the widows who weep over Tabitha (9.36–43). Each of these episodes will be discussed below.

6 Other women who are mentioned in Luke and Acts who may have been widows include: Simon's mother-in-law (Lk. 4.38–39), the Galilean women who followed and ministered to Jesus (Lk. 8.1–3), the women of Jerusalem who lamented Jesus on the way of the cross (Lk. 23.27), Mary, the mother of Jesus and the women who devoted themselves to prayer in the upper room with the other disciples awaiting the Holy Spirit (Acts 1.14), Mary, the mother of John Mark, in whose house the Jerusalem community gathered (Acts 12.12), Lydia and the women of her household (Acts 16.14–15, 40), the prominent women of Thessalonica (Acts 17.4), and those of Beroea (Acts 17.12).

Anna, Temple Prophet (Luke 2.36-38)

Anna is the first widow to appear in the Lukan narrative. She is a prophet with impeccable credentials: her lineage is honorable and her advanced age (v. 36) makes her a reliable figure of maturity and wisdom.[7] With the number seven signifying perfection or completeness in biblical parlance, Anna's seven-year marriage evokes the image of one who has been an ideal wife. She now devotes herself to worshiping in the Temple night and day with fasting and prayer, practices that prefigure Jesus' own and those that would be continued by his disciples.[8] Like Simeon,[9] she recognizes the child Jesus as the one whom they awaited for the redemption of Israel (v. 38). The function of this scene is to confirm for the reader that Jesus is the one in whom to believe. In the context of expectant Israel, two venerable prophets attest that he is the awaited one. The focus of the episode is to assure the reader that faith in Jesus is the proper response.

What is not so apparent in the narrative is the power that Anna exercised as a temple prophet. First, one wonders why Anna did not remarry after her brief marriage.[10] It was not unusual for women to be married several times, as they were often very young when married to older men.[11] The first hint of Anna's exercise of power is found in her decision to resist the pressures of her culture to remarry in order to dedicate herself to her prophetic mission. One may reflect on what kind of power it takes for a young widow to decide to exercise a countercultural ministry and then to remain faithful to this for 84 years.[12] Luke's portrayal of her, however, reflects his mixed estimation of women prophets in the early church. He diminishes the character of Anna, who, unlike Simeon with whom she is paired, has not been given a voice. Whereas the words of his prophecy are conveyed in vv. 29–32, and continue to be prayed nightly in the church, the substance of Anna's words are conveyed not in quotation, but in a single phrase in third-person. Nor is any reaction to her prophecy related. Whereas Simeon's prophecy evokes amazement (v. 33),[13] the reader is not

---

7 See the regulations in 1 Tim. 5.3–16, where enrolled widows are expected to be over 60 years old (v. 9) and younger widows are encouraged to marry (vv. 11, 14).

8 Luke tells of Jesus spending the night in communion with God (6.12), fasting (4.1–13) and praying frequently (3.21; 9.18, 28, 29; 11.1; 22.32, 41–45). His followers acted similarly: Lk. 24.53; Acts 1.14; 2.42, 46; 3.1; 4.31; 6.4, 6; 7.59; 8.15; 9.11, 40; 10.2, 9; 11.15; 12.5, 12; 13.2–3; 14.23; 16.25; 20.36; 21.5; 22.17; 26.29; 27.29; 28.8.

9 On Lukan pairs and their function, see D'Angelo, 'Women in Luke–Acts', pp. 443–48.

10 Paul's advice to widows not to remarry in 1 Cor. 7 presumes the more usual practice is to remarry. The regulation in 1 Tim. 5.9 that widows be married only once in order to be enrolled in the ministry would have been very difficult for most women to fulfill. See below on Lk. 20.27–40 which presumes that a childless widow would marry her husband's brother in the attempt to provide progeny to him. For another perspective, see Peter Walcot, 'On Widows and their Reputation in Antiquity', *Symbola Osloenses* 66 (1991), pp. 5–26, who explores the ideal in the ancient world that a woman should have just a single husband and that the widow, therefore, ought not to remarry. This ideal, he shows, was reinforced by a fear of the sexually experienced widow and of the sexually voracious older woman. The concept of the virtuous widow was balanced by that of the widow as predator, and both concepts persisted throughout antiquity.

11 Seim, *Double Message*, p. 192.

12 The Greek is ambiguous: ἕως ἐτῶν ὀγδοήκοντα τεσσάρων can mean either her present age is 84 or she has been a widow for 84 years.

13 'Amazement' (θαυμάζω) is a favorite Lukan word. It is the response to the message of the shepherds (2.18), to the naming of John by Elizabeth and Zechariah (1.63), and is the constant reaction to Jesus' words (4.22; 20.26) and deeds (8.25; 9.43; 11.14, 38; 24.12, 41).

led to respond similarly to hers. By giving Anna no concrete audience and no response, Luke discourages the reader from giving her much notice. The same can be said for Philip's four unmarried daughters gifted with prophecy (Acts 21.9). Nothing of their prophecy or how it was received is preserved, whereas that of the prophet Agabus, which immediately follows, is told in detail (Acts 21.10–14).

In other biblical portraits of prophets, those who exercise this ministry are powerful in word and deed, decisive in their message, and self-possessed agents of God. They act in ways that are independent of the approval of others, knowing that their message will provoke controversy, and they are willing to suffer the consequences. In the Old Testament women as well as men prophets exercise this powerful ministry: Miriam (Exod. 15.20), Deborah (Judg. 4–5) and Huldah (2 Kgs 22.14; 2 Chron. 34.22). But in the Gospel of Luke only Jesus is given this role. He is the prophet par excellence.[14] He is cast as the 'prophet like Moses' of Deut. 18.15 (Lk. 9.28–36; Acts 3.22–23; 7.37). He emulates the prophets Elijah and Elisha in his miracle working.[15] And a particularly Lukan theme is that of Jesus as the rejected prophet.[16]

In Acts, although the prophecy of Joel (3.1–5) that both men and women would prophesy is seen to be fulfilled at Pentecost (Acts 2.18), all the prophets named in Acts are male, save the brief notice about Philip's daughters. In Acts 11.27–30 Luke tells of some prophets that came down from Jerusalem to Antioch, one of whom was named Agabus. He predicted a severe famine which prompted a relief collection for the Christians in Judea. This same prophet later announced that Paul would be bound by the Jews and handed over to the Gentiles (Acts 21.10–11). In Acts 13.1 the names of prophets and teachers at Antioch are listed: 'Barnabas, Symeon who was called Niger, Lucius of Cyrene, Manaen who was a close friend of Herod the tetrarch, and Saul'. In 15.32 Judas and Silas also exhort the community in Antioch as prophets. A Jewish false prophet, Bar-Jesus, is mentioned in 13.6. In Ephesus, Paul laid hands on twelve men, upon whom the Holy Spirit came, and they spoke in tongues and prophesied (19.6–7).

The first of the widow stories in Luke–Acts sets the stage for Luke's ambiguous treatment of women overall. His account preserves the memory of women who exercised decisive power in prophetic ministry, while, at the same time, he diminishes the impact of this in his narrative. Luke builds up the image of this ministry as one that pertains primarily to men by the number of male prophets he mentions and by relating their words in detail and elaborating on their effect. The double message concerning women results, as Mary Rose D'Angelo observes, 'from the tension between the necessity of catechizing women converts who are still of real political importance to the church of Luke's day and the anxiety that an expanded role for

---

14 In addition to Anna, the only other prophets mentioned in the Gospel of Luke besides Jesus are Zechariah, whose canticle is cast as prophecy (1.67), and John the Baptist, who 'will be called prophet of the Most High' (1.76; see also 3.2; 7.26; 20.6). Though the term is not used of Mary and Elizabeth, in some ways they are cast in the mold of women prophets of the Old Testament. See further Reid, *Choosing the Better Part?*, pp. 55–95.

15 Lk. 4.25–27; 7.11–17; 9.8, 10–17, 19, 30–33, 51. See Joseph A. Fitzmyer, *The Gospel according to Luke* (2 vols.; AB, 28A; New York: Doubleday, 1981), I, pp. 213–15; R. O'Toole, 'The Parallels between Jesus and Moses', *BTB* 20 (1990), pp. 22–29; R.E. Brown, 'Jesus and Elisha', *Perspective* 12 (1971), pp. 84–104.

16 Lk. 4.24, 39; 13.33; 24.19–20; Acts 7.52.

women may cause Christians to be seen as practitioners of "un-Roman" activities'.[17] A similar effort to silence widows can be seen in the *Didascalia Apostolorum*, where widows are forbidden to teach and baptize and 'gad about', which refers, probably, to their answering and asking theological questions.[18]

Widows in Israel and the Widow at Zarephath (Luke 4.25–26)

The second reference to widows comes in the context of Jesus' inaugural proclamation of his mission in the synagogue at Nazareth. He has just read from the prophet Isaiah about liberating the oppressed and the reaction is most favorable (v. 22). The assembly then turns on Jesus when he speaks about the prophet Elijah having been sent not to the many widows in Israel, but to the widow at Zarephath in Sidon (see 1 Kgs 17.8–24).

In this episode, the widow is not the focus of the story. Rather, Jesus' ministry to outsiders is at issue. Luke sounds this theme early on and alerts the reader to the controversy that is created by Jesus' attention to the marginalized and outcast, of which the widow at Zarephath is an example. The function of this episode is to confront the readers with the decision that they will have to make repeatedly: Will you follow the prophet Jesus, or not? Will you marvel at his gracious words and deeds (4.22) or will you be enraged and drive him out (4.28–29)?

A Widow at Nain (Luke 7.11–17)[19]

This woman is cast in a traditional widow's role. She is a nameless, silent object of pity. Her grief is heightened by the notation that the dead man is her only son, her only means of support and status.[20] Like the other accounts of resuscitations and healings in the beginning of Luke's Gospel, this story's main effect is to point to Jesus and the power of God at work in him. The crowd reacts by glorifying God and acclaiming Jesus as a prophet (v. 16). The widow fades into the background. We hear nothing of her reaction. There is no mention of faith in this story. We know nothing more about whether the widow became a disciple of Jesus or whether others were drawn to him through her subsequent testimony. Luke concludes the story by attesting that 'this report about him spread through the whole of Judea and in all the surrounding region' (v. 17) but who it is that spreads the word is left unspecified.[21]

The image Luke presents of this widow is one of an utterly destitute person who is the object of Jesus' compassion and whose dire plight heightens his own power.

---

17 See further D'Angelo, 'Women in Luke–Acts', pp. 441–61 (443).
18 See R.H. Connolly (ed.), *Didascalia Apostolorum* (Oxford: Clarendon Press, 1929), pp. 133, 134, 142.
19 See further Reid, *Choosing the Better Part?*, pp. 103–106.
20 In two other episodes, Lk. 8.42 (cf. Mk 5.23) and Lk. 9.38 (cf. Mk 9.17) Luke heightens the distress of the parents by making the ill child an only child.
21 There are many parallels between Luke's account and that of 1 Kgs 17. See T.L. Brodie, 'Towards Unravelling Luke's Use of the Old Testament: Luke 7.11–17 as an Imitatio of 1 Kings 17.17–24', *NTS* 32 (1986), pp. 247–67. This is one of many episodes in which Jesus is cast as Elijah come again. See also Lk. 9.61–62 (cf. 1 Kgs 19.19–21); Lk. 9.54 and 12.49 (cf. 1 Kgs 1.10, 12); Lk. 19.1 (cf. 2 Kgs 2.4); Lk. 22.33 (cf. 2 Kgs 2.4); Lk. 24.49 (cf. 2 Kgs 2.13).

Yet a reality that Luke masks is the power often exercised by widowed women who refuse to be victims of their grievous circumstances. In the narrative the widow's tears have the power to bring Jesus to compassion and to move him to restore her son to life. She and the group of mourners that surround her can be likened to the groups of contemporary women who gather in many different places to protest against death. The Madres de la Plaza de Mayo are one such group, who march in silence every Thursday, demanding to know the fate of their disappeared husbands and brothers and sons from Argentina's 'dirty war' of the 1970s. The power of their decision not to acquiesce silently to the deaths that left them widowed has resulted in the disclosure of the fates of at least one-third of the men. The power of the protests of these widows has been thought to be partially responsible for the collapse of the military dictatorship in 1982. This is not, however, the kind of image that Luke wants to present of widows. Luke gives his patron assurance (ἀσφάλεια, 1.4) that the Christian message is not only theologically sound, but politically nonthreatening.[22]

A Widow Pursuing Justice (Luke 18.1–8)[23]

The next reference to a widow is found in this provocative parable, in which a widow repeatedly[24] confronts an unjust judge with her demands for justice. She does not relent, even though the judge delays (v. 4) and is utterly shameless (vv. 2, 4). The judge finally gives her a just verdict out of fear that she will blacken his eye.[25] This parable portrays a widow who is needy, but she does not passively accept her lot. In fact, quite the opposite. We have here a most unconventional woman who ventures into the world of men to argue her own case before the judge. Adjudication of her complaint would have been the responsibility of her nearest male relative. But he is absent from the scene and may even be the culprit against whom she lodges her protest. Her persistence is an exercise of power that finally accomplishes its end. The comic twist in v. 5, where the judge actually fears she will do him physical violence,[26] underscores all the more the power she possesses over against the one who is supposedly the mighty one in the story.

The nameless widow of this parable is not unique in her assertive action for justice. The stories of Ruth and Tamar also preserve the memory of widows who take critical action in unconventional ways for the salvation of their people.[27] She also embodies the kind of godly power that is evident in the crucified Jesus, giving a female face to the same paradox: the one who is seemingly most vulnerable and

---

22 D'Angelo, 'Women in Luke–Acts', p. 448.
23 See further B. Reid, 'Beyond Petty Pursuits, and Wearisome Widows', *Int* 56 (2002), pp. 284–94.
24 The verb ἤρχετο in v. 3 connotes repeated, persistent coming.
25 This is the literal meaning of ὑπωπιάζω in v. 5, a term that comes from the world of boxing. See also Paul's use of the term in 1 Cor. 9.26–27.
26 BAGD, p. 848, also suggests that in Lk. 18.5 ὑπωπιαζω may be taken in a weakened sense, 'annoy greatly, wear out' (so the NRSV translation). But this is the only example where ὑπωπιάζω is thought to have this nuance. To propose this connotation dilutes the irony of the literal 'strike', which is part of the twist of the story.
27 See Don C. Benjamin, 'The Persistent Widow', *TBT* 28 (1990), pp. 213–19.

powerless is, indeed, the very embodiment of the power of God. Just as Jesus' seeming helplessness in the face of his executioners is transformed into the defeat of the powers of sin and death through his persistent faith and forgiveness, so does this seemingly powerless widow achieve righteousness over the recalcitrant judge through her persistent demands for justice that unmask his viciousness.

But that is not the image Luke would have us see. Rather, in his redaction of the parable,[28] Luke skews the reader's perception from the very first verse. By introducing the parable as one that concerns 'the need to pray always and not to lose heart' (v. 1), Luke tames this provocative widow, casting her in a role more akin to Anna, who prays ceaselessly in the Temple. There is nothing controversial about widows who stay put and pray all day. But it is quite another matter to have them venturing into court and challenging the powers that be. Even more unsettling for the ruling powers is to have a widow emerge victorious.

The last verses (vv. 6–8) take us further afield. Verse 6 puts the judge back into the center, insisting that the reader focus on the judge and not the widow. The absolute use of ὁ κύριος ('the Lord') is out of step with the narrative flow and is a sign of later interpretation. Calling Jesus 'Lord' is a post-resurrection insight that has been retrojected into the time of Jesus' ministry. Verses 7 and 8 then try to answer the question of whether God hears the prayers of those who are just; and, if so, why does God delay in responding? The last half of v. 8 takes the applications even farther afield by asking if the Son of Humanity will find faith on earth at his coming. It links loosely to the notion of delay in vv. 7b–8a, but is unrelated to the parable proper, which makes no mention of faith. It appears to be a transplant from the discussion of the coming of the Son of Humanity in Luke 17, which immediately precedes the parable.

Once again we meet Lukan ambiguity: Luke preserves an authentic parable of Jesus from the tradition, the only one in which a widow is given her own voice; but he tries to hush her by his redaction. In the core of the parable from the Jesus tradition, the widow is decisive, independent, forceful in her persistence, and takes unconventional measures, emerging victorious over a seemingly insurmountable obstacle through her relentless insistence on justice. The theological and pastoral potential of this parable is enormous. When the widow is the central character, she can easily be seen to be the one who embodies the godly qualities to be emulated by a disciple. As one who doggedly resists injustice, faces it, names it, and denounces it until right is achieved, she is acting as God does. Moreover, she is an icon of Christ, as she exhibits the kind of power he claims in his passion and resurrection. As this upright widow seems powerless before a corrupt and potent judge, so Jesus appears helpless in the face of Pilate and his executioners. Just as Jesus defeats the very powers of sin and death by his persistent pursuit of justice and his faithfulness to God, so this upright and aggrieved widow draws on godly power in apparent weakness to overcome death-dealing powers by her relentless demand for justice. But Luke recasts the story in a way that diminishes this impact. By insisting in v. 6 that the hearer pay attention to the judge instead of the widow, he reinforces the tendency of Christians to gravitate to images of powerful males as the

---

28 Most scholars agree that vv. 2–5 are the core of Jesus' original parable, with secondary interpretations attached by Luke in vv. 1, 6–8.

god-like figures. He succeeds in keeping a female image of God and Christ at bay.[29] By framing the parable as one that concerns prayer he would have us see this widow like the harmless Anna, whose ceaseless prayers disturb no one. These redactional moves create a further theological difficulty: now the parable says that if one badgers God persistently enough in prayer, one can eventually wear God down and get a positive response. Such a notion of God is flatly contradicted by texts such as Lk. 11.9–13 and Sir. 35.14–19, which insist that God is eager and willing to give all good things to those who ask, particularly to those who are poorest.

Finally, Luke, like other good story-tellers, often presents two single contrasting characters, representing opposite positions, so as to make a point.[30] In this parable, he would have us see the widow as poor, pitiable, and powerless. The judge is almighty, shameless, and immovable. She is a victim of injustice; he is corrupt and cares not a whit. He would seem to have all the power; she none at all. In reality, however, both widows and judges have networks of relationships that undergird their power. His may be more openly known, but she also knows how to navigate these and how to turn them to her advantage. But such an image does not fit Luke's ideal. To countless women who are oppressed by multiple systems of injustice, Luke's redacted parable advises ceaseless prayer as their only recourse. An image of widowed women who brashly transgress acceptable bounds, and who are outside the control of a husband, creating havoc by tenaciously voicing their demands, is not to be countenanced by Luke. But try as he may, the deliciously humorous image of the judge cowering before the widow who won't get out of his face cannot be erased by Luke from the parable.

Widows at the Resurrection (Luke 20.27–40)

In this passage, which also has parallels in Mark (12.18–27) and Matthew (22.23–33), some Sadducees pose a question to Jesus concerning resurrection. In all three Synoptic accounts the episode is set among the controversies between Jesus and the Jerusalem authorities after he has entered the holy city. The other questions posed to Jesus concern the source of his authority (Lk. 20.1–8), whether taxes are to be paid to Caesar (Lk. 20.20–26), and a question about David's son (Lk. 20.41–44). They are not sincere inquiries, but are meant to trap Jesus (20.20). The hostility of the religious authorities toward Jesus is mounting. The scribes and the chief priests have tried to lay hands on him, but they delay for fear of the people (20.19). That the questioners are not sincere in Lk. 20.27–40 is also clear from the introductory verse: the Sadducees do not believe in the resurrection. They create a preposterous scenario to make Jesus look foolish.

---

29 Countless commentators on this parable (e.g. Fitzmyer, *Luke*, II, p. 1177) try to smooth out the difficulty created by vv. 2 and 4, where the judge's words clearly show he is not like God (he has respect for neither God nor people), by proposing that the parable is a negative example, one that makes its point by argument *a minori ad maius* (from the lesser to the greater): if an unjust judge would give in to the relentless pleas of a widow, how much more will God, who is upright?

30 E.g. Zechariah's disbelief and Mary's ready fiat (1.18–20, 38), the active Martha vs. the passive Mary (10.38–42), an obedient older son and a profligate younger son (15.11–32), a rich man and the destitute Lazarus (16.19–30), a Pharisee and a tax collector (18.8–19).

The case they pose to Jesus involves a woman whose husband dies childless, and then, in compliance with Deut. 25.5 (see also Gen. 38.8), she marries each of his six brothers, all of whom die without producing an heir with her to her husband's name. The Sadducees want to know whose wife she will be at the resurrection. Jesus' reply dodges the trap. He affirms that, indeed, the dead are raised, that all are alive to God (vv. 37–38), but the Sadducees' query is based on a false understanding of the nature of that life. As Jesus quotes Scripture in his rebuttal he unmasks the inconsistency of the Sadducees—they quote the law of Moses about levirite marriage, but they don't listen to him about resurrection and immortality.[31]

The function of this pronouncement story is to show Jesus as authoritative interpreter and teacher of the Law and to point ahead to Jesus' vindication on this question through his own resurrection. The widow at the center of the controversy has no voice and is an object of discussion. She has no power in the decisions made about her life. The Sadducees pose the problem in terms of the man and his brothers; no consciousness of the woman is evident. Even the begetting of children seems to leave the woman aside, as it is said to be done by a man for his brother: 'If a man's brother dies, leaving a wife but no children, the man shall marry the widow and raise up children for his brother' (v. 28). This story presumes a patriarchal world in which the men controlling this widow's life give no thought to what she wants or thinks. They even envision that this situation perdures into the afterlife. Would women who hear Jesus' response hear an assurance of freedom from the strictures of patriarchal marriages? Would widows who were ministering in the Lukan communities and who were encountering resistance from men find an affirmation in this story that the new era of post-resurrection life in the Christian community already embodies different arrangements from patriarchal marriages? If so, perhaps they would concur with the scribes, whose reaction to the exchange is, 'Teacher, you have spoken well' (v. 39). That the scribes, however, are no less sincere than the Sadducees is revealed in the next episode.

Devouring the Houses of Widows (Luke 20.45–47)[32]

Among the things for which Jesus denounces the scribes are their love of long robes, salutations in the marketplaces, the best seats in the synagogues, places of honor at feasts, pretentiously long prayers, and, finally, that they 'devour (κατεσθίουσιν) the houses of widows' (v. 47). Fitzmyer lists six possible ways in which scribes 'devoured' widows' houses. They may have: (1) accepted payment for legal aid to widows, even though such was forbidden; (2) cheated widows of what was rightfully theirs; (3) sponged on the hospitality of these women of limited means; (4) mismanaged the widows' property; (5) taken large sums of money from credulous widows in return for promised prolonged prayer on their behalf; (6) taken their houses as pledges for debts which could not be paid.[33] Here again, Luke paints widows as vulnerable victims. But when coupled with the next episode, it takes on an interesting function.

---

31 Fitzmyer, *Luke*, p. 1299.
32 This episode also appears in Mt. 23.1–7 and Mk 12.38–40.
33 Fitzmyer, *Luke*, p. 1318.

A Widow Who Gives her Life (Luke 21.1–4)[34]

This widow has traditionally been held up as the epitome of generosity, giving from her want, and not from surplus. Contemporary Christian development campaigns often appeal to her as the model donor. In Luke's community her story would have presented a real challenge to the richer members: the large contributions of the wealthy have not the weight of the paltry two coins[35] of the poor.

The final verse has a double meaning. The Greek word βίος means both 'life itself' and 'means of subsistence'. There are two nuances, 'she put in all the means she had to live on' and 'she put in all the life she had'. This latter connotation is highlighted by the literary context. This episode comes shortly before the passion narrative. The widow who gives her whole life prefigures Jesus' own handing over of his very life on behalf of others.[36] She and the widow Anna (2.37) frame the gospel story with their pouring out of their very lives in the Temple. One function of this story is to invite the hearer to do the same.

There is, however, another possible interpretation of this episode. There is a question as to whether or not the widow's sacrifice is meant to be lauded and emulated. When read in tandem with Lk. 20.45–47, which immediately precedes the widow's offering, another meaning altogether emerges. The widow's sacrifice in 21.1–4 may be an illustration of how the scribes 'devour the houses of widows'. As such, Jesus is not praising the woman's generosity, but rather laments the religious system that takes advantage of her by prompting her to give her last cent.[37]

Her misdirected support of a system that oppresses her is not unlike that of the woman with the hemorrhages who 'spent all she had ὅλον τὸν βίον) on physicians' (Lk. 8.43) to no avail. Moreover, the verses immediately following the poor widow's action show that her gift to the Temple is a waste. Jesus asserts that 'not one stone will be left upon another; all will be thrown down' (21.6).

In the text of 21.1–4 there is nothing that reveals which way the story is to be taken. In vv. 3–4 Jesus simply remarks on the amount that the widow puts into the treasury. We do not know whether it is with a tone of praise or lament. Moreover, there is no exhortation to imitate her. Perhaps, like a parable, it is multivalent. If a disciple hears it from the perspective of one who has power, privilege, or status, then the story issues a warning.[38] Jesus advises such followers to guard against acting like the voracious scribes, who feed off the poorest, particularly under the guise of religion.[39]

---

34 The discussion of this passage is taken in large part from Reid, *Choosing the Better Part?*, pp. 195–97.
35 The two coins, λεπτὰ δύο, were small copper coins, the smallest in use in Palestine at the time. They were worth about one-eighth of a cent each. In Lk. 12.59 λεπτόν is usually translated 'penny'.
36 Elizabeth Struthers Malbon, 'The Poor Widow in Mark and her Poor Rich Readers', *CBQ* 53 (1991), pp. 589–604.
37 Addison G. Wright, 'The Widow's Mites: Praise or Lament? A Matter of Context', *CBQ* 44 (1982), pp. 256–65.
38 Eugene LaVerdiere, 'The Widow's Mite', *Emmanuel* 92 (1986), pp. 316–21, 341.
39 Note that the scribes are portrayed negatively throughout the whole Gospel. They team with the Pharisees, chief priests, and the elders in challenging Jesus (5.21, 30; 6.7; 11.53; 15.2; 20.1) and in looking for a way to kill him (9.22; 19.47; 20.19; 22.2, 66; 23.10). The only favorable remark about scribes occurs in 20.39 where they admit that Jesus has answered well the Sadducees' question about resurrection. But their lack of sincerity is revealed in Jesus' challenge to them about David's son (20.41–44) and in his denunciation of them (20.45–47).

Rather than emulate the scribes' poor example of leadership, Jesus' disciples are to follow his way: that of the leader as the servant (22.26–27). From the perspective of people who are victims of systems that devour them, this passage could help them reject giving support to those very systems that treat them unjustly. The struggles of widows against such oppression exemplify the struggles of women through every age against being swallowed up by multiple systems of oppression. The paradox is a poignant one: a widow who, as an icon of Christ, so readily offers up her whole life to God, is in danger of being 'eaten up' by the very institution that feeds her faith. In many ways Lk. 21.1–4 prepares the reader for the struggle in Acts 6 over widows' feeding and getting fed.

Widows of the Hellenists and of the Hebrews (Acts 6.1–7)[40]

We now return to questions we raised earlier about the conflict involving the widows of the Hellenists and those of the Hebrews in Acts 6.1–7. We have seen how all the episodes concerning widows in the Third Gospel have an ambiguous message. On the one hand widows are depicted as needy and oppressed: one in Zarephath is starving (Lk. 4.25–26), another in Nain is grieving the death of her only son (7.11–17), one is done an injustice by an enemy (18.1–8), another is married off seven times and is still without children or husband (20.27–40), some have had their houses devoured by scribes (20.45–57), and one widow who is poor is co-opted into giving her entire life to the Temple (21.1–4). One thread of Luke's message is that needy widows are objects of compassion to be cared for by the community. But there is another strand that underlies a number of these episodes. Widows also exercise important ministerial functions: Anna is a venerable prophet, constant and true in her witness (2.36–38). The grieving mother can be a force for protest against death (7.11–17). The widow who confronts the judge exercises a ministry of advocacy for justice (18.1–8). The widow who gives her life foreshadows Jesus' own total self-donation on behalf of others (21.1–4). But, as we have seen, with the way he redacts the tradition, Luke suppresses hints of the unconventional nature of widows' exercise of these ministries. He attempts to keep the spotlight on the compassionate treatment of widows, rather than their exemplary responses as disciples in ministry.

In Acts 6.1–7 the issue is clearly a struggle involving ministry. But it may not be the simple problem of division of responsibilities as is usually thought. The complaint of the Hellenists to the Hebrews is that their widows are being overlooked in the 'daily distribution' (ἐν τῇ διακονίᾳ τῇ καθημερινῇ). But the nature of their protest is not clear. The noun διακονία, along with the verb διακονεῖν, has a wide variety of ministerial connotations.[41] In Acts 1.17, 25 it refers to apostolic ministry; in Lk. 8.3; Acts 11.29; 12.25 it connotes financial administration; in Acts 20.24 it refers to Paul's testifying to the good news; at Acts 21.19 it sums up the whole of Paul's ministry. In Luke's Last Supper scene Jesus instructs his disciples to be as

---

40 See Clarice J. Martin, 'The Acts of the Apostles', in Schüssler Fiorenza (ed.), *Searching the Scriptures*, II, pp. 763–99 (esp. pp. 780–82); Gail R. O'Day, 'Acts', in Newsom and Ringe (eds.), *The Women's Bible Commentary* (exp. edn, 1998), pp. 394–402 (esp. pp. 397–99).

41 See further, BDAG, p. 229; H.W. Beyer, 'διακονέω', *TDNT*, II, pp. 81–94; John N. Collins, *DIAKONIA: Re-interpreting the Ancient Sources* (New York: Oxford University Press, 1990).

ὁ διακονῶν, 'one who serves', particularly those who would lead, since that is his own stance (22.26–27).

What remains unclear in Acts 6 is whether the problem is that the widows of the Hellenists are not receiving their due in the 'daily distribution' or whether they are being overlooked in the assignment of ministries, that is, not being given their proper turn to serve. It is notable that nothing in the text indicates that these widows were poor, and thus in need of goods distributed by the community.[42]

Moreover, when Luke is speaking of distribution of possessions to those in need in the community in Acts 2.45 and 4.32–37, he does not use the verb διακονεῖν. It fits Luke's pattern that the widows' exercise of ministry is submerged as Luke shifts the focus of the episode to the male apostles.[43] It is notable that in the Gospel there are three episodes in which διακονεῖν and διακονία are used of women (4.39; 8.3; 10.40), but none in Acts. These terms are used only of male disciples in Luke's second volume, as he focuses on their leadership. As Peter, followed by Paul, occupies center stage, they overshadow the reality of the ministering women.

The solution that the twelve offer to the problem involving the widows in Acts 6.1–7 is to divide the exercise of the ministry of the Word (διακονία τοῦ λόγου, v. 4) and the ministry of the table (διακονεῖν τραπέζαις, v. 2). The twelve dedicate themselves to the former, saying, 'it is not right for us to neglect the word of God to serve at table' (v. 2) and so they appoint seven 'reputable men full of the Spirit and wisdom' (v. 3) to the latter task.[44]

In light of the way that Luke links the breaking of bread and the breaking open of the Scriptures (e.g. Lk. 24.30–32), it is startling that he should dichotomize the two in Acts 6. Moreover, this separation of ministerial functions does not hold in subsequent episodes, as Stephen, one of the Seven, is portrayed as working wonders and signs (6.8), debating in the synagogue with wisdom and spirit (6.8–9), and preaching before the Sanhedrin (7.1–53). Philip likewise devotes himself to preaching the word in 8.4–5, becoming known as 'the evangelist' (21.8). Later in Acts Luke portrays the apostle Paul engaged both in preaching (20.7) and in breaking bread (20.11).

---

42 Elisabeth Schüssler Fiorenza was the first to make these observations in *In Memory of Her: A Feminist Theological Reconstruction of Christian Origins* (New York: Crossroad, 1983), pp. 164–66.

43 For further elaboration of Luke's depiction of women's participation in discipleship and mission, see Reid, *Choosing the Better Part?*, pp. 21–54. Women in Luke and Acts are depicted mostly in silent, passive roles. Women disciples receive (δέχομαι) the word, believe (πιστύειν), follow (ἀκολουθέω), minister (διακονεῖν), witness Jesus' crucifixion and burial (Lk. 23.49, 55), are the first to discover the empty tomb, and are commissioned to proclaim the resurrection (Lk. 24.1–11). They are recipients of the promised Spirit (Acts 1.13–14; 2.1–13), but there are no call stories of women disciples. They are not depicted as proclaiming (κηρύσσω, ἀναγγέλλω, ἀπαγγέλλω, διαγέλλω, καταγέλλω), witnessing (μαρτύρομαι), healing, exorcising, resuscitating, forgiving, feeding, enduring persecution, nor imparting the Spirit to others, as are the male disciples.

44 As Turid Karlsen Seim notes, the explicit direction that ἀνδρῶν, 'men', be chosen (6.3; so also Acts 1.21 when Matthias is chosen to take the place of Judas) reveals that it is not automatically taken for granted that men would exercise the leadership: 'The presentation of women in the gospel story has actually launched them as natural candidates—not least for the task of which Acts 6.1–3 speaks' (*Double Message*, pp. 111–12).

What is more likely at issue in Acts 6.1–7 is a conflict over the exercise of ministry by widows.⁴⁵ The kind of ministry denoted by ἐν τῇ διακονίᾳ τῇ καθημερινῇ (v. 1) is not entirely clear. Elisabeth Schüssler Fiorenza⁴⁶ posits that the conflict between the Hellenists and the Hebrews involved the role and participation of women at the eucharistic meal. 'Serving at table' (v. 2) denotes service at a meal, as also in Lk. 12.37; 17.8. And in 1 Cor. 10.21 the 'table of the Lord' is the eucharistic table. Moreover, table sharing, according to Acts 2.46, took place 'day by day' (καθ' ἡμέραν). Eucharistic table ministry included preparation of a meal, purchase and distribution of food, actual serving during the meal, and probably cleaning up afterwards. The Hellenist women, more accustomed to participating in symposia and festive dinners, probably took for granted their participation in eucharistic meals in the Christian house churches,⁴⁷ whereas such a practice would have been more problematic for the Hebrews. The ensuing difficulties would have been not unlike the problems that emerged in Antioch concerning table sharing between Gentile and Jewish Christians.

Another possibility is that διακονεῖν τραπέζαις (6.2) may refer to financial administration, not food distribution, since τράπεζα is the word used for the table on which money changers do their transactions (thus the term is still used in Greece for 'bank'). In this case, the widows in Acts 6 may have been exercising a ministry akin to that of Mary Magdalene, Susanna, and Joanna (Lk. 8.3), who ministered to Jesus and his followers out of their own financial resources (διηκόνουν αὐτοῖς ἐκ τῶν ὑπαρχόντων αὐταῖς).⁴⁸

---

45 Another Lukan episode that concerns conflicts over the exercise of διακονία by women is that of Mary and Martha (Lk. 10.38–42). See Elisabeth Schüssler Fiorenza, 'A Feminist Critical Interpretation for Liberation: Martha and Mary: Luke 10.38–42', *Religion and Intellectual Life* 3 (1986), pp. 16–36; Reid, *Choosing the Better Part?*, pp. 144–62; W. Carter, 'Getting Martha out of the Kitchen: Luke 10.38–42', *CBQ* 58 (1996), pp. 264–80.

46 Schüssler Fiorenza, *In Memory of Her*, pp. 165–66. See also Ivoni Richter Reimer, *Women in the Acts of the Apostles: A Feminist Liberation Perspective* (trans. L.M. Maloney; Minneapolis: Fortress Press, 1995), pp. 234–37.

47 On women's roles within households and house churches, see Carolyn Osiek and David L. Balch, *Families in the New Testament World: Households and Churches* (The Family, Religion and Culture Series; Louisville, KY: Westminster/John Knox Press, 1997). On the roles of women at meals see Kathleen E. Corley, *Private Women, Public Meals: Social Conflict in the Synoptic Tradition* (Peabody, MA: Hendrickson, 1993).

48 The word ὑπαρχόντων, 'resources', always means possessions, property, money, or goods in Luke and Acts (Lk. 11.21; 12.15, 33, 44; 14.33; 16.1; 19.8; Acts 4.32). The feminine plural possessive pronoun, αὐταῖς, indicates that the money belonged to the women, and was not money from the common purse that they administered (cf. Jn 12.6). While in patriarchal societies women are economically dependent on men, and are very restricted in their possession of and control over money, there were at least some women in Jesus' day who had money and had control of it. Under some circumstances women could inherit money and property (Num. 27.8). Many women earned money by working, as did Lydia (Acts 16.14), who appears to have been either single or widowed and running her own business. Prisca shared her husband's work of tent-making (Acts 18.3). Other occupations in which Greco-Roman women were employed include: weavers, midwives, doctors, hairdressers, wet nurses, masseuses, attendants, and musicians. The parable of the woman who loses one of her ten coins in Lk. 15.8–10 presumes that she has charge of the family finances. A similar situation is reflected in Pliny the Younger's approving comment that his wife is sensible and careful with their money (*Letters* 4, 19.2–4). Inscriptions from Jewish women who were donors to synagogues show that at least some women had money or property and the power to donate it. On

The reality was that not all widows were economically destitute; some had means and the power to use them.⁴⁹ Luke, however, deflects attention from the ministry of the widows by shifting the focus to that of male leadership from within the Hellenists in the community. The episode becomes one that narrates an orderly transition in leadership. As the geographic and ethnic boundaries of the community are expanding, Luke depicts how the leadership shifts from Peter and the twelve in Jerusalem to Hellenists who will take the lead in spreading the good news beyond the borders of Palestine to the Greek-speaking world.⁵⁰

Whatever the exact nature of the controversy in Acts 6.1–7, the resolution of it reflects a completely androcentric approach. The problem involves widows, but at no point are they involved in the resolution of the difficulty. The two groups of widows are not asked to give their sides of the story. The differing perspectives are not weighed or discussed. There is no consultation, no invocation of the Spirit in the process,⁵¹ no consensus, nor acclamation of the decision. Rather, the twelve see the problem as involving their own ministerial leadership (v. 2). They empower the Hellenist men to choose their own leaders from among their own ranks, but the widows, the subjects of the controversy, remain invisible. One wonders if the proposal of Peter and the twelve did, indeed, please the whole community (v. 5), or if the widows would have had another opinion.⁵²

---

this last point see further Bernadette Brooten, *Women Leaders in the Ancient Synagogue: Inscriptional Evidence and Background Issues* (BJS, 36; Chico, CA: Scholars Press, 1982). See also Matthew S. Collins, 'Money, Sex, and Power: An Examination of the Role of Women as Patrons of the Ancient Synagogue', in Peter J. Haas (ed.), *Recovering the Role of Women: Power and Authority in Rabbinic Jewish Society* (South Florida Studies in the History of Judaism, 59; Atlanta: Scholars Press, 1992), pp. 5–22. See Richard Atwood, *Mary Magdalene in the New Testament Gospels and Early Tradition* (European University Studies. Series 23.457; Bern: Peter Lang, 1993), p. 17 n. 23 for examples of women who gave monetary aid and property to rabbis. Ben Witherington III, 'On the Road with Mary Magdalen, Joanna, Susanna, and Other Disciples—Luke 8.1–3', *ZNW* 70 (1979), pp. 243–48 (244 n. 9) lists rabbinic texts that refer to women offering support to rabbis and their disciples in the form of money, property, or foodstuffs. See Moshe Meiselman, *Jewish Woman in Jewish Law* (New York: Ktav, 1978), pp. 84–95, for information on inheritance by women in rabbinic tradition. He also demonstrates Jewish women's financial independence by entering into contracts to acquire and dispose of property (pp. 81–83).

49 See Shelly Matthews, *First Converts: Rich Pagan Women and the Rhetoric of Mission in Early Judaism and Christianity* (Contraversions: Jews and Other Differences; Stanford: Stanford University Press, 2001), who analyzes the stories of rich women's associations with religion, comparing the evidence from pagan cults and Hellenistic Judaism with that of early Christianity. In the current debate about whether Hellenistic Jews engaged in proselytism, she takes the position that they did engage in religious apologetics and propaganda and that early Christian missionary activity was an extension of this. Matthews shows the importance of women of high standing who were attracted to Judaism and Christianity and how they actively propagated these religions, and in this volume, Beverly Gaventa 'What Ever Happened to Those Prophesying Daughters?' pp. 49–60.

50 See Joseph B. Tyson, 'The Emerging Church and the Problem of Authority in Acts', *Int* 42 (1988), pp. 132–45.

51 The twelve instruct the Hellenists to pick out seven men full of the Spirit (v. 3), and the apostles pray and lay hands on them after they have been chosen, a gesture of commissioning (v. 6), but there is no mention of prayer or invocation of the Spirit in the decision-making process itself.

52 F. Scott Spencer ('Neglected Widows in Acts 6.1–7', *CBQ* 56 [1994], pp. 715–33) argues that the twelve are ambivalent figures in the Lukan narrative, and their appraisal of the widows' situation in Acts 6.1–7 shows the twelve not to be an entirely reliable voice. Their approach to needy widows

It is notable that the way this decision is reached contrasts considerably with the way Luke portrays the resolution of the question of Gentile circumcision and dietary observance in Acts 15. In that instance, Paul and Barnabas are sent to Jerusalem by the church at Antioch to represent their views (v. 3). The leaders in Jerusalem listen to testimony from both sides (vv. 4–7, 12) and there is much debate (v. 7). They turn to the Scriptures for guidance (vv. 15–18), and the decision is made in concert with the Holy Spirit (v. 28). Not only the apostles and presbyters, but the whole church (v. 22) is involved in determining how to implement the decision. The result is that the whole assembly in Antioch was delighted with the decision (v. 31). While it is anachronistic to think that in this meeting of the leaders of the early Christian community in Jerusalem they used what today would be called an inclusive, consensus decision-making process, it is interesting to note the differences between the processes described in the two different episodes in Acts.

Weeping Widows at the Death of Tabitha (Acts 9.36–43)[53]

The final Lukan episode in which widows appear is at the deathbed of Tabitha. Notably, Tabitha is identified as a 'disciple' (μαθήτρια). This is the only occurrence of the feminine form of the word in the New Testament. Her ministry in the community at Joppa is described as 'good works and acts of charity' (ἔργων ἀγαθῶν καὶ ἐλεημοσυνῶν). Some of this work included making tunics and other garments (v. 39), presumably for the poor. While many commentators envision the widows weeping at her bedside as the objects of her charity, it may rather have been the case that Tabitha was herself a widow, and a leader of widows, having opened her house to them, and coordinating their ministries. Such a situation is referred to in 1 Tim. 5.16, which reads literally, 'If a believing woman has widows, let her assist them; let the church not be burdened, so that it can assist those who are real widows.' While the presenting issue in 1 Tim. 5 is the financial support of widows, this text also reveals that there were women who maintained households for other Christian widows, providing communal homes and a support network for them apart from patriarchal households.[54]

Verses 3–16 reveal the anxiety of the male leaders in the early church for control over these women, as highly restrictive qualifications for age, type of ministerial

---

is partly in line with the way that Jesus approaches widows with prayer and compassionate service, but it is also partly affiliated with the scribes, who deceitfully mix the practice of prayer with the neglect of widows. He sees a proclivity on the part of the twelve to promote the ministry of teaching and preaching at the expense of the service of food at table, in contrast to Jesus' pattern of blending the two vocations (Lk. 9.1–6, 10–17; 12.37–42; 17.7–10; 22.14–27). He sees a certain conversion on the part of Peter in the episode with Tabitha, where he combines prayer and service in an exemplary support system for needy widows. While I do not agree with Spencer that all Luke's widows were needy, I think he has important insights into the passage.

53 For a much fuller treatment of this passage see Reimer, *Women in the Acts of the Apostles*, pp. 31–69.

54 Joanna Dewey, '1 Timothy', in Newsom and Ringe (eds.), *The Women's Bible Commentary* (exp. edn, 1998), pp. 444–49, esp. 448. See also Dennis MacDonald, 'Virgins, Widows, and Paul in Second Century Asia Minor', in Paul J. Achtemeier (ed.), *SBLSP* (Missoula, MT: Scholars Press, 1979), pp. 169–84. On the sociological advantages derived by widows by membership in their circle see Jouette M. Bassler, 'The Widows' Tale: A Fresh Look at 1 Tim. 5.3–16', *JBL* 103.1 (1984), pp. 23–41.

activities, and payment⁵⁵ are laid out (vv. 3-16). Luke may be similarly concerned about the control of widows in his communities, as he characterizes Tabitha's ministry not as διακονία, which he uses only for male disciples in Acts, but as charity, which poses no threat to good order.⁵⁶ Tabitha's power and that of the women who minister with her is overshadowed by Luke's focus on Peter. It is his authority and power to resuscitate the dead that is central. Just as Jesus brought the dead son of a widow back to life, causing people to glorify God and spread the word about him (Lk. 7.11–17), so Peter's resuscitation of Tabitha functions the same way: 'This became known throughout Joppa, and many believed in the Lord' (v. 42). Moreover, Luke contains women's ministries as ministry only to other women (as in Tit. 2.3–5), while male disciples minister to the whole community.

Conclusion

The ministry of widows was most vibrant from the third to the fifth centuries. From early church writings we have evidence that women enrolled as widows were treated as part of the church hierarchy. Their duties included prayer and petition, theological instruction, testing of deaconesses, anointing of women at baptism, caring for the sick, and receiving offerings.⁵⁷

Already in Luke's day the number of ministering widows was growing. There is a pattern in his writings of an attempt to mask the growing power of widows, and of downplaying the ministry of women in general and the controversies around that.⁵⁸

For Luke power and decision-making are in the hands of the male disciples. It is important for the aware reader in contemporary times to recognize the slant with

---

55 The verb τιμάω means not only 'honor, or esteem', but also connotes payment, i.e. 'to set a price on' their services (BDAG, p. 1004).

56 For a study of widows in the apocryphal Acts and their rejection of patriarchal constraints see Stevan L. Davies, *The Revolt of the Widows: The Social World of the Apocryphal Acts* (Carbondale: Southern Illinois University Press, 1980). For an attempt to read the widow traditions in Luke and Acts as stemming from the same milieu see Robert M. Price, *The Widow Traditions in Luke–Acts: A Feminist-Critical Scrutiny* (SBLDS, 155; Atlanta: Scholars Press, 1997).

57 For these texts see Ross S. Kraemer (ed.), *Maenads, Martyrs, Matrons, Monastics: A Sourcebook on Women's Religions in the Greco-Roman World* (Philadelphia: Fortress Press, 1988), pp. 232–40. For details on the inscriptional evidence see Ute Eisen, *Women Officeholders in Early Christianity: Epigraphical and Literary Studies* (Collegeville, MN: Liturgical Press, 2000), pp. 143–57. For a fuller treatment on the development of the ministry of widows from New Testament times through the apostolic period see Thurston, *The Widows*.

58 See Carolyn Osiek, 'The Widow as Altar: The Rise and Fall of a Symbol', *Second Century* 3 (1983), pp. 159–69, who shows how the texts that refer to widows as 'altar' reflect a change in their social status and a change in the religious symbolism associated with them. Widows were likened to the 'altar' on which the community placed their offerings of charity. In the early centuries they occupied a special place in the piety and religious symbolism of the church, even to the point of being seated with the clergy at eucharistic celebrations. As esteem for virginity and its ecclesiastical status rose, so did increasingly repressive polemic aimed at subordinating widows to both virgins and male clergy. Osiek observes that no other group comes under such sharp criticism as do widows in texts such as *Didascalia* 3.5–11. The length and vehemence of the texts about the conduct of widows is exceptional, indicating a reaction to some real or imagined threatening situation. The symbolism of widow as 'altar' shifts, as widows are told that just as the altar does not wander about but stays in one place, so should they remain at home (*Didascalia* 3.6.3).

which Luke tells the story, to retrieve traditions that give a fuller picture, and to resist the androcentrism of Luke's narrative by reading against the grain. A word of hope for women can be taken from the speech of Gamaliel in Acts 5.38-39. He assures the council that if a work is of human origin it will fail, but if it is of God, 'you will not be able to overthrow them—in that case you may even be found fighting against God!' The power given to women by the Spirit for ministry, exemplified by Luke's widows, cannot ultimately be squelched.

'KNOCK, KNOCK—WHO'S THERE?' ACTS 12.6–17 AS A COMEDY OF ERRORS

KATHY CHAMBERS

While the Gospel of John tells us 'Jesus wept' (11.35), nowhere in the New Testament does he laugh.[1] However, Luke realized what his Israelite forebears[2] as well as his modern clerical counterparts have always known: it is from the repository of popular culture, and especially from the comedic, that serious lessons are profitably inculcated and ecclesial history is profitably taught. Luke and his original audiences knew Greek and Roman comedic traditions—almost every city mentioned in the New Testament had a theatre,[3] and even the smallest village would have had its raconteur—and Luke drew upon their traditions both formal and folk to shape the *kerygma* in an engaging manner appropriate for house churches and missionary activity.

Epitomizing this evangelistic art is Acts 12.6–17, the conjoined stories of the apostle Peter and the slave Rhoda (otherwise appropriately titled 'a tale of two prisons'). These scenes reveal more than Luke's invocation of comedic elements; they demonstrate how Christian adaptations of comedic tropes challenged the dominant cultural construction of status and gender, of ecclesial authority, slaves, and women.

Unfortunately, both modern readers in general and, I fear, New Testament scholars in particular, like Rhoda, slavishly keep tightly shut the door to the comedic. Scholars interested in disciplinary diversity turn toward literature rather than the stage; programs on Acts are today incomplete without some citation from Homer, Dionysius of Halicarnassus, or Josephus, but Aristophanes, Terence, and Menander never get the spotlight. Further, the idea of serious work is often in both academy and church confused with seriousness, and the presumed sobriety of Holy Writ coupled with the New Testament's focus on the cross discourages the search for humor. Third, such reluctance to recognize Luke's use of humor is exacerbated by the fact that this humor often comes at the expense of the church leaders: doctors of the church and doctors in the classroom are reluctant if not unable to see themselves as satirical targets. Finally, humor is often carried by minor characters whereas studies of Acts tend to focus on the major male figures—Peter, Paul, and James; Stephen and

---

1 The only teaching concerning laughter attributed to Jesus is, 'Blessed are the ones who weep now, for you will laugh' (Mt. 6.21b); the decrease in eschatological urgency presented by the Acts of the Apostles might even suggest that laughter was a part of the house churches' quotidian demeanor.

2 See, for example, Gen. 29.9–30 and the convention of mistaken identities in the account of Jacob and Rachel/Leah; Balaam and his talking donkey (Num. 22.22–35); Saul ignominiously hiding among the baggage (1 Sam. 10.17–27); and Abigail's dramatic response when she first sees Nabal (1 Sam. 25).

3 John McRay, *Archaeology and the New Testament* (Grand Rapids: Baker Book House, 1991), p. 57.

Philip; Cornelius and the Roman officials—who either have a consistent story line, or have extra-canonical attestation, or change the focus of the mission. But minor characters, that is, characters such as slaves and women, have only recently gained the attention of the scholarly community.[4] And even in these cases, humor typically yields to more serious questions such as women's leadership roles, the level of Luke's misogyny, and the sexual servitude of slaves rather than to an analysis of how humor serves as the vehicle by which such issues are addressed.

Comedy is the ideal genre for instructing the elite, and theorists of humor have convincingly articulated comedy's subversive and even liberationist traits.[5] Whereas in antiquity (and in most cases today as well) comedy served ultimately to reinforce the status quo—the 'happy ending' puts everything back in place—it also gives an alternative vision. David Konstan writes: 'In making fun of conventions and characters, [Greek comedic playwrights] revealed what is arbitrary in them ... comic playwrights test what is possible in their comedies.'[6] What is possible includes an increasing respect for women and slaves, even if they are stereotyped and finally constrained, for as outsiders to the male citizenry they can serve to critique the pretensions of their 'betters'.[7]

Thus, it is insufficient merely to note that a line or a scene has comic potential; interpretation requires the serious business of determining what attitudes and roles are questioned as well as who benefits from the resolution. It is this second step that scholarship on Acts 12 often fails to take. The literature offers sobering examples of how the effects of the comedic are trivialized. James Dunn, for example, states: 'whoever first told this story evidently had a sense of humour: Peter who has just walked through gates manned by soldiers is left standing at the door by a maid servant and has to keep knocking to gain attention'.[8] While correctly noting the humor in the second part of the pericope—humor gained at the expense of Rhoda and the female-identified church in the home of John Mark's mother—he misses the humor in Peter's somnabulatory engagement with the angel.[9] Further, although he correctly observes Peter's frustration, he incorrectly names the problem: Peter has gotten Rhoda's attention; it is the slave's continual insistence upon Peter's presence at the gate that goes unanswered by the free Christians busy at prayer.

Haenchen relegates the pericope's comedic aspects to indicators of miraculous occurrences.[10] Matching Acts 12.14 where Rhoda 'los[es] her wits for the very joy'[11]

---

4 E.g., Jennifer A. Glancy, *Slavery in Early Christianity* (Oxford: Oxford University Press, 2002); see also F. Scott Spencer, 'Out of Mind, Out of Voice: Slave-Girls and Prophetic Daughters in Luke–Acts', *BibInt* 7 (1999), pp. 132–53; and Ivoni Richter Reimer, *Women in the Acts of the Apostles: A Feminist Liberation Perspective* (trans. L.M. Maloney; Minneapolis: Fortress Press, 1995).

5 For more information on the subversive function of Greco-Roman comedy, see Erich Segal, *Roman Laughter: The Comedy of Plautus* (New York: Oxford University Press, 1987). For a discussion of the subversive function of comedy in the Bible, see J. William Whedbee, *The Bible and the Comic Vision* (Cambridge: Cambridge University Press, 1998).

6 David Konstan, *Greek Comedy and Ideology* (New York: Oxford University Press, 1995), p. 6.

7 An example of a slave that appears more 'clued in' than his superiors is Geta in Terence's *Phormio*, whose approach makes Antipho nervous because of the news Geta might bring to him.

8 James D.G. Dunn, *The Acts of the Apostles* (Valley Forge, PA: Trinity Press International, 1996), p. 164.

9 Dunn, *Acts of the Apostles*, p. 161.

10 Ernst Haenchen, *The Acts of the Apostles: A Commentary* (trans. B. Noble and G. Shinn; rev. R.M. Wilson; Philadelphia: Westminster Press, 1971), p. 385.

11 Haenchen, *Acts of the Apostles*, p. 385.

(ἀπὸ τῆς χαπᾶς) with Lk. 24.41, in which Jesus appears to the disciples, and 'from their joy' (ἀπὸ τῆς χαρᾶς) they react in disbelief and wonderment, he finds examples of 'Lucan psychology'.[12] Yet the correct analogy between Rhoda's joyful reaction to Peter's miraculous appearance and the disciples' joyful reaction to Jesus' miraculous appearance makes all the more stark Haenchen's incorrect and perhaps patronizing view of the female slave, for he does not conclude that the disciples 'have lost their wits'. Indeed, whereas Lk. 24.41 goes on to state that the disciples' reaction was accompanied by *disbelief* and wonder, Rhoda never ceased to believe Peter's presence. The only person who appears to have kept her wits is the female slave: Peter had earlier lost his in the prison escape, as we see in his completely befuddled relationship to the angel, and those assembled in the home of 'Mary the mother of John Mark' (Acts 12.12) hardly exemplify consistency of faith.

Richard Pervo, who recognizes the connections of Acts to popular literature, notes that Rhoda is 'like a figure from New Comedy'.[13] Unfortunately, he gives us no further direction concerning the import of that statement. Placing Acts 12.6–17 under the subheading of 'Burlesque and Rowdy Episodes' (defined as 'scornful laughter ... at the misfortunes of others' as evidenced in the plays of Aristophanes, Menander, and Shakespeare),[14] he remarks only that Rhoda is 'a flighty slave girl' who 'answers [Peter's] knock and foolishly leaves him in the hostile street as she rushes back in with the good news'.[15] Ironically, however, the street is the one place in the pericope which is not 'hostile'; Peter has just escaped from the obviously hostile prison, and the house church is at best unwelcoming. When he is finally granted entry, Peter himself chooses to remain in the street. One plausible interpretation of this scene is that it is safer in the street than in a Jerusalem house church run by a woman. Peter is much safer in Joppa, but only because Dorcas (or Tabitha), who is the central figure in what might be a house church, is dead throughout most of the pericope.

Finally, J. Albert Harrill, reading Acts 12 in light of Plautus and Terence, correctly notes that the conventions of the *servus currens*—one of the most familiar of the stock characters in Roman comedy—provide the best interpretive context by which to understand Rhoda's depiction.[16] The run-down on the *servus currens*, the 'running slave', goes like this: the character 'sees' invisible people on the street, dares to lecture social betters, and delivers a message with the expectation of reward.[17] Commenting on Acts 12.14, 'and recognizing Peter's voice, she did not open the door because of her joy, but running in she announced that Peter was at the gate', Harrill offers: 'For a brief moment Rhoda holds the narrative spotlight in Acts, and blows it.'[18] Indeed, he suggests that ancient audiences would recognize Rhoda's

---

12 Haenchen, *Acts of the Apostles*, p. 385 n. 3.
13 Richard Pervo, *Profit with Delight: The Literary Genre of the Acts of the Apostles* (Philadelphia: Fortress Press, 1987), p. 63.
14 Pervo, *Profit with Delight*, p. 61.
15 Pervo, *Profit with Delight*, p. 62.
16 J. Albert Harrill, 'The Dramatic Function of the Running Slave Rhoda (Acts 12.15–16): A Piece of Greco-Roman Comedy', *NTS* 46 (2000), pp. 151–57. Harrill notes the presence of the *servus currens* in Terence's *Self-Tormentor*, *The Eunuch*, and *Adelphoe* and Plautus's *Stichus* and *Captivi*.
17 Harrill, 'Dramatic Function', p. 156.
18 Harrill, 'Dramatic Function', p. 156.

'flighty delight' as more a result of her 'lust for a reward such as extra food or even manumission [rather than her faith], the ultimate prize imaginable that motivates slave exuberance'.[19]

Were Luke to have depicted only Rhoda's failure to open the door and omitted both Peter's humorous escape from prison and the failure of the house church to believe Rhoda's persistent words, Harrill would have a stronger case regarding Rhoda's 'blown' chance.

As for why Luke includes this scene, Harrill offers several reasons: the 'fictional' Rhoda is designed to highlight the audience's involvement with Peter, to heighten audience expectation for more realism in the following scene (Acts 12.16b–17 in which the 'apostles' encounter the 'miraculously rescued Peter'[20]), and to parallel Acts 12.13–15 with Lk. 24.11, where the first witnesses to Jesus' resurrection are women whose words are not believed by the apostles.[21] Finally, Harrill proposes that the elaborate sequence of events in Acts 12 serves to entertain with humor that dishonors slaves, and, he observes parenthetically, also women.

The kerygmatic aspects of the scene, aspects that offer alternatives to Harrill's thesis, emerge when Rhoda is compared to the *servus currens* convention. Rhoda recognizes not fiction but fact: Peter really is at the door. She does not 'lecture' her social betters; to the contrary, they silence her. Indeed, the narrative never grants Rhoda direct discourse. Moreover, Luke's juxtaposition of Peter's passive escape from prison and difficulty at the door with the failure of the prayerful Christians to heed Rhoda's announcement actually serves to enhance her status, and it does so at the expense of the apostle and the (free) members of the house church. Similarly, the comparison of Acts 12 with Luke 24 can be seen both to heighten the importance of a woman's voice and to critique the movement's purported leaders. If we read in light of the *servus currens* convention but apply a hermeneutic informed by liberationist concerns, we still find that Mary and her colleagues remain targets of critique. In Luke's account, Rhoda does not ask for reward: her joy at Peter's escape is sufficient. Nevertheless, in this new household of faith, all are to be fed, and, by extension, all are to be free. Rhoda, conventionally, would only be asking for what the Christian message (ideally) promises.

Rhoda's joy does confirm Harrill's claim that the slave highlights audience involvement with Peter, but the type of involvement should also be noted: the humor comes much more at Peter's expense than at Rhoda's. Peter's helplessness would have come as no surprise to Luke's audience; he had already been shown as unable to orchestrate his release from prison and even unable to understand what was happening with the angel until he was on the street. His inability to gain entry to the house is also a comedic convention. Frost, analyzing entrances and exits in Greek comedy, asserts: 'Only once in the extant comedies is knocking successfully carried out in a serious scene (*Aspis* 499) where the door is, apparently, immediately answered at the first knock.'[22] Had the audience not recognized the humor in Peter's

---

19 Harrill, 'Dramatic Function', p. 156.
20 Harrill, 'Dramatic Function', p. 157.
21 Harrill, 'Dramatic Function', p. 157. Regarding the heightened expectation for more realism, Harrill notes, 'the sequence is a piece of escapist comedy that siphons implausibility from the scene, by which the subsequent action could be made to seem more real' (p. 157).
22 K.B. Frost, *Exits and Entrances in Menander* (Oxford: Clarendon Press, 1988), p. 9.

escape from prison, they would have seen it in the 'knock, knock joke' at the door. The joke at Peter's expense is confirmed at the end of the pericope, for he never achieves his original goal: he never actually enters the house. The scene instead ends with the too-vague notice, 'he went off elsewhere' (12.17 [καὶ ἐξελθὼν ἐπορεύθη εἰς ἕτερον τόπον]).[23] This lack of fulfillment of expectations is yet another indicator of Greco-Roman comedy,[24] and the lack of specific location enhances both the humor of the scene and the critique of the house church.

When we turn to feminist criticism, we find both recognition and denial of Luke's liberative aspects as well as occasional recognition of humor. Yet again, the critique does not address the significance of the humor. Richter Reimer, for example, sees Acts 12 as providing a liberative message to both slaves and women, but she frames her argument in terms of expected master–slave relations and by appealing to Rhoda's vindication through truthful speech.[25] But it is the comedic trope that makes Rhoda's speech powerful, for the *servus currens* convention prompts an expectation of foolish speech. The power of Rhoda's announcement lies not only in its surprising message; it also lies in the surprise of the messenger. The import of the juxtaposition of Rhoda's scene with Peter's escape has not received much attention in feminist scholarship,[26] perhaps because such scholarship tends to focus just on the women characters. Nor is there much comment on slavery itself: Luke does not explicitly state that Rhoda is owned by Mary, but if this is the case, then the critique of the house church is sharpened. The ideal in Acts is that all in Jerusalem shared their resources, but Mary keeps a house in the high-rent district, and in that house she keeps slaves. That Luke's other Mary, the mother of Jesus, utters the Magnificat's rejection of the power of the elite seals the critique of John Mark's mother. The second Mary is the negative foil to the first.

James Arlandson notes in Acts 12 both liberation and reduction: 'Rhoda is vindicated (an exaltation); the rest are humorously shown to be unbelievers (a demotion) even though they are praying for Peter.'[27] Observing that when Rhoda is seen in conjunction with Mary, the master–slave relationship takes priority over gender concerns, Arlandson concludes: 'Luke is not afraid of exalting a slave woman at the

---

23 Heinrich Greeven (ed.), *Martin Dibelius: Studies in the Acts of the Apostles* (Mifflintown: Sigler Press, 1999), p. 21. Dibelius argues that the notation 'he went off elsewhere' came at the end of an originally isolated story that was not concerned with further Petrine journeys; Dunn, *Acts of the Apostles*, p. 164, writes that Peter presumably had to withdraw from public appearances because of Herod's pursuit; C.K. Barrett, *A Critical and Exegetical Commentary on the Acts of the Apostles* (ICC; 2 vols.; Edinburgh: T. & T. Clark, 1994), I, p. 587, argues that while the Greek might imply that Peter left Jerusalem, whether to travel to another town or embark on another missionary journey, had Luke meant this the text would be more explicit. He finds it most probable that Luke may have simply been 'running out of information about Peter; probably he meant only that Peter got clean away'.

24 Netta Zagagi, *The Comedy of Menander: Convention, Variation and Originality* (Bloomington: Indiana University Press, 1995), p. 120.

25 Reimer, *Women in the Acts of the Apostles*, pp. 241–43.

26 Robert C. Tannehill, *The Narrative Unity of Luke–Acts: A Literary Interpretation*. II. *The Acts of the Apostles* (Minneapolis: Fortress Press, 1990), p. 155, does note that it is primarily Peter and the assembly who fail to understand, seemingly letting Rhoda 'off the hook'.

27 James Malcolm Arlandson, *Women, Class, and Society in Early Christianity: Models from Luke–Acts* (Peabody, MA: Hendrickson, 1997), p. 196.

expense of a wealthy, slave-owning woman.'[28] The same argument, however, would not hold for the other appearance of a slave girl in Acts. In the case of Paul and the Pythoness, the slave girl's status is not exalted.[29] A female slave can be exalted over a female slave-owner, but there is no such exaltation of a female slave over her male slave-owners, even if those owners are pagans.

In *The Women's Bible Commentary*, Gail O'Day writes, 'Rhoda's announcement that Peter is standing at the gate is taken first as a sign of Rhoda's mental instability, then a sign of her delusion.'[30] Rhoda lacked the necessary authority to have her message taken seriously because of her status of both woman and slave, and the resistance of her listeners completely prevented her message from being delivered.[31] Perhaps because of the constraints of the commentary genre, she was unable to develop the humorous aspects of the pericope. These aspects, as we have seen, complement O'Day's politically informed exposition.

The gap between the slave's insistence and the church's resistance indicates that the relationship between the two named women—Rhoda and Mary the mother of John Mark—is not one of solidarity. As the slave attempts to deliver her good news to the prayerful church, Luke's comedic focus turns to the pietistic believers. Rather than accepting Rhoda's news as delivered, the very news that (likely) they had been praying to hear, the house church castigates her: 'And they said to her, "You are out of your mind!" [εἶπαν μαίνῃ] But she insisted that it was so' (Acts 12.15). They would rather believe that Peter is dead and so in the *inefficacy* of their prayer than heed the words of a female slave.[32]

While the house-church members refuse to recognize the truth of Rhoda's claim, Rhoda herself immediately recognizes—from the sound of Peter's voice, no less— that the apostle is at the door (Acts 12.14).[33] Rather than allowing the house church to silence her, she doggedly insists on the veracity of her claim. Thus, Rhoda effectively takes over the characteristics that one might expect to be accorded to a free, male, apostle: she announces the truth despite the refusal of her audience to listen, and despite their insistence that she is mad. The scene thus suggests a parallel to Paul's experience in Athens. Aristophanes, whose comedies, Elizabeth Bobrick tells us, present 'an upside-down world in which traditional social roles are reversed or abandoned altogether',[34] has found an heir in Luke.

The absurdity of the house church's reaction is compounded by their explication of what Rhoda did hear: 'They were saying, "It is his angel"' (12.15). Since when do

---

28 Arlandson, *Women, Class, and Society*, p. 196.

29 For further discussion on this pericope, please see Kathy Chambers Williams, 'At the Expense of Women: Humor (?) in Acts 16.14–40', in A. Brenner (ed.), *Are We Amused? Humour about Women in the Biblical Worlds* (BTC, 2; New York: Continuum, 2003), pp. 79–89.

30 Gail R. O'Day, 'Acts', in Carol A. Newsom and Sharon H. Ringe (eds.), *The Women's Bible Commentary* (Louisville, KY: Westminster/John Knox, exp. edn, 1998), pp. 394–402.

31 O'Day, 'Acts', pp. 394–402.

32 On guardian angels in early Jewish thought, see Charles H. Talbert, *Reading Acts: A Literary and Theological Commentary on the Acts of the Apostles* (New York: Crossroad Publishing Company, 1997), p. 120; Barrett, *Critical and Exegetical Commentary*, p. 585.

33 Spencer, 'Out of Mind'.

34 Elizabeth Bobrick, 'The Tyranny of Roles: Playacting and Privilege in Aristophanes' *Thesmophoriazusae*', in Gregory W. Dobrov (ed.), *The City as Comedy: Society and Representation in Athenian Drama* (Chapel Hill: The University of North Carolina Press, 1997), p. 177.

angels need to knock? And if there really is an angel knocking, might they not through curiosity, if not hospitality or piety, open the door? The comedy at the expense of the assembled worshipers is heightened all the more by the context of the scene, for Luke has just depicted an angel who rescues Peter from prison by miraculously opening numerous doors and gates. According to this pericope, then, it is easier to escape from prison than it is to join the members of Mary's household in prayer. We may even hear in Peter's knocking faint echoes of Lk. 18.1–15, the parable of the widow and the unjust judge. Here, however, Mary (a widow?) is cast in the role of the unjust judge who cares for neither 'man' (read: Rhoda) nor 'God' (read: presumed angel) while Peter assumes the importuning widow's role.

Those familiar with Menander's plays would at this point expect a complex, dramatic moment surrounding the identification of a main character—and Luke does not disappoint. Rhoda's trouble convincing the group delays Peter's entrance, and thus the slave does exactly what she is supposed to do, namely, heighten the suspense.

Eventually Mary and company open the door: whether they finally heeded Rhoda's words or wished to shut her up (as Paul reacts to the female slave in Philippi) remains unclear. Acts 12.16 states, 'And opening [the door], they saw him and were amazed (beside themselves)' (ἀνοίξαντες δὲ εἶδαν αὐτὸν καὶ ἐξέστησαν).[35] The members of the church now fulfill the slave's role: free people serve as doorkeepers, and now it is their mental state, not Rhoda's, that receives comment. When the church members had proclaimed Rhoda to be 'mad' (μαίνῃ), they were incorrect; it is the omniscient narrator who correctly identifies those who are 'beside themselves'. Only when the prayerful believers leave their routine way of thinking do they recognize the truth; only when they are willing to take the word of a slave or at least to be influenced by her message do they gain access to the truth. Thus to Spencer's comment—'No matter that Peter has been knocking at the gate the whole while, rapping out a confirming signal of Rhoda's message. Only when the group belatedly opens that gate and sees Peter for themselves do they believe her report'[36]—a correlate is needed: the house church had already 'believed' the slave, or at least attended to her words, or they would not have opened the door at all.

But if Rhoda's voice—the voice of the woman and the slave—is now, like the voice of the women at the tomb, to be treated with respect, the same cannot be said for poor Peter. Most benignly, it could be argued that Luke told this story in conformity with the standard comedic interest in making 'friendly fun of others, who may enjoy the joke'.[37] However, the juxtaposition of Peter's situation with that of Rhoda suggests more. Just as Menander tends 'to highlight the differences of character between the two by means of their different reactions to one and the same situation',[38] so Luke highlights the differences between Peter and Rhoda, to the woman's benefit.

---

35 LSJ define εξίστνμι as 'displace', 'alter utterly', 'to drive one out of his senses', and 'to derange'; they define μαίνη ('to be driven mad' and 'madness').
36 Spencer, 'Out of Mind', pp. 144–45.
37 F.H. Sandbach, *The Comic Theatre of Greece and Rome* (New York: W.W. Norton & Company, Inc., 1977), p. 37. This tendency to make jokes at the expense of others is a remnant from Aristophanes.
38 Zagagi, *Comedy of Menander*, p. 85.

Peter enters Acts 12 as completely passive, and completely clueless: the angel must instruct him not only to get up, but also to dress. Even the angel's role can be seen as humorous, for his attention to sartorial propriety is not only unexpected, but completely unneeded. As Pervo notes, 'All of this will madden anxious readers. Why spend all of this time perfecting the outfit? He is breaking out of jail, not going to a papal reception.'[39] Humorous elements continue as Peter, now outfitted for escape, continues in his ignorance, for Luke remarks that 'Peter had no idea that the angel's intervention was real' (καὶ οὐκ ᾔδει ὅτι ἀληθές ἐστιν γινόμενον διὰ τοῦ ἀγγέλου, 12.9). Whereas the members of the house church choose to believe that Peter's angel is at the door, Peter himself doesn't recognize his own angel. Such mistaken identity—at the gentle expense of the church leaders—permeates the plot. The same motif will continue in Acts, when Paul and Silas are mistaken for, respectively, Hermes (the deity known for convincing speech) and Zeus. The mistake is doubled in that Hermes is subordinate to Zeus, but Paul is by no means subordinate to Silas (at least in Luke's presentation). Comparable also is Paul's experience on Malta, where first he is rejected as cursed because he had been bitten by a viper, and then is hailed as divine because he did not drop dead (Acts 28.3–6).

Passing through the second gate (πύλην) of the prison, the angel and Peter come to the iron gate of the city. What might seem like an obstacle to anyone else poses no problem for them; this gate opens of its own accord. The contrast to the gate (πυλῶνος) at Mary's house heightens the irony of the scene. Just as the members of the house church finally come to full belief when they open the gate but at this point are 'beside themselves', only when the city gate is open and the angel departs does Peter 'come to himself' (12.11 ἑαυτῷ γενόμενος).

Preventing all of these elements from creating farce is the broader content of the narrative. Much of the dramatic effect in Acts 12.6–17 stems from the juxtaposition of the humorous with the serious, for Peter's escape follows immediately upon the death of the apostle James (Acts 12.1–2). The reference to another 'James' along with 'the members of the church' (12.17) at the end of the scene concerning the house church frames the story and returns the text to the seriousness of the message. Despite the humor, the spreading of the gospel can be, literally, deadly serious. And with this final line, Luke returns the reader to the status quo: James and his fellow disciples are in charge; Mary is dropped from the story; Peter—the object of the humor who is now replaced by James—has wandered off the stage.

The good news for those seeking liberative readings from Acts 12 is that Rhoda's appearance, especially when compared to that of Peter, confirms the import of the voice of women and slaves. Rather than reinforcing the status quo, Luke's play upon comedic conventions can be seen as challenging constructions of status and gender.

Luke, however, is no social revolutionary. Attention to women and slaves is one thing; placing them ahead of men and the free is something else entirely. That Peter next appears in the home of the dead widow Tabitha may remind us of Mary's home: widows in Acts are assets to the church, as long as they are not running it. Comparable also is the account of Mary and Martha in Luke 10: although Martha owns the house, her effort at ministry is not as valued (if it is valued at all) as is Mary's silent listening. Completing this trope of an apostle in the home of a single

---

39 Pervo, *Profit with Delight*, p. 62.

woman is Paul's sojourning with Lydia. Whereas Peter could not gain entry to Rhoda's house, Paul is compelled, even bullied (παρεβιάσατο) by Lydia to remain with her. The single women who receive praise are those who recognize, either actively or passively, the importance of the men. Those who retain any leadership status—for example Martha, Mary the mother of John Mark—are either silenced or made the fools.

In like manner, the voice of the slave girl (παιδίσκη) is ultimately of little consequence. No matter how true Rhoda's proclamation of Peter's escape, she still fails to welcome Peter into the house. When the assembled members do invite in the apostle, he is no longer interested in gaining access. Thus the slave's efforts had at best minimal consequence. In the Gospel (Lk. 22.56), a 'slave girl' (παιδίσκη) in the high priest's courtyard correctly identifies Peter, but he denies the truth of her claim that he was with Jesus. A third dismissal of a slave girl who knew—again, perhaps miraculously—the true identity of an apostle appears in Acts 16, the same chapter where we encounter Lydia. Not only have we another house church run by a woman, we have a slave (παιδίσκη, Acts 16.6) who proclaims the truth that no one wants to hear. The slave girl announces that Paul is 'a servant of the most high God', but the apostle himself refuses to accept her (true) message, let alone permit it to be promoted. Rather, finding her proclamation annoying, Paul exorcises from the 'Pythoness' her 'spirit of divination'. The move is counterproductive, both because the slave girl provides Paul 'free advertising'[40] from no less a sponsor than the god Apollo and because the consequent loss of income for the girls' owners eventuates in Paul's being imprisoned.

Luke follows the comedic convention promoted by Aristophanes: 'The women's emerging voice and its subsequent silencing follows a pattern ... ordinarily voiceless women claim a public voice only to reorder wayward men [here we add a reference also to elite women]. Once that reordering has taken place, the women retreat from the public arena and are heard from no more.'[41] According to Harrill, the *servus currens* model makes Rhoda 'a running cliché which encourages laughter at her as a moral inferior even when her news is true'.[42] Yet textual silence need not lead to hermeneutical silence, and ancient convention need no longer be taken as normative. As warnings to the elite of any system, be it religious, political, or economic, the voices of the slave girl in the high priest's court, the slave girl in the Jerusalem church, and the slave girl in Philippi—all of whom insisted on the truth even when it was denied—echo still. To laugh at the leaders of any community is a sign of freedom; for the leaders to be able to appreciate that laughter enough to accept its promptings in a canonical document is a sign of health; to celebrate that such humor disrupts the status quo in a way of benefit to those outside traditional bases of authority is a sign of the *Basileia*.

---

40 Pervo, *Profit with Delight*, p. 63.
41 Pervo, *Profit with Delight*, pp. 187–88.
42 Harrill, 'Dramatic Function', p. 157.

RHODA AND PENELOPE: TWO MORE CASES OF LUKE'S SUPPRESSION OF WOMEN

ROBERT M. PRICE

In *The Widow Traditions in Luke–Acts: A Feminist-Critical Scrutiny*,[1] I tried to show how the second-century author of that double document had rewritten a number of Jesus-traditions and apostolic stories stemming from communities of celibate, charismatic women, in order to put women in the place assigned to them by the strictures of, for example, the Pastoral Epistles. In the present article it will be my aim to reinforce my characterization of Luke's agenda by outlining two more instances, these involving the suppression of important women characters (or their deeds) in his sources; these two do not, however, involve consecrated widows. If Luke's agenda was as I described it in *The Widow Traditions in Luke–Acts*, there is no obvious reason he should have restricted his efforts to the widows' materials. Presumably he would have manifested the same biases in other cases where women received a bit too much prominence for his tastes.

The first of the cases occurs in the Gospel of Luke's parable of the prodigal son. The second comes from the Acts of the Apostles: the story of Peter's miraculous escape from martyrdom at the hands of Herod Agrippa I. In the course of the analysis I hope to show that while the suppression of women is by no means the most striking or important feature of the Lukan redaction, recognizing it will nonetheless help us recognize other, equally suggestive features (and vice versa).

Penelope and the Prodigal

Dennis R. MacDonald has recently drawn attention to the great interest taken by early Christians in Homer's epics.[2] This may surprise those who prefer to see the New Testament writers taking their inspiration solely from Jewish materials, but this interest is only natural in view of the status in the Hellenistic world of both *Iliad* and *Odyssey* as canonical scriptures themselves. Early Christians could hardly have avoided the *Iliad* and the *Odyssey*. MacDonald shows, in *Christianizing Homer*, how the *Acts of Andrew* essentially rewrote the *Odyssey* along Christian lines. And in *The Homeric Epics and the Gospel of Mark*, MacDonald also argues that Mark's Gospel is similarly a Christianized *Odyssey*.

But in the meantime, I would suggest, *contra* MacDonald, that Mark is not the only New Testament writer to draw upon the *Odyssey*. Luke, too, has done it. This makes perfect sense, not only in view of Luke's well-known penchant for garnishing his own writings with quoted snippets from Diodorus Siculus, Plato, Euripides,

---

[1] Robert M. Price, *The Widow Traditions in Luke–Acts: A Feminist-Critical Scrutiny* (SBLDS, 155; Atlanta, GA: Scholars Press, 1997).

[2] Dennis Ronald MacDonald, *Christianizing Homer:* The Odyssey, *Plato, and* The Acts of Andrew (New York: Oxford University Press, 1994) and *idem, The Homeric Epics and the Gospel of Mark* (New Haven: Yale University Press, 2000).

Epimenides, and Arratus, but also from Luke–Acts' notable similarity and probable kinship[3] with the ancient novels and the Apocryphal Acts which were in some measure based upon them. Once we see that the *Acts of Andrew* could use the *Odyssey*, it should not seem far-fetched to suggest that a kindred writer like Luke could use it, too. If he is making the same general sort of sandwich, he might as well use the same meat.

Specifically, my suggestion is that Luke has modeled his parable of the prodigal son upon the *Odyssey* episode of Penelope's suitors. That the parable is Luke's work and does not go back to the historical Jesus is evident not least from its length, but also from its signature feature of character introspection: 'What shall I do? I shall ...' Compare other Lukan creations such as the unjust judge (Lk. 18.4–5, 'He said to himself, I will ...'), the dishonest steward (16.3–4, 'What shall I do? I will ...'), and the rich fool (1.16–21, 'What shall I do? I will ...'). How did Luke go about composing his parable? Here I take a leaf from the book of Thomas L. Brodie, who shows how Luke frequently deconstructed stories from the Deuteronomic histories and reshuffled their elements into new tales, a technique widespread, as he shows, in ancient literature.[4] We will see what Luke has derived from Homer and what he has left out, as well as the permutations he has wrought. Luke has combined traits from different characters in some cases, while dividing single characters into multiple ones in others.

The character of the prodigal himself has been suggested by both the long-absent Odysseus and his son Telemachus who returns from a long quest in search of his missing father. Both the parable's elements of wandering far from home and of the father–son reunion stem from here. The cavorting of the prodigal with loose women in far lands was suggested by Odysseus's dalliance with Calypso. But the motif of the prodigal's having 'devoured [his father's] estate with loose living' is based on the similar judgment passed more than once by Telemachus and Eumaeus on the 'gang of profligates' infesting Odysseus's estate during his absence, the suitors.

The prodigal's taking a job as a swineherd, a galling 'transformation' for a Jew, might reflect the transformation of Odysseus's men into swine by Circe, especially since the hungry prodigal would like to fill his aching stomach with the pods on which his porcine charges feed. This is but another way of saying he envies their lot and would like to turn into one of them. Is Luke also thinking of Augustus's joke, 'I would rather be Herod's swine, ὑιγός, than his son, υἱός'? It is the same implicit pun in any case.

---

3 Richard I. Pervo, *Profit with Delight: The Literary Genre of the Acts of the Apostles* (Philadelphia: Fortress Press, 1987), pp. 122–35.

4 Thomas L. Brodie, 'Luke the Literary Interpreter: Luke–Acts as a Systematic Rewriting and Updating of the Elijah–Elisha Narrative in 1 and 2 Kings' (PhD diss., Pontifical University of St Thomas Aquinas, 1981); 'The Accusing and Stoning of Naboth (1 Kgs 21.8–13) as One Component of the Stephen Text (Acts 6.9–14; 7.58a)', *CBQ* 45 (1983) pp. 417–43; 'Luke–Acts as an Imitation and Emulation of the Elijah–Elisha Narrative', in Earl Richard (ed.), *New Views of Luke and Acts* (Collegeville, MN: Liturgical Press, 1990), pp. 78–85; 'Luke 7, 36–50 as an Internalization of 2 Kings 4.1–37: A Study in Luke's Use of Rhetorical Imitation', *Biblica* 64 (1983), pp. 457–85; 'Reopening the Quest for Proto-Luke: The Systematic Use of Judges 6–12 in Luke 16.1–18.8', *Journal of Higher Criticism* 2.1 (Spring 1995), pp. 68–101.

Then again, the prodigal's job as a swineherd might stem from Eumaeus's occupation as a swineherd. The latter's oft characterization as a 'righteous swineherd' may be linked with the characterization of the prodigal as a repentant swineherd. (Eumaeus, remember, is the faithful servant of Odysseus who befriends both the returning Odysseus, whom he does not first recognize, and the returning Telemachus, whom he does.)

The return of the prodigal is of course suggested by the late return of Odysseus, but no less of Telemachus, who together share the same actantial role. The prodigal hopes to enter the company of his father's household slaves, while Odysseus returns in disguise and does find shelter among Eumaeus and the household slaves. The glad reception afforded the prodigal by his father recalls the reunion of Odysseus and Telemachus, also father and son, but even more the reunion of Telemachus and Eumaeus:

> The last words were not out of his mouth when his [Odysseus's] own son appeared in the gateway. Eumaeus jumped up in amazement, and the bowls in which he had been busy mixing the sparkling wine tumbled out of his grasp. He ran forward to meet his young master, he kissed his lovely eyes, and then kissed his right hand and his left, while the tears streamed down his cheeks. Like a fond father welcoming back his son after nine years abroad, his only son, the apple of his eye and the center of all his anxious cares, the admirable swineherd threw his arms around Prince Telemachus and showered kisses on him as though he had just escaped from death.[5]

Next Luke splits Odysseus into two characters, the two brothers. The elder son also returns from being away, albeit only out in the field (the scene of conflict between two other famous brothers, Cain and Abel). But he does return, and is dismayed, like Odysseus, to discover a feast in progress. (Neither can we miss the echo of the disgust of the returned Moses: 'It is not the sound of shouting for victory, or the sound of the cry of defeat, but the sound of ... *singing* that I hear!' [Exod. 32.18].) It is a feast in honor of a profligate, as the elder brother is quick to point out, like that of the suitors. And just as their feast is predicated on their supposition of Odysseus's death, the prodigal's father explains to the elder son that they must feast since the prodigal was dead and has now returned alive, as Odysseus is about to do.

A puzzling feature of the Lukan parable now approaches solution, for is it not evident that the prodigal's planned hand-wringing confession of unworthiness is a mere tactic aimed at mollifying his father enough to be accepted as a slave? The prodigal, knee-deep in hog-slop, 'comes to himself', but his realization has nothing to do with his having sinned. It is merely the realization that a better menu than he presently enjoys is available in the slave quarters of his father. He seems to intend genuine remorse as little as he expects the extravagant forgiveness of his father. Thus his forgiveness seems in the long run to be doubly undeserved. It is not surprising that Luke might have sought to depict God as doubly forgiving—the point of the parable on any reading—but it may seem strange for Luke so to reward an unrepentant schemer. Or does it? Luke is happy enough to use the obviously Machiavellian unjust steward as a lesson in repentance over in Luke 16, so why not here? But that just pushes the problem back a step. Why there? Because Luke was

---

5 Homer, *The Odyssey* (trans. E.V. Rieu; Baltimore, MD: Penguin, 1961), p. 245.

thinking of Odysseus as much as Jacob, both scheming rogues whose guile was considered a singular virtue by ancient readers who envied it.

Malherbe reviews the ancient debate over Odysseus.[6] He was a favorite model for resourcefulness among the Cynic and Stoic preachers, and recall how Luke associates resourcefulness with repentance. Theognis praised Odysseus for his chameleon-like character (cf. 1 Cor. 9.19–22). On the other hand, Pindar, Sophocles, and Euripides condemned the very same trait in Odysseus. Yes, Odysseus was ambivalent, a good example in the eyes of some, a bad one in the eyes of others. But then how natural for Luke to split the character up, as I have suggested, into a good Odysseus (the elder brother) and a bad one (the prodigal), who must finally be reconciled!

Bruno Bettelheim, in *The Uses of Enchantment*,[7] observes how many 'two brother' fairy tales involve the separation of the two brothers, one leaving home and falling into danger or even death, the other, bound to the apron strings, finally leaving the safety of home to rescue him. In these tales, Bettelheim suggests, the siblings stand for two aspects of every individual, the desire to stay in the nest and the desire to sow one's wild oats. The story helps hearers integrate both tendencies within themselves. I think Luke has something of the same aim as he splits up Odysseus into the two returning brothers and anticipates their reconciliation.

When the elder brother grouses about never having been given so much as a goat to share with his poker buddies, do we not see a reflection of Eumaeus's apology to the disguised Odysseus that all he can scrape together as victuals are a couple of pigs left over from the suitors' feast? There is also the obvious parallel that the suitors (= the prodigal) have been consuming the fare that rightly belongs to Odysseus himself (= the elder brother).

Finally, let me suggest that a good deal of the reshuffling Luke has put the Homeric original through was necessitated by one aim: *eliminating Penelope*. In the original, Penelope was a loving parent welcoming home two beloved family members. She had tolerated the presence of the suitors but given in to none of them; thus, she demonstrated a degree of marital faithfulness unmatched by her absent husband. And her faith was rewarded by his return. Had Penelope retained her place in the parable of the prodigal son, as she might have, in the role of a widowed mother dependent upon the labors of her sons (cf. Lk. 7.12), what would we have had? Luke would have provided us a sterling use of a woman standing for the forgiving God, a compassionate heavenly mother. But no. And it is no accident that Luke has replaced her with a father.

Peter and his Passion

I have already made glancing reference to Richard I. Pervo's comparative study of the Apocryphal and canonical Acts, in which he shows that the supposedly unbridgeable gulf separating the two genres is largely an illusion generated by

---

6 Abraham J. Malherbe, *Paul and the Popular Philosophers* (Minneapolis: Fortress Press, 1989), pp. 98–101.

7 Bruno Bettelheim, *The Uses of Enchantment: The Meaning and Importance of Fairy Tales* (New York: Random House Vintage Books, 1977), pp. 90–96.

scholars zealous to fortify the boundaries of the canon of Scripture. One striking feature of several major Apocryphal Acts is the manner in which the martyrdoms of their eponymous heroes precisely parallel that of Jesus in the Gospels, in some cases even issuing in empty tombs and postmortem appearances to disciples! But does Luke's Acts feature any such parallel? Of course it does: Paul's recapitulation of Jesus' own journey to Jerusalem, passion predictions, tumult at the Temple, being taken into Roman custody, trial before the Sanhedrin, getting slapped for sassing the high priest, trial before both Herodian kings and Roman procurators, and final journey to (an implicit) execution at the hands of Rome. Luke is just a bit more subtle than the *Acts of Paul* in this regard, where the beheaded Paul appears to Nero, warning him of divine vengeance, and later ascends from an empty tomb.

But there is a second passion parallel, a second apostolic passion narrative in Acts, that has never to my knowledge been adequately explored. Given the tendency (with Knox, I make it anti-Marcionite)[8] of Acts to parallel Paul with Peter, we ought to expect at least as detailed—if not as long—a passion narrative for Peter as Luke provides for Paul. And we find it in ch. 12. It is a commonplace to note a few basic similarities between this episode and the passion narrative of Jesus, especially the Passover setting. But the parallels are much more extensive. Peter languishes in a prison; Jesus didn't. Or did he? Peter's time in the jail cell matches Jesus' three days in the tomb. As angels greeted the women at the empty tomb of Jesus, an angel greets Peter and 'empties' his cell of him. The angel's command to 'wrap your mantle around you' (v. 8) recalls Luke's references to Joseph of Arimathea, who 'wrapped' the body of Jesus 'in a linen shroud' (Lk. 23.53). The chains which fell from Peter's hands recall Peter's own earlier preaching about the resurrection of Jesus: 'But God raised him up, having loosed the pangs of death, because it was not possible for him to be held by it' (Acts 2.24).

Peter is guarded by two Roman soldiers in the cell, with at least another pair stationed between the cell and the outer door. He escapes despite their presence, apparently invisible to their eyes, as the angel has, like the Shadow, 'clouded men's minds'. In light of the extensive parallels to the passion of Jesus, a striking new possibility emerges just at this point. What if Peter's guards reflect the presence of Matthew's Roman guards at Jesus' tomb? Luke's tendency to save this or that gospel element for later use in Acts (e.g., the slapping of Jesus omitted from the Gospel, where we find it in Jn 18.22, and used for Paul's trial instead [Acts 23.2–4], or the accusation that Jesus will destroy the Temple, removed from the trial scene of Jesus and transferred to Stephen's trial in Acts 6) is well known. What if this is another instance of the same tendency? It would imply that the tomb guards, though a subsequent development to Mark's account, was not quite so late an embellishment as generally thought. Perhaps Matthew and Luke both knew it but made different uses of it.

As the jail gate opens miraculously of itself, by angelic telekinesis, we are inevitably reminded of the stone door of Jesus' tomb being rolled back by angelic sinews. As the Risen Christ came to his assembled disciples on Easter, so the newly sprung Peter arrives at the house of Mary where the church is gathered, praying for

---

8 John Knox, *Marcion and the New Testament: An Essay in the Early History of the Canon* (Chicago, IL: University of Chicago Press, 1942), pp. 119–21.

him. His appearance calls forth the very same reaction: utter skepticism (a riotously funny piece of Lukan irony!). Just as the eleven disciples in Luke 24 jumped to the conclusion that they were seeing a spirit, the assembled Christians first believe Peter must be dead, and it is merely his ghost, his guardian angel, who has appeared to say good-bye. And as it was women who first brought the news of Jesus' escape from the tomb, only to meet with incredulity, so does Rhoda the maidservant (cf. Lk. 1.38, 'Behold, I am the handmaid of the Lord') encounter stubborn disbelief.

As it takes the appearance of Jesus himself to banish the doubts of the eleven, so does the entrance of Peter himself have the same effect. Just as the Risen Christ was caught up to heaven to be seen no more (save for occasional emergency visions vouchsafed to Stephen and Paul), so does Peter vanish mysteriously 'to another place', effectively quitting Acts' narrative (again, except for a strategic appearance at the Apostolic Council in ch. 15, which is just Luke's way of reminding the reader of the events of ch. 10). Peter's parting words, 'Tell this to James and the brethren' (12.17), recall those of the young man in the tomb in Mk 16.7, 'But go, tell his disciples and Peter ...'

Now how does any of the preceding bear on Luke's redactional suppression of women's roles in early Christianity? It is simple, really. Luke has transparently derived the passion of Peter sequence from Jesus' passion in his sources. Aside from the fact that, for obvious narrative reasons, Peter does not literally die and rise, the single important departure from the Jesus version, as we can see by comparing Luke's Peter passion with his Jesus passion, is that while, for Luke, Mary Magdalene and her sisters did not see the Risen Christ at the empty tomb (and are not said to have been present with the eleven when Jesus subsequently appeared to them), Rhoda does see the 'risen' Peter and bears not merely the tidings of angels but of the man himself to the skeptical disciples. Of course what this implies is that Luke knew good and well that the female disciples of Jesus were supposed to have seen the Risen Christ himself, such an account underlying his story of Rhoda and Peter, but when he wrote his Jesus version, he eliminated this element, purposely excising any possible basis for women's appeal to the empty tomb story as a precedent for their own apostolic ministry.

Rhoda (whether under this or some other name like Mary, Joanna, or Salome) did originally (in Luke's sources) behold the Risen Christ and was commissioned to take his message to the eleven, but Luke has changed all that. If she saw someone, it was not Jesus, only Peter. If she bore tidings of the resurrection to the eleven, they were secondhand, from two men at the tomb, not from the Risen One himself. That such a distinction was no minor one can be seen in Gal. 1.11–12, 'For I would have you know, brethren, that the gospel which was preached by me is not according to man [or, one might say, two men!], nor was I taught it, but it came through a revelation of Jesus Christ himself.' In Luke's redaction, I maintain, we are witnessing the other side of an analogous and equally urgent dispute.

Widows After All?

I have argued that Luke's redactional agenda to suppress the role of women in his sources was not restricted to the traditions he derived, and co-opted, from the circle of ministering celibate widows, but extended to other stories involving prominent women. One of these was Homer's *Odyssey*, in which Penelope played an important role, the other a version of the passion and resurrection in which a woman or women beheld the Risen Christ and reported these tidings to the eleven. In the first case, Luke replaced the female model of forgiving parental love with a male one, substituting the prodigal's father for Penelope; in the second he allowed the woman to have beheld only the escaped Peter, not the Risen Jesus.

Finally, it is worth noting that even these two passages may rest ultimately upon widow-community traditions, though the links are slender and speculative. First, I have already noted above how a female Penelope analog in the prodigal-son parable would have formed a parallel with the widow of Nain; this might suggest that it was someone in the widow community who had borrowed from the *Odyssey*, already before Luke. As we would have read that version, the abandonment of the mother by one son, taking his share of the assets with him, would have been especially outrageous as well as poignant, and the ensuing forgiveness all the more miraculous. Perhaps it was a widow tradition that Luke took over and redacted. Then he would have been using Homer secondhand.

Second, given the parallel between Rhoda and the Virgin Mary as 'handmaids of the Lord', we might wonder if Rhoda was already understood as a young consecrated widow/virgin such as sex-shunning piety soon made of Mary. The link between spiritual virginity and susceptibility to visions, for example, of the Risen Christ, is widespread in early Christian thinking, as was the case with Philip's daughters, 'prophesying virgins', and the prophesying widow Anna, who, like Mary in early Christian apocrypha, dwelt day and night in the Temple. But these are mere shadows of possibilities. I like to think that the foregoing analyses of the prodigal-son parable and the passion of Peter rest upon a firmer foundation.

LYDIA AND HER SISTERS AS LUKAN FICTIONS

DENNIS R. MACDONALD

According to ch. 16 of the Acts of the Apostles, Paul's first convert in Europe was a woman and not a European at all: Lydia of Thyatira from western Asia Minor. She emigrated along a route similar to Paul's own journey from Troas to Philippi. The story of her conversion:

> On the Sabbath day we went outside the gate by the river, where we supposed there was a place of prayer, and we sat down and spoke to the women who had gathered there. A certain woman named Lydia, a worshiper of God, was listening to us; she was from the city of Thyatira and a dealer in purple cloth. The Lord opened her heart to listen eagerly to what was said by Paul. When she and her household were baptized, she urged us, saying, 'If you have judged me to be faithful to the Lord, come and stay at my home.' And she prevailed upon us (16.13–15).

Although there is nothing inherently implausible about this tale, it contains several peculiarities that have befuddled interpreters. Luke calls the place where the women convened a προσευχή, a 'prayer', metonymically a place of prayer. Although it is possible to take the word to designate a synagogue,[1] it more likely designates a wild, natural setting where the women convened for worship.[2] Surely Luke did not have in mind a building recognizable as a synagogue: Paul and company 'surmised' (ἐνομίζομεν) the place was a *proseuche*. The total absence of men likewise speaks against taking the reference to refer to a synagogue. Furthermore, all other synagogues in Luke–Acts (invariably called synagogues) seem to be buildings within the city gates.[3] These women are outside the male-dominated city, in the wild, worshiping their god.

The name Lydia is suspicious insofar as it is the same name as the province she had left; Thyatira was in Lydia. Furthermore, Lydia from Lydia sold purple garments, which seems to be a gratuitous reference to her means of support. Perhaps Luke wished to call attention to her as a woman of independent means; after all, it is said that she had a household, implying dependants and perhaps slaves.

The next episode in Acts once again concerns a woman outside the city, this time a slave girl possessed of a 'Pythian spirit', viz. a divining demon, who enabled the girl to prophesy (μαντευομένη), and by so doing provided her owners a good living.[4] She persisted on following Paul and his entourage, shouting, 'these people are slaves of the Most High God, who proclaim to you the way of salvation'.[5] This young

---

1 BAGD, s.v. προσευχή.
2 This is even more likely if one prefers the conjectural variant οὗ ἐνομίζεν προσευχβ'υ εἶναι ('where they were accustomed to be at prayer'), BDF 397.2.
3 The location of synagogues within city confines is explicit in Acts 9.2, 20; 13.5; 14.1; 17.1, 10, 17; 18.4, 19, 26; 19.8, 24.
4 Acts 16.16; cf. Euripides, *Bacchae* 256–57 on financial gain from fortune-telling.
5 Acts 16.17.

woman correctly identified Paul—none of the men did!—but her unbidden mantic pestering so annoyed Paul that he exorcised the spirit.

> But when her owners saw that their hope of making money was gone, they seized Paul and Silas and dragged them into the marketplace before the authorities. When they had brought them before the magistrates, they said, 'These men are disturbing our city; they are Jews and are advocating customs that are not lawful for us as Romans to adopt or observe.'

Paul's reception in Europe thus faced opposition by men, including men in positions of power, whereas the only women mentioned in the story were favorable to the new religion.

The next story in Acts tells of the earthquake and prison break in Philippi that resulted in the conversion of the jailer and his family and the release of Paul and Silas. Several interpreters have called attention to the similarities between this story and the prison break of Dionysus in Euripides' *Bacchae*. I will argue that Luke not only modeled the prison break after the *Bacchae* but created the character of Lydia, her sisters, and the mantic slave girl to invite the reader to compare Paul's arrival in Europe preaching a new religion with the arrival of Dionysus in Europe preaching his new and disturbing religion. Put bluntly: Lydia never existed apart from her literary depiction in Acts. But as we shall see, she is an important fiction, for she allows Luke to contrast the influence of Paul and his God on women with the influence of Dionysus on women.

Elsewhere in Acts Luke seems nearly to quote from the *Bacchae*. Three times Paul narrates a vision on his way to Damascus to persecute followers of Jesus,[6] and each account repeats the same question from the heavenly voice: 'Saul, Saul, why do you persecute me?'[7] In the third version, however, Luke adds a statement not found in the previous two: 'It is hard for you to kick against the goads.'[8] Paul claims he heard this utterance in Aramaic, but Agrippa and his court, as well as Luke's readers, may well have recognized it as a near quotation from Euripides' *Bacchae*, in which Dionysus, in disguise, tells Pentheus, king of Thebes: 'I would rather slay sacrifices to him [Dionysus] than, as a mortal raging against a god, a kick against the goads' (πρὸς κέντρα λακτίζοιμι; cf. Acts 26.14; πρὸς κέντρα λακτίζειν).[9]

The parallel contexts for this proverb in the *Bacchae* and Acts suggest that Luke might have known it not as a free-floating, uncontextualized proverb but as a line from the famous play.[10] Euripides told how Dionysus, having established his cult in

---

6 Acts 9.1–29; 22.3–21; 26.9–20.
7 Acts 9.4; 22.7; 26.14.
8 Some manuscripts add this proverb to the end of Acts 9.4; others to the end of 9.5.
9 *Bacchae* 794–95.
10 'The author of Acts uses it... exactly as Euripides does, as a warning to the θεομάχος: he may in fact have borrowed it from the present passage' (E.R. Dodds, *Euripides' Bacchae* [Oxford: Oxford University Press, 2nd edn, 1960], p. 173). Dodds notes, however, that the proverb was traditional independent of Euripides. The classicist Wilhelm Nestle likewise argued for Luke's dependence on Euripides for this line and suggested that Paul's conversion was inspired by *Bacchae* 1078–85, where a 'voice (φωνή)' came 'from heaven' accompanied by a 'light (φῶς) of awful flame' (cf. Acts 9.3 [φῶς] and 4 [φωνήν], 22.6 [φῶς] and 7 [φωνῆς], and 26.13 [φῶς] and 14 [φωνήν]); 'Anklänge an Euripides in der Apostelgeschichte', in his *Griechische Studien: Untersuchungen zur Religion, Dichtung und Philosophie der Griechen* (Aalen: Scientia Verlag, 1968), pp. 232–33.

central Asia Minor, introduced himself to Greek soil, more specifically, Thebes, his mother's home and his birthplace. He arrived in disguise with an entourage of female followers from Lydia, who worshiped the god in Corybantic ecstasy. These Maenads provided Euripides his chorus throughout the play. Dionysus immediately drove Theban women outside the city into the hills to worship him in divinely induced madness.[11] King Pentheus, whose own mother, Agave, raged among the Maenads, found this new cult so outrageous, so out of keeping with Greek society, that he incarcerated some of the women as well as the god himself, whom he took to be merely a priest.[12]

During the night, Dionysus invoked an earthquake that freed him from his shackles and cell. Pentheus drew his sword and vainly stabbed at a phantom of the god, trying to slay him lest he escape. The subsequent dialogue contains the lines about kicking against the goads. Despite this earthshaking display of divine power, the king remained defiant, and, driven mad by the god, disguised himself as a woman to spy on the women in the hills and put an end to this madness. The women, likewise demented by deity, mistook Pentheus for a lion and dismembered him as they did other animals in their rites. In a hideously memorable episode, Agave returned triumphant from the hills with the head of her son impaled on a *thyrsus*, still thinking it was that of a lion. When she returned to her senses, she was numb with grief. Euripides thus drove home the point that it was indeed hard for mortals to kick against divine goads.

Considering Jesus a mere mortal, Saul persecuted his followers, 'both men and women'.[13] Like Dionysus, Jesus demonstrated his divinity through a supernatural act that sent people falling to the earth.[14] Dionysus and Jesus both warned their persecutors not to 'kick against the goads'. Unlike Pentheus, Saul succumbed to the new god and thus avoided a tragic ending.[15]

The *Bacchae* has more parallels to ch. 16 of Acts. Both in the play and in Acts, the preacher of a new god arrives on European soil from Asia Minor and immediately gains acceptance by women, like the Maenads of Euripides worshiping Dionysus in the hills.[16] Dionysus drove women mad, allowing them to prophesy;[17]

Nestle also observed evidence of the *Bacchae* in the use of θεομάχοι, 'god-fighters', in Acts 5.39 (cf. *Bacchae* 45, 325, 635–36, and 1255; 'Anklänge', pp. 228–31) and in the charge against Paul for preaching 'foreign divinities (ξένων δαιμονίων)' (Acts 17.18b), advocating a 'new teaching (καινή... διδαχή)' (17.19), and 'introducing some strange (deity?) (ξενίζοντα... τινα εἰσφέρεις)' (17.20; 'Anklänge', pp. 235–36). See especially *Bacchae* 219 (τὸν νεωστὶ δαίμονα); 256 (τὸν δαίμον' ἀνθρώποισιν ἐσφέρων νέον); 272 (ὁ δαίμων ὁ νέος); 353–54 (ἐσφέρει νόσον καινήν); and 650 (ἐσφέρεις καινούς). Euripides repeatedly refers to Dionysus himself as ξένος, 'stranger' (*Bacchae* 233, 253, 441, 453, 642, 800, 1063, 1068, and 1077). For Nestle's discussion of Paul's 'kicking against the goads', see 'Anklänge', pp. 231–33.

11 *Bacchae* 32–38 and 217–20.

12 *Bacchae* 215–41, 434–40, 497.

13 Acts 9.2 and 22.4.

14 *Bacchae* 605–606: 'Are you so struck with fear that you fell to the earth (πρὸς πέδῳ πεπτώκατ')?' Compare Pentheus's falling to earth with Acts 9.4: πεσὼν ἐπὶ τὴν γῆν, 22.7: ἔπεσά εἰς τὸ ἔδαφος, and 26.14: καταπεσόντων εἰς τὴν γῆν.

15 Jesus and Dionysus are similar in other respects. See Martin Hengel, 'The Dionysian Messiah', in *idem*, *Studies in Early Christology* (Edinburgh: T. & T. Clark, 1995), pp. 293–331.

16 According to Euripides, the only Theban men who worshiped Dionysus were Tiresias and Cadmus (*Bacchae* 195–96).

17 *Bacchae* 298–301.

Paul did the opposite: he drove the possessed girl sane. Paul, like Dionysus, ended up in prison because of the girl. Her hostile owners hauled him and Silas off to the authorities, claiming that 'these men are disturbing our city; they are Jews and are advocating customs that are not lawful for us as Romans to adopt or observe'.[18] This charge resembles Pentheus's complaint that Dionysus had introduced disturbing, barbaric practices in Hellas.[19] In both books, without a formal trial, hostile men incarcerated the messengers of the new god, binding them in chains in the darkest regions of the prisons.[20]

Neither prison held its captive for long thanks to an earthquake. In Euripides, Dionysus called from the prison: 'Shake (σεῖε) the floor of the world, sovereign Spirit of Earthquake!'[21] A quake then shook the palace to rubble, freeing the god from his chains (δεσμίοισιν).[22] According to Acts, 'About midnight Paul and Silas were praying and singing hymns to God, and the prisoners were listening to them. Suddenly there was an earthquake (σεισμός), so violent that the foundations of the prison were shaken; and immediately all the doors (θύραι) were opened and everyone's chains (δεσμά) were unfastened.'[23]

The earthquake woke the Philippian jailer and he 'saw the prison doors wide open', so 'he drew his sword and was about to kill himself, since he supposed that the prisoners had escaped (ἐκπεφενγέναι)'.[24] The response of Pentheus to the earthquake in Thebes likewise was to draw his sword, not to kill himself but to kill Dionysus, whom he feared had escaped (πεφευγόντος).[25] The god created a phantom of himself, at which Pentheus lunged to no avail. Dionysus then totally collapsed the building, so that Pentheus fainted, dropping his sword.[26] Regaining his composure, the king came forth from the rubble, convinced that the prisoner had escaped (διαπέφευγε).[27] Instead, he found the god waiting for him, ready to tranquilize him.[28] Dionysus reassured Pentheus that he would stay and not flee (οὐ φευξούμεθα).[29]

The sword of the Philippian jailer, too, went unused. 'Paul shouted in a loud voice, "Do not harm yourself, for we are all here." '[30] After the jailer had convinced himself that all the prisoners were still there, he brought everyone out of the prison and

---

18. Acts 16.20–21.
19. *Bacchae passim*; e.g. 215–62. See especially 481–84 and 778–79.
20. Cf. *Bacchae* 498 (εἰρκταῖσί τ' ἔνδον σῶμα σὸν φυλάξομεν; 'We will guard your body inside the prison') and Acts 16.24 (εἰς τὴν ἐσωτέραν φυλακήν; 'into the innermost prison'). See also *Bacchae* 509–11, 549, 610.
21. *Bacchae* 585.
22. *Bacchae* 586–93 and 615; cf. 616–19.
23. Acts 16.25–26. This passage also resembles an earlier prison escape in the *Bacchae*, when Dionysus freed his incarcerated Maenads (443–48). Particularly noteworthy are lines 447–48: 'Of themselves (αὐτόματα) the bonds (δεσμά) were loosed from their feet and the bolts unlocked the doors (θύρετρ') without a mortal hand.' See also Acts 12.7 ('the chains fell off his hands') and 12.10 ('It [the iron gate] opened for them of its own accord [αὐτομάτη]').
24. Acts 16.27.
25. *Bacchae* 627–28.
26. *Bacchae* 633–35.
27. *Bacchae* 642–43.
28. *Bacchae* 644–47.
29. *Bacchae* 659.
30. Acts 16.28. Notice the use of the first-person plural by individuals both in *Bacchae* 659 and Acts 16.28.

asked, 'Sirs, what must I do to be saved?' Paul and Silas told him to believe 'on the Lord Jesus'. Whereas Pentheus continued to rage against Dionysus, the Philippian jailer believed in Paul's God.

The parallels between the two stories are too dense and sequential to be accidental. Luke consciously modeled this story after Euripides' play. Luke's story also retains distinctive features from Euripides that further bind the two stories together. The most obvious of these is Luke's near quotation of *Bacchae* 794–95, the statement concerning the goads. Prison breaks were popular type-scenes in ancient fiction,[31] but the prison breaks of Dionysus and Paul share unusual details that set them apart: incarcerations by men because of raving women, earthquakes opening the doors and loosening the chains, refusals to flee, drawn but unused swords, and discussions with jailers about religion.

Furthermore, Luke's indebtedness to Euripides would explain peculiarities in his account, such as the place of prayer exclusively for women outside the city, which corresponds to Euripides' worshiping women in the wild. Even more impressive is the ability of this reading of Acts to account for Luke's detailed description of Lydia from Lydia. The coincidence of her name and the name of her home region could be coincidental, but it also might suggest that Luke wished to emphasize the woman's connections with Lydia.[32]

According to Euripides, Lydia was the cult center of Dionysus; when Pentheus questioned the god about his place of origin, he replied, 'Lydia is my fatherland.'[33] More relevant to Luke's Lydia is Euripides' chorus comprised exclusively women who had accompanied the god from that very region. Dionysus addressed them as 'women who had left [Mount] Tmolus, bulwark of Lydia, throng of women, whom I carried away from barbarians as companions at rest and march'.[34] Some worshipers of the god in the Hellenistic period referred to themselves as Λυδαί, 'Lydian women'.[35] Furthermore, like Euripides' Maenads who worshiped the god in the hills outside Thebes, Lydia and her sisters worshiped their god at a river outside Philippi.

The other distinction of Luke's Lydia is her profession as 'a seller of purple cloth (πορφυρόπωλις)'.[36] As one might expect, the god of wine was intimately related to the color purple. One of his most celebrated depictions appears in *Homeric Hymn* 7, where he is described as wearing 'a purple cloak (πορφύρεον)'.[37] A certain Callixinus of Rhodes regaled Alexandrians under the rule of Ptolemy Philadephus (c. third century BCE) with the description of a Dionysiac parade). Many of the participants wore purple,[38] as did the two statues of the deity himself. '[I]n this [cart]

---

31 Richard I. Pervo, *Profit with Delight: The Literary Genre of the Acts of the Apostles* (Philadelphia: Fortress Press, 1987), pp. 18–24.

32 The word Lydia appears nowhere else in Luke's writings, or in the New Testament, for that matter.

33 *Bacchae* 464. See also 13, 140, and 234.

34 *Bacchae* 55–57.

35 Athenaeus, *Deipnosophists* 5.198e.

36 Acts 16.14.

37 *Homeric Hymn* 7 (to Dionysus), line 6.

38 According to Athenaeus, the procession included Sileni 'dressed in purple *chlamyses* (πορφυρᾶς χλαμύδας)' (*Deipnosophists* 5.197e), 120 boys 'in purple tunics (ἐν χιτῶσιν πορφυροῖς)' (197f), Satyrs with bodies smeared in purple (ὀστρείῳ), and two more Sileni 'in purple *chlamys* (πορφυραῖς χλαμύσι)' (198a).

stood a statue of Dionysus, fifteen feet tall, pouring a libation from a gold goblet, and wearing a purple tunic (χιτῶνα πορφυροῦν) extending to the feet, over which was a transparent saffron coat; but round his shoulders was thrown a purple mantle (ἱμάτιον πορφυροῦν) spangled with gold.'[39] 'In another cart, which contained "the return of Dionysus from India," there was a Dionysus measuring eighteen feet who reclined upon an elephant's back, clad in a purple coat (πορφυρίδα) and wearing a gold crown .... This cart was followed by five hundred young girls dressed in purple tunics (χιτῶσι πορφυροῖς) with golden girdles.'[40] One must use this evidence from Callixinus with caution: he obviously exaggerated the extravagance of the occasion, but even allowing for hyperbole, this passage surely attests to an association between the god of wine and purple clothing.[41]

Insofar as every detail about Lydia in Acts points to her as a Christian Maenad, it would appear that by making the first convert in Europe a woman from Lydia, named Lydia, a seller of purple garments, Luke broadcast the similarities between Paul's mission to Greece and that of Dionysus. The parallels between the *Bacchae* and Paul's adventures in Philippi are intentional, indeed strategic.

If Luke's readers detected this antecedent, they might well have compared Paul positively against Dionysus. Whereas Dionysus sent women into dangerous frenzies, Paul exorcised the mantic slave girl. Whereas Dionysus's earthquake resulted in Pentheus's even more adamant unbelief and ultimate destruction (along with the anguish of his mother Agave and his grandfather Cadmus), Paul's earthquake resulted in the salvation of the Philippian jailer 'and his household'.[42]

If the argument here is correct, it provides a warning to feminist biblical interpreters. Insofar as women are largely absent from early Christian sources, one understandably may lament the migration of women in this story from history to fiction. But they are larger in fiction than they ever could be in history, because they represent what the author and probably some of his readers understood to be their symbolic significance as Maenads in a Christian mode. Lydia is not a wild woman in the hills in raving ecstasy. The mantic slave girl, exploited by her male owners, returns to her senses. Many Greeks and Romans considered Dionysian worship objectionable because of its irrationality, and Luke precludes such criticisms of Christian women by portraying Lydia and her sisters as altogether noble, sane, and faithful.

---

39 Athenaeus, *Deipnosophists* 5.198c.
40 Athenaeus, *Deipnosophists* 5.20d.
41 Nonnus's massive epic, *Dionysiaca*, recasts Euripides' play in Books 44–46. Here again the god is related to Lydia and purple (e.g. 44.135; 45.18; and 46.109 and 123).
42 Acts 16.31.

ELITE WOMEN, PUBLIC RELIGION, AND CHRISTIAN PROPAGANDA IN ACTS 16*

SHELLY MATTHEWS

The argument that in Hellenistic and early Roman society men uniformly viewed women's participation in 'foreign' cults as subversive often functions as an apologia for the church's reining in of its female members. As this line of argument goes, it was pagan pressure, usually coupled with the 'rabbinic' insistence on women's subordination, that *forced* Christians both to remove women from the public sphere of religion and to insist upon their obedience to husbands and ecclesial (male) elders. But good theology cannot be based on bad history, and this apologia is bad history. Not only did some Christian groups contemporaneous with the restrictive measures proposed in the Pastoral Epistles and 1 Peter foster women's leadership—'Jezebel' of Thyatira (Rev. 2.20–23) is one example; Syntyche and Euodia of Philippi are two others—had Christians wanted to (continue to) privilege women's participation in and leadership of their communities, they could have pointed to pagan precedent attested in narrative as well as archaeological sources.

The Acts of the Apostles does acknowledge the influential role of elite, or at least economically secure women, as church benefactors. But the narrative also recollects another topos, often overlooked, in order both to justify and to domesticate such women. The stories in Acts 16.11–40 of Lydia, the 'god-fearing' businesswoman from Thyatira, and the unnamed mantic slave girl whom Paul encounters in Philippi, draw on the motif of elite women as mediators between the religious movement and the larger culture. Further, like the conjoined presentation in Josephus's *Antiquities* 18 of the elite, proper Fulvia and the contemptible freedwoman Ida, Acts demonstrates that members of the new religious movement are socially respectable. Indeed, Luke's obedient, accommodating Lydia, from Thyatira, is the counterpart both to Revelation's 'heretical' 'Jezebel' and to the two women whom Paul addresses in Philippians.

Acts, the Bacchae, *Sexual Immorality, and State Subversion*

Complete with valiant prisoners singing hymns in jail, the miraculous loosening of chains subsequent to an earthquake, the conversion of the jailor, and the legal vindication of the missionaries newly arrived in Philippi, Acts 16.19–40 is an exemplary instance of a type of Hellenistic religious propaganda, the divinely effected prison escape.[1] The scene is so closely patterned on the escape of Dionysos in Euripides'

---

* Reprinted from Shelly Matthews, *First Converts: Rich Pagan Women and the Rhetoric of Mission in Early Judaism and Christianity* (Contraversions: Jews and Other Differences; Stanford: Stanford University Press, 2001). Used by permission.

1 The classic discussion of the prison escape as a topos of Hellenistic religious propaganda is O. Weinreich, 'Gebet und Wunder', in Friedrich Focke, *et al.* (eds.), *Genethliakon: Wilhelm Schmid zum siebzigstend Geburstag* (Tübingen Beiträge zur Altertumswissenschaft, 5; Stuttgart:

Bacchae that Otto Weinreich argued that the redactor of Acts was directly dependent on this classic Athenian drama.[2] Lilian Portefaix then broadened the discussion of the links between the Philippian mission according to Acts and the Dionysos tradition by noting that not only the incarceration proper but also the prefatory scene, Acts 16.11–18, resonates with the missionary pattern of the *Bacchae*.[3]

Identifying Acts 16.11–18 as conforming to a pattern of missionary activity such as that presented by Euripides helps to clarify one of the exegetical puzzles in the narrative of Paul's Philippian mission. Typically in Acts, the synagogue visit is integrally connected to Paul's entry *into* a city and preaching to 'the Jews'.[4] But in 16.11–15, Paul and his companions travel *outside* of the city to search for a synagogue on the Sabbath. They do find a meeting place, designated with the term προσευχή[5] rather than the typically Lukan συναγωγή. Moreover, those congregated are not said to be 'Jews and God-fearers' or 'Jews and Greeks', but 'women': 'On the Sabbath day we went outside the gate by the river, where we supposed there was a synagogue, and we sat down and spoke to the women who had gathered there' (τῇ τε ἡμέρᾳ τῶν σαββάτων ἐξήλθομεν ἔξω τῆς πύλης παρὰ ποταμὸν οὗ ἐνομίζομεν προσευχὴν εἶναι, καὶ καθίσαντες ἐλαλοῦμεν ταῖς συνελθούσαις γυναιξίν). Also, according to Acts (although unmentioned in Paul's own epistle to the Philippians), the first convert in Philippi is Lydia, a woman originally from Thyatira who, as a dealer in purple, is apparently of some means.[6]

The visit to the 'synagogue of women' and the conversion of Lydia resonate with Dionysiac propagandistic themes. In Euripides' *Bacchae* the prophet/god of the Dionysos cult claims Lydia in Asia Minor as his homeland and travels to Europe to spread his religion; on his missionary journey he is not just accompanied by but also supported by Lydian women. Although the play centers around the persecution of Dionysos at Pentheus's hands, and the ultimate vindication of Dionysos, the story is

---

Kohlhammer, 1929), pp. 200–462. See also W. Nestle, 'Anklänge an Euripides in der Apostelgeschichte', *Philologus* 13 (1900), pp. 46–57; and for a more recent discussion, Richard I. Pervo, *Profit with Delight: The Literary Genre of the Acts of the Apostles* (Philadelphia: Fortress Press, 1987), pp. 18–24.

2 Weinreich, 'Gebet und Wunder', pp. 309–41, esp. 332–41. Pervo (*Profit with Delight*, p. 21) does not argue for textual dependence but speaks more generally of the Dionysos tradition as the 'apparent home' of this type.

3 Lilian Portefaix, *Sisters Rejoice: Paul's Letter to the Philippians and Luke–Acts as Seen by First-Century Philippian Women* (ConBNT, 20; Stockholm: Almqvist & Wiksell International, 1988), pp. 169–71.

4 Cf. 13.14–16; 14.1; 17.1–2, 10; 18.4, 19; 19.8.

5 I will generally translate προσευχή in Acts 16.13 as 'synagogue', a well-attested meaning for the term. See Bernadette Brooten, *Women Leaders in the Ancient Synagogue: Inscriptional Evidence and Background Issues* (BJS, 36; Atlanta: Scholars Press, 1982), pp. 139–40; Ivoni Richter Reimer, *Women in the Acts of the Apostles: A Feminist Liberation Perspective* (trans. Linda M. Maloney; Minneapolis: Fortress Press, 1995), pp. 78–92. A primary reason that scholars question whether the προσευχή in Acts 16 is really a synagogue is because only women appear to be in attendance (cf. BAG, s.v. προσευχή: 'Esp. used among Jews, this word is nearly always equivalent to συναγωγή ... But many consider that the προσευχή in Acts 16.13, 16 was not a regular synagogue because it was attended only by women ... and because the word συναγωγή is frequently used elsewhere in Acts').

6 For my argument that Lydia is best understood as a Gentile God-fearer, rather than a Jew, see my *First Converts*, p. 59. For argument about Lydia's status, see below, pp. 124–27.

prefaced by Dionysos's encounter with Theban women upon whom he imposes a maenadic trance. In Acts 16, Paul, the missionary of the new religion, travels from Asia Minor to Philippi, a major city in Macedonia. He meets fierce resistance within the city: he is dragged before authorities, attacked by the crowd, flogged by magistrates, thrown in prison, and, with feet bound in stocks, is secured within the 'innermost cell' (16:19–24). But before Paul encounters the male officials in the city, he brings his message to the women gathered in the προσευχή outside the city gate. His first convert there is a woman from Thyatira, a city in Lydia, who bears 'Lydia' as a personal name. Both stories, then, center on the (negative) reception of the new religion by important male officials of the locality. This dramatic center is prefaced by the new religion's initial reception by women.[7]

Such parallels would be more tantalizing if one could argue for direct dependence of Luke on the *Bacchae*, as did Weinreich.[8] Without going so far as to suggest Luke had a copy of the *Bacchae* before him, I do posit that the basic pattern of the play was widely known and therefore available to Luke.[9] That the Dionysos cult and the Jewish and Christian cults were frequently conflated provides additional support for this conclusion.[10]

Richard Pervo classifies the pattern—common to the *Bacchae*, several passages in Acts—as well as the Apocryphal Acts—as 'mission aretalogy' and outlines it as follows: '(1) Missionaries of a new god appear; (2) they achieve success (usually

---

7 My outline of parallels differs somewhat from that offered by Portefaix, *Sisters Rejoice*, p. 170.

8 Weinrich, 'Gebet und Wunder', pp. 326–41, points to verbal idiosyncrasies and literary motifs in Acts that he felt were best explained by such a connection. One of his more compelling arguments is the association between the prison escapes and the *Bacchae* made by 'Celsus's Jew' in Origen's *Contra Celsum* 2.34. The Jew quotes from the play a line spoken by the imprisoned Bacchus: 'The god himself will free me, whenever I wish' (*Bacchae* 498), and then asks why Jesus could not do the same. Origen responds that his God could, and did, free the imprisoned Peter (Acts 12.6–9) as well as the imprisoned Paul and Silas (Acts 16.24–26).

9 Indications of the *Bacchae*'s popularity include a papyrus fragment from Oxyrhynchus preserving the opening lines of the play as a school exercise (Roger A. Pack, *Greek and Latin Literary Texts from Greco-Roman Egypt* [Ann Arbor: University of Michigan Press, 2nd edn, 1965], p. 40); a reference in Lucian to an uneducated person (ἀπαίδευτος) reading the *Bacchae* (*The Ignorant Book Collector* 19); Plutarch's *Crassus* 33.1–4, which speaks of a performance of the *Bacchae* at a banquet at which the audience is presumed to know the story's plot; references in Artemidoros to people dreaming of slave women and poor people reciting passages from Euripides (4.59) as well as to people dreaming of Dionysiac figures belonging to the *Bacchae* (4.39). See also the passage in *Contra Celsum* cited in n. 8. Portefaix (*Sisters Rejoice*, pp. 98–114) argues that women in Philippi would have known the *Bacchae* because of the enduring popularity of Euripides in the region and the mythic associations of Dionysos with the neighboring Mt Pangaion. For indications of the general popularity of Euripides in the Roman era, see Lucian, *Quomodo Historia Conscribenda Sit* 1; Dio Chrysostom, *Discourses* 18.6.7; the discussion in Louis H. Feldman, *Josephus's Interpretation of the Bible* (Hellenistic Culture and Society, 27; Berkeley: University of California Press, 1998), p. 175 n. 20; P.E. Easterling, 'From Repertoire to Canon', in *idem* (ed.), *The Cambridge Companion to Greek Tragedy* (Cambridge: Cambridge University Press, 1997), pp. 211–27, esp. 225.

10 See especially the dialogue in Plutarch's *Quaest. conv.* 671C–672C and the commentary in Menachem Stern, *Greek and Latin Authors on Jews and Judaism* (3 vols.; Jerusalem: Academy of Sciences and Humanities, 1974–84), II, pp. 558–62. On confusion of Dionysian and Christian practice, see Robert Wilken, *The Christians as the Romans Saw Them* (New Haven, CT: Yale University Press, 1984), p. 17.

with women, foreigners, slaves, or some other less "respectable" group); (3) The establishment is jealous, and opposition develops; (4) That leads to persecution and punishment (arrests, martyrdoms, suits, etc.); (5) The mission is vindicated by what believers see as a miracle; (6) There follow the defeat and punishment of the opponents, possibly ending with their conversion'.[11] However, when this pattern is assessed in relation to Acts 16, modification of element 2, the initial encounter of the missionaries with the 'less respectable' group, is required. Lydia, the one who represents the women who are part of Paul's first missionary encounter in Philippi, is depicted as a woman of high standing.[12]

The motif of missionaries who encounter women also appears in Josephus's recounting of the conversion of the royal house of Adiabene (*Ant.* 20). Although Josephus's narrative lacks several of the aretalogical elements present in Acts 16 and the *Bacchae*, the connections among the three in terms of gender depictions are striking. While the narrative focuses on the conversion to Judaism of King Izates, Josephus begins by carefully noting the missionary's initial contact with royal women:

> Now during the time when Izates resided in Charax Spasini, a certain Jewish merchant named Ananias visited the king's wives and taught them to worship God after the manner of the Jewish tradition ['Ιουδαῖός τις ἔμπορος . . . πρὸς τὰς γυναῖκας εἰσιὼν τοῦ βασιλέως ἐδίδασκεν αὐτὰς τὸν θεὸν σέβειν, ὡς 'Ιουδαίοις πάτριον ἦν]. It was through their agency [καὶ δὴ δι᾽ αὐτῶν] that he was brought to the notice of Izates, whom he similarly won over with the cooperation of the women[13] (*Ant.* 20.34–35).

Such thematic parallels among the *Bacchae*, Acts, and *Antiquities*—and especially their notable attention to women—prompt consideration of how gender functions both in polemics against and in support for Dionysiac rites. As Dionysos worship evolves from ancient Greece to imperial Rome, women's cultic function also changes. Most notably, the ecstatic rites of groups made up exclusively of women give way to more somber ceremonies involving men as well.[14] But despite the multiform and evolving nature of Dionysos rites, a polemical topos concerning women's involvement varies little from the time of Aristophanes to that of Tacitus. Throughout the Hellenistic and Roman periods, elite writers stereotyped practitioners of 'foreign rites' as primarily women involved in sexual immorality that subverted state order.

In the *Bacchae*, Pentheus, king of Thebes, is chief spokesman for this common prejudice:

---

11 Pervo, *Profit with Delight*, p. 19. For his expanded definition of aretalogy as encompassing not only hymns but also 'various literary media and structures employed for proclaiming the virtues of a god or divine figure', see p. 146 n. 11.

12 On Lydia's status, see my argument below, pp. 124–27.

13 For discussion of the story of the Royal Family of Adiabene as a historical 'novel', see Lawrence Wills, *The Jewish Novel in the Ancient World* (Myth and Poetics; Ithaca, NY: Cornell University Press, 1995), pp. 206–11.

14 Ross Shepard Kraemer, *Her Share of the Blessings: Women's Religions Among Pagans, Jews, and Christians in the Greco-Roman World* (Oxford: Oxford University Press, 1992), pp. 36–49. See also the conclusions of Albert Henrichs, 'Greek Maenadism from Olympias to Messalina', *HSCP* 82 (1978), pp.121–60.

I happened to be traveling outside this land
But now I hear of strange and vile deeds in this city —
That our women have gone forth from their homes,
Feigning Bacchic rapture, darting among the thickly wooded hills,
Honoring with their dances this new god Dionysos, whoever he is;
That the wine-bowls stand in the middle of each *thiasos* full to the brim,
And that one by one they go
Crouching in the wilderness to serve the lechery of men.
While they profess to be Maenads making sacrifice,
They honor Aphrodite more than Bacchus[15] (*Bacchae* 215–25).

Livy appropriates this topos in his depiction of the Bacchanalia in Rome in 186 BCE.[16] Cicero even more explicitly identifies Dionysos worship as emblematic of the orgiastic revelry that subverts the Roman state. As precedent for the legislation prohibiting the participation of women in nocturnal cults in his *Leg.* 2.35–37, he first cites the Senate action against the Bacchanalia of 186: 'The strictness of our ancestors in matters of this character is shown by the ancient decree of the Senate with respect to the Bacchanalia, and the investigation and punishment conducted by the consuls and with the assistance of a specially enrolled military force' (*Quo in genere severitatem maiorum senatus vetus auctoritas de Bacchanalibus et consulum exercitu adhibito quaestio animadversioque declarat*). As further precedent, he reminds his dialogue partner that in one of the plays of Aristophanes, Sabazios, a god often confused with Dionysos and who also required nightly vigils by women, is banished from the state.[17]

To these depictions of the Dionysos cult as the locus of sexual immorality and subversion can be added Tacitus's early second-century description of the empress Messalina's Bacchic 'garden party'. This description follows immediately upon his narration of Messalina's divorce of the emperor Claudius and traitorous marriage to Silius. Tacitus underscores her treason by referring to her Bacchic revelry:

> But Messalina had never given voluptuousness a freer reign [*At Messalina non alias solutior luxu*]. It was the height of autumn and she was celebrating a mimic vintage throughout the household. Presses were being trodden, vats flowed, while women girded in skins were bounding like Bacchanals excited by sacrifice or delirium. She herself was there with flowing hair and waving thyrsus; and next to her, Silius with an ivy crown, wearing the buskins and tossing his head, while around him rose the din of a wanton chorus[18] (*Ann.* 11.31.2).

---

15 See also *Bacchae* 233ff., 260, 352.
16 See Livy, *Hist.* 39.8–18, esp. 39.5.9.
17 The Sabazios incident in question may have been contained in the no-longer-extant play by Aristophanes, *Horae*. See E.R. Dodds, 'Introduction', in *Euripides' Bacchae* (Oxford: Clarendon Press, 2nd edn, 1960), p. xxiv. On the close correlation between the rites of Dionysos and Sabazios, see Ross Shepard Kraemer, 'Ecstasy and Possession: The Attraction of Women to the Cult of Dionysus', *HTR* 72 (1979), pp. 55–80, esp. 61–63.
18 While Henrichs ('Greek Maenadism', pp. 156–59) cautions that Tacitus's account is an 'inseparable blend of fact and fiction', he does assume that the assignment to Messalina of a flair for Bacchic ostentation is correct. For the difficulties in reconstructing imperial women's history from anything Tacitus says, see Sandra R. Joshel, 'Female Desire and the Discourse of Empire: Tacitus's Messalina', *Signs* 21.1 (1995), pp. 50–82.

Although these texts imply that women's involvement in Dionysos rites was a primary cause for suspicion of the cult, disapproval of women's worship was not unvarying. This condemnation contended with the view that women's participation in this cult—even in its nocturnal, ecstatic rites—was proper. Indications of this alternative perception surface throughout the period in a variety of literary forms.

The Bacchae
Although Pentheus articulates a common prejudice concerning women's involvement in maenadic worship, he is not a hero in the *Bacchae*; he is, rather, a *theomachos*, one who foolishly resists the god; this folly causes the downfall of his house.[19] Pentheus's charges equating Bacchic worship with sexual promiscuity prove unsubstantiated: they are deflected by the prophet Teiresias (314–18) as well as by Dionysos himself (485–88), and they are refuted most fully by the herdsman who reports to Pentheus that he has spied the maenads at rest in the high pastures:

> [They lay on the ground] modestly [σωφρόνως], not—as you say—drunk with wine and flute-music, hunting for love in the solitary woods ... They were a sight to marvel at for good order [εὐκοσμία];[20] women both old and young, girls still unmarried (686–88, 693–94).

Pentheus does indeed make a conventional assessment of the nature of Bacchic worship. No sharper modifier could be used to refute his view, however, than σωφρόνως, a word difficult to translate, but encompassing self-control, deference, modesty, and—above all for women—chastity. The *Bacchae* challenges viewers to reconsider standard distinctions between established religions and new, 'foreign' cults. Euripides' paradoxical portrait of maenads as chaste and well ordered is constituent of that challenge.[21]

The Senatus consultum de Bacchanalibus
Although both Livy and Cicero employ the familiar topos of women/foreign religion/sexual misconduct to justify the repression of the Bacchanalia in 186 BCE another source detailing the repression of Dionysiac worship in Rome, the so-called *Senatus consultum de Bacchanalibus* (*ILS* 18), suggests that women's cultic involvement was not intrinsically problematic. The decree does set severe restrictions on Dionysiac worship, but it does not bar women from participation. To the contrary, the decree permits women, but not men, to become priests of Bacchus. Furthermore, it allows for women to outnumber men in the small congregations

---

19 Pentheus is notorious in antiquity for his impiety. See Horace, *Odes* 2.19.14–15; Pausanius, *Description of Greece* 2.2.7; Diodorus Siculus, *Bibliotheca historica* 4.3.4.
20 On the meaning of this term here, see Barbara K. Gold, εὐκοσμία in Euripides' Bacchae', *AJP* 98 (1977), pp. 3–15.
21 For further discussions of gender in the *Bacchae*, see Helene P. Foley, 'The Conception of Women in Athenian Drama', in *idem* (ed.), *Reflections of Women in Antiquity* (New York: Gordon & Breach, 1981), pp.127–68, esp.142–45; and Froma I. Zeitlin, 'Cultic Models of the Female: Rites of Dionysos and Demeter', *Arethusa* 15 (1982), pp. 129–57. See also H.S. Versnel, *Inconsistencies in Greek and Roman Religion,* 1 (Studies in Greek and Roman Religion, 6; Leiden: Brill, 1990), I, pp. 156–205.

organized around Bacchic worship.[22] These provisions prompted Albert Henrichs to conclude that for Roman authorities, Bacchic rites were primarily 'women's business'.[23]

Cicero's De legibus

Cicero's proposed prohibition of sacrifice by women at night (*Leg.* 2.21) and his dialogue concerning this prohibition (*Leg.* 2.35–37) are often cited to prove the unfavorable view of women's involvement in 'foreign' religions. Although Cicero himself clearly holds this view, the structure of his dialogue with Atticus indicates his awareness that his proposed universal law will not meet with universal acceptance. He begins by questioning whether Atticus can accede to his proposed legislation, 'In regard to what follows, I am wondering, Titus, how you can agree with me or how I can attack your position' (*At vero quod sequitur quo modo aut tu adsentiare aut ego reprehendam sane quaero, Tite*). Atticus responds that he does accede since the law is not without exception: 'But I am in agreement with you, especially as the law itself makes an exception of the customary public sacrifice' (*Ego vero adsentior, excepto praesertim in ipsa lege sollemni sacrificio ac publico*). Cicero presses further, suggesting that his regulation could be detrimental to the widespread and impressive rites of Dionysos and the Eleusinian mysteries, since he is making legislation 'not for the Roman people in particular, but for all virtuous and stable nations' (*non enim populo Romano, sed omnibus bonis firmisque populis leges damus*). Again Atticus responds by assuming that Cicero will make further exceptions: 'I take it for granted that you make an exception of those rites into which we ourselves have been initiated' (*Excipis, credo, illa, quibus ipsi initiati sumus*). After first agreeing that such an exception would be granted and then praising the divine mysteries, Cicero explains that his general objection to nocturnal rites is due to the potential licentiousness they could inspire among the Roman people. Atticus meets this objection by suggesting a further exception: 'Very well, then; propose such a law for Rome, but do not deprive us of our customs' (*Tu vero istam Romae legem rogato; nobis nostras ne ademeris*). Cicero concedes: 'I will then return to our own enactments' (*Ad nostra igitur revertor*).

This is the only place in his treatise, otherwise concerned with laws for the ideal state, where Cicero limits the application of a law specifically to Rome. Further, anticipating that some will still find the legislation too harsh, he supports it by citing Greek legal precedent, '*That we may not possibly seem too severe*, I may cite the fact that in the very center of Greece, by a law enacted by Diagondas of Thebes, all nocturnal rites were abolished for ever' (*atque omnia nocturna, ne nos duriores forte*

---

22 *CIL* 1.581, lines 10, 19–20, 'No man shall be a priest of, nor shall any man or woman be master of such an organization ... No one in company of more than five persons altogether, men and women, shall perform such rites; nor in that company shall more than two men or three women be present, unless it is in accordance with the opinion of the urban praetor and the Senate ...' (trans. Mary R. Lefkowitz and Maureen B. Fant [eds.], *Women's Life in Greece and Rome: A Sourcebook in Translation* [Baltimore, MD: Johns Hopkins University Press, 2nd edn, 1992], p. 275).

23 Henrichs, 'Greek Maenadism', p. 135. David L. Balch, *Let Wives Be Submissive: The Domestic Code in I Peter* (SBLMS, 26; Atlanta: Scholars Press, 1981), p. 69, does not consider this inscription when he concludes that 'the main problem [with the Dionysos cult in Rome] was that Roman women joined the cult'.

videamur, in media graecia Diagondas Thebanus lege perpetua sustulit) (my emphasis).

When this passage is read as indicating Cicero's apprehension concerning the acceptability of his proposed legislation restricting women's involvement in nocturnal rites, it cannot be held up as an unqualified demonstration that 'the fear of women misbehaving with men at nocturnal wine-feasts of some god must be described as general or typical'.[24] Cicero is aware that his proposal to restrict women's involvement in such rites would be contested by many of his Roman peers and especially by educated readers outside the capital.

Philo

The notion that the association of women, nontraditional gods, nocturnal rites, and ecstatic practices was always perceived negatively in antiquity is called into question also by Philo's remarkable description in his *On the Contemplative Life* of the Therapeutics. The treatise extols the community of celibate men (Therapeutae) and women (Therapeutrides) living outside of Alexandria as the preeminent example of virtuous contemplative life. Although the literary and religious purposes of this treatise are complex and frequently debated, scholars do agree that Philo aims to portray the Therapeutics favorably.[25]

A close reading of the treatise describing the vigil celebrated on the feast of Pentecost clearly counters the conventional understanding of the Bacchic rites as socially subversive.

> After the supper they hold the sacred vigil which is conducted in the following way. They rise up all together and standing in the middle of the refectory form themselves first into two choirs, one of men and one of women ... Then they sing hymns to God ... and brimming with enthusiasm reproduce sometimes the lyrics of the procession, sometimes of the halt and of the wheeling and counter-wheeling of a choric dance. Then when each choir has separately done its own part in the feast, having drunk as in the Bacchic rites of the strong wine of God's love, they mix and both together become a single choir [καθάπερ ἐν ταῖς βακχείαις ἀκράτου σπάσαντες τοῦ θεοφιλοῦς, ἀναμίγνυνται καὶ γίνονται χορὸς εἷς ἐξ ἀμφοῖς], a copy of the choir set up of old beside the Red Sea in honor of the wonders worked there (*Vita Cont.* 83–85).

To be sure, this is metaphorical language. Philo's 'mixing' is a blending of voices in song, not of bodies in sexual union. The metaphors would exemplify for a Pentheus, or Livy, or Cicero the depravity of ecstatic, Bacchic worship: a nocturnal vigil, dancing, 'drunkenness', the mixing of male and female. For Philo, however, the Therapeutic vigil is paradigmatic of the virtuous life:

> Utterly good/beautiful [πάγκαλα] are the thoughts; utterly good/beautiful [πάγκαλα] are the words; worthy of reverence are the choristers, and the end and aim of thoughts, words and choristers alike is piety [εὐσέβεια]. Thus they continue until dawn, drunk with this honorable drunkenness [τὴν καλὴν ταύτην μέθην] (*Vita Cont.* 88).

24 This is Balch's argument, *Let Wives Be Submissive*, p. 66.
25 See, for example, David M. Hay, 'Things Philo Did and Did Not Say about the Therapeutae', SBLSP (1992), pp. 673–93, esp. 677; Ross Shepard Kraemer, 'Monastic Jewish Women in Greco-Roman Egypt: Philo on the Therapeutrides', *Signs* 14.1 (1989), pp. 342–70.

By characterizing the nocturnal mixing of Therapeutae and Therapeutrides with the phrases 'most excellent/beautiful' (πάγκαλα), 'piety' (εὐσέβεια), and 'honorable drunkenness' (καλὴ μέθη),[26] Philo takes the anti-Bacchanalian tradition and turns it on its head. Hans Lewy has suggested that in *On the Contemplative Life* the honorable drunkenness (καλὴ μέθη) of the Therapeutics serves as a paradoxical contrast to the wicked drunkenness (κακὴ μέθη) of those who attend Greek symposia, for before turning to the Therapeutics Philo speaks at length about the depravity of the Greeks at table.[27] Although this contrast is certainly operative, it is not a sufficient explanation for Philo's elaborate and favorable description of the nocturnal mixing of the sexes. He could have argued for the superiority of the Therapeutics over Greek dining practices without resorting to metaphors of ecstatic Bacchic practice. Moreover, Philo did not need to provide an account of men and women 'mixing' at night in order to be true to the Scriptures he interprets. He speaks of the celebration of the fifty-day feast as modeled on the biblical celebration following the parting of the Red Sea. But Exodus 15 does not mention a 'single choir'. Rather, it tells first of Moses leading the singing of the 'Israelites' and then of Miriam leading the singing women. At no point does the biblical account speak of the choir of Moses joining together with the choir of Miriam. Philo's use of this Bacchanalian imagery suggests he does not view it as damaging to his apologetic aims. He seems, instead, to be working within a tradition that views these practices as virtuous.[28]

Plutarch
Approval of women's participation in Dionysiac worship is also apparent in Plutarch's references to maenadic practice.[29] His treatise *Mulierum virtutes* is

26 Philo frequently employs the paradoxical phrase 'sober drunkenness' (μέθη νηφάλιος). See *On Drunkenness* 145–46; *On Flight and Finding* 31, 166; *Special Laws* 1.82–83; *That Every Good Person is Free* 12–13; *On the Creation of the World* 70; *Moses* 1.187. For discussion, see Hans Lewy, *Sobria Ebrietas: Untersuchungen zur Geschichte der Antiken Mystik* (Geissen: Töpelmann, 1929), esp. pp. 3–41. On Philo's taxonomies of ecstasy, see Laura Nasrallah, *An Ecstasy of Folly: Prophecy and Authority in Early Christianity* (HTS, 52; Cambridge, MA: Harvard University Press, 2003). That Philo is stressing the virtue of the Therapeutics here is apparent in his shift from the typical pairing, sober/drunken, to virtuous/drunken.

27 Lewy, *Sobria Ebrietas*, pp. 31–34.

28 Plato, for example, speaks of Dionysian frenzy as a blessing (*Phaedrus* 244B). For discussion, see Ivan M. Linforth, 'The Corybantic Rites in Plato', *University of California Publications in Classical Philology* 13.5 (1946), pp. 121–62; idem, 'Telestic Madness in Plato, *Phaedrus* 244DE', *University of California Publications in Classical Philology* 13.6 (1946), pp. 163–72. See also Sze-Kar Wan, 'Charismatic Exegesis: Philo and Paul Compared', *Studia Philonica* 6 (1994), pp. 54–82. That Philo is working with Platonic ideas here is evident from his descriptions of the two choirs dissolving finally into 'one choir'. The Platonic ideal of the dissolution of male and female into oneness informs many discussions of Gal. 3.28. See, for example, Dennis Ronald MacDonald, *There Is No Male and Female: The Fate of a Dominical Saying in Paul and Gnosticism* (HDR, 20; Philadelphia: Fortress Press, 1987). For discussions of Gal. 3.28 in relation to Philo's Therapeutics, see Daniel Boyarin, *A Radical Jew: Paul and the Politics of Identity* (Contraversions, 1; Berkeley: University of California Press, 1994), pp. 188–89; and idem, 'Paul and the Genealogy of Gender', in A.-J. Levine (ed.), *A Feminist Companion to Paul* (FCNT, 6; London: T. & T. Clark, 2004), pp. 13–41.

29 In addition to passages discussed here, see also *Mulierum virtutes* 251–53; *De primo frigido* 953C, and *Quaestiones romanae et graecae* 293C–F.

dedicated to Clea, one of his highly educated women friends and the priestess of Osiris at Delphi, whom he acknowledges in another work as 'the leader of the Delphic maenads' (ἀρχηίδα ἐν Δελφοῖς τῶν Θυιάδων) (*De Iside de Osiride* 364E). Plutarch offers no indication that his respect for Clea is somehow mitigated by her holding this office.[30] Furthermore, he singles out an incident involving women's practice of maenadic rites as an exemplary act of women's virtue. In *Mulierum virtutes* 249E–F Plutarch tells the story of maenads who, in Bacchic frenzy, wander into a city under enemy control.[31] When they are found sleeping in the marketplace the next morning, the women of the city first provide for their needs and then secure permission from their husbands to escort them safely from the hostile territory. In Plutarch's telling these nocturnal rites are neither suspicious nor offensive. The vulnerable sleeping women are protected by the women of the city; the men of the city respect their right to safe passage.

Plutarch's well-known and oft-quoted proscription against women's independent religious practice in his *Conjugalia praecepta* 140D, then, stands in tension with his narrative of maenadic rites. His denunciation there of women's 'stealthy and surreptitious rites' is not brought to bear on his sympathetic description of the maenadic practice of wandering off at night in ecstatic trances.[32]

Discussing sexual conduct among Dionysiac worshipers, Albert Henrichs argues that despite the many accusations of sexual licentiousness directed against Dionysos devotees, in reality such practice was not pervasive.[33] In other words, Henrichs proposes (1) a stereotypical propagandist theme that condemned women's participation in the cult on the grounds of sexual impropriety, often coupled with charges of subversion; and (2) a 'historical reality' in which such impropriety cannot be documented on a wide scale. The sources discussed above suggest a third factor: a line of argumentation, apparent in the writings of the elite as well as in popular literary forms, that respected, supported, and even promoted women's prominent role in Dionysiac rites. Philo's easy identification of Bacchic with Therapeutic ecstasy is especially noteworthy, since it indicates Hellenistic Jewish use of Dionysian concepts in apologetic presentation of women's cultic worship.[34] That

---

30 For more on Clea, see Philip A. Stadter, '*Philosophos kai Philandros*: Plutarch's View of Women in the *Moralia* and the *Lives*', in Sarah B. Pomeroy (ed.), *Plutarch's* Advice to the Bride and Groom *and* A Consolation to his Wife (Oxford: Oxford University Press, 1999), pp. 173–82, esp. 173–75.

31 On this passage, see also Henrichs, 'Greek Maenadism', p. 136.

32 This inconsistency can be explained in part by the different focus of each work. In *Conjugalia praecepta*, Plutarch lauds women's private virtue. Only in *Mulierum virtutes* does he consider their public virtue. See Kathleen O'Brien Wicker, '*Mulierum Virtutes* (*Moralia* 242E–263C)', in Hans D. Betz (ed.), *Plutarch's Ethical Writings and Early Christian Literatures* (Leiden: Brill, 1978), pp. 106–34. For another instance of Plutarch's inconsistency on a wife's place, see Sarah B. Pomeroy, 'Reflections on Plutarch, *Advice to the Bride and Groom*', in *idem* (ed.), *Plutarch's* Advice, pp. 33–42.

33 Albert Henrichs, 'Changing Dionysiac Identities', in Ben F. Meyer and E.P. Sanders (eds.), *Jewish and Christian Self-Definition* (3 vols.; Philadelphia, Fortress Press, 1982), III, pp. 137–60, esp. 147–48.

34 A second source interpreting female cultic activity in Judaism by analogy to Bacchic worship is Plutarch's *Quaestionum convivialum*. Here Plutarch offers a speech by the Athenian Moirangenes that links the Dionysos and Jewish cults. For example, Moirangenes notes that in both Jewish and

such a line of argumentation can be identified with respect to Dionysos worship helps to clarify why Josephus and Luke include narratives of high-standing women converts.

Women, Religion, and the Public Life

The identification of two lines of argumentation concerning the function of women in religions that encourage and accept converts—one that views their participation as subversive and one that views it as proper—can be set within the discussion of women's roles within the religious sphere in general. Several texts from antiquity deride not only missionary religions but also religion in general, because it is associated with women. Hence, Ross Kraemer begins her important book on women's religions: 'It was a commonplace in Graeco-Roman antiquity that religion was women's business, and it was not a compliment.'[35] Such a statement requires further nuance. There is high praise in Greek and Roman texts for women's religious activity, along with an understanding that women's public religious function can be exercised positively for the state.

From the *Iliad* on, the importance of women's religious or ritual function receives prominent attention in Greek literature. For example, Homer assigns the role of sacrificing and offering supplications to Hecuba and the other Trojan women (*Iliad* 6.312–65).[36] The women in Aristophanes's *Lysistrata* justify their takeover of the Acropolis by reference to their roles in the city's most important religious cults.[37] The privileged place of women in the religious sphere is articulated most eloquently in Greek literature by Melanippe, the protagonist of Euripides' *Melanippe Captive*:

> [Women] manage the home, and guard within the house the sea-borne wares. No house is clean or prosperous if the wife is absent. And in religion—highest I judge this claim—we play the greatest part. In the oracles of Phoebus, women expound Apollo's will; and at the holy seat of Dodona, beside the sacred oak, woman conveys the will of Zeus to all Greeks who may desire it. As for the holy rites performed for the Fates and the Nameless

---

Dionysian festivals, female 'nurses of the God' take on liturgical roles: '[The Jews] also have noise as an element in their nocturnal festivals, and call the nurses of the god "bronze rattlers"' (ψόφοις δὲ χρῶνται περὶ τὰ νυκτέλια, καὶ χαλκοκρότους τὰς τοῦ θεοῦ τιθήνας προσαγορεύουσιν). Notably, Plutarch does not link female and Jewish Bacchic cultic activity in derision, but rather makes the analogy while drawing a sympathetic portrait of Jewish practice.

35 Kraemer, *Her Share of the Blessings*, p. 3.

36 Consider especially Hector's reply to his mother Hecuba after she exhorts him to make libations to the gods on his return to Troy: 'I'd be ashamed to pour a glistening cup to Zeus with unwashed hands. I'm splattered with blood and filth—how could I pray to the lord of storm and lightning? *No, mother, you are the one to pray*. Go to Athena's shrine ... go with offerings, gather the older noble women and take a robe ... and spread it out across the sleek-haired goddess' knees. Then promise to sacrifice twelve heifers in her shrine ... if only she'll pity Troy ...' (*Iliad* 6.315–25, trans. Robert Fagels, my emphasis).

37 For further discussion of these texts, see Helene P. Foley, 'The Female "Intruder" Reconsidered: Women in Aristophanes' *Lysistrata* and *Ecclesiazusae*', *CP* 77.1 (1982), pp. 1–21; *idem*, 'Conception of Women'; Froma I. Zeitlin, 'The Dynamics of Misogyny: Myth and Mythmaking in the *Oresteia*', *Arethusa* 11.2 (1978), pp. 149–83, esp. 172–73; and Jeffrey Henderson, '*Lysistrate*: The Play and its Themes', *Yale Classical Studies* 26 (1980), pp. 153–218.

Goddesses—they are not holy in the hands of men; among women they flourish all. So righteousness is woman's part in holy service. How then should her kind be fairly abused?[38]

The view that women's public participation in religious practices is for the good of the state appears in Latin texts as well. In the *Aeneid* (2.501–15; 11.477–87), Hecuba and 'her hundred daughters' perform religious duties similar to those assigned them in the *Iliad*. Livy also gives key roles to Roman matrons who offer supplication at critical junctures. For example, he notes that during Hannibal's march on Rome, the women poured into the streets to offer their prayers at altars and temples of the gods (*Hist.* 26.9.7–8).[39] Arguing against the view that women held only peripheral roles in Roman religion, Ariadne Staples has shown that women's participation is essential to several important public rituals and festivals of the Roman civic calendar, including the cults of Bona Dea, Ceres, Flora, and Venus.[40]

The prominence of women in the civic, religious sphere[41] is obfuscated in scholarship that adopts the public/private binary to conceptualize the social roles of men and women in antiquity, without attention to how religious obligations destabilized this binary. These arguments generally posit that since Greco-Roman ideology restricted women to domestic space and reserved public speech and political action for men, Jews and Christians who wanted to conform to standard mores exhorted their women to stay at home.[42] In the case of early Christianity, Karen Jo Torjesen

---

38 D.L. Page (ed.), *Select Papyri* (3 vols.; LCL; Cambridge, MA: Harvard University Press, 1970), III, pp. 113–14.

39 Cf. 22.1.18; 27.37.8–10. For further citation and discussion of Latin texts which privilege women's public religious function, see Alan Wardman, *Religion and Statecraft among the Romans* (Baltimore, MD: Johns Hopkins University Press, 1982), pp. 37–39.

40 Ariadne Staples, *From Good Goddesses to Vestal Virgins: Sex and Category in Roman Religion* (London: Routledge, 1998).

41 For the widely accepted argument that approval of elite Hellenistic women's benefaction owed to the extension of the private sphere into the public, see Riet van Bremen, 'Women and Wealth', in Averil Cameron and Amélie Kuhrt (eds), *Images of Women in Antiquity* (Detroit, MI: Wayne State University Press, 1983), pp. 223–41; idem, *The Limits of Participation: Women and Civic Life in the Greek East in the Hellenistic and Roman Periods* (Amsterdam: Gieben, 1996). On the social innovations of the Roman period that allowed for women's participation in public meals, see Kathleen E. Corley, *Private Women, Public Meals: Social Conflict in the Synoptic Tradition* (Peabody, MA: Hendrickson, 1993). See also Carolyn Osiek, 'The Family in Early Christianity: "Family Values" Revisited', *CBQ* 58.1 (1996), pp.1–24, and Carolyn Osiek and David L. Balch, *Families in the New Testament World: Households and Churches* (The Family, Religion, and Culture Series; Louisville, KY: Westminster/John Knox Press, 1997), pp. 43–47, 54–56. For a useful critique of public/private models in terms of the conceptualization of the family in antiquity, see Miriam Peskowitz, ' "Family/ies" in Antiquity: Evidence from Tannaitic Literature and Roman Galilean Architecture', in Shaye J.D. Cohen (ed.), *The Jewish Family in Antiquity* (BJS, 289; Atlanta: Scholars Press, 1993), pp. 9–36, esp. 24–28. See also the insightful comments on public rhetoric of 'private' life in Kate Cooper, *The Virgin and the Bride: Idealized Womanhood in Late Antiquity* (Cambridge, MA: Harvard University Press, 1996).

42 See, for example, Léonie J. Archer, *Her Price is Beyond Rubies: The Jewish Woman in Graeco-Roman Palestine* (JSOTSup, 60; Sheffield: Sheffield Academic Press, 1990), pp. 85–86, 113–22; Deborah F. Sawyer, *Women and Religion in the First Christian Centuries* (London: Routledge, 1996), pp. 36–40, 76–77; Balch, *Let Wives Be Submissive*, pp. 52–56. See also Jerome Neyrey's rigid adherence to the public/private binary in arguing that the Johannine community defied standard mores ('What's Wrong with This Picture? John 4, Cultural Stereotypes of Women, and Public and Private Space', *BTB* 24.2 [1994], pp. 77–91), reprinted in Amy-Jill Levine (ed.) *A Feminist Companion to John* (2 vols.; FCNT 4–5; London: Sheffield Academic Press, 2003) I, pp. 98–125.

has proposed that women's leadership in religious affairs was tolerated only so long as it was confined to the private sphere, and that as the church moved into public space, women were no longer granted leadership roles.[43] The locus classicus for this understanding of how the public/private dichotomy informed Jewish, and later Christian, thinking is Philo's *Spec. Leg.* 3.169:

> Market places and council-halls and law courts and gatherings and meetings where a large number of people are assembled, and open-air life with full scope for discussion and action—all these are suitable to men both in war and peace. The women are best suited to the indoor life which never strays from the house, within which the middle door is taken by the maidens as their boundary, and the outer door by those who have reached full womanhood [θηλείαις δὲ οἰκουρία καὶ ἡ ἔνδον μονή, παρθένοις μὲν εἴσω κλισιάδων τὴν μέσαυλον ὅρον πεποιημέναις, τελείαις δὲ ἤδη γυναιξὶ τὴν αὔλειον] (*Spec. Leg.* 3.169 [Colson, LCL]).

Philo's articulation of Greco-Roman public/private ideology, however, should not be analyzed in isolation from a subsequent paragraph, which destabilizes the public/private binary:

> A woman, then, should not be a busybody, meddling with matters outside her household concerns, but should seek a life of seclusion. She should not show herself off like a vagrant in the streets before the eyes of other men, except when she has to go to the temple [πλὴν εἰς ἱερὸν ὁπότε δέοι βαδίζειν], and even then she should take pains to go, not when the market is full, but when most people have gone home, and so like a free-born lady worthy of the name [ἐλευθέρας τρόπον καὶ τῷ ὄντι ἀστῆς], with everything quiet around her, make her oblations, and offer her prayers to avert the evil and gain the good (*Spec. Leg.* 3.171 [Colson, LCL]).

This paragraph is intriguing on several counts. The terms 'freeborn' (ἐλευθέρας) and 'female citizen' (ἀστή) used as attributes of 'woman' indicate that Philo's public/private gender ideology pertains only to elite women.[44] References to local temple worship and offering of sacrifices indicate that he is adopting the language of gentile communal worship in Alexandria. The prescriptive nature of this and subsequent paragraphs (172–77) indicates that Philo knows women who are not conforming to the ideology of domestic confinement. Notably, he adopts not only the standard rule concerning elite women's domestic confinement but also the standard exception to the rule. Even a most rigid formulation of the ideology inscribing elite women's seclusion must allow for ventures into public space for performing religious duties.[45]

---

43 Karen Jo Torjesen, *When Women Were Priests: Women's Leadership in the Early Church and the Scandal of their Subordination in the Rise of Christianity* (San Francisco: HarperSanFrancisco, 1993), pp. 126–28.

44 On the connotations of ἀστή in Philo, see Dorothy Sly, *Philo's Perception of Women* (BJS, 209; Atlanta: Scholars Press, 1990), pp. 95–97.

45 Compare Philo's public/private formulation with the treatise attributed to Phintys, a female member of the Pythagorean community in southern Italy (third to second century BCE), which also provides for prominent women to leave the house in order to make sacrifice. Holger Thesleff (ed.), *The Pythagorean Texts of the Hellenistic Period* (Åbo, Finland: Åbo Akademi, 1965), pp. 151–54, esp. 154; and the English translation in Lefkowitz and Fant, *Women's Life*, pp. 163–64.

In light of the privileged place of elite women in the religious sphere as promoted in the texts discussed above, it is fitting that apologists such as Josephus and Luke would construct narratives featuring the initial reception of their religions by women. To do so serves as a gesture of recognition that in Greco-Roman society women were associated with certain public religious festivals and, hence, would provide a bridge between these cults and the larger society. To understand these apologists as appropriating such a motif is not to say that in Acts 16.11–15 or in *Ant.* 20.34–48 the narratives place women at the center of Christianity or Judaism. As with the *Bacchae*, so in Acts and *Antiquities*, the prefatory nature of the material on women's involvement with the new religion is an expression of the marginal nature of their religious experience in the narrative's structure. At the center of all three stories is the resolution of conflict between the male worthies of a locality and the male missionary/god.

The Status of Lydia as a Rhetorical Strategy in Acts

Acts 16.14 introduces Paul's first convert in Philippi as 'a woman named Lydia, a dealer in purple from the city of Thyatira' (γυνὴ ὀνόματι Λυδία, πορφυρόπωλις πόλεως Θυατείρων). The narrative suggests further that Lydia is a householder (16.15, 40). Given Luke's skill at creating symbolic characters, the string of modifiers attached to Lydia's name is clearly intended to import much about who Lydia is. How precisely to interpret these modifiers with respect to Lydia's status is a question of dispute among scholars. The disagreement stems in part from conflicting views concerning the respectability of merchants in antiquity. Clarification on this issue is further hindered by the tendency among scholars to read the narrative as a window onto the 'historical Lydia', without first raising the issue of Luke's rhetorical strategies.

By citing stereotypical views of elite writers who denigrate anyone involved in small-scale trade (for example, Cicero, *De officiis* 1.42), some scholars argue that Lydia should be regarded as a member of a despised profession and hence of low status and with little wealth.[46] Others assert that Lydia, although not from the highest stratum of society, would have been 'somewhat well-to-do'.[47] And still others, pointing to the wealth needed to deal in purple as well as to epigraphic sources indicating that some (male) purple-sellers held prominent civic offices, set Lydia

---

46 This view of trade as 'dirty work' provides the basis for the readings of Schottroff and Richter Reimer discussed below. Richard L. Rohrbaugh also stresses the low status of merchants by arguing that all but the largest-scale traders were outcasts living on the edges or outside of the city (see Richard L. Rohrbaugh, 'The Pre-Industrial City in Luke–Acts: Urban Social Relations', in Jerome H. Neyrey (ed.), *The Social World of Luke–Acts: Models for Interpretation* [Peabody, MA: Hendrickson, 1991], pp. 125–49, esp. 133–37). For a more nuanced view of social and spatial relations between the urban elite and merchants, see Andrew Wallace-Hadrill, 'Ethics and Trade in the Roman Town', in John Rich and Andrew Wallace-Hadrill (eds.), *City and Country in the Ancient World* (London: Routledge, 1991), pp. 241–69.

47 Marianne Palmer Bonz, *The Past as Legacy: Luke–Acts and Ancient Epic* (Minneapolis: Fortress Press, 2000), p. 167. Bonz cites John H. D'Arms, *Commerce and Social Standing in Ancient Rome* (Cambridge, MA: Harvard University Press, 1981), who argues that the freedman Trimalchio from Petronius's *Satyricon* serves as the fictional paradigm for the quasi-elite.

among the 'urban elite'.[48] Lydia's name is often taken as indicating her freedwoman status, since slaves and freedpersons often bore names reflecting their geographical origin,[49] although there are both first- and second-century inscriptions describing socially elite women also named Lydia.[50]

It is difficult to ascertain Lydia's status primarily on the basis of four words: Λυδία, πορφυρόπωλις, πόλεως Θυατείρων. Drawing from their study of the social history of the dye professions, feminist scholars Luise Schottroff and Ivoni Richter Reimer argue that Lydia should be understood as a member of a despised profession, of humble status and modest means. From this understanding, they produce liberationist readings in which Lydia epitomizes the 'last who became first', and the household that she heads signifies a 'contrast society' (*Gegengesellschaft*) within a Roman colony.[51] Although Schottroff and, more extensively, Richter Reimer provide a valuable social history of the manufacture of dye, their arguments that trade in purple necessarily involved work in manufacturing are less compelling. Furthermore, readings that foreground Lydia's lowliness ignore Luke's rhetorical strategies concerning class and status. They also gloss over the rather troubling question of the relationship of Lydia's own conversion to the conversion of 'her house' (ὁ οἶκος αὐτῆς), language that could suggest the forced conversion of slaves.[52]

A dominant theme of Luke–Acts is that those in the 'center' of Jewish society reject the message of Jesus, and those on the 'margins' respond favorably to it. Marginal and thus favored groups in the Third Gospel include tax collectors, sinners, and the poorest of the poor. In Acts, however, a major shift occurs in depictions of those who are 'marginal' and hence the true recipients of divine grace. The 'outsiders' who are brought in are no longer the poorest of the poor, but the gentiles.[53] Many of these gentiles hold explicitly prominent social status, including the Ethiopian chamberlain (8.26–40), Cornelius, a centurion (10.1–48), the proconsul Sergius Paulus (13.7–12), the women of high standing in Thessalonica (17.4), the leading men and women of Beroea (17.12), and Dionysius the Areopagite (17.33). Moreover, Asiarchs and Roman governors, even though they do not convert

---

48 David W.J. Gill, 'Acts and the Urban Elites', in David W.J. Gill and Conrad Gempf (eds.), *The Book of Acts in its First Century Setting*. II. *The Book of Acts in its Graeco-Roman Setting* (Grand Rapids: Eerdmans, 1994), pp. 105–18, esp. 114–17. Gill builds on the work of H.W. Pleket, 'Urban Elites and Business in the Greek Part of the Roman Empire', in P. Garnsey, *et al.* (eds.), *Trade in the Ancient Economy* (London: Chatto & Windus, 1983), pp. 131–44, esp. 141–43.

49 G.H.R. Horsley, *New Documents Illustrating Early Christianity* (7 vols.; North Ryde, New South Wales, Australia: Ancient History Documentary Research Centre, Macquarie University, 1981–94), II, p. 27; Wayne A. Meeks, *The First Urban Christians: The Social World of the Apostle Paul* (New Haven, CT: Yale University Press, 1983), p. 203 n. 93.

50 From Sardis comes the well-placed Julia Lydia, and from Ephesus, Julia Lydia Laterane. See discussion in Gill, 'Acts and the Urban Elites', p. 114.

51 Luise Schottroff, 'Lydia: A New Quality of Power', in *idem*, *Let the Oppressed Go Free: Feminist Perspectives on the New Testament* (trans. Annemarie S. Kidder; Louisville, KY: Westminster/John Knox Press, 1993), pp. 131–37; Reimer, *Women in the Acts of the Apostles*, pp. 98–130.

52 See discussion of Jennifer A. Glancy, *Slavery in Early Christianity* (Oxford: Oxford University Press, 2002), pp. 46–47.

53 See Jack T. Sanders, *The Jews in Luke–Acts* (Philadelphia: Fortress Press, 1987), pp. 132–53.

to Christianity, protect its emissaries. The shift in emphasis from *les misérables* in the Third Gospel to the social elite is the primary reason for Richard Pervo's wry observation: 'One would be somewhat hard-pressed to illustrate the Sermon on the Plain (Lk. 6.20–49) by reference to Acts.'[54] In light of this narrative strategy in which the designation 'marginal, yet saved' is transferred from the poor of the Gospels to the (well-placed) gentiles of Acts, it is not convincing to argue that Lydia's conversion vindicates the 'poorest of the poor'. Indeed, those who undoubtedly are of this low status, namely, the mantic slave girl (16.16–18) and the prisoners in the Philippian jail (16.25–34), are not recipients of salvation. As Yann Redalié notes:

> [The slave girl] is introduced only in order to demonstrate the power of the apostle... Paul enters into a relationship with her only when his patience has been exceeded, and he heals her only in order to get rid of her... The same goes for the prisoners. Freed by the miraculous earthquake, they remain in prison so that the jailer may be converted. The power of God is expressed by Luke not in order to deliver the powerless prisoners, but to convert the officer.[55]

Although elite readers like Cicero or Pliny would have despised someone like Lydia because of her involvement in a trading profession, they would have held the hero of the story, Paul, in at least as much contempt. Despite his many high status markers in Acts, Paul is nevertheless involved in the lowly craft of tent-making. That characters involved in trade could be portrayed as having more respectability than Cicero or Pliny would grant them makes sense for an audience that includes neither a Cicero nor a Pliny. Luke's audience is more appropriately identified as a group with some wealth and education, in which persons of low status but (relatively) high income were included.[56] Such an audience would view characters involved in trade, who had also achieved a measure of respectability, as mirroring their own social and economic aspirations. Lydia's status markers—a dealer in purple who is also a householder—thus position her among the ranks of this same 'quasi-elite' class.

In addition to being a merchant of purple from Thyatira, Lydia is also designated as 'God-fearing' (σεβομένη τὸν θεόν, 16.14). Thus, she may be understood as the Cornelius of the European phase of Paul's ministry. Like Cornelius, the archetypal godfearer, she converts to Christianity and subsequently extends hospitality to the one who has baptized her (cf. 16.15 and 10.48). But such a comparison requires

---

54 Mikeal C. Parsons and Richard I. Pervo, *Rethinking the Unity of Luke and Acts* (Minneapolis: Fortress Press, 1993), p. 39. Richard J. Cassidy, *Society and Politics in the Acts of the Apostles* (Maryknoll, NY: Orbis Press, 1987), pp. 57–59, glosses over this shift in tone in part by arguing that in its affirmation of 'women', Acts still shows concern for the 'less regarded groups'. This argument ignores the high status of many women in Acts. Pervo argues that Luke's focus on the elite is best understood as 'propagandistic fiction' rather than mere apologetics: 'The upward mobility of many new religions encourages fictional propaganda about their adherents' social status' (*Profit with Delight*, p. 79).

55 Yann Redalié, 'Conversion ou libération? Notes sur Actes 16, 11–40', *Bulletin du centre protestant d'études* 26.7 (1974), pp. 6–17, esp. 12.

56 On the presentation of class in Acts, see Pervo, *Profit with Delight*, p. 79, as well as his insightful comments on 'rich' Christians of the late first and early second centuries in *idem*, 'Wisdom and Power', *ATR* 67 (1985), pp. 307–25.

qualification, since one crucial element of the Cornelius episode is displaced in the story of Lydia.

The issue of table fellowship with a gentile is central to Peter's baptism of Cornelius, as evident in the twice-narrated vision of unclean animals that Peter is commanded to eat (10.9–16; 11.5–10). The hospitality that Cornelius extends includes table fellowship, as indicated by the question the 'circumcised' address to Peter in 11.3: 'Why do you go to the uncircumcised men and eat with them?' (εἰσῆλθες πρὸς ἄνδρας ἀκροβυστίαν ἔχοντας καὶ συνέφαγες αὐτοῖς). According to Esler, the issue of table fellowship is of such concern in Acts that Paul's 'going to the gentiles' can be understood primarily as his public establishment of table fellowship between Jew and gentile.[57]

Lydia's invitation to Paul to stay in her house may be read as an implicit extension of table fellowship from a gentile to a Jew.[58] Luke explicitly narrates a story of a common meal shared by Jew and gentile in Philippi, however, only after Paul baptizes the jailor. 'Bringing them into his house, the jailor set food before them. He and his entire household rejoiced that he had become a believer' [ἀναγαγών τε αὐτοὺς εἰς τὸν οἶκον παρέθηκεν τράπεζαν καὶ ἠγαλλιάσατο πανοικεὶ πεπιστευκὼς τῷ θεῷ]' (Acts 16.34). Luke reserves the acknowledgment of Jewish–gentile table fellowship in Philippi until after the (male) jailor is baptized. This coincides with the avoidance of narratives of women at public tables in his Gospel.[59] His hesitancy to acknowledge meal sharing between Paul and a gentile woman may help to account for the inclusion of this second conversion narrative of the jailor in his story of the Christian community in Philippi.[60] Lydia is the first convert, but she is not the first (explicitly) to share a table with Paul.

The Mantic Slave Girl's Religious Allegiance

The first words of the brief narrative of the mantic slave girl, 'and it happened as we were preceding to the synagogue', Ἐγένετο δὲ πορευομένων ἡμῶν εἰς τὴν προσευχήν, (Acts 16.16), link it to the story of Paul's encounter with Lydia in the προσευχή of women (16.13) and so establish a contrast between the status and demeanor of female Christian convert and female pagan missionary. Paul and his companion receive hospitality from the well-to-do purple merchant; they are harassed by a slave girl (παιδίσκη) The range of meaning for παιδίσκη extends from young female, to servant, to slave, to prostitute.[61] In light of the context, in which the παιδίσκη is controlled by her owners (κύριοι), the girl is undoubtedly a

---

57 Philip Francis Esler, *Community and Gospel in Luke–Acts* (SNTSMS, 57; Cambridge: Cambridge University Press, 1987), pp. 93–109.
58 So Esler, *Community and Gospel*, pp. 99–100. For my argument that Lydia is gentile, see *First Converts*, p. 59.
59 Corley, *Private Women*, pp. 108–46.
60 Gottfried Schille, *Die Apostelgeschichte des Lukas* (THKNT, 5; Berlin: Evangelische Verlagsanstalt, 1983), pp. 340–49, proposes an alternative reason for the double foundation story in Philippi, namely, that since one story must be superfluous, the account of Lydia's conversion must be understood as a secondary addition to the conversion of the jailor, the original foundation story.
61 LSJ, s.v., παιδίσκη.

slave. The report that she earns money for her masters by her performance on the city streets indicates that her work is not clearly differentiated from prostitution.[62]

The narrative creates a contrast to Luke's depiction of Christian women prophets. Although the Pentecost narrative includes Joel's promise that both sons and daughters will prophesy and that the Spirit will fall even upon male and female slaves (τοὺς δούλους καὶ τὰς δούλας, 2.17–18), the only Christian women Acts describes as prophesying (προφητεύω) are Philip's virgin daughters in Caesarea (21.9). Later reports indicate that Christians in Asia Minor held these four daughters in high regard (cf. Eusebius, *Ecc. Hist.* 3.31), but Acts devotes only one verse to them and records none of their prophecies.[63] The only inspired woman's speech Acts records is that of the παιδίσκη who stands outside the Church and whose words are said to be mantic rather than prophetic.[64]

The narrative has several verbal connections to the exorcism stories of the Synoptics, but this is not a typical exorcism.[65] The slave girl is not depicted as physically tormented by the possessing spirit (cf. Lk. 8.29), no crowd witnesses in astonishment the miraculous event, and no one proclaims it (cf. Mk 1.27, 45; 5.14–17; Lk. 8.35–39).[66] Although Jesus characteristically heals on his first encounter with an unclean spirit, Paul exorcises the slave girl only after becoming annoyed by her continued utterance over the course of several days. Rather than affirming her as healed, Luke makes no further mention of the slave girl after the spirit departs (cf. Lk. 8.35–39). Uncharacteristically not only for Luke but for the entire Synoptic tradition, the possessing spirit here is not designated as unclean (πνεῦμα ἀκάθαρτον) or demonic (πνεῦμα πονηρόν).[67] Instead, the slave girl is said to have a 'Pythonian spirit' (πνεῦμα πύθωνα). Finally, unlike the possessed in the Synoptics, the slave girl is said to earn large sums of money for her owners through her prophesying (μαντεύομαι).

---

62 On the sexual availability of slaves, see now Glancy, *Slavery in Early Christianity*.

63 François Bovon reads 21.8–9 as suggesting the strength of the Christian community in Caesarea and its independence from Paul; see his 'Der Heilige Geist, die Kirche und die menschlichen Beziehungen nach Apostelgeschichte 20, 36–21, 16', in his *Lukas in neuer Sicht* (Biblisch-Theologische Studien, 8; Neukirchen–Vluyn: Neukirchener Verlag, 1985), pp. 181–204.

64 For an important discussion of women prophets in Acts, see Turid Karlsen Seim, *The Double Message: Patterns of Gender in Luke–Acts* (Studies of the New Testament and its World; Edinburgh: T. & T. Clark, 1994), pp. 164–84; I do disagree with her argument, p. 174, that gender plays no explicit role in Acts 16.16–18. See also Mary Rose D'Angelo, 'Women in Luke–Acts: A Redactional View', *JBL* 109 (1990), pp. 441–61, esp. 451–53, who argues, as I do, that Luke distances women from prophetic roles.

65 For example, the narrative incorporates the word ὑπαντάω, a verb commonly used to describe the meeting of the exorcist and the possessed; ἀνακράζω, associated with the possessing spirit's cry; and ἐξέρχομαι, associated with the exorcist's command. Further, like the demons in the Synoptics who proclaim publicly the true identity of Jesus of Nazareth, the spirit in the girl utters a recognition oracle on meeting Paul. There are especially close connections between this story and the report of the exorcism of the Gerasene demoniac in Lk. 8.26–39, because both share all of the verbal parallels mentioned above, and in both cases the possessed is a gentile who uses the epithet 'Most High God' (θεός ὕψιστος) in the recognition oracle. Robert Tannehill, *The Narrative Unity of Luke–Acts: A Literary Interpretation* (2 vols.; Minneapolis: Fortress Press, 1990), II, p. 197.

66 For discussion of this story in relation to Synoptic exorcisms, see Reimer, *Women in the Acts of the Apostles*, pp. 154–74, esp. 171–74.

67 Cf., for example, Mk 1.23; 3.11; 5.2; Mt. 8.32; 17.18; Lk. 7.21; 8.2; Acts 8.7; 19.13.

Both πνεῦμα πύθωνα and μαντεύομαι are *hapax legomena* in the New Testament. Ivoni Richter Reimer argues convincingly that the word cluster πνεῦμα πύθωνα and μαντεύομαι evokes associations with the Pythian priestess of Apollo at Delphi.[68] Πύθων is the name of the serpent guarding the Delphic oracle who is slain by Apollo. Although Plutarch states that the word came to designate a ventriloquist,[69] the initial association of the word with Delphic prophecy remained.[70] The girl is not called a 'ventriloquist' πύθων herself, but is rather said to have a πνεῦμα πύθωνα. This designation is consistent with the broad tradition that the odor of the snake's decomposed body inspires the Pythia.[71] Synonyms for the Pythia include μάντις and πρόμαντις, and μαντεύομαι is the verb frequently associated with her oracular utterances.[72] In view of these associations, Acts 16.16 presents, as Werner de Boor argues, a Pythia in miniature.[73]

In this reading, πνεῦμα πύθωνα indicates the slave girl's cultic allegiance, and Acts 16.18 thus represents a religious competition in which Paul's deity prevails over Apollo, the god of the slave girl. The mantic slave is best understood not as someone tormented by evil spirits along the lines of the possessed in the Gospels but as a prophet/missionary of the greatest of the oracular gods, yet one who is compelled to identify Paul and his companion as 'slaves of the Most High God' (θεός ὕψιστος). That Luke reports how her owners profit from her prophecies also suggests missionary competition.[74] Charges that missionaries are hucksters motivated by financial gain are conventional features of invective against religious movements.[75]

Luke's depiction of the only female who speaks prophetically as a παιδίσκη whose source of inspiration is the πνεῦμα πύθωνα lies on a trajectory of Christian criticism of female religious functionaries of Apollo articulated most fully in extant

---

68 Reimer, *Women in the Acts of the Apostles*, pp. 154–56.

69 Plutarch, *De defectu oraculorum* 414E. Cf. Hans Conzelmann, *Acts of the Apostles: A Commentary on the Acts of the Apostles* (ed. E.J. Epp and C.R. Matthews; trans. J. Limburg, A.T. Kraabel, and D.H. Juel; Hermeneia; Philadelphia: Fortress Press, 1987), p.131.

70 *Pace* Werner Foerster, 'πύθων', in *TDNT*, VI, pp. 917–20.

71 Pierre Amandry, *La mantique apollinienne à Delphes: Essai sur le fonctionnement de l'oracle*, Bibliothèque des écoles français d'Athènes et de Rome (Paris: Boccard, 1950), p. 65.

72 Wolfgang Fauth, 'Pythia', *PW*, XXIV, pp. 515–48, esp. 516–17.

73 Werner de Boor, *Die Apostelgeschichte* (Wuppertaler Studienbibel; Wuppertal: Brockhaus, 1965), p. 298 n. 364; see also Otto Bauernfeind, *Kommentar und Studien zur Apostelgeschichte* (WUNT, 22; Tübingen: Mohr, 1980), pp. 208–209.

74 Because of the way it varies from the traditional exorcism account and the manner in which Paul triumphs over the rival spirit, Pervo rightly notes the story's entertainment value (*Profit with Delight*, p. 63). Scholars who do not appreciate the humor can construct elaborate theories to explain Paul's rationale for the exorcism. See, for example, Paul R. Trebilco, 'Paul and Silas—"Servants of the Most High God"' (Acts 16.16–18)' *JSNT* 36 (1989), pp. 51–73.

75 The critique of religious practice motivated by profit occurs in Acts 19 as well as 16.16–18. For additional examples of such accusation, see Lucian's *Alexander the False Prophet*; the depiction of the female religious functionary Oenothea in Petronius's *Satyricon* 134–38; Juvenal's begging Jewish woman, *Sat.* 6.543–47; and the discussion of Dieter Georgi, *The Opponents of Paul in Second Corinthians* (Philadelphia, PA: Fortress Press, 1986), pp. 98–101; Paul's attempts to distance himself from popular philosophers who seek monetary gain (1 Thess. 2), and the discussion of Abraham J. Malherbe, ' "Gentle as a Nurse", the Cynic Background to I Thessalonians 2', *NovT* 12 (1970), pp. 203–17, reprinted in his *Paul and the Pagan Philosophers* (Minneapolis: Fortress Press, 1989), pp. 35–48.

literature by Origen (*Contra Celsum* 3.25; 7.3–7). Origen derides Delphic prophecy by noting that the Pythian priestess receives the prophetic spirit through her womb (*Contra Celsum* 3.25; 7.3). Chrysostom articulates the same criticism:

> This same Pythoness then is said, being a female, to sit at times upon the tripod of Apollo astride, and thus an evil spirit ascending from beneath and entering the lower part of her body, fills the woman with madness, and she with disheveled hair begins to play the bacchanal and to foam at the mouth, and thus being in a frenzy to utter the words of her madness. (*Homilae in epistulam i ad Corinthios* 29.2).[76]

Origen and Chrysostom show nothing but contempt for the notion, attested much earlier, that sacred intercourse with Apollo is the source of the Pythia's inspiration.[77] If this hostile evaluation of Pythian inspiration was shared by Luke's readers, they would find a slave girl possessed by a πνεῦμα πύθωνα especially unseemly.

But even if πνεῦμα πύθωνα were not read in this way, Origen's more general criticism of Delphic religion still illuminates the propagandistic function of Luke's story:

> If the Delphic Apollo were a god, as the Greeks imagine, shouldn't he have chosen as his prophet some wise man or, if such a man could not be found, at least one who had made progress in that direction? And why did he not prefer to prophesy through a man rather than a woman? If, however, he even preferred the female ... shouldn't he have chosen a virgin rather than a married woman to prophesy his will? In fact, the Pythian Apollo admired by the Greeks did not deem any wise man, or indeed any man at all, to be worthy of what the Greeks take to be divine inspiration. And from the female sex he did not choose a virgin or a wise person who had been helped by philosophy, but some vulgar woman [Ἀλλ᾽ οὐδ᾽ ἐν τῷ θήλει γένει παρθένον τινὰ ἢ σοφὴν καὶ ἀπὸ φιλοσοφίας ὠφελημένην ἀλλά τινα γυναῖκα ἰδιῶτιν] (*Contra Celsum* 7.5–6).

Origen's critique is at one with Luke's. Unlike the prophecies of Paul's God, which are delivered in Acts solely by men, the prophets of the Pythian Apollo, both in Luke's time and in Origen's, are women. In Acts, this Pythian prophet is depicted not only as a woman, but as a slave girl παιδίσκη, far removed from acceptable categories for women prophets—that is, virgins and educated women.[78]

From Rhetorical Analysis to Historical Situation

The stories of Philippian women engaged in religious activities in Acts 16 are part of a larger group of literary sources indicating women's prominence among

---

76 John Chrysostom, 'Homilies on the Epistles of Paul to the Corinthians', in Philip Schaff (trans. and ed.), *A Select Library of the Nicene and Post-Nicene Fathers of the Christian Church* (14 vols.; Grand Rapids: Eerdmans, 1982), XII, p. 170.

77 See Herodotus, *Hist.* 1.182; Strabo, *Geographica* 9.3.5; and the discussions of Arthur Bernard Cook, *Zeus: A Study in Ancient Religion* (1914–40; reprint, 3 vols. in 2, New York: Biblo & Tannen, 1965), II, pp. 207–10; and Herman Kleinknecht, 'πνεῦμα, πνευματικός', *TDNT*, VI (1968), pp. 332–451, esp. 345–46.

78 Origen, *Contra Celsum*, translated into French by Marcel Borret, *Sources chrétiennes*, nos. 132, 136, 147, 150, 227 (5 vols.; Paris: Editions du Cerf, 1967–76), III, p. 26.

Christians at Philippi.⁷⁹ These include Paul's exhortations concerning Euodiaand Syntyche in his letter to the Philippians (4.2–3), Polycarp's exhortation in his *Letter to the Philippians* concerning women's celibacy and discretion (4.1–3), and a fragment from the *Acts of Paul* that speaks of a female Christian martyr named Frontina in Philippi.⁸⁰

Since Acts is the only source for Lydia, it is difficult to make the case that she is herself a historical figure rather than Luke's creation. Factors weighing against her historicity include Paul's own letter to the Philippian congregation, in which he addresses several members by name, but does not acknowledge Lydia.⁸¹ Supporting this argument from silence, I read the symbolic richness of Lydia's name as a further indication that she is a fictional character.⁸²

This is not to say that Luke invented Lydia because he did not know of women who were prominent in the early Philippian church. It may be that Luke knows all too well that women were leaders in the congregation there, especially the two named in Phil. 4.2–3. On the basis of her rhetorical analysis of Philippians, Cynthia Kittredge argues convincingly that these two women held leadership positions independent of Paul, and that Paul's conflict with them is an important aspect of the situation his letter addresses.⁸³ Acts can be read, then, as substituting the narrative of a female convert generously accommodating the Pauline mission for a more conflictual account of Paul's relations with Philippi's female leadership.⁸⁴ Such a reading coincides with Luke's aim to portray the early church as unencumbered by conflict.⁸⁵

Although Luke's positioning of the mission's base in Lydia's household in Philippi may not reflect actual history, this is not to say that women did not host house churches. Paul's letters reveal that they did.⁸⁶ What is most suspect in Acts'

---

79 Valerie Abrahamsen, 'Women at Philippi: The Pagan and Christian Evidence', *JFSR* 3.2 (1987), pp. 17–30; Portefaix, *Sisters Rejoice*, pp. 169–73.

80 Edgar Hennecke, *New Testament Apocrypha* (ed. Wilhelm Schneemelcher; 2 vols.; Philadelphia: Westminster Press, 1964), II, pp. 373–78.

81 Compare 1 Cor. 16.15, where Paul acknowledges the household of Stephanus as the first converts of Achaia.

82 As Marianne Bonz notes, Lydia's 'felicitious combinations of name, occupation, and place of origin suggest that Luke is presenting the reader with a fictional character ... A felicitious combination in the sense that Lydia is the name of a region of western Asia Minor, fabled for its wealth ever since the days of its sixth century B.C.E. king Croesus. Thyatira is a city within the region of Lydia that was famous for its purple dye industry' (*Past as Legacy,* p. 137). For my argument that Stephen is also a fictional character in Acts, see 'The Need for the Stoning of Stephen', in E. Leigh Gibson and Shelly Matthews (eds.), *Violence in the New Testament* (T. & T. Clark, 2005).

83 Cynthia Briggs Kittredge, *Community and Authority: The Rhetoric of Obedience in the Pauline Tradition* (HTS, 45; Harrisburg, PA: Trinity Press International, 1998), pp. 105–108.

84 My reading coincides with that of Valerie Abrahamsen, 'Women at Philippi and Paul's Philippian Correspondence' (paper delivered at the SBL Annual Meeting, 1987), cited in Reimer, *Women in the Acts of the Apostles*, p. 128. Reimer herself dismisses the possibility that Lydia could be Luke's creation.

85 Consider, for example, the conformity of the speeches of Peter, Stephen, and Paul, and see Helmut Koester, *Introduction to the New Testament* (2 vols.; New York and Berlin: De Gruyter, 1982), II, pp. 318–23. On the rhetorical aims of Acts, see now Christopher Mount, *Pauline Christianity: Luke–Acts and the Legacy of Paul* (NovTSup, 54; Leiden: Brill, 2002).

depiction of Lydia is not the suggestion that such a woman could have hosted an assembly in her house, but rather her portrayal only as a convert accommodating Paul and his mission, and not as a missionary/leader in her own right.[87]

While the mantic slave girl is not portrayed as a member of the Christian community, her story also indicates the tensions concerning the status and roles of women in the early church. Josephus responds to charges that the Jews attract men and women from the lower classes by deflecting those charges onto the devotees of Isis. He does so by contrasting the status and demeanor of Fulvia, the Roman matron of senatorial rank and a convert to Judaism, with that of Ida, the cunning, immoral freedwoman whom he places at the heart of Rome's Isis scandal.[88] A similar deflection occurs through Luke's juxtaposition of Lydia and the mantic slave girl. Lydia is a well-to-do Christian convert and patroness who extends hospitality to the missionaries. The enslaved female missionary/prophet openly proclaiming her message on public streets has no place in Luke's church, but only in an inferior religious practice until she is ultimately defeated and discarded.

When the accounts of Tacitus and Suetonius are read against Josephus's description of the expulsion of the Jews in Rome, one finds indications that, despite Josephus's refusal to say so, members of the lower classes were attracted to Judaism in significant numbers. A similar confusion emerges from reading Luke's apologetic narrative against the famous letter of his near-contemporary, Pliny, to Trajan concerning Christians in Bithynia (*Ep.* 10.96). Although no female slave takes on a leadership role in Acts, Pliny recounts how he found it necessary to torture two female slaves who were deacons of the Christian congregation, for information concerning the cult (*'Quo magis necessarium credidi ex duabus ancillis, quae minstrae dicebantur, quid esset veri et per tormenta quaerere'* [10.96.8]). Here is an indication that slave women took on prominent roles in the early church in Asia Minor, in spite of their absence in Acts.

---

86 For example, the mention of Apphia in Phlm. 2; Prisca in 1 Cor. 16.19 and Rom. 16.3; Nympha in Col. 4.15, and discussion in E. Schüssler Fiorenza, *In Memory of Her: A Feminist Theological Reconstruction of Christian Origins* (New York: Crossroad, 1983), pp. 175–84. While Lydia may be fictional, the mention of Prisca by both Paul and Luke (Acts 18) suggests that Luke knows of her prominence in the early tradition.

87 On the leadership role the host of a house church was expected to hold, see 3 Jn 9–10 and the reading of these verses by Abraham J. Malherbe, 'Hospitality and Inhospitality in the Church', in idem, *Social Aspects of Early Christianity* (Philadelphia: Fortress Press, 2nd edn, 1983), pp. 92–112; originally published as 'The Inhospitality of Diotrephes', in Jacob Jervell and Wayne A. Meeks (eds.), *God's Christ and his People: Studies in Honor of Nils Alstrup Dahl* (Oslo: Universitetsforlaget, 1977), pp. 222–32. Reading Luke's depiction of Lydia as reflecting her active leadership in Philippi, Richter Reimer stresses the report in 16.15 that she 'prevailed upon' (παραβι-άζομαι) the missionaries to stay in her home (*Women in the Acts of the Apostles*, pp. 117–25) and suggests that given Roman disapproval of Jewish missionary activity in Philippi, Lydia thereby put herself at risk. Luise Schottroff makes a similar argument (*Lydia's Impatient Sisters: A Feminist Social History of Early Christianity* [trans. B. and M. Rumscheidt; Louisville, KY: Westminster/John Knox Press, 1995], pp. 109–11) as does Wolfgang Stegemann, *Zwischen Synagoge und Obrigkeit: Zur historischen Situation der lukanischen Christen* (FRLANT, 152; Göttingen: Vandenhoeck & Ruprecht, 1991), pp. 213–14.

88 For discussion, see Matthews, *First Converts*, pp. 21–28.

Finally, Luke gives just one verse to the prophesying daughters of Philip and attributes the only inspired speech of a female character to the mantic slave girl. Thus distancing Christian women from prophecy, Acts belies the historical importance of women prophets to the early church. Eusebius's preservation of two sources about Philip's daughters in his *Ecclesiastical History* (3.31) suggests that they were long revered in Asia Minor.[89] Another text that may be brought to bear on the displacement of female prophetic speech onto the missionary of a defeated religion is Rev. 2.20–23. Here the author of the Apocalypse derides a female prophet in Thyatira as 'Jezebel'. The rhetorical strategies of these two authors differ greatly. Acts, which does not wish to portray conflict among Christians, suggests that 'unseemly' women's prophecy is a problem only for other religious cults. Revelation, which makes no secret of intra-sectarian disputes, vilifies a woman prophet by encoding her as a fornicating Jezebel.[90] Both sources suggest exalted, if disputed, roles for women prophets in the early church at the turn of the first century CE.

The depictions of Lydia and the slave girl in Acts are in line with Luke's rhetorical strategy of presenting a history of Christian origins in which a reader who identifies with 'most excellent Theophilus' may find 'surety' (ἀσφάλεια).[91] The Christian Lydia is respectable and deferential; the female speaking 'prophet' and sexual threat belongs to a defeated religion. Although the stories are not liberatory when taken at face value, the task of a feminist commentator is not to take such texts at face value. It is, rather, to read them against the grain in order to reconstruct the counter discourse that Luke's ideologically driven apologetic history is attempting to mask.

---

89 Eusebius's sources are somewhat contradictory. One, a letter of Polycrates, speaks of Philip, 'who sleeps at Hierapolis with his two daughters who grew old as virgins and his third daughter who lived in the Holy Spirit and rests in Ephesus'. The other, a dialogue of Gaius and Proclus, says that all four daughters rest at Hierapolis with their father.

90 For discussion, see Elisabeth Schüssler Fiorenza, *Revelation: Vision of a Just World* (Proclamation Commentaries; Minneapolis: Fortress Press, 1991), pp. 132–35.

91 For discussion of how depictions of women change from Luke to Acts, see Seim, *Double Message*, pp. 249–60.

WOMEN OF 'THE CLOTH' IN ACTS: SEWING THE WORD

F. SCOTT SPENCER

HOW TO CURSE A TREACHEROUS VILLAIN: Witness David's fivefold declamation of the house of Joab after the latter's vengeful murder of the diplomatic Abner:

> May the house of Joab never be
> without one who has a discharge,
> or who is leprous,
> or who holds a spindle,
> or who falls by the sword,
> or who lacks food! (2 Sam. 3.29)

At the heart of this ominous list of disasters, flanked by paired imprecations of dreaded disease (discharge/leprosy) and death (war/famine) is the surprising threat of *spinsterhood*. Is 'holding a spindle' really a fate equal to, if not worse than, death?[1] It was, apparently, in the macho, militaristic culture of ancient Israel's Davidic kingdom. Spinning, weaving, knitting, and other forms of textile labor were quintessentially women's work—domestic drudgeries that no self-respecting commander like Joab would be caught dead doing. To consign his male descendants to such effeminate employment would effectively emasculate Joab's legacy; it would be difficult to imagine any more shameful fate in that society.[2]

This scenario reflects a pervasive stereotype, confirmed in both literary and material remains, concerning the production of clothing in the ancient Mediterranean world: such arduous labor was performed principally by women in the private confines of the patriarchal household. In short, women were responsible for clothing

---

1 Some ambiguity surrounds the meaning of the Hebrew text. P. Kyle McCarter, Jr, suggests that one who 'clings to a crutch' makes better sense in the present context, presumably because it depicts another physical impairment to military service (*II Samuel* [AB, 9; Garden City, NY: Doubleday, 1984] p. 118). Bruce C. Birch, however, notes that one who 'holds a spindle' (NRSV) aptly fits the situation by 'imply[ing] men who are not fit for battle and must do women's work' ('The First and Second Books of Samuel', *NIB*, II, pp. 949–1383 [1225]).

2 See David D. Gilmore, 'Introduction: The Shame of Dishonor', in *idem* (ed.), *Honor and Shame and the Unity of the Mediterranean* (Washington, DC: American Anthropological Association, 1987), pp. 2–21; F. Scott Spencer, 'The Ethiopian Eunuch and his Bible: A Social-Science Analysis', *BTB* 22 (1992), pp. 156–58. On the perpetuation of this stigma into the Roman period, note the assessment of Judith P. Hallett: 'Roman authors such as Cicero and Ovid emphasize that the representation of wool-working as a quintessentially female pursuit served as a form of distinguishing proper female from proper male behavior: each author characterizes men as effeminate and homosexually passive merely by attributing them with working in wool' ('Women's Lives in the Ancient Mediterranean', in Ross Shepard Kraemer and Mary Rose D'Angelo [eds.], *Women and Christian Origins* [Oxford: Oxford University Press, 1999], pp. 13–34 [33–34]).

their families in conjunction with other standard domestic chores such as cooking, cleaning, and child care.³

While women's historic preoccupation with spinning and sewing can scarcely be denied, questions may be raised regarding the relationship of such labor to other spheres of activity beyond the domestic environment. In her analysis of women's roles within early Christianity, Luise Schottroff invites us to explore a 'triple track' of possible channels for women's work: (1) 'providing for others', (2) 'earning an income', and/or (3) 'building up the congregation'.⁴ Alternatively, we may relate Schottroff's first category to *domestic/menial duty in the home*; the second to *public/commercial work in the marketplace*; and the third to *religious/communal service in the church*. This heuristic framework leads us to wonder whether women's textile labor in biblical antiquity ever extended beyond the domestic realm into the wider commercial and religious sectors, and if so, how did such pursuits undergird and/or undermine women's traditional roles within the family and male-dominated society at large.

Interestingly, within the androcentric world of the New Testament book of Acts, we discover three prominent Jewish-Christian women of 'the cloth'—Tabitha, Lydia, and Priscilla—who utilize their textile skills—sewing tunics, dyeing fabrics, and stitching tents—in various business ventures within the Roman marketplace and ministerial efforts within the Christian community. The domestic status, both marital and maternal, of these women is uncertain, except for Priscilla's identity as Aquila's wife; but clearly, though working with cloth in their homes, they are not monochrome, housebound 'spinsters'. This study aims to provide a multilevel profile of these women of 'the cloth' in Acts in terms of Schottroff's triad of domestic, commercial, and religious spheres of occupation.

The pun on 'the cloth'—while anachronistic to Acts—particularly focuses our attention on the interplay between women's domestic and religious identities and between 'material' and 'spiritual' forms of service. While Acts can scarcely be read as endorsing full-dress 'ordained' ministry for women or anyone else beyond the Twelve (cf. 1.15–26), cloth-dealing women like Tabitha, Lydia, and Priscilla who also actively participate in synagogue and church provide excellent cases for reflecting on the nexus between matter and spirit, hand and heart, labor and ministry. Such reflection on the ideological implications of 'women's traditional textile work' coordinates with what Elaine Hedges has shown to be 'a widespread and peculiarly interesting development in contemporary feminist thinking'. Writing in 1991, she notes:

---

3 Hallett stresses that this stereotype of women-as-weavers cut across class boundaries in the ancient world: 'Employing symbolic designations for women as a group, most notably by associating all women with wool-working, was perhaps the most visible way of erasing class distinctions and of positing a domestically defined gender unity among all females' ('Women's Lives', p. 33). See further Elizabeth W. Barber, *Women's Work: The First 20,000 Years. Women, Cloth, and Society in Early Times* (New York/London: Norton, 1994); Carol Meyers, *Discovering Eve: Ancient Israelite Women in Context* (New York/Oxford: Oxford University Press, 1988), pp. 142–49; Phyllis A. Bird, *Missing Persons and Mistaken Identities: Women and Gender in Ancient Israel* (OBT; Minneapolis: Fortress Press, 1997), p. 59.

4 Luise Schottroff, Silvia Shroer, and Marie-Theres Wacker (eds.), *Feminist Interpretation: The Bible in Women's Perspective* (Minneapolis: Fortress Press, 1998), p. 199.

In the past two decades visual artists and art historians, social historians, folklorists, poets and novelists, and most recently literary critics and theorists have discovered in the processes and products of the spindle, shuttle, and needle a major source for understanding women of the past, and as well, a source of subject matter and of images and metaphors for new creative work.[5]

As for religious scholars, Hedges cites the pioneering efforts of Mary Daly to redefine women's spiritual experience in terms of a radical appropriation of 'spinning' as a root metaphor for the 'creative enterprise of mind and imagination' and 'connectedness within the cosmos'.[6] More recently, Elizabeth A. Johnson has tapped into a similar metaphorical heritage in designing her own 'feminist-theological' vision, no less creative than Daly's but much more interwoven with classical Christian tradition:

> Feminist artisans and poets have been designing evocative metaphors for the creative work women do. Spinning, weaving, and quilting, all taken from women's domestic chores, provide an evocative description of scholarship as it seeks to articulate new patterns from bits of contemporary experiences and ancient sources. In the spirit of these metaphors, this exploration attempts to braid a footbridge between the ledges of classical and feminist Christian wisdom.[7]

Feminist interpreters of the New Testament and Christian origins have also turned for fresh inspiration and guidance to women's work of weaving, spinning, and quilting, discovering that more than etymology links the production of textiles and texts. Building on the insights of poet Adrienne Rich[8] and literary critic Nancy Miller,[9] Elisabeth Schüssler Fiorenza has employed a 'hermeneutics of remembrance' which 'resemble[s] the activity of a quilt-maker who stitches all surviving historical patches together into a new overall design'.[10] Balancing this creative and connective dimension of feminist biblical-historical research is a counteractive and deconstructive component which 'seeks to move against the grain' (or 'read against the weave', in Miller's terms) 'of the androcentric text to the life and struggles of

---

5 Elaine Hedges, 'The Needle or the Pen: The Literary Rediscovery of Women's Textile Work', in Florence Howe (ed.), *Tradition and the Talents of Women* (Urbana: University of Illinois Press, 1991), pp. 338–64 (338).

6 Mary Daly, *Gyn/Ecology: The Metaethics of Radical Feminism* (Boston: Beacon Press, 1978), pp. 389–90; cf. the entire concluding chapter, 'Spinning: Cosmic Tapestries', pp. 385–424; Hedges, 'Needle', p. 339.

7 Elizabeth A. Johnson, *She Who Is: The Mystery of God in Feminist Theological Discourse* (New York: Crossroad, 1992), p. 10; cf. Shannon Shrein, *Quilting and Braiding: The Feminist Christologies of Sallie McFague and Elizabeth A. Johnson in Conversation* (Collegeville, MN: Liturgical Press, 1998).

8 Rich's poetry, replete with vivid textile imagery, has been appropriated by a number of modern feminist thinkers, religious and otherwise. For a useful synopsis of her work, see Hedges, 'Needle', pp. 348–54.

9 Nancy K. Miller, 'Arachnologies: The Woman, The Text, and the Critic', in *idem* (ed.), *The Poetics of Gender* (New York: Columbia University Press, 1986), pp. 270–95.

10 Elisabeth Schüssler Fiorenza, *But She Said: Feminist Practices of Biblical Interpretation* (Boston: Beacon Press, 1992), pp. 52–54; cf. *idem*, 'The "Quilting" of Women's History: Phoebe of Cenchreae', in Paula M. Cooey, Sharon A. Farmer, and Mary Ellen Ross (eds.), *Embodied Love: Sensuality and Relationship as Feminist Values* (San Francisco: Harper & Row, 1987), pp. 35–49.

women in the early churches'.[11] Applied to the study of Luke–Acts, Schüssler Fiorenza detects that the ostensible pattern of women's equality and even leadership in the early church—suggested, for example, by Jesus' acceptance of wealthy women patrons (Lk. 8.1–3) and special affirmation of Mary's discipleship (10.38–42)—is effectively 'undercut' or unraveled by the overall dominance in Acts of male preachers of the word and officers of the church.[12]

In a similar fashion, appreciating the close analogy between 'putting together a text' and 'the weaving of a textile', Brigitte Kahl offers a 'materialist-feminist' reading of Luke both in light of intertextual threads with the Jewish Scriptures and against the weave of Luke's own narrative fabric.[13] The birth stories in Luke 1, for example, betray a 'close interwovenness' with well-known biblical narratives from Genesis and Samuel. At the same time Luke creates a new 'feminist-egalitarian' pattern out of these materials:

> The age-old rivalry between one woman and another woman, between firstborn and younger son, which is inherent in the rules of patriarchy, finally turns into sisterhood and brotherhood: Hagar and Sarah, Leah and Rachel, Hannah and Penninah as well as Cain and Abel, Ishmael and Isaac, Esau and Jacob finally become reconciled in Elizabeth and Mary, John and Jesus.[14]

Unfortunately, this magnificent, inclusive web is severely stretched and strained in the balance of Luke's work. Clear marks of 'repatriarchalization' predominate from Luke 2 to the end of Acts. What began in the Magnificat as a female prophet's (Mary's) revolutionary announcement of liberation for the poor and oppressed in occupied Palestine is 'fully replaced by a socially neutral "gospel for the Gentiles"' proclaimed by the male missionary (Paul) in the heart of imperial Rome (Acts 28.28–31). Still, as Kahl argues, the radical vision of Luke 1 remains 'as something like a "feminist code" woven into the texture of the biblical "textile"', functioning as a persistent, obstinate 'challenge to reinterpret and reanimate the Pauline gospel for the Gentiles by the "original" spirit of an inclusive and ecumenical justice and liberation for poor men and women'.[15]

These feminist-critical appropriations of textile work rooted in historical analysis and postmodern literary theory guard against the trap of romanticizing the ancient tradition of women's weaving as some sort of pristine model of modern women's liberation. Focusing on the American scene, Hedges has demonstrated that women's celebration of textile labor as a stimulus to independent creative and scholarly endeavors is largely a recent phenomenon, emerging in the last half of the twentieth

---

11 Schüssler Fiorenza, *But She Said*, p. 62; Miller, 'Arachnologies', p. 272. David M. Gunn and Danna Nolan Fewell have compared their deconstructive reading of biblical narratives with another textile operation: '"Deconstructive" criticism seeks to expound the gaps, the silences, the contradictions which inhabit all texts, like loose threads in a sweater, waiting to be pulled' (*Narrative in the Hebrew Bible* [Oxford: Oxford University Press, 1993], p. 10).

12 'Acts does not tell us a single story of a woman preaching the word, leading a congregation, or presiding over a house-church' (Schüssler Fiorenza, *But She Said*, pp. 65–66).

13 Brigitte Kahl, 'Toward a Materialist-Feminist Reading', in Elisabeth Schüssler Fiorenza (ed.), *Searching the Scriptures* (2 vols.; New York: Crossroad, 1993), I, pp. 225–40.

14 Kahl, 'Toward a Materialist-Feminist Reading', p. 237.

15 Kahl, 'Toward a Materialist-Feminist Reading', pp. 237–38.

century. Before that, aspiring female artists and intellectuals encountered the stereotype of the stay-at-home seamstress as a marked 'deterrent to ambition and achievement'. When daring to branch out in new directions, with a pen, say, rather than a needle, thoughtful women had to assure the male hierarchy that nothing was really changing, that their new ventures were just 'an innocuous extension of domesticity'.[16] Hence we find adroit nineteenth-century writers like Harriet Beecher Stowe deprecating their compositions as an 'ill-arranged patchwork' of characters and even concealing their 'scribblings' in a sewing basket, the perduring symbol of 'proper' ladies' labor.[17]

If this 'adversarial relationship'[18] between women's textile and textual work, between their domestic, commercial, and religious 'weavings', characterized nineteenth-century American society, how much more, we might imagine, would such conditions have typified the first-century eastern Mediterranean world. In any event, in assessing the various roles of women of 'the cloth' in Acts, it is incumbent that we firmly anchor such investigation in the ancient historical and literary contexts undergirding this material.

Weaving the Contexts[19]

In narrowing ideological proximity to the portraits of Jewish-Christian women of 'the cloth' in Acts, three broad 'intertexts' merit examination: (1) pagan Greek and Roman classics;[20] (2) Jewish Scriptures in Greek (LXX);[21] and (3) the Christian Gospel of Luke, the 'first' volume in the Luke–Acts set (cf. Acts 1.1; Lk. 1.3).[22]

Of particular relevance to tracking the thread between women's domestic, religious, and other creative outlets of textile work, we consider two poetic rendi-

---

16 Hedges, 'Needle', pp. 340–41.

17 Hedges, 'Needle', pp. 341–42. Gerda Lerner also notes the strong domestic ties maintained by Stowe and other women writers: 'When, like so many wives before her, she [Stowe] took up the pen to supplement her husband's inadequate earnings, she did it for the sake of the family' (*The Female Experience: An American Documentary* [Indianapolis: Bobbs–Merrill, 1977], p. 58).

18 Hedges, 'Needle', p. 340.

19 I am focusing here on significant literary 'intertexts'. A full investigation of relevant contexts would also include a variety of inscriptional and archaeological data. I will hint at some of this information in later notes. For a thorough and careful examination of material as well as literary artifacts pertaining to weaving in Jewish and Greco-Roman antiquity, see Miriam B. Peskowitz, *Spinning Fantasies: Rabbis, Gender, and History* (Berkeley: University of California Press, 1997).

20 As evidence of his broad familiarity with Greco-Roman culture, Luke actually cites—on the lips of Paul in Athens—snippets from the Greek poets Epimenides and Aratus in Acts 17.28–29.

21 The Lukan writings in Greek were heavily influenced by the Greek-Jewish Scriptures in both form and content. As John Darr states, 'Luke–Acts is saturated with the language, imagery, settings, and flavor of the Septuagint (LXX). It is hard to find a part of Luke's narrative that has not been affected by this intertextual linkage' (*On Character Building: The Reader and the Rhetoric of Characterization in Luke–Acts* [Louisville, KY: Westminster/John Knox, 1992], p. 28).

22 Scholars continue to argue about the precise relationship between Luke and Acts (see Mikeal C. Parsons and Richard I. Pervo, *Rethinking the Unity of Luke and Acts* [Minneapolis: Fortress Press, 1993]), but no one seriously disputes their common authorship; see I. Howard Marshall, 'Acts and the "Former Treatise"', in Bruce W. Winter and Andrew D. Clarke (eds.), *The Book of Acts in its First Century Setting. I. The Book of Acts in its Ancient Literary Setting* (Grand Rapids, MI: Eerdmans, 1993), pp. 163–82.

tions of Greek mythology. The first encounter between a man and woman in Homer's *Odyssey* features a conflict between Telemachus and Penelope, the son and wife of the long-absent hero, Odysseus. In this scene, the 'wary and reserved' Penelope emerges from her upstairs chamber deeply offended by the musical entertainment offered to her son and suitors in her own home. She demands that the bard 'break off this song' about returning warriors, since it only served to deepen her grief over Odysseus's loss. In response, Telemachus, shamed by Penelope's intrusion, puts his mother back in her place in no uncertain terms:

> So, mother
> go back to your quarters. Tend to your own tasks,
> the distaff and the loom, and keep the women
> working hard as well. As for giving orders,
> men will see to that, but I most of all:
> *I* hold the reins of power in this house (1.409–14).[23]

Clearly, Telemachus's view is that women should diligently and silently carry out their weaving duties in the home, isolated from and subordinate to male rulers. And Penelope agrees!: 'she withdrew to her own room ... and took to heart the clear good sense in what her son had said' (1.415–16). Later, however, she uses her weaving skills not only to confirm her domestic identity but also to connive against her suitors and control her own destiny. She announces that she cannot remarry in good conscience until she has completed weaving a burial shroud for her departed husband's father, Laertes. The project winds up extending over three years because each night Penelope secretly unravels her web, to start anew the next morning. When Penelope is finally exposed, one of her deceived suitors, Antinous, cannot help but admire this 'matchless queen of cunning' who has so frustrated his plans: 'she persists in tormenting us, quick to exploit the gifts Athena gave her—a skilled hand for elegant work, a fine mind and subtle wiles too—we've never heard the like' (2.127–30). Here is the tension: on the one hand, Penelope's weaving 'wiles' reinforce her exclusive, chaste devotion to her lord and husband Odysseus, even in his assumed death; on the other hand, they also demonstrate her considerable god-given intellectual and political talents beyond her expected manual-domestic skills.[24]

Athena's patronage of women's textile labor is also the subject—and problem—of the tale of Arachne spun by the first-century Roman poet Ovid (43 BCE–17 CE). In Book VI of *The Metamorphoses*, Arachne is introduced as a young woman of lowly birth, the daughter of a common Lydian artisan who made his living as a purple-dyer. Arachne herself becomes known throughout Lydia for her consummate skills at all levels of cloth production—carding, spinning, weaving, embroidering. Whether she used these talents to enhance her father's business or supplement the family's

---

23 Citations from Homer, *The Odyssey* (trans. Robert Fagles; introduction and notes Bernard Knox; New York: Viking Penguin, 1996); on this incident, see Knox's notes on pp. 50–52 and the parallel scene in 21.389–93.

24 See Helene P. Foley, 'Penelope as Moral Agent', in Beth Cohen (ed.), *The Distaff Side: Representing the Female in Homer's* Odyssey (Oxford: Oxford University Press, 1995), pp. 94–97. Note also Peskowitz's discussion of both the popularity and ambiguity of the Penelope tradition in Roman-period Judaism (*Spinning Fantasies*, pp. 1–10).

income is never mentioned. In any event, she captures the attention of admiring nymphs as well as mortals and is assumed to be great Athena's prize pupil. Arachne, however, spurns such tutelage and defiantly challenges Athena to a weaving duel. So each contestant—girl and goddess—fashions her finest tapestry out of gold and purple threads. Athena's displays a central battle scene between her and Neptune, establishing her superior claim to the city of Athens, surrounded in each corner by vivid depictions of divine retribution against human, especially female, pride. Arachne's work intricately details a series of gross violations of mortal women by rapacious gods. The two tapestries thus inscribe the basic power struggle within conventional divine/human and masculine/feminine hierarchies.[25]

Arachne both wins and loses. Shockingly, she wins the battle in Ovid's account (a notable reversal from earlier versions) by virtue of her 'flawless' creation conceded by Athena and 'even Envy personified'; ultimately, however, she loses the war, as an irate Athena bashes Arachne four times on the forehead and transforms her into a spider. That will teach uppity young women who dare to step outside their proper domestic sphere of modest, mortal, menial weaving. Nevertheless, that Arachne's work outstrips Athena's in the latter's 'masculine, military mode' and that, even as a spider, she continues to spin her web (to 'exercise her old-time weaver-art') may suggest Ovid's admiration for Arachne's subversive activity; perhaps she is a model for his own 'verbal tapestries' and 'skillful *ecphrases* of textile skill', as Ann Rosalind Jones surmises.[26]

In considering the context of Jewish Scripture, we have already noted the traditional image of spinning as domestic women's work in David's curse of Joab's lineage (2 Sam. 3.29). A wider survey of biblical literature both sharpens and complicates this basic portrait. The first attempt at sewing comes very early with the famous fig-leaf project, carried out by the man and woman *together* (Gen. 3.7) just before God stipulates a gender-divided system of labor (3.16–19). In this new order, however, nothing is said about who should be responsible for clothing duties. As it happens, *God himself* takes on the role of tailor, outfitting the first couple in leather coats to replace their pathetic leaf coverings (3.21).[27]

Perhaps this sets the stage for certain links between worship and weaving which emerge in the construction of various curtains, screens, coverings, hangings, and vestments for use in Israel's tabernacle, following a detailed pattern which 'the Lord commanded Moses' in Exodus 35–40. Initially, colored yarns, fine linen, and goats' hair were provided by 'all the skillful women [who] spun with their hands' (35.25).[28]

---

25 See Ann Rosalind Jones, 'Dematerializations: Textile and Textual Properties in Ovid, Sandys, and Spenser', in Margreta de Grazia, Maureen Quilligan, and Peter Stallybrass (eds.), *Subject and Object in Renaissance Culture* (Cambridge: Cambridge University Press, 1996), pp. 189–209 (194–96).

26 Jones, 'Dematerializations', pp. 195–96.

27 In light of the typical portrayal of sewing elsewhere in the Bible as women's work, one might appropriately envisage God as 'seamstress'. But 'tailor' seems better suited to the Genesis narrative, which consistently employs masculine language for God. Of course, such language is metaphorical and anthropomorphic, not essentialist; the image of 'tailor' complements that of potter, gardener, and surgeon in Gen. 2.

28 Exod. 35.23 also mentions 'tanned rams' skins' and 'fine leather', but these materials are not specifically linked with women's production in 35.25.

Thus we find biblical precedent for weaving both as women's work and as a channel for women's worship of YHWH, as was also true in the service of Asherah (2 Kgs 23.7), Artemis, and other ancient female deities.[29] In building YHWH's tabernacle, however, while women supplied the raw materials, the task of producing and finishing the grand project fell primarily to two divinely inspired crafts*men*, Bezalel and Oholiab (Exod. 35.35–40). To what extent they were aided by other weavers, male or female, is not certain.[30] It may well be that women were involved strictly in a cottage industry, working out of their homes to provide fabrics for professional male artisans. In any case, if women were involved in making priestly vestments, they certainly did not wear them.

Not surprisingly, the ideal wife in Proverbs 31 diligently works in the home to manufacture clothing for her family. Indeed, the poem presents spinning wool and flax as the woman's first specific duty (31.13) and thereafter adds three supplemental references to textile labor (31.19, 21–22, 24) interlaced with other standard household responsibilities for providing food, tending children, and honoring her husband. Beyond this domestic realm, however, the female paragon also 'engages in public economic enterprise'[31] and certain expressions of religious service. On the commercial front, 'she makes linen garments and sells them; she supplies the merchant with sashes' (31.24); in terms of ministry, the same hands that hold the distaff/spindle reach out to clothe the poor/needy (31.19–20), and as a mortal model of Woman Wisdom, the 'capable wife ... opens her mouth with wisdom' to 'teach' the simple to 'fear the Lord' (31.10, 26, 31).[32] Still, we must be careful not to make too much of this woman's independence: her business efforts, while 'profitable' (31.18), seem limited to a cottage avocation (supplying cloth goods to merchants); her conveyance of wisdom, while praiseworthy, seems directed chiefly to children within her household (31.27). Throughout the poem, the woman's remarkable achievements in textile and other types of employment redound to the pleasure and glory of her husband, who sits among the ruling elders 'in the city gates' (31.23; cf. vv. 11–12, 28).[33]

From this idyllic portrait of a happy, honored husband supported by his wise, weaving wife, we turn to a messier snapshot of marital conflict surrounding women's textile work in the book of Tobit (2.11–14). The once prominent Assyrian exile, Tobit, now stripped of all his property and stricken blind despite his tenacious

---

29 On the link between women's weaving and the worship of certain ancient Greek goddesses, see Ross Shepard Kraemer, *Her Share of the Blessings: Women's Religions among Pagans, Jews, and Christians in the Greco-Roman World* (Oxford: Oxford University Press, 1992), pp. 22–29.

30 The general reference to 'all those with skill among the workers' in Exod. 36.8 opens the door for a variety of helpers, both male and female. But throughout Exod. 35–40, Bezalel is especially singled out as the tabernacle's master-builder. See Bird, *Missing Persons*, p. 95 n. 36.

31 Claudia V. Camp and Carole R. Fontaine, 'Proverbs', in Wayne A. Meeks (ed.), *The HarperCollins Study Bible: New Revised Standard Version* (New York: HarperCollins, 1993), pp. 984–85.

32 On the wife in Prov. 31 as a symbolic representation of Woman Wisdom, see Thomas P. McCreesh, 'Wisdom as Wife: Proverbs 31:10–31', *RB* 92 (1985), pp. 25–46.

33 The final line in the poem enters a plea that 'her works praise her in the city gates' (Prov. 31.31), thus calling for public recognition alongside her husband. The fact is that the husband needs no one to trumpet his honor, since he is already known personally as a civic leader, thanks in large measure to his wife's domestic support.

devotion to Jewish law, bemoans the added disgrace of having to depend on his wife Anna's income from selling material she had woven.[34] The struggle comes to a head when Anna receives not only the usual wages from her employers, but also 'a young goat for a meal'. Tobit angrily accuses his wife of stealing the animal and demands she return it. Insisting that the goat was a charitable 'gift', Anna lashes back at her husband: 'Where are your acts of charity? Where are your righteous deeds? These things are known about you!' (2.14). Formerly proud of his many good deeds—including feeding the hungry and clothing the naked (1.16)—Tobit cannot even manage to feed and clothe himself now. What has he to show for all his piety?[35] A wife forced to peddle homespun goods, a wife whom he thinks (wrongly) is a thief! There is little left for Tobit now except to pray for death (3.1–6).

Once again, tensions emerge. The male ideal of a submissive, weaving, stay-at-home wife is challenged by the reality, born of necessity, of women's earning wages from textile labor, wages paid by businessmen other than their husbands.[36] Still, Anna is scarcely an example of a successful career woman. She works at a subsistence level and stays firmly rooted in the home ('she cut off a piece she had woven and *sent it to the owners*', 2.14). Overall she appears to be no happier about her situation than Tobit.

Moving to the most immediate literary context for interpreting Acts, namely, Luke's Gospel, we encounter women in many other traditional domestic occupations—cooking, catering, cleaning, child-bearing—but no spinning, weaving, or the like. On closer examination, however, some important relevant material emerges. While women are not specifically cast as seamstresses in Luke, *Jesus* twice utilizes sewing metaphors to depict the kingdom of God. First, to illustrate the fundamental breach between an eroding social, political, and religious establishment—coming apart at the seams—and the restorative eschatological kingdom of God, Jesus cites a general maxim of sewing practice: 'No one [οὐδείς, a generic masculine plural pronoun] tears a piece from a new garment and sews it on an old garment' (Lk. 5.36; cf. 5.27–39). Second, Jesus more specifically describes the activity of God the Father as a tailor (reminiscent of Gen. 3) clothing the destitute in his inclusive royal household:

> Consider the lilies, how they grow: they neither toil nor spin; yet I tell you even Solomon in all his glory was not clothed like one of these. But if God so clothes the grass of the field, which is alive today and tomorrow is thrown into the oven, how much more will he clothe you—you of little faith! ... Do not be afraid, little flock, for it is your Father's good pleasure to give you the kingdom (Lk. 12.27–28, 32).

---

34 Carey A. Moore notes that 'this must have been a bitter pill for Tobit to swallow', particularly if he endorsed the conventional wisdom of Sir. 25.22: 'There is wrath and impudence and great disgrace when a wife supports her husband' (*Tobit: A New Translation with Introduction and Commentary* [AB, 40A; New York: Doubleday, 1996], pp. 132–33). Similarly, Amy-Jill Levine correlates Tobit's consternation over Anna's working with a typical scenario in Hellenistic Jewish literature: 'when women leave the confines of the home, confusion and marital disharmony result' ('Tobit: Teaching Jews How to Live in the Diaspora', *BR* 8 [1992], pp. 42–51, 64 ([51]).

35 Cf. Moore's translation of the end of Tob. 2.14: 'Where are your righteous deeds? Look where they've got you!' (Moore, *Tobit*, p. 126).

36 See Tal Ilan, *Jewish Women in Greco-Roman Palestine* (Peabody, MA: Hendrickson, 1996), pp. 184–90.

These images of sewing and spinning from the lips of the male Jesus pertaining to the kingdom of God the Father scarcely eradicate the pattern of weaving as typical women's work. Luke does not liberate women from domestic duty, but he does significantly ennoble household service (διακονία) as a paradigm of honorable divine and human activity, both male and female, governing even the ministry of Jesus himself: 'I am among you as one who serves (διακονῶν)' (22.27).[37] Alongside feeding and table-waiting, clothing the poor—including sharing one's own clothes as well as making new garments—constitutes a major expression of true religious piety in Luke (cf. 3.11; 6.29–30).[38]

Having explored the broad tapestry of women's textile work from Greco-Roman, Jewish, and Lukan sources, we are now prepared to examine the particular texture of stories of cloth-handling women in Acts along domestic, commercial, and religious lines. While seeking to coordinate this material with relevant contexts and intertexts, we must remain open to the possibility that depictions of women of 'the cloth' in Acts might also run 'against the weave'—as Schüssler Fiorenza and Kahl have put it—of previous literary patterns.

Tabitha: The Charitable Seamstress

The Tabitha story features the resuscitation from death of a beloved female disciple (μαθήτρια)[39] in the Christian community at Joppa, known chiefly for her abundant 'good deeds and the alms which she made (ἐποίει)'[40]—especially garments which 'she made' (ἐποίει) for needy widows (Acts 9.36, 39). While it is commonly assumed that such philanthropy intimates Tabitha's status as an independent, wealthy patroness,[41] the fact that she actually *makes* the clothing, as Ivoni Richter Reimer observes, rather than gives from her own surplus, may suggest a more lowly social location.[42] In truth, we know little about Tabitha's identity beyond the fact that she is a Jew with an Aramaic name meaning 'gazelle' ('Dorcas' in Greek, 9.36),

---

37 See F. Scott Spencer, 'Neglected Widows in Acts 6.1–7', *CBQ* 56 (1994), pp. 715–33 (728–31); idem, *The Portrait of Philip in Acts: A Study of Roles and Relations* (JSNTSup, 67; Sheffield: Sheffield Academic Press, 1992), pp. 199–206.

38 A similar point underlies Jesus' critique of wealthy elites bedecked in 'soft robes', 'fine clothing' and 'purple and fine linen' (16.19), in contrast to the desert prophet John and the diseased beggar Lazarus (Lk. 7.24–26; 16.19–23).

39 The only use of a feminine form for 'disciple' in the NT.

40 Joseph A. Fitzmyer, *The Acts of the Apostles: A New Translation with Introduction and Commentary* (AB, 31; New York: Doubleday, 1998), p. 445. The imperfect tense implies a typical, ongoing pattern of conduct.

41 So most commentators, including feminist interpreters: e.g. Gail R. O'Day, 'Acts', in Carol A. Newsom and Sharon H. Ringe (eds.), *The Women's Bible Commentary* (London: SPCK; Louisville, KY: Westminster/John Knox, 1992), pp. 305–12 (309–10); and Turid Karlsen Seim, *The Double Message: Patterns of Gender in Luke–Acts* (Nashville: Abingdon, 1994), pp. 242–43.

42 Ivoni Richter Reimer, *Women in the Acts of the Apostles: A Feminist Liberation Perspective* (Minneapolis: Fortress Press, 1995) pp. 43–44. Robert C. Tannehill pictures Tabitha as 'one of the poor' but largely because he assumes, without warrant (see below), that she was a widow ('"Cornelius" and "Tabitha" Encounter Luke's Jesus', *Int* 48 [1994], pp. 347–56 [354]).

which, contrary to early interpreters, probably has nothing to do with her being light on her feet.[43]

As for Tabitha's domestic status, because she appears as a single, autonomous woman, without male supporters, many interpreters classify her as a widow. But the term for 'widow', χήρα, commonly used in Luke and Acts, is never applied to her; she helps poor χήραι, but not necessarily as one of them.[44] If not a χήρα, which Luke reserves for particularly destitute widows,[45] perhaps Tabitha is financially better off than the widows she assists; but again, that need not make her a wealthy aristocrat.

It is also not certain where Tabitha resided prior to her death. Since her corpse is prepared and laid in 'a room upstairs', it is often thought that she had owned this two-story dwelling. But neither of the two references to the upper room (ὑπερῷον, 9.37, 39) specifically labels it as *her* quarters. Moreover, upper rooms are common gathering places for Christian communities or 'house-churches' in Acts (1.13; 20.7–12; cf. Lk. 22.12). As such, the upper room may also represent a suitable site for mourning and memorializing respected members of the community—like Tabitha—who had died.[46] It is possible that Tabitha hosted the Joppan congregation in her own home (as we see later with Lydia and Priscilla), but that scenario is never made explicit in the text.

Wherever she lived, we can safely presume that Tabitha produced her handsewn tunics and cloaks[47] out of her domicile. How many garments she made and how organized or how extensive her outreach to widows might have been, we do not know. James Arlandson's suppositions that she had 'a small team helping her' manufacture 'a sizeable surplus of goods' and that 'she also sold part of the surplus to those capable of buying it, thereby making a profit' constitute pure speculation.[48] We have no accounting of the number of widows Tabitha was supplying or even whether she was their sole provider, and commercial interests—which Luke often displays elsewhere—play no role in the present narrative.

The prime significance of Tabitha's work in Acts 9 lies in its *religious* dimension. The performance of 'good works and acts of charity' such as clothing the naked reflects standard Jewish piety demanded of God-fearing persons, both male and female (cf. Tob. 1.17; 4.16; Mt. 25.36-46; Acts 10.1-2). Domestic manufacturing of garments to help the poor especially recalls the model of the ideal woman in Proverbs 31 sketched above (31.19). In Luke's Gospel, John the Baptist's first requirement of penance for would-be converts was that 'whoever has two coats

---

43 John Chrysostom described Tabitha 'as active and wakeful as an antelope'. On the whole, the church fathers regarded her name as a positive attribute, except for John Calvin's rather raw rendering of Tabitha/Dorcas as 'wild she-goat'. See the helpful survey of interpretation in Janice Capel Anderson, 'Reading Tabitha: A Feminist Reception History', in Elizabeth S. Malbon and Edgar V. McKnight (eds), *The New Literary Criticism and the New Testament* (JSNTSup, 109; Sheffield: Sheffield Academic Press, 1994), pp. 108-44, reprinted in this volume, pp. 22-48.

44 See Spencer, 'Neglected Widows', p. 732 n. 47.

45 Spencer, 'Neglected Widows', pp. 715-33; Seim, *Double Message*, pp. 241-43.

46 Death is much on the mind of Jesus in the Last Supper scene in the upper room, and the account of Eutychus's fall from the upper room in Acts 20 focuses on his death and resuscitation (like Tabitha).

47 χιτῶνας καὶ ἱμάτια (9.39), basic under- and outer-garments.

48 James Malcolm Arlandson, *Women, Class, and Society in Early Christianity: Models from Luke–Acts* (Peabody, MA: Hendrickson, 1997), pp. 143-44.

(χιτῶνας) must share with anyone who has none' (3.11). Tabitha goes one better by not merely lending an extra coat but actually making multiple new coats for needy widows (χιτῶνας, Acts 9.39).[49] Particular caretaking of vulnerable widows represents another hallmark of Jewish piety, exemplified by YHWH (Exod. 22.22–23; Ps. 68.5; Prov. 15.25) and his prophets, Elijah (1 Kgs 17.8–24), Elisha (2 Kgs 4.1–37), and Jesus (Lk. 7.11–17; 18.1–8; 20.45–21.6).[50] Although, admittedly, the male apostle Peter gets star billing in Acts 9 for assisting the widows at Joppa by restoring their deceased benefactress—mirroring the resuscitation miracles of Elijah, Elisha, and Jesus—Tabitha obviously plays a vital supporting role. Widows owed their clothing most directly to *Tabitha's* diligent labor, both before and (presumably) after her death (Peter immediately leaves and turns to other business [9.43–10.23]).

Apart from Tabitha's subordination to Peter in Luke's story, certain feminist critics have also been suspicious of Luke's apparent hesitance to characterize Tabitha's work as διακονία or 'ministry'—a 'good work' (ἔργον ἀγαθόν), to be sure, but not 'ministry'. The problem is further complicated by Luke's willingness to describe the care of hungry widows by a seven-*man* committee as διακονία (Acts 6.1–7).[51] Why not use the same term for Tabitha's service? While Luke often employs some form of διακονία / διακονέω to identify authentic ministry, he is not limited to it. For example, in a key text summarizing Jesus' entire ministry, Luke announces through Peter—'he [Jesus] went about doing good (εὐεργέτον)' (Acts 10.38)—utilizing the verb form εὐεργετέω, closely related to Tabitha's 'good works' (ἔργα ἀγαθά). Further, Tabitha's 'almsdeeds' (ἐλεημοσύνας) are matched by the God-fearing Cornelius in the next story (10.2, 4) and by the missionary Paul later in Acts (24.17).

A salient feature of διακονία in Luke's writings stresses a 'holistic' rather than dichotomized view of religious 'ministry' or 'service'. The Lukan Jesus who proclaims the gospel does so as 'one who serves [at table]' (ὁ διακονῶν; Lk. 22.27); 'serving tables' (διακονεῖν τραπέζαις) and 'serving the word' (διακονία τοῦ λόγου) comprise complementary forms of true ministry (Acts 6.2, 4).[52] Such a perspective fits well with the focus on the home/household (οἶκος) as the primary locus of Christian fellowship, worship, and care, thus breaking down, to some extent, traditional domestic and cultic boundaries.[53] Therefore, while, on one level, Tabitha's benevolent clothing of widows appears to be merely an 'innocuous extension of domesticity',[54] on another level, fully appreciating Luke's pastoral emphasis on caring materially for every member of God's household, such work may not be so innocuous or quotidian after all.

---

49 Tannehill, ' "Cornelius" and "Tabitha" ', p. 352.

50 Spencer, 'Neglected Widows'.

51 O'Day, 'Acts', pp. 309–10; Clarice J. Martin, 'The Acts of the Apostles', in Elisabeth Schüssler Fiorenza (ed.), *Searching the Scriptures* (2 vols.; New York: Crossroad, 1994), II, pp. 763–99 (782); Mary Rose D'Angelo, 'Women in Luke–Acts: A Redactional View', *JBL* 109 (1990), pp. 441–61 (455).

52 See Spencer, 'Neglected Widows', pp. 728–31; *idem, Portrait of Philip*, pp. 199–206.

53 See John H. Elliott, 'Temple versus Household in Luke–Acts: A Contrast in Social Institutions', in Jerome H. Neyrey (ed.), *The Social World of Luke–Acts: Models for Interpretation* (Peabody, MA: Hendrickson, 1991), pp. 211–40.

54 Hedges's phrase cited above ('Needle', p. 341).

Does Luke then take us to the brink of women's ordination, that had there been the tradition of ministers donning 'the cloth', Tabitha could have worn it as easily as Peter? Not exactly. As suggested above, Luke's ideals of equal ministerial opportunity for men and women often run 'against the weave' of the actual stories he spins, particularly when it comes to who really has *a say* in church affairs.[55] Likewise, the ideal that *acts* of charity speak as loudly as actual *words* of proclamation becomes frayed in light of Acts' mounting preference for the latter form of ministry. It is difficult to ignore that a lot of speechmaking goes on in Acts and that it all comes from male voices. Reimer's opinion that labeling Tabitha a 'disciple' implies her role as a missionary-proclaimer of the gospel stretches the meaning of the term beyond what it can bear.[56] Peter stands out as the sole spokes*man* in this story and, indeed, throughout much of the first half of Acts. The old Puritan commentator, Matthew Henry, got it right when he asserted that 'Tabitha was a great doer, [but] no great talker'—right, that is, on the final level of Luke's narrative, but not necessarily from the view of history behind the story and certainly not from that of many feminist critics.[57]

Lydia: The Hospitable Purple-Dealer

The Lydia story presents a God-fearing 'dealer in purple cloth' (πορφυρόπωλις), transplanted from Thyatira to Philippi, who welcomes the message proclaimed by Paul, receives baptism along with her household, and hosts the visiting missionaries and new community of believers in her home (Acts 16.13-15, 40). Again we encounter a single woman of 'the cloth', with no mention of male kin. Whether Lydia was widowed, divorced, or married to a forgettable husband is anyone's guess.[58] Whatever the case, in contrast to Tabitha's ambiguous domestic status, Lydia clearly functions as the head of 'her household' (οἶκος αὐτῆς) and owner of 'my home' (οἶκος μοῦ) (16.15).

Other dimensions of Lydia's identity remain a matter of debate, including the significance of her name. It is commonly noted that she bears a regional rather than individual appellation—'a certain Lydian woman'—befitting someone of 'servile

---

55 Parity between male and female ministers may seem to be suggested in the well-known pattern of pairing incidents involving men and women in Luke–Acts. But juxtaposition does not mean equality. Tabitha's story is sandwiched between similar healing/conversion episodes featuring two men, Aeneas (9.32–35) and Cornelius (10.1–48). Her story is longer than the former's but much shorter than the latter's. But in terms of voice and power, Peter overshadows all of them (see below). See M.R. D'Angelo, '(Re)Presentations of Women in The Gospel of Matthew and Luke–Acts', in Ross Shepard Kraemer and Mary Rose D'Angelo (eds.) *Women and Christian Origins*: (Oxford: Oxford University, 1999), pp. 171–95; and F. Scott Spencer, 'Out of Mind, Out of Voice: Slave-Girls and Prophetic Daughters in Luke–Acts', *BibInt* 7 (1999), pp. 132–53.

56 Reimer, *Women in the Acts of the Apostles*, p. 54.

57 See the trenchant analysis of the 'dark side' of Henry's interpretation in Anderson, 'Reading Tabitha', p. 120.

58 See the discussion of various possibilities in Bradley Blue, 'Acts and the House Church', in David W.J. Gill and Conrad Gempf (eds.), *The Book of Acts in its First Century Setting*. II. *The Book of Acts in its Graeco–Roman Setting* (Grand Rapids: Eerdmans; Carlisle: Paternoster, 1994), pp. 184–86.

origin'.⁵⁹ The area of Lydia in western Asia Minor in fact encompassed the city of Thyatira, where the character Lydia formerly resided. We may also recall another famous cloth-working girl from Lydia and daughter of a humble purple-dyer, who, however, is also remembered by her given name (Arachne). Some inscriptional evidence also attests to 'Lydia' as a personal as well as place name, supporting Ben Witherington's contention that Luke intentionally highlights Lydia in Acts 16 as a wealthy, independent, *named* woman, prominent in her own right.⁶⁰

However we evaluate her name, the key factor in determining Lydia's social location concerns her occupation. Here we move beyond Tabitha's homespun sphere of charitable garment-making to truly *commercial* production and distribution of material goods, specifically, purple-tinted fabrics. Of course, we might still picture Lydia's running her business out of a home office and workshop where she employed members of her household.⁶¹ But more seems to be involved than a simple cottage industry like that carried out by Tobit's wife, Anna, and the woman of Proverbs 31. For one thing, Lydia does not have to reckon with a husband (like Tobit) hassling her about her work or being preoccupied with his own public honor. And whereas the dutiful wife of Proverbs 31 outfits her family in elegant crimson and purple fashions to support her husband's high position *within the city gates* (an ancient 'dress for success' strategy [Prov. 31.21–23]), the purple-peddling Lydia may well live and work where she worships—in a marginal spot *outside the city gates* (Acts 16.13). Also, whereas the women in Proverbs and Tobit supply local merchants with cloth goods, Lydia functions more like a merchant herself, having transferred her business from Thyatira—a well-known center for dyed textiles⁶²—to the booming Roman colony of Philippi.

Most commentators, like Witherington, assume that Lydia's employment in the purple trade brought her considerable wealth and prestige, making her one of the 'high-standing' women Luke likes to feature (Acts 13.50; 17.4, 12), even though he does not explicitly label Lydia as such. The logic runs that, since purple garments were expensive items fit for kings and other elites, purple merchants must also have been rather well-to-do, perhaps even part of Caesar's civil service.⁶³ In short, a

---

59 Wayne A. Meeks, *The First Urban Christians: The Social World of the Apostle Paul* (New Haven, CT: Yale University Press, 1983), p. 203 n. 93; see the discussion in Colin J. Hemer, *The Book of Acts in the Setting of Hellenistic History* (ed. C.H. Gempf; Winona Lake, IN: Eisenbrauns, 1990), pp. 114–15, 231; Luise Schottroff, 'Lydia: A New Quality of Power', in *idem*, *Let the Oppressed Go Free: Feminist Perspectives on the New Testament* (Louisville, KY: Westminster/John Knox Press, 1993), pp. 131–37 (132–33).

60 Ben Witherington, III, *The Acts of the Apostles: A Socio-Rhetorical Commentary* (Grand Rapids, MI: Eerdmans; Carlisle: Paternoster, 1998), pp. 491–92; cf. Hemer, *Book of Acts*, pp. 114–15, 231; Florence M. Gillman, *Women Who Knew Paul* (Zacchaeus Studies; Collegeville, MN: Liturgical Press, 1992), p. 31.

61 See Karen Jo Torjesen, *When Women Were Priests: Women's Leadership in the Early Church and the Scandal of their Subordination in the Rise of Christianity* (San Francisco: HarperSanFrancisco, 1993), pp. 14–15, 54–56.

62 See Reimer, *Women in the Acts of the Apostles*, pp. 99–100.

63 Witherington, *Acts*, p. 492. While the processing and management of luxury purple dye derived from the Tyrian mollusk was an imperial monopoly, less expensive sources of purple, like the madder plant, were not under government control. See Hemer, *Book of Acts*, pp. 114–15; F.M. Gillman, *Women Who Knew Paul*, pp. 34–35.

luxury product makes a lucrative profit. A somewhat quirky variation on this theme arises in Lilian Portefaix's suggestion that Lydia's profession, while lucrative, was still 'entirely connected to the feminine sphere', since purple dye was purchased chiefly by wealthy women for party dresses, cheek rouge, and lipstick. Accordingly, 'a woman dealer in purple needed to be well dressed herself in order to advertise her goods as her appearance would place her high in the estimation of other women'.[64] Such a profile makes Lydia out to be something of a first-century Avon lady or Mary Kay representative (with the exception, presumably, that she ran around in a *purple* chariot instead of a pink one).

An entirely different strand of recent feminist-historical analysis challenges not only Lydia's supposed engagement in male-dominated commercial affairs, but also her high social standing. Both Schottroff and Reimer make a fundamental class distinction between purple-*wearers* and purple-*workers*.[65] The exploitation and marginalization of textile laborers is a sad, but staple element of social life up to the modern day. In the ancient world, Plutarch clearly stated the common opinion: 'Often we take pleasure in a thing, but we despise the one who made it. Thus we value aromatic salves and purple clothing, but the dyers and salve-makers remain for us common and low craftspersons.'[66] In the case of purple-dyeing, the stigma was compounded by the filthy, 'sordid', smelly process of extracting dye from plants or mollusks and treating materials with animal urine. It was a business typically zoned outside city limits, geographically matching the marginal social location of its practitioners. Purple-dyers might well have been wealthier than other artisans, but money was not the only or even supreme status marker in the ancient world.[67]

The case for Lydia's lower social status can only be made, of course, if we assume that her purple business included processing the dye and producing the colored fabrics as well as selling them.[68] We cannot be certain, but placing Lydia 'outside the gate by the river' (16.13)—where smells would not offend those with noses in the

---

64 Lilian Portefaix, *Sisters Rejoice: Paul's Letter to the Philippians and Luke–Acts as Seen by First-Century Philippian Women* (ConBNT, 20; Stockholm: Almqvist & Wiksell International, 1988), pp. 170–71; cf. F.M. Gillman, *Women Who Knew Paul*, p. 34.

65 Schottroff, 'Lydia', pp. 131–37; Reimer, *Women in the Acts of the Apostles*, pp. 101–109.

66 Plutarch, *Pericles* 1.3–4; cited in Reimer, *Women in the Acts of the Apostles*, p. 107.

67 Public honor—a 'pivotal value' in the ancient Mediterranean world (see Bruce J. Malina, *The New Testament World: Insights from Cultural Anthropology* [Louisville, KY: Westminster/John Knox, rev. edn, 1993], pp. 28–62)—had more to do with family heritage and patronal networks than sheer accumulation of wealth. To be sure, generous sharing of wealth could enhance one's public standing, but money made at a 'dirty' profession like dyeing would not have compensated for its lowly reputation.

68 *Contra* Rosalie Ryan, who assumes that Lydia was only a prosperous merchant, with no involvement in manufacturing. She cites the parallel of the famous Stoic philosopher Zeno, who made a fortune in the purple trade ('Lydia, A Dealer in Purple Goods', *Bible Today* 2 [1984], pp. 287–89). Similarly, David W.J. Gill observes that 'frequently it was the men who dealt with purple who were able to become members of the civic councils and therefore have a major role in the life of their communities'. In Hierapolis, for example, an inscription identified one M. Aurelius Alexander Moschianus as both 'purple-seller' and 'town councillor' ('Acts and the Urban Elites', in D.W.J. Gill and C. Gempf [eds.], *The Book of Acts in its First Century Setting*. II. *The Book of Acts in its Graeco-Roman Setting*, pp. 105–18 [114–15]). In Lydia's case, however, we have no evidence concerning any possible involvement in local politics, and the fact that she is situated *outside* the city gates may suggest a degree of marginalization (see more below).

air and plenty of water would be available for treating garments—supports the identity of a peripheral artisan. If it be objected that Luke would never portray his missionary heroes lodging with such folk, we need only recall Peter's sojourn in the house of Simon the *tanner* (9.39; 10.6, 32), another profession of questionable odor.[69]

Whatever the demands of Lydia's occupation, they do not distract her from an active *religious* life. As Tabitha was introduced as a 'disciple', Lydia first appears as a 'worshiper of God' (σεβομένη τὸν θεόν), probably denoting here a Gentile sympathizer with the Jewish faith, perhaps even a proselyte (cf. 13.43; 17.4, 17; 18.7). Appropriately, Paul first encounters Lydia along with other worshiping women 'on the sabbath day' at a riverside 'place of prayer' (προσευχή) or synagogue. As Bernadette Brooten has established, women's participation, even leadership, in synagogue services is amply attested in Luke's text and environment (cf. Lk. 13.10–17; Acts 17.4, 10–12; 18.26).[70] While we do not know Lydia's precise role in the Jewish assembly, we do learn of her significant contribution to the new community of believers in Paul's gospel. She stands out as the first Christian convert on European soil and chief patron of the visiting missionaries and the emerging Philippian church congregating in her house. Along with being head of her economic household, Lydia apparently holds a similar place of authority in the fictive family of faith which she hosts, comprised of both male and female members ('brothers', ἀδελφοί, 16.40).[71] Far from being a perfunctory service, hospitality constitutes an honorable, indispensable form of ministry in Luke and Acts, which leading figures like Jesus and Paul not only benefit from, but also practice.[72] In Lydia's case, her hospitality certainly goes beyond mere maid-service to represent a courageous act of support in a politically charged situation. As Schottroff puts it:

> Each detail of the story speaks of Lydia's power ... She 'compelled' Paul and other men to be her guests. She took initiative to such an extent that even our source—Acts—briefly cites her speech ... She insisted on having a house church in her home, knowing well that she thereby became conspicuous in the city and could possibly be persecuted for it ... The power growing in this community was not the kind that makes others small but a power that is shared and wants to make others great when they are small and in misery. Lydia's 'compelling' was an expression of a power not directed toward rule but toward justice.[73]

While personally applauding this assessment of Lydia's 'power', I fear that it glosses over less liberating aspects of Luke's story. Lydia's 'speech', as Schottroff calls it, simply recounts Lydia's offer of hospitality. Though reflecting a degree of boldness on Lydia's part, her discourse is hardly up to the standards of Peter or Paul's sermons

---

69 Schottroff, 'Lydia', pp. 132–34.

70 Bernadette J. Brooten, *Women Leaders in the Ancient Synagogue: Inscriptional Evidence and Background Issues* (BJS, 36; Atlanta and Chico, CA: Scholars Press, 1982), pp. 139–41.

71 See John Gillman, 'Hospitality in Acts 16', *LS* 17 (1992), pp. 189–91.

72 See Lk. 2.1–7; 5.27–32; 7.36–50; 10.38–42; 11.37–52; 14.1–24; 22.14–27; 24.28–30, 36–43; Acts 9.10–19; 16.27–34; 17.5–9; 18.2–3; 28.7–10, 30–31; John Koenig, *New Testament Hospitality: Partnership with Strangers as Promise and Mission* (OBT, 17; Philadelphia: Fortress Press, 1985), pp. 85–123; Spencer, *Portrait of Philip*, pp. 253–62.

73 Schottroff, 'Lydia', pp. 135–36.

in Acts. And her wider involvement with the dynamic proclamation of God's word is much more passive than active. A double emphasis falls on her 'listening' to Paul's message, and even here she does not receive full credit: '*the Lord* opened her heart to listen' (16.14).[74] As elsewhere in Luke and Acts, despite the ideal of women prophets (Lk. 1.26–56; Acts 2.17–18), the 'better part' assigned to women is usually that of silent listening rather than eloquent proclaiming.[75]

While Lydia's clothing business does not hinder her religious pursuits, is there any sense in which it might actually enhance her ministry? Unlike Tabitha, for whom making clothing for the poor *was* her ministry, Lydia does not, as far as we know, donate any of her purple goods to charity; indeed, supplying the rich with fancy garments might even be viewed as legitimating an oppressive hierarchy ('There was a rich man who was dressed in purple ...', Lk. 16.19–31). At the risk of over-interpreting the Lydia account, I suggest a possible metaphorical link between her purple and church work, inspired by the tradition (sketched above) of women's textile labor as a model of women's wider creative endeavors. As Lydia employed her household in transforming ordinary materials into regal purple fabrics through a washing–dyeing process, so she leads her household—and others who gather in her house—to spiritual renewal through Christian faith and baptism. Paul himself might well have regarded Lydia's home as an inclusive center for 'Jew and Greek, slave and free, male and female'—for all who 'were baptized into Christ' and 'clothed with Christ' (Gal. 3.27–28).[76]

Priscilla: The Teaching Tentmaker

The story of Priscilla features a woman employed alongside her husband Aquila as a tentmaker, who hosts the itinerant missionary Paul in her home in Corinth, journeys with Aquila and Paul to Ephesus, and participates in catechizing another traveling teacher, an erudite Alexandrian named Apollos (Acts 18.1–4, 18–28). Unlike the two preceding women of 'the cloth', Priscilla's marital status is clear and consistent. She is the wife of Aquila, a Jew from Pontus, and is never mentioned apart from him (18.2, 18, 26). Interestingly, however, in two of the three named references in Acts, Priscilla is cited first (18.18, 26), matching the exact pattern of Paul's letters.[77] This inversion of the typical 'Mr and Mrs' order may point to Priscilla's dominance in the relationship, in terms of either social status,[78] ministerial

---

74 See F. Scott Spencer, *Acts* (Readings: A New Biblical Commentary; Sheffield: Sheffield Academic Press, 1997), pp. 165–66.

75 See Lk. 10.42; Barbara E. Reid, *Choosing the Better Part? Women in the Gospel of Luke* (Collegeville, MN: Liturgical Press, 1996); Spencer, 'Out of Mind', pp. 132–53.

76 Cf. J. Gillman, 'Hospitality', pp. 188–89.

77 In Rom. 16.3 and 2 Tim. 4.19, Prisca (Priscilla's more formal name) appears first; she is listed after Aquila only in 1 Cor. 16.19. Luke's use of the diminutive 'Priscilla' surely reflects a term of endearment or familiarity rather than 'a put-down', as Jerome Murphy-O'Connor suggests ('Prisca and Aquila: Traveling Tentmakers and Church Builders', *BR* 8 [1992], pp. 40–51, 62 [40]).

78 Her name recalls the *gens Prisca*, a venerable Roman family, perhaps suggesting her elite background. Her inclusion in the Jews' expulsion from Rome under Claudius (Acts 18.2) may owe more to her marital tie with Aquila than her ancestry. Only Aquila is specifically labeled 'a Jew ... a native of Pontus' (18.2); we know nothing of Priscilla's origins. See F.F. Bruce, *The Pauline Circle* (Grand Rapids: Eerdmans; Exeter: Paternoster, 1985), pp. 45–47.

function or both. In any case, she is no subordinate cipher in the most reliable text (the revised Western version is another story).[79] Like the other Christian couple featured in Acts, the ill-fated Ananias and Sapphira, Aquila and Priscilla appear as collaborative associates in business and ministry.[80] Priscilla does not, however, simply follow her husband's lead as Sapphira did (all the way to her grave).

According to the most natural reading of the text, the partnership between Priscilla and Aquila extended to their craft of tentmaking: 'he [Paul] stayed with *them* [αὐτοῖς, Aquila and Priscilla], and he was working [with them], for by trade *they were tentmakers* (ἦσαν σκηνοποιοί)' (18.3). There is no good grammatical reason to exclude Priscilla from the 'they/them' team. On sociohistorical grounds, however, Ronald Hock has argued that 'tentmaking' in this context referred primarily to the stout, manual—that is, manly—labor of leather-working, as opposed to the more delicate occupation of linen-weaving performed chiefly by women.[81] While Hock provides some valuable insights into the manufacture of leather goods in the ancient world, he goes too far in constructing unnecessarily sharp labor and gender dichotomies.[82] The great leather–linen debate, for example, is largely moot, as Jerome Murphy-O'Connor has shown. Why not both means of making tents and related goods? In addition to the evidence that Hock marshals for leather-working, Murphy-O'Connor details the demand for colored woven linen ship-sails—like Cleopatra's royal purple sail in her voyages with Mark Antony—and decorative linen awnings draped around forums and theaters as sun-screens—such as the 'star-spangled, sky blue' curtains around Nero's amphitheater in Rome.[83] We may recall similar tapestries of dyed linen and goats' hair (along with tanned hides and fine leather), fashioned by skilled women and men, adorning the wilderness tabernacle (Exod. 35.23–26). Also, actual tents used for market booths and temporary lodging—at the popular Isthmian Games near Corinth, for example—could also be made of durable canvas as well as leather. In sum, tentmakers like Paul, Aquila and Priscilla were probably 'equally at home in sewing together strips of leather or different weights of canvas', using various awls, knives, needles, and waxed threads in the process.[84] Such work was unquestionably strenuous, time-consuming, even

---

79 As part of an apparent agenda 'to reduce the prominence of Priscilla', the Western reviser (in codex D) adds Aquila's name in 18.3, 18, 21—without also mentioning Priscilla—and reverses the order to put Aquila first in 18.26 (Bruce M. Metzger, *A Textual Commentary on the Greek New Testament* [New York: United Bible Societies, 1971], pp. 460–61, 466–67).

80 See Acts 5.1–2—'But a man named Ananias, *with the consent of his wife Sapphira*, sold a piece of property; *with his wife's knowledge*, he kept back some of the proceeds' (cf. 5.7–10).

81 Ronald F. Hock, *The Social Context of Paul's Ministry: Tentmaking and Apostleship* (Philadelphia: Fortress Press, 1980), p. 81 n. 46. Throughout this study, Hock typically refers only to Aquila the tentmaker, thus effacing Priscilla's potential contribution to the family business (see e.g. pp. 31, 50, 59, 67).

82 See a similar critique in F.M. Gillman, *Women Who Knew Paul*, pp. 18, 51–52. In two studies, Luise Schottroff suggests that wives were often required to assist their husbands in difficult manual trades like tentmaking, simply to make ends meet: 'Women as Followers of Jesus in New Testament Times', in Norman K. Gottwald and Richard A. Horsley (eds.), *The Bible and Liberation: Political and Social Hermeneutics* (Maryknoll, NY: Orbis; London: SPCK, rev. edn, 1993), pp. 458–59; and in her *Let the Oppressed Go Free*, pp. 90–91.

83 Jerome Murphy-O'Connor, *Paul: A Critical Life* (Oxford: Oxford University Press, 1997), pp. 86–87, citing Pliny, *Natural History* 19.22–24; cf. *idem*, 'Prisca and Aquila', pp. 43–49.

84 Murphy-O'Connor, *Paul*, pp. 87–88.

slavish, as Paul himself attests (1 Cor. 4.10–12; 9.6, 19; 2 Cor. 4.5; 6.5, 10; 11.27; 1 Thess. 2.9), but there is no reason to think that Priscilla and other women were not up to the task (cf. Rom. 16.3-4). There is also no reason to assume that Priscilla, Aquila, and other tentmakers were especially well-off economically or socially. Like other members of the toiling artisan class, they may have struggled to make ends meet and been snubbed by ruling elites and leisured aristocrats.[85]

The *religious* service of Priscilla and Aquila may be tracked in three stages of increasing authority. First, they provide material support in the form of lodging and employment for the itinerant missionary Paul, who proclaims his message in the local Corinthian synagogue and in the nearby home of the God-fearing Titius Justus (Acts 18.1–8). At this stage, Priscilla and Aquila's ministry in Corinth seems more limited than Lydia's in Philippi: the married couple make no converts, from their household or otherwise, and their residence does not appear to be the headquarters of a 'house church'.[86] In the second stage, however, their involvement intensifies as they accompany Paul to Ephesus and are left in charge of the developing mission there when Paul moves on to other areas (18.18–23). At this point, Priscilla and Aquila function much like Barnabas, Timothy, Silas, and other Pauline missionary partners. Finally, their leadership becomes most evident in a climactic encounter with another visiting teacher, the 'eloquent' and 'enthusiastic' Apollos of Alexandria. While teaching 'accurately concerning the things of Jesus' in the Ephesian synagogue, Apollos needed more advanced, sophisticated instruction. Enter the master teachers, Priscilla and Aquila (note the order), who 'took him aside and explained the way of God to him *more accurately*' (18.24–26). This is as close as we get in Acts to a woman proclaiming the word to a man. To be sure, the scene is normalized somewhat by the presence of her husband; nonetheless, Priscilla takes the lead and more than holds her own in debating and correcting the learned Alexandrian. Whether she (and Aquila) 'take him aside' in a corner of the synagogue[87] or in their home[88] is uncertain; in any case, Priscilla takes the initiative and assumes the role of an authoritative teacher.

How might her teaching and tentmaking correlate? Here we may rely more on logical inference than metaphorical imagination. Recent appraisals of tentmaking in the Pauline world have accented its particular compatibility with missionary vocations and various intellectual pursuits.[89] The portability of requisite tools of the

---

85 Hock, *Social Context*, pp. 31–37; Murphy-O'Connor, *Paul*, pp. 88–89; Schottroff, *Let the Oppressed Go Free*, pp. 88–91, 106. Utilizing the social stratification model of Gerhard Lenksi, Jerome Neyrey classifies urban artisans like Priscilla and Aquila as 'landless peasants, either dispossessed or non-inheriting ones', positioned just above the 'unclean, degraded and expendables' on the social ladder. Still, artisans could either be 'well-off or penurious'. Where Priscilla and Aquila fit on this economic scale remains uncertain (Jerome H. Neyrey, 'Luke's Social Location of Paul: Cultural Anthropology and the Status of Paul in Acts', in B. Witherington, III (ed.), *History, Literature and Society in the Book of Acts* [Cambridge: Cambridge University Press, 1996], pp. 251–79 [258, 266]).

86 Murphy-O'Connor opines that Paul's appropriation of the house of Titius Justus rather than that of Priscilla and Aquila may imply that the latter residence was not large enough to accommodate the congregation. He even entertains the possibility that the couple rented, rather than owned, workshop space in Corinth, befitting their station as artisans of modest means ('Prisca and Aquila', p. 49).

87 Brooten, *Women Leaders*, p. 140.

88 Seim, *Double Message*, p. 130.

89 Reimer, *Women in the Acts of the Apostles*, pp. 208–209; Hock, *Social Context*, pp. 37–42; Murphy-O'Connor, *Paul*, pp. 86–89.

trade and high demand for its products in bustling urban centers made tentmaking an apt profession for itinerant evangelists. Priscilla and Aquila would thus be able to transfer their business and ministry from Rome to Corinth to Ephesus with relative ease. The tentmaking workshop itself, perhaps located at the front or first floor of a residence, would afford a reasonably quiet and relaxed atmosphere for concurrent work and conversation with customers and other visitors, not only about the job at hand but also the issues of the day. The shop of Simon the shoemaker became a famous venue for philosophical discussion in Athens, including such notables as Socrates and Pericles. Other Cynic philosophers also combined artisanship and scholarship, stitching and teaching, establishing the craftshop 'as a conventional social setting for intellectual discourse'.[90] Paul's reminder to the Thessalonians that 'we worked night and day ... *while* we proclaimed to you the gospel of God' (1 Thess. 2.9) may also intimate a more direct link between manual labor and evangelical witness than is often assumed.[91] Sewing cloth or leather to make tents may go hand in hand with sowing the word or gospel to make disciples.

Stitching the Pieces Together

In our sampling of weaving stories from Greco-Roman, Jewish, and Lukan sources, we uncovered certain tensions between women's textile work as isolated domestic labor in support of the patriarchal family, on the one hand, and as a wider creative outlet for both economic profit and religious service, on the other hand. The three working women of 'the cloth' in Acts negotiate these tensions in both similar and distinctive ways.

On the *domestic* front, all three women seem to ply their craft, at least partly, in a residential setting. That is, they use their homes as a base of operation, a workshop of sorts. Beyond this common foundation, however, different household structures emerge: Tabitha appears to work alone as a single woman; Lydia seems to be equally independent of paterfamilial rule at the same time she manages a working household of her own; and Priscilla labors alongside—but not subordinate to—her husband and at least one other male employee and household guest (Paul).

The *commercial* extension of domestic cloth production also varies: whereas Tabitha simply gives away her garments to needy widows, both Lydia and Priscilla market their goods for profit. While these two women's textile businesses may have brought them a measure of financial security, as hard-working artisans engaged in menial labor they probably did not enjoy high status among society's true, leisured nobility. Luke is happy to identify upper-crust women within early Christianity when he can; the fact that he does not so label Tabitha, Lydia, and Priscilla likely means that they did not fit the bill.

All three women of 'the cloth' stand out as models of *religious* devotion, but each illustrates her own unique interface between textile work and Christian ministry. Tabitha's case offers the most *direct* and *material* connection: clothing widows *was* her ministry, the prime evidence of her 'good deeds' and discipleship. Lydia's purple business, by contrast, while not incompatible with ministry, seems related to it only

---

90 Hock, *Social Context*, p. 41.
91 Hock, *Social Context*, pp. 47–49.

in an *indirect* and *metaphorical* fashion: handling dyed garments may be compared symbolically to hosting baptized converts. Finally, *inference* and *circumstantial* evidence suggest a plausible tie between Priscilla's tentmaking and her missionizing and teaching: her manual occupation provided an optimal setting for her ministerial vocation.

However we parse the precise relationship between women's cloth work and religious service in Acts, a clear case is made for 'braiding a footbridge', to reprise Elizabeth Johnson's image, rather than driving a wedge between so-called 'menial' and 'spiritual' pursuits. I might wish that Luke had woven tighter specific links between women's practical service and *prophetic* opportunities, between sewing cloth and sowing the word. Priscilla's portrayal as a teaching tentmaker points in the right direction, but unfortunately it stands too alone in Acts and too much in the shadow of Paul's dominant witness. If Christian women are ever to fit 'the cloth' of ordained ministry as easily as men, they must be given a great deal more *authoritative voice* than Luke allows. Still, it is good for all in the church, both men and women—especially those within heavily word-centered traditions—to be reminded that acts of service can themselves speak volumes. As the earthly Jesus announced to his disciples in the upper room—'I am among you as one who serves'—so the risen Jesus embodied in Tabitha might well have proclaimed in another upper room—'I am among you as one who *sews*.'

LIFESTYLES OF THE RICH AND CHRISTIAN: WOMEN, WEALTH, AND SOCIAL FREEDOM*

JAMES M. ARLANDSON

After much struggle and with more struggle left to do, Christian women in the Western world today enjoy unprecedented wealth and social freedom. In honor of these advancements we would not be amiss if we looked at some wealthy women in Luke–Acts, all of whom became followers of Jesus, so that from their lives both men and women today can glean some insights into how to handle wealth: the 'leading' women in Acts 17.4; the 'prominent' women in Acts 17.12; Mary, the wealthy landowner in Acts 12.12–17; and Joanna in Lk. 8.1–3. Luke's depiction of their lives in a narrative that is normative for Christians can clarify our attitudes towards wealth, status, career, public involvement, and gender roles even though their lives are separated from ours by twenty centuries.

What was life like for women of their class location? Did money gain them public power, official or otherwise, or were they restricted to the domestic sphere? Did they have any control over money, or did men in their patriarchal society deprive them and control them? Worse, does Luke's narrative deprive or oppress them?

Answering these questions involves a two-step process. First, the women's class and their roles within it need to be determined. Once this is done, we can then investigate their social and economic freedoms by comparing their portraits with descriptions of contemporaneous Mediterranean women.

The Ruling Class

Throughout the Roman empire in cities smaller than *metropoleis* like Ephesus, Antioch, and Jerusalem, the ruling class could achieve high levels of wealth if they had large estates. Within their own cities, the wealthy enjoyed high esteem and could obtain strong political power by joining the council (βουλή) or by holding political offices, which involved overseeing and contributing money to civic life.

'First' and 'Prominent' Women (Acts 17.4, 12). Paul and his colleagues arrived in Thessalonica and converted 'first' or 'leading' (πρώτη) women to the faith (v. 4). Next, in Beroea, they converted 'prominent' or 'respectable' (εὐσχήμων) women. It is not, though, clear to the modern reader where these women were situated socially and politically. Were they public office-holders? Wives of council members such as Roman *decurions* or Greek *bouleutai*? However, the two adjectives Luke accords them would have been sufficient for any first-century audience to know that the

---

* This article can be considered as an alternative to ch. 4 in my book, *Women, Class, and Society in Early Christianity: Models from Luke–Acts* (Peabody, MA: Hendrickson, 1996), pp. 120–50, though I'm happy with ch. 4 as it is.

women came from the same ruling class, a class with certain privileges, and certain duties.[1]

In Chariton's novel *Chaereas and Callirhoe* (first century CE), Dionysius is called the 'first man' (πρῶτος) of Miletus, and Hermocrates is the 'first man' (πρῶτος) of Syracuse, and each, respectively, the 'first man' of Ionia and Sicily.[2] Thus, both men occupy the highest levels of political power. As usual in Chariton's novel, fictional descriptions mirror social reality. In Acts 28.7 a certain Publius, whose father Paul healed of a fever and dysentery, is the 'first man' (πρῶτος) of the island of Malta. Josephus, Luke's contemporary, uses the term repeatedly for the leading men of a tribe, people, and priesthood, most of whom either have political power or compete for it.[3] Strabo (c. 64 BCE–21 CE) the geographer, who traveled the Mediterranean world, praises the city of Mytilene for producing famous artists and politicians, one of whom became the 'first' among the friends of the Emperor Tiberius.[4]

In addition to these literary references are inscriptions. 'Symmachus, son of Symmachus, orator and first (πρῶτον) [in] the city, financial overseer of the council and the council of elders ...'[5] The governing bodies in Aphrodisias in Asia Minor set up an honorary decree for a woman named Tata, who lived in the second century CE: 'The council, the assembly, and the council of elders honored with first honors (ταῖς πρώταις τειμαῖς) Tata, daughter of Diodorus, son of Leon, sacred priestess of Hera for life, mother of the city, who became and remained wife of Attalus, son of Pytheas, Wreath-bearer, herself from a leading and illustrious family (αὐτὴν γένους πρώτου καὶ λαμπροῦ) ...'[6] The inscription further records that Tata was a priestess of the imperial cult, twice supplied oil for athletes, became a *Stephanephorus* (see below), offered sacrifices for the health of the imperial family, held banquets for the people many times, and imported the foremost actors and dancers in Asia; she was a woman 'who spared no expense', that is, she used her own money generously. These passages and inscriptions reveal that πρῶτος and πρώτη are used of men and women of wealth, prestige, and political power.

As πρώτη is used for 'first' or 'leading' people, similarly, εὐσχήμων is used for 'prominent' or 'respectable' persons from the same class. Acts 13.50 joins 'prominent' women (γυναῖκας τὰς εὐσχήμονας) with 'leading' men (τοὺς πρώτους) of Pisidian Antioch, who persecute Paul and his colleagues. These two adjectives are

---

1 I. Richter Reimer, *Women in the Acts of the Apostles: A Feminist Liberation Perspective* (trans. L.M. Maloney; Minneapolis: Fortress Press, 1995), pp. 244–46, incorrectly separates the two adjectives as representing two groups. But both words connote the wealthy, powerful, and prestigious men and women from the same upper class. See n. 15 below.

2 Chariton, 'Chaereas and Callirhoe', in B.P. Reardon (ed. and trans.), *Collected Ancient Greek Novels* (Los Angeles: University of California Press, 1989), pp. 41 and 43 for Dionysius (2.4, 5); and pp. 22 and 49 for Hermocrates (1.1, 2.11).

3 W. Michaelis, 'πρῶτος', *TDNT*, VI, p. 866.

4 Strabo, *Geography* (trans. H. Jones; LCL; Cambridge, MA: Harvard University Press, 1941–55), 13.3.

5 W.M. Ramsay, *The Cities and Bishoprics of Phrygia* (New York: Arno Press, 1975 [1895–97]), p. 642. He explains why λογισ[τή]ν should be translated 'financial overseer'.

6 H.W. Pleket (ed.), *Epigraphica. II: Texts on the Social History of the Greek World* (Leiden: Brill, 1969), p. 31 (n. 18). See also M.R. Lefkowitz and M.B. Fant (trans. and eds.), *Women's Life in Greece and Rome: A Sourcebook in Translation* (Baltimore, MD: Johns Hopkins University Press, 2nd edn, 1992), p. 302 (#432).

synonymous in signifying the ruling class: since classes at widely divergent levels did not mix, the reference cannot be to lower-class but 'respectable' women ('lower-class and prominent' is a contradiction) who join forces with upper-class men. Nor is it likely that Luke would describe the women who persecuted Christians as 'respectable' in the moral sense. Rather, these women correspond to the leading men: both are from the ruling class. Indeed, many other occurrences of εὐσχήμων, accompanied by the adjective πρῶτος or not, are found in reference to the upper classes.

In Mk 15.43 Joseph of Arimathea is called a εὐσχήμων βουλευτής ('prominent member of the council'). This prominence agrees with inscriptions that use the adjective and praise an office-holder for effective administration.[7] Josephus uses the term to refer to 'prominent' men who support Rome and oppose two other factions, one of which was composed of 'the most insignificant' persons, and both of which had an anti-Roman agenda.[8] Clearly, in this context the men who supported Rome were the best in leadership, wisdom, and judgment. Plutarch (c. 50–120 CE) does mention a certain Tarpeia, one of 'the maidens of prominence' (τῶν εὐσχημόνων παρθένων) who was punished for betraying her high office by arranging a bribe,[9] so the adjective does not always mean only morally upright. According to the grammarian Phrynicus (third century CE), εὐσχήμων refers to all persons of rank; he implies that they also have wisdom.[10]

Finally, a second-century CE inscription records an honorary decree awarded to a certain Aba for her generosity to the city of Histria in Dacia: 'With Good Fortune. The council and the assembly decreed, Ulpius Demetrius proposed, when Diogenes Theodorus brought it to a vote: Whereas, Aba, daughter of Hekataios, son of Euxenides, wife of Herakôn, being from a distinguished family and illustrious ancestors, a family that declined not one act of honor or exemplary civic service (φιλοτιμίαν ἢ λειτουργίαν εὐσχήμονα)...'[11] The phrase 'act of honor or exemplary civic service' is translated thus because other inscriptions link φιλοτιμία (lit. 'love of honor') with generous contributions and donations,[12] and λειτουργία is the service or duty imposed on the rich for the benefit of city life and development.[13] It is not often in inscriptions that the adjective 'exemplary' (εὐσχήμων) is attached to terms like 'civic service'; all contributions and donations would be considered exemplary, thus making the adjective redundant. It is almost as if the governing bodies wanted to elevate the service of Aba's family beyond that of others in the ruling class, even when the governing members knew that only their class could perform such services in the first place. Similarly, calling Nicodemus a 'prominent'

---

7 H. Greeven, 'εὐσχήμων', *TDNT*, II, p. 770. Effective administration is usually mentioned with καλός.

8 Josephus, *The Life* (trans. H.St.J. Thackeray; LCL; Cambridge, MA: Harvard University Press, 1926), 9.32–37.

9 Plutarch, 'Parallel Stories', in *Moralia* (trans. F.C. Babbitt *et al.*; LCL; Cambridge, MA: Harvard University Press, 1927–69), 309C.

10 W.G. Rutherford (ed.), *The New Phrynicus* (Hildesheim: Georg Olms, 1968 [1881]) p. 417.

11 Pleket, *Epigraphica*, II, p. 33 (#21), my translation.

12 A.R. Hands, *Charities and Social Aid in Greece and Rome* (Ithaca, NY: Cornell University Press, 1968), pp. 175–209, translates many inscriptions and notes whenever φιλοτιμία appears.

13 Arlandson, *Women, Class, and Society*, pp. 27–36.

member of the council means that compared with only council members, Nicodemus was at the top. This inscription, like the literary references, links εὐσχήμων with the ruling class by going on to record the offices Aba's family held, such as *Stephanophori*, priests, and *archons* (civic magistrates).

The common factor in all these diverse examples is that εὐσχήμων always refers to the highest level of society and implies political power and a display of wealth. Not only does it mean respectable or exemplary behavior,[14] it also elevates the people to whom it is attached more highly than everyone else in society and sometimes in their own high class as well: the adjective is found invariably in that context, as in Acts 13.50, for example, which unambiguously connects it with πρῶτος, both signifying persons from the same upper class. It is not the case that if references to εὐσχήμων were found in the context of ordinary things or people, the ordinary suddenly becomes elite. Rather, in a context with other data supporting the presence of the upper class, εὐσχήμων refers to them. This is true in Acts 17.12 which differentiates the 'many' or commoners who converted from a second group of converts, the 'prominent' women and men. Since first-century readers lived in a society divided by class—much more than our own in the West—they would automatically know who were intended by πολλοὶ μὲν οὖν ἐξ αὐτῶν ἐπίστευσαν ('and many of them therefore believed') and by καὶ τῶν Ἑλληνίδων γυναικῶν τῶν εὐσχήμων καὶ ἀνδρῶν οὐκ ὀλίγοι ('and not a few prominent Greek women and men').

Thus, as signified by the adjectives πρωτή and εὐσχήμων, the newly converted women in Thessalonica and Beroea were wealthy, powerful, and enjoyed a high measure of political power and social prestige in their own city, just like their eastern Greek analogues.[15] Both adjectives denote that the women belonged to the ruling class within their own cities. And while the adjectives alone do not indicate how much social freedom and power these 'first' and 'prominent' women had, the literature does indicate something about their lives.

Social Freedom

Often they donated their own money to help people or to improve the city's appearance with new buildings or other structures. Philê lived in the first century BCE in Western Asia Minor, near Miletus, in the city of Priene to which she became a benefactor: 'Philê, daughter of Apollonius, wife of Thessalus, son of Polydeuces, first woman *Stephanephorus* (στεφανηφορήσασα πρώτη γυναικῶν) dedicated with her own means the water receptacle and the water channels in the city.'[16] The

---

14 Pleket, *Epigraphica*, II, p. 38 (#25), concerns Berenice, whose manner of life or conduct was 'good' and 'respectable.'

15 This conclusion contradicts that of Reimer, *Women in the Acts of the Apostles*, pp. 243–45, which separates 'leading' from 'prominent'. In the aggregate, there is no difference between having wealth, noble birth, and high status, even among those aristocrats who foolishly lost their wealth, because losing wealth in high levels happened rarely in the aggregate. Ancestry or family connections could block the wealthy from official political power if they did not have the proper background, but across the Roman empire, this did not occur very often, and certainly no evidence in Acts 13.50 supports this claim. My conclusion also contradicts W.A. Meeks's statement, in *The First Urban Christians: The Social World of the Apostle Paul* (New Haven, CT: Yale University Press, 1983), p. 73, that no landed aristocrats were found among the Christians.

16 Pleket, *Epigraphica*, II, p. 16, my translation. In this case, πρώτη refers to chronology, not social rank; that is, she was the first woman to become Wreath-bearer in her city.

Stephanephorus or 'wreath-bearer' is a political and religious office that included wearing a wreath or possibly even a gold crown and standing in a prominent place at sacrifices and civic festivals.[17] Whatever the requirements, Philê occupied a place of prominence in her city. Significantly, this inscription shows that she controlled her own money even though her husband is explicitly mentioned. As we will see, this fact illumines the example of Joanna in Lk. 8.1–3 who also gave out of her own resources even though her husband, Chusa, is mentioned.

The following inscriptions confirm that women had independent financial control. The first concerns a woman named Epiê honored with an inscription from the people of the island of Thasos (N. Aegean Sea). 'With unanimous consent. Whereas, Epiê, daughter of Dionysius, conducts herself piously before the gods and philanthropically before the people, and willingly gave herself for all the upkeep of the temples, by which not only did she strive eagerly for the public good, but she also repaired the temples from her own resources; she was first (πρώτη) to give willingly votive offerings for the Artemision and for the temple of Aphrodite ...'[18] The lengthy inscription goes on to record how she gave for the refurbishing of the front gates and doors of the Artemision, for bearing the costs of holding the office of priestess, which, the inscription says, were expensive, and for paying for various objects, some golden, devoted to goddesses. The inscription spells out not only in this excerpt but at least two more times that she gave from her own funds.

The ultimate charitable act comes from Menodora who lived in the third century CE. From a powerful family, Menodora was the wealthiest person in her hometown of Syllium in Pisidia. Her generosity is typical of many wealthy women in the Hellenistic and Roman eras, though theirs is not so lavish.[19] In gratitude for her benefaction to the city, the council of elders and the assembly paid for this inscription:

The council of elders (ἡ γερουσία) and the people (ὁ δῆμός) have honored the priestess of all the gods, hierophant for life, and a member of the Finance Committee (δεκάπρωτον), demiourgos, and gymnasiarch for the provision of oil, Menodora, daughter of Megacles, demiourgos, a member of the Finance Committee, and gymnasiarch for the provision of oil; on behalf of her son Megacles, she willingly gave to her homeland 300,000 silver denarii for the maintenance of children; and she further gave willingly in her own *gymnasiarchy*, and in her son's office as *demiourgos*, and in her own office as *demiourgos*, and in the *gymnasiarchy* of her daughter, to each councilor, 86 *denarii*; to each member of the council of elders, 80 *denarii*; to each member of the assembly, 77 *denarii*; to the wives of each of

---

17 See also Lefkowitz and Fant, *Women's Life*, p. 346 n. 50. For the crown being gold, see the inscription for Archippê in Pleket, *Epigraphica*, II, p. 13, lines 13–14.

18 Pleket, *Epigraphica*, II, p. 18 (#7), my translation. Pleket gives the date as ranging from the first century BCE to the first century CE. Here πρώτη means chronologically, not socially 'first', although the two meanings in this case may not be mutually exclusive: the inscription says she was the only woman in her class and community wealthy enough to bear the costs of performing civic obligations; thus, she is ranked first among her peers. The inscription further implies that the other women were unwilling (or hardly willing or willing but with difficulty) to bear the costs. The clause, 'by which things not only did she strive eagerly for the public good', is ἐν οἷς οὐ τὰ κοινὰ ἐφιλοτιμήθη μόνον, which could also mean that Epiê strives eagerly for the public domain and, by extension, public affairs, since τὰ κοινά is plural.

19 Hands, *Charities*, pp. 175–209, has a list of inscriptions that show the generosity of the wealthy—many of whom were women acting in their own behalf with their own wealth.

these, 3 *denarii*; to each citizen, 9 *denarii*; and to the *vindictariis*, freedmen and resident aliens, 3 *denarii* ...[20]

This inscription, rich in data, shows that she gave an enormous sum to the children's maintenance. And despite this expenditure, she had enough money to contribute handsomely to many others. The council and assembly could number close to a hundred in a small city and several hundreds in a large one. Moreover, she held four political and religious offices: priesthood for life; *hierophant* (an office that teaches religion); *demiourgos* (chief architect or city planner, which means she gave money for building or maintaining structures); *gymnasiarch* (overseer or contributor to the cultural center); membership in 'the Finance Committee', which oversaw the city's finances. In no way does she appear restricted from using her own money or barred from economic and social life.

These inscriptions and others indicate both that women contributed their own finances to civic life and that they played prominent public roles. Indeed, one way wealthy women gained status and power was to hold political office. The following list includes some of the offices that women held, their number, cities, and dates (as far as the information is known).[21]

Hipparchos, Highest Civic Office (five women in Cyzicus, Troas; first to third century CE);
Prytanis, Ruler (28 eponymous women in eight cities; first to third century CE);
Stephanephoros, Wreath-bearer, related to a secular magistracy and a priesthood (37 in 17 cities—second century BCE to third CE);
Dekaprôtos, Member of the Finance Committee (one woman, Menodora, third CE);
Dêmiourgos, Chief Artificer or Chief Architect (ten in six cities; second century BCE to 3rd CE);
Archôn, Civic Magistrate, a general title (three in three cities);
Agônothete, Sponsor of the Contests (18 in 14 cities; first to third century CE);
Panêgyriarch, Sponsor of the Sacrifices and Banquets (one woman in one city);
Gymnasiarch, Ruler of the Cultural and Educational Center (48 in 23 cities; first to third century CE);
Timouchos, Honor-holder, where there was no *prytanis* (one woman);
Priestess, presided over and paid for cultic ceremonies in local temples (many women in many cities);
Stratêgos, Member of Magisterial Board (one woman in Aegiale);

---

20 The inscription concludes with a note that the 'tribe' or society of Meäleitides put up the statue. Document in G. Radet and P. Paris, 'Inscriptions de Syllion en Pamphylie', *Bulletin de correspondence hellénique* 13 (1889), pp. 486–97. Δεκάπρωτον is a Finance Committee, with its members, presumably ten, chosen from the *boulê* (p. 495). 'Maintenance' is from Hands's translation (*Charities*, p. 192) for τροφάς but could also mean 'food', especially since another inscription shows Menodora giving wheat to the members of the ruling bodies (Radet and Paris, 'Inscriptions', p. 487). The *vindictariis* (in m. dat. pl. οὐδικταρίοις so the Lat m. dat. pl. is used) are slaves that have been freed with the 'rod', through a ceremony using that instrument (pp. 496–97).

21 See Arlandson, *Women, Class, and Society*, pp. 31–33, for the sources and discussion of the roles in the inscriptions.

Gerousiarchissa, President of the Council of Elders (one woman in Thessalonica; third century CE);
Lyciarch, Presiding Officer over the Federation of Lycia (two women);
Pontarch, Presiding Officer over the Federation of Pontus (one woman);
Asiarch, Highest Provincial Office in Asia Minor (one woman).

It seems, then, that women held positions of power and were active in public life without incurring any shame or loss of modesty. Furthermore, these inscriptions do not at all correspond to the maximum number of women who held offices from the third century BCE to the third century CE. They *represent* far more women than the surviving records are able to show, since many of the offices were vacated and filled yearly or within a few years.

Thus, throughout the Greek East, 'leading' and 'prominent' women were politically involved and wielded their money and power freely and publicly. So even though in Acts 17 Luke is silent on the women's day-to-day leadership, it is more likely than not that they participated in city life or held public office. It is also more likely than not that they used their money in the same way that their counterparts did throughout the Greek East (except, after their conversions, for sacrifices; cf. Acts 15.20–29).

Luke's silence on the women's leadership does not mean that he restricts them.[22] Rather, he is silent for two straightforward reasons. First, Luke's omission of details means that his theme in Acts is centered on something bigger, such as Christianity's spread. It should be noted that, likewise, Luke omits data about Bartholomew, Thomas, and Matthew, to name only a few, but it can be assumed that they carried out their mission. The leading and prominent women in Acts 17.4, 12 are, for Luke, merely one more stop along the way in the inexorable, worldwide march of the church. Second, Luke did not need to detail the women's roles because his first-century audience, hearing the two adjectives, would have already known about them; this is especially the case for πρῶτος and πρωτή since they were often used in inscriptions found in city centers.

Moreover, Luke's silence works in favor of the political, social, and economic freedom of the Christian women because in no way does he *explicitly* restrict them; he never proscribes their involvement in the duties and customs required for their class, even after their conversion, provided they did not hold an office that entailed overseeing sacrifices to pagan gods. It is as if in his silence he expects that the newly converted women, provided they obey the call of the gospel first, should carry out their regular civic duties, and should thereby use their monies responsibly.

The issue of fiscal responsibility or, more broadly, questions of wealth and poverty, are complicated in Luke–Acts.[23] On the one hand, in Lk. 16.13, Jesus sums

---

22 E. Schüssler Fiorenza, *In Memory of Her: A Feminist Theological Reconstruction of Christian Origins* (New York: Crossroad, 10th anniversary edn, 1994), p. 161, points out that Luke is silent about the details of women's lives and ministry; this 'Lukan silence' restricts women, according to her hermeneutics of suspicion.

23 For more on the wealthy and poor in Luke–Acts, see *inter alia* W. Pilgrim, *Good News to the Poor: Wealth and Poverty in Luke–Acts* (Minneapolis: Augsburg, 1981), and D.P. Secombe, *Possessions and the Poor in Luke–Acts* (Linz: Studien zum Neuen Testament und seiner Umwelt, 1983).

up his parable about the dishonest manager with the pronouncement, 'You cannot serve God and wealth.' Luke also informs the reader that the pronouncement is told to the Pharisees who were lovers of money, φιλάργυροι (v. 14), a word that appears also in 1 Tim. 6.10. This denunciation of wealth fits the story of the rich man who confronted Jesus with the question of what he must do to inherit eternal life. Jesus told him to sell all he had, give to the poor, and follow him (18.18–30). When the rich man became sad because he did not want to relinquish his wealth, 'Jesus looked at him and said, "How hard it is for those who have wealth to enter the kingdom of God!"'

On the other hand, shortly after the episode of the rich man is the story of Zacchaeus, the rich tax collector (Lk. 19.1–9). In response to Jesus, Zacchaeus said that he would give half—not all—of his possessions to the poor and repay for any fraud four times the amount. Upon hearing this statement, Jesus announces that salvation has come to Zacchaeus's house (v. 9). Nowhere does the text say that Jesus required Zacchaeus to give away all of his possessions, or that Zacchaeus was barred from the kingdom of God because of his wealth. As we shall see, this absence of denouncing wealth complements the case of Joanna, Susanna, and the other women who supported Jesus out of their resources (Lk. 8.1–3). Nowhere does Jesus condemn them for having wealth, especially since they too were generous with their money. This endorsement of the rich living according to their class but being generous finds confirmation in another New Testament writing, 1 Timothy (cf. 6.6–10, 17–19), as its author grappled with more and more leading and prominent women (and men) who converted and probably stayed involved in city life. For both Luke and 1 Timothy, loving and holding tightly on to wealth is wrong, but wealth per se is not wrong if used appropriately and generously.

Despite the lack of detail in Acts 17.4 and 12, the adjectives 'prominent' and 'first' were sufficient for the audiences in Luke's day to understand that the women (and men) who converted came from the ruling class. And if the gospel does not bar a Christian from participating in daily life—and it does not, according to Luke—it is much more probable than not that at least some of these leading and prominent Christian women participated in the political and economic life of their city. Indeed, it would be surprising if they did not fulfill these roles, becoming benefactors and holding political offices, just as Philê, Epiê, Tata, Aba, and Menodora did in eastern cities.

Landowners

In antiquity, the almost exclusive source of wealth was land. All the men and women in the ruling class owned estates, and some city councils required land ownership for membership.[24] This class, though sometimes distinct from the ruling class since not all the elite chose to become public benefactors or hold office, can still overlap widely with it.

Mary, mother of John Mark (Acts 12.12–17). According to Luke, Mary lived in Jerusalem and had a son who joined Paul and Barnabas on their missionary travels.

---

24 Arlandson, *Women, Class, and Society*, pp. 68–73.

She also hosted a church in her house. It was there that Peter, after miraculously escaping from prison, sought refuge for a few moments before departing for a place unknown. Her house size, along with one other very revealing fact, means that she was a landowner, and a wealthy one.

Mary owns a house large enough for 'many [to be] gathered together' (Acts 12.12). Haenchen states, 'It was a house of some size, with a gateway (πυλών) on the street, from which the house proper was separated by the intervening courtyard.'[25] Large cities around the Mediterranean were limited in space, so urban property was always more expensive then rural land,[26] so that a house with a gate and courtyard in Jerusalem, the capital, must have been quite expensive. It is no wonder that according to tradition it was in Mary's house that Jesus and the disciples ate the Last Supper and the disciples were praying when Pentecost arrived.[27] If this last datum is true, then the upper room had a capacity of at least 120 persons. Mary's house is an independent factor that reveals her wealth; the urban and rural poor—the vast majority of the population in the entire empire—could never have afforded a house large enough to hold a congregation implied in the 'many' who gathered there.

One other datum demonstrates both how Mary obtained her wealth and that she belongs in the landowning class. Colossians 4.10 identifies John Mark, Mary's son, as a cousin to Barnabas,[28] a Levite[29] (4.36–37) of no small status in the Christian community. Barnabas, nicknamed 'son of encouragement', was the one who reintroduced Paul the recent convert to the Christian community (Acts 11.25). Barnabas was also a landowner; motivated by his faith, he sold the tract and laid the proceeds at the feet of the apostles to be distributed to the less fortunate (4.37). It is impossible to know precisely where and how big the parcel of land was, but if Barnabas's case is typical, then it was out of town, likely at least a medium-sized tract of 50–315 acres,[30] and it supported his living in Jerusalem. He is too active in the Christian community in Jerusalem to have owned anything smaller, which would have forced

---

25 E. Haenchen, *The Acts of the Apostles: A Commentary* (trans. B. Noble and G. Shinn; rev. R.M. Wilson; Philadelphia: Westminster Press, 1971), p. 385. Reimer, *Women in the Acts of the Apostles*, p. 241, cross-references Simon the Tanner's gated house to Mary's gated house and concludes that the gate does not indicate wealth because Simon, being a tanner, could not have earned much money. However, it is entirely possible that Lydia and Simon could have earned enough money with their occupations to buy houses large enough to host Christian communities. See Arlandson, *Women, Class, and Society*, pp. 79–84, 92–98. Richter Reimer implies that because Simon's trade was despised, it was not particularly lucrative (p. 241). She also says this of Lydia (p. 112), but her proof—a passage from Cicero, whose view on trades and occupations she claims 'represents the common, dominant opinion' (p. 106)—is problematic. Cicero is a member of the elite class and so does not 'represent the common, dominant position'. Commoners had quite a different attitude.

26 T.R.S. Broughton, 'Roman Asia Minor', in Tenney Frank (ed.), *An Economic Survey of Ancient Rome* (6 vols.; Paterson, NJ: Pageant Books, 1959), IV, pp. 499–918 (689).

27 Haenchen, *Acts of the Apostles*, p. 384 n. 11.

28 This section depends on Arlandson, *Women, Class, and Society*, pp. 138–40.

29 Levites were not allowed 'an inheritance' in the land (Num. 18 but cf. Neh. 13.10), and many in Palestine interpreted this as forbidden to *work* the land, so they *owned* land instead, with retainers serving as intermediaries. See E.P. Sanders, *Judaism: Practice and Belief, 63 BCE–66 CE* (Philadelphia: Trinity Press International, 1992), p. 77.

30 David Fiensy, *The Social History of Palestine in the Herodian Period: The Land Is Mine* (Studies in the Bible and Early Christianity, 20; Lewiston, NY: Edwin Mellen Press, 1991), pp. 23–24.

him to live outside the city and work the land from sunrise to sunset. If he owned property within the city, it is impossible to find out how much it was worth, though it is reasonable to infer that it was profitable since city property was at a premium price.

In the ancient world elite families maintained rigid class distinctions, and preserved their properties, through arranged marriages. Land ownership of any substantial size was thus the privilege of only a few. And since Barnabas was a landowner of a sizeable tract and a cousin to John Mark, son of Mary, it is therefore highly likely that Mary was a prosperous landowner too.

Social Freedom

Throughout the Greek East, including Israel, women who were landowners but without known political positions or connections had a great deal of power over their own property and wealth, like women in the ruling class had. No one exemplifies this power more clearly than Babatha and Nicerata, who represent not only many other women whose inscriptions and papyri have survived, but also many others whose inscriptions and papyri have not.

Babatha lived in the small settlement, Maoza, on the southern shore of the Dead Sea, from c. 80 CE to the Bar Kokhba rebellion in 132–35 CE. She was a rural landowner who could not read or write, but over 25 of her legal documents—dating from 94 to 132 CE and ranging in content from land sales, marriage contracts, and loans to summonses and a counter-summons—have been found in a cave near the Dead Sea where she hid them during the rebellion.[31] Her feisty attitude and independence permeate the corpus.

For example, Babatha's first husband, Jesus, set up a trust fund for their son and, through the council in Petra, appointed guardians to keep the fund.[32] Very soon after Jesus died, Babatha sued the guardians for mishandling the fund. Seeking control of it on security of her own property, she claimed that she could invest more wisely than the guardians and get 'threefold' more interest than they earned; she would be the one to maintain the orphaned boy 'in splendid style'.[33] However, a year later she evidently dropped the legal action because she was satisfied with the amount that the guardians paid out.[34] Thus, that outcome notwithstanding, Babatha was confident in her own skill to earn money with her own investments.

In another case revealing her independence and financial acumen, she lent her second husband, Judah, a sizeable sum under strict terms:

---

[31] N. Lewis, Y. Yadin, and J. Greenfield (eds.), *The Documents from the Bar Kokhba Period in the Cave of Letters* (Jerusalem: Israel Exploration Society, 1989), p. 29. This section of this article updates and corrects information in my book, *Women, Class, and Society*, pp. 57–58; 78–79.

[32] Lewis, Yadin, and Greenfield, *Documents*, pp. 56–61. It is not clear why Jesus appoints guardians and not Babatha over the fund, but to judge from all of the surviving documents, they kept their incomes and property separate.

[33] Lewis, Yadin, and Greenfield, *Documents*, pp. 58–61.

[34] Lewis, Yadin, and Greenfield, *Documents*, pp. 116–17. Apparently the guardians were unwilling to relinquish the trust fund over to her.

Judah has received from her on account of a deposit three hundred *denarii* of silver coin of genuine legal tender, on condition that he have and owe them [as debt] on deposit until such time as it may please Babatha, or anyone acting through her or for her, to request the aforesaid *denarii* of the deposit from the said Judah. And if Judah when so requested does not promptly repay, in accordance with the law of deposit he shall be liable to repay the deposit to her twofold in addition to damages ...[35]

Finally, guardians of Babatha's deceased brother-in-law's orphans brought a lawsuit against her because she seized by force three productive date palm orchards that they claim did not devolve to her at her husband's death. Babatha countered, however, that they belonged to her in lieu of unpaid debts, which were likely connected to her loan to Judah.[36] Seizing 'by force' implies violence, a charge that Babatha rejected as false,[37] although something may have happened that the plaintiffs interpreted as 'force'.[38] At the very least their claim means that she was aggressive. Even though the documents do not say who won the case, 'the fact that Babatha kept these documents presumably implies that she emerged victorious in this litigation'.[39]

Another case three or so centuries earlier in another part of the Greek East complements Babatha's independent power in litigation. Nicerata lived in the town of Thespies in Boeotia, Greece, sometime between 223 and 170 BCE.[40] Her father, Theron, lent a sizeable sum of money, 18,883 drachmas, to a neighboring town, Orchomenus. When her father died, the burden of collecting the loan fell to Nicerata. After a year-long dispute, she still had difficulty collecting the full amount.[41] A long inscription (178 lines), recording the loan and the terms, shows that Nicerata, not her husband Dexippos, was in charge of collecting the debt; the city leaders of Orchomenus negotiated with her; it is her name that is mentioned as wielding the power. And it is she who arrived in Orchomenus on certain due dates to ensure that she got repaid.

Despite these two examples, it is always difficult to apply the details of one case to another. Mary comes from a different time and different place from either Babatha or Nicerata. Nor have we evidence that Mary was litigious. However, it is evident from our survey thus far that women who came from the ruling or landowning classes both before and after Luke's time and in various parts of the Greek East enjoyed a great deal of economic freedom. It is clear from Acts 12.12 that Mary owned her home: Peter went to the 'house of Mary', not to the 'house of John Mark' or the house of some unnamed husband.[42] Luke's language reflects the inscriptions

---

35 Lewis, Yadin, and Greenfield, *Documents*, p. 73. Judah was married to Miriam while married to Babatha, and his two wives sue each other because Babatha took some of his possessions (p. 114).

36 Lewis, Yadin, and Greenfield, *Documents*, pp. 103–104; 110.

37 Lewis, Yadin, and Greenfield, *Documents*, p. 110.

38 Arlandson, *Women, Class, and Society*, pp. 55–58.

39 Arlandson, *Women, Class, and Society*, p. 102.

40 R. Dareste, B. Haussoulier, and T. Reinach (eds. and trans.), *Recueil des inscriptions juridiques grecques* (Rome: 'L'Erma' di Bretschneider, 1965), pp. 276–311. It is unknown from the inscriptions whether Nicerata was part of the ruling class, so she is included among landowners.

41 Dareste, Haussoulier, and Reinach, *Recueil des inscriptions*, p. 31.

42 If Mary were a widow, then even according to rabbinic laws and traditions, she would be allowed to exercise control over her estate and money. See J.R. Wegner, *Chattel or Person? The Status of Women in the Mishnah* (New York: Oxford University Press, 1988), pp. 138–42.

and papyri describing women in charge of their households and resources.[43] Moreover, to judge from the remaining verses in Acts, Mary exercised leadership in the church in her house, a role which involved paying for food and other needs, as the following demonstrates.

Junia Theodora, a Roman woman who had large estates[44] in Lycia (Asia Minor) near the city of Patara in the first half of the first century, was honored with the following decree:

> The people of Patara have decreed: Whereas, Junia Theodora, a Roman residing in Corinth a woman whom the residents hold (τῶν κατοικουσῶν ... καθεστηκειῶν) in highest honor, who lives wisely, is a friend of Lycia, and lives her life for the gratitude of all the Lycians, has provided generously of her means for the majority of our citizens, for benefaction; and she does not hesitate to show the greatness of her own soul out of good will, to provide of her means her own hospitality to every Lycian, and to welcome them into her house; and, in particular, to our citizens and to all she does not hesitate to communicate kindnesses; because of which, the majority of our citizens, gathering in the assembly, have offered testimony for her ...[45]

A Roman citizen living in Corinth, Junia received into her home citizens of Lycia and others on diplomatic assignments, some of whom settled (κατοικέω) in Corinth. This residency of aliens is similar to a situation described in Acts 2.5 (cf. 9.22): 'Now there were devout Jews from every nation under heaven living (κατοικοῦντς) in Jerusalem.' As Junia received Lycians, perhaps Mary received such Jewish residents into her house (v. 46); she certainly received Christians into her home during persecution (12.12) and thus practiced the hospitality appropriate to her class.

To conclude, as seen with the 'first' and 'prominent' women, no first-century reader would think it strange that a woman could own her own house, a large one at that, and control her own affairs: not only inscriptions but also daily contacts in cities and towns would make this clear. Thus, Luke had no need to detail Mary's economic situation: the connections among wealth, community status, and power, if not in official terms, were obvious. It should be recalled that Luke is silent about Peter after he left Mary's house. Surely this 'Lukan silence' was not intended to restrict him from carrying out his mission. Likewise, Luke's silence about Mary's daily life does not restrict her, either. Rather, his omission means merely that his narrative is focused on bigger themes, related to the spread of Christianity through Paul.

---

43 The Babatha papyri in Lewis, Yadin, and Greenfield, *Documents*, pp. 84–85; 90–92, to cite only these documents, use the genitive to express possession, which is also found in Acts 12.12, 'Mary's house'.
44 Louis Robert, 'Recherches épigraphiques', *Revue des études anciennes* 62 (1960), p. 330.
45 Pleket, *Epigraphica*, II, p. 22 (n. 8), my translation, which differs somewhat from a French translation: D.I. Pallas and S. Charitonides, 'Inscriptions Lyciennes trouvées à Solômos près de Corinthe', *Bulletin de correspondence hellénique* 83.2 (1959), pp. 496–508. For an alternative translation see Lefkowitz and Fant, *Women's Life*, p. 160 (n. 197), who give only excerpts. As to Junia living among other colonists in Corinth, Pallas and Charitonides speculate that they were Lycian businessmen who had not achieved citizenship (pp. 503–504). This decree sent from Patara mistakenly groups Junia, who had citizenship, with the colonists (cf. l.17).

Retainers

Retainers occupied the place between the ruling class and rich, and the 90 or more per cent of the peasants and city dwellers who had little or no wealth or power. They carried out the policies, laws, and day-to-day business of the landowners and ruling class.

Joanna (Luke 8.1–3). Joanna was one of the women who accompanied Jesus and the twelve throughout the towns and countryside and provided for them 'out of their own resources'. Luke describes her as the wife of a certain Chusa, Herod's estate or financial manager (ἐπίτροπος); thus, Joanna had some contact with the highest circles of government in that small Roman province.[46]

Landowners employed managers to oversee ensuring that the estates were productive, debts were paid, property bought or sold, the necessary products reached the household to sustain it, receipts were taken, and expenditures logged. Most important, they enjoyed substantial leeway in spending their employer's money and wielding their employer's power. An example of this power is seen in the following inscription from early second-century CE Galatia: 'Eutyches, steward of the Augusti of the Considian estates, and his children, Faustinus, Nicerotianus, and Hermes, built the temple with the cult statues. Claudius Valerianus, the most eminent procurator, made provision.'[47] The procurator worked with the estate manager in carrying out the building program. Perhaps Eutyches, associating with a procurator and working at such a high level in society, parallels Chusa, Joanna's husband.

Social Freedom

Little evidence for female managers has been found, and what remains does not detail their duties. Irene, who lived in the second or third century CE, was an estate manager for two landowners whose property bordered Pisidia and Phrygia in Asia Minor: 'Irene, estate manager (οἰκονόμισσα) of Longillianus and Severus, to her own most respected husband, Stachys, for a memorial.'[48] For female estate managers, literature rather than inscriptions is more informative.

In the fictional book of Judith, which is set in Israel, Judith's unnamed servant is the one 'who was in charge (τὴν ἐφεστῶσαν) of all she [Judith] possessed' (8.10; NRSV). That the unnamed servant is a slave raises the possibility that Irene and

---

46 Babatha's papyri often use ἐπίτροπος for legal guardian in her court cases. Broughton, 'Roman', pp. 648-95, has many examples of landowners and their holdings, which also have numerous references to an ἐπίτροπος. Broughton consistently translates the term as 'procurator'; however, in one context it appears to mean no more than an assistant to a government official, and in another context it seems to be synonymous with οἰκονόμος. This latter word he translates consistently as 'steward'. See the next inscription about Eutyches, which has both an ἐπίτροπος ('procurator') and οἰκονόμος ('estate manager'). Whichever is true for Chusa, he still occupies a high-level position. The more common word for financial or estate manager is οἰκονόμος which illuminates the function of the ἐπίτροπος. O. Michel, 'οἰκονόμος', *TDNT*, V, pp. 149-51. The description that follows of a manager comes from these pages, along with Chariton's *Chaereas and Callirhoe*.

47 Broughton, 'Roman', p. 654, his translation. The Greek word for procurator is ἐπίτροπος, which shows how closely the two positions can work together and perhaps overlap.

48 Pleket, *Epigraphica*, II, p. 39 (#28), my translation.

Joanna were slaves as well. Yet even if they were slaves, this does not mean that they lived miserable lives; rather, their attachment to the ruling class appears to have provided them substantial economic and social freedom.[49] Just as Judith's unnamed female retainer and Eutyches were in charge of their employer's property, Irene had charge of Longillianus and Severus's possessions in much the same way; it would not have surprised original passers-by who read Irene's inscription if they found out that she paid for the monument with the remuneration from her management. Into this class and with these privileges then, perhaps, we can situate Joanna.[50]

That Joanna traveled with Jesus was somewhat unusual but not without precedent: women sometimes accompanied wandering prophets and philosophers.[51] Commoners observing her commitment would not have been scandalized by it. Luke further states that Joanna was among the women who gave to Jesus and his disciples ἐκ τῶν ὑπαρχόντων αὐταῖς, 'out of their resources'. This language reflects Babatha's papyri and the inscriptions of Junia Theodora, Philê, Epiê, and Tata.[52] This connection suggests that Joanna, too, had independent access to funds. Perhaps she, like her husband, even had some official responsibility in Herod's court.

Joanna's introduction, along with that of the other women who followed Jesus (Lk. 8.1–3), follows a specific narrative pattern. Luke says that Jesus taught in the cities and countryside; then he mentions that 'the twelve were with him, as well as some women' (8.1). Next, he inserts personal details about the women: they had been cured of sicknesses and evil spirits.[53] Finally, he mentions that the women were contributing to Jesus and the twelve 'out of their own resources'. The pattern that emerges has four steps: Jesus arrives and preaches; some people, in this case women, gather around him; they are healed; and they respond. Thus the reference to the women follows the same sequence Luke depicts from the beginning of Jesus' ministry after the temptation (4.1–13). In this case, the response is not praise or anointing or weeping: the response is financial support. Like the sinful woman who poured her own expensive ointment on Jesus' feet (Lk. 7.36–50), they also were healed of much, so they loved much through giving out of their own resources.

Luke, as usual in his rapid narrative, omits the details of Joanna's source of wealth to emphasize a higher, theological value: wealthy people who have been forgiven or healed and have decided to follow Jesus and join the fledgling church. Those who have wealth should adopt Joanna's example and give generously out of gratitude. That Luke does not give many details about Joanna and the other women is not an

---

49 See Arlandson, *Women, Class, and Society*, pp. 45–52.

50 Conversely, D. Sim, 'The Women Followers of Jesus: The Implications of Luke 8.1–3', *Heythrop Journal* 30 (1989), pp. 52–53, wrongly argues that Joanna comes from a wealthy home but is as good as poor since women could not control financial resources.

51 Plato had women pupils: cf. Lefkowitz and Fant, *Women's Life*, p. 167. At least three women, Axothea from Arcadia then to Athens; Apollonia from Asia Minor; and Euphrosyne from Rome were philosophers (pp. 167 and 169). A certain Hipparchia adopted the life of a wandering Cynic (p. 167). Finally, Thecla is said to have followed Paul (pp. 311–13).

52 Lewis, Yadin, and Greenfield, *Documents*, pp. 66–67; see the following women in Pleket, *Epigraphica*, II: Junia Theodora, p. 22 (n. 8); Philê, p. 16 (n. 5); Epiê, pp. 18–19 (n. 7); see also Archippe, p. 15 (n. 3); Phanis, p. 36 (n. 23); and Berenice, p. 38 (n. 25).

53 E. Schüssler Fiorenza, 'Luke 13.10–17: Interpretation for Liberation and Transformation', *Theology Digest* 36 (1989), pp. 303–19 (310), wrongly suggests that when Luke mentions the illness and demonic possession of the women, he is suppressing their chance of social status.

indication of androcentric disregard for women: Luke is more concerned about the big picture, the formation of the Jesus movement and the church. Moreover, Luke does not elaborate on Joanna's use of her wealth and status, because Luke's audience was well aware of the social freedom wealthy, powerful women had in their society and would have assumed what her actions were. Historical evidence demonstrates that a woman like Joanna could have her own wealth and contribute it in any way she wished without incurring the least bit of social stigma or patriarchal opposition; that Luke does not comment on it proves that he does not find these actions unusual or inappropriate for a woman.

Summary and Application

All writings, secular or sacred, majestic epic or bare inscription, have two sides, like a two-way mirror. Like scientists clandestinely looking in on patients, we can look from one side to examine others without their knowledge. When the experiment is over, we may walk around to the other side and see a reflection of ourselves open to self-examination. So it is with Luke–Acts. When we look *through* the narrative, we analyze the characters in their own context, in their own world. But when we look *into* Luke–Acts, we are more self-conscious; we see ourselves in the characters living lives not too different from our own. Accordingly, in our conclusion we first review two groups and two individuals in Luke–Acts; then we examine ourselves as we encounter them.

The two groups of women converts in Thessalonica (17.4) and Beroea (17.12) who are described as 'leading' and 'prominent' came from the same ruling class in their own cities. Luke's narrative strongly suggests that they did not have to renounce their status or wealth in order to join the church. The Gospel does depicts a tension between total renunciation and retention of possessions (cf. 16.13; 18.18–30; 19.1–10, and so on)—a tension likely felt within Luke's own community—but the tension is resolved when the wealthy and prestigious are generous with their money. That is, the wealthy should continue to practice their roles as benefactors, a role the women had likely already assumed. Given their commitment to the church, it would be surprising if they ceased to be benefactors.

Luke's silence concerning the details of the social freedom and privileges of these newly converted women in Acts 17.4 and 12 was not designed to oppress or restrict them; rather, he did not need to go into detail because he knew his audience would understand the women's role because of the language he used, such as 'first', 'prominent', and ἐπίτροπος, and because of other clues, such as the size of Mary's house and Joanna's contributions to Jesus *on her own*.

Acts 12.12–17 introduces Mary in the context of persecution by Herod. The passage shows that her house had been open to the Christian community for quite some time. These verses, coupled with Col. 4.10 which ties Barnabas the Levite and landowner (see also Acts 4.37) to her family, indicate that Mary was a wealthy landowner. Because Acts 12.2 says that 'many' were gathered in her house, it is reasonable to infer that her house was large. As we saw with the 'leading' and 'prominent' women, Luke is silent on the details of Mary's role, and this silence can be explained in the same way: Luke could trust his audience to recognize Mary's status, wealth, and hospitality based on their own personal knowledge of the actions and responsibilities of the elite. Just as Junia, spending her own money, received Lycians from Asia Minor and Lycians residing in Corinth into her home, so Mary welcomed Christians and missionaries into her home.

Joanna (Lk. 8.1–3) was married to Chusa, Herod's estate manager, and so likely had contacts among the highest circles of the province. She controlled her own resources, out of which she provided support to Jesus and the twelve. This announcement would not have surprised Luke's original readers; women did have such financial freedom.

Thus the people we look at *through* the mirror in Luke–Acts and its larger context enjoy a high quality of life: all of the women kept their wealth and the social freedom that it brought. They appeared in public, spent their money as they saw fit, and even occupied political offices for the improvement of their city. They could exercise hospitality or initiate lawsuits; they could give to maintain children or to benefit foreigners living in their cities. However, the one image *of ourselves* in Luke–Acts that is the clearest is this: the first priority of the wealthy should be generosity towards the needy. It is one thing to give money to the city and so improve one's status and collect the official praises; it is quite another to give to the poor. Therefore, according to Luke–Acts, prosperous women—and men as well—may maintain their status and resources and social freedom, provided they live according to the dominant social value that the Gospel imposes on anyone of either gender: generosity.

Afterword to 'Household Management and Women's Authority'*

Virginia Burrus and Karen Torjesen

'No cultural barrier to women assuming leadership roles' in early Christian house churches? Looking back from the vantage point of the year 2001 in an essay first drafted in the mid 1980s, we are struck by the tactical optimism of its argument. There, we suggested that the commonplace exercise of authority by ancient Mediterranean women in their roles as householders and patrons should form the context for interpretations, not only of the scattered references to women in early Christian writings, but also of the copious silences all too frequently (and noisily) filled with a presumption of patriarchy. Our argument was not couched in theological terms and we certainly did not intend to present ancient Christian women's roles as ideal, much less normative. Rather, the goal was that of much women's history: to retrieve the agency of women in our retelling of the past.

The basic goal still seems not only valid but relevant—surprisingly so, perhaps. As feminist analyses of early Christian materials have grown both sharper and more subtle, we now understand texts like Luke–Acts, once lauded for their 'inclusion' of women, as mixed blessings, conveying double messages at best.[1] In the end, silence may seem preferable to talk about women that exalts their submissiveness, a visibly gapped text better than an apparently fuller account that has cast females in supporting roles only. Meanwhile, we have become more aware than ever of the difficulty (perhaps the impossibility) of moving from textual representations of women (almost inevitably androcentric) to the 'social reality' outside the text. And, yet, are we not in danger of overshooting our goal, if feminist critique results in the loss of all purchase on female subjectivity in ancient texts and the bracketing of women's agency in the making of history?

---

* This 'Afterword' is a reflection on a chapter co-authored by Virginia Burrus and Karen Torjesen, 'Household Management and Women's Authority', in Karen Jo Torjesen, *When Women Were Priests: Women's Leadership in the Early Church and the Scandal of their Subordination in the Rise of Christianity* (San Francisco: HarperSanFrancisco, 1993), pp. 53–87. The material in this article is all new and not copyright protected.

1 As registered in the title of Turid Karlsen Seim, *The Double Message: Patterns of Gender in Luke–Acts* (Studies of the New Testament and its World; Edinburgh: T. & T. Clark; (Nashville: Abingdon, 1994). Other relatively recent feminist studies reflecting this consensus include Mary Rose D'Angelo, 'Women in Luke–Acts: A Redactional View', *JBL* 109 (1990), pp. 441–61; *idem*, '(Re)Presentations of Women in the Gospel of Matthew and Luke–Acts', in Ross Shepard Kraemer and Mary Rose D'Angelo (eds.), *Women and Christian Origins* (Oxford: Oxford University Press, 1999), pp. 171–95; Clarice J. Martin, 'The Acts of the Apostles', in Elisabeth Schüssler Fiorenza (ed.), *Searching the Scriptures*. II. *A Feminist Commentary* (2 vols.; Crossroad, 1994), pp. 763–99; Gail R. O'Day, 'Acts', in Carol A. Newsom and Sharon H. Ringe (eds.), *The Women's Bible Commentary* (Louisville, KY: Westminster/John Knox Press, 1992), pp. 305–12; Jane Schaberg, 'Luke', in Newsom and Ringe (eds.), *The Women's Bible Commentary*, pp. 275–92; and Turid Karlsen Seim, 'The Gospel of Luke', in Schüssler Fiorenza (ed.), *Searching the Scriptures*, II, pp. 728–62.

Interpreting the figures of female householders and patrons in Luke–Acts requires direct engagement of the challenges and dilemmas. The crucial passage is perhaps Lk. 8.1–3: 'Afterward [Jesus] was journeying through city and village preaching and proclaiming the reign of God, and the twelve were with him, and some women who had been cured of evil spirits and diseases; Mary, called Magdalene, from whom seven demons had gone out, and Joanna wife of Chuza the steward of Herod, and Susanna, and many other women, who used to minister to them from their resources.' Here as elsewhere the Lukan text plays with gendered doublings; here as elsewhere the parallelism is inexact. Indeed, the women almost seem to have barged into the sentence unexpectedly—if not uninvited. Their presence requires explanation (as that of the twelve men does not), and yet when the explanations themselves are doubled, the result is still more unsettling. Initially identified by what they now lack (evil spirits and diseases), the women are subsequently identified by what they still have (resources); recipients of the gifts of healing, they are also presented as ministerial donors. The larger Lukan framing repeats and intensifies the portrayal of women as both takers and givers who are strongly defined by their positions within relational webs of power complexly ordered by class, wealth, and spiritual gifts, as well as gender.

Joanna is merely 'the first of many women of wealth and status mentioned by Luke', as Jane Schaberg notes.[2] Some of these women appear in anonymous civic collectives: we read that 'devout women of high standing and the leading men of the city' stirred up persecution against Paul and Barnabas in Pisidian Antioch (Acts 13.50); in Thessalonica, however, 'a great many of the devout Greeks and not a few of the leading women' supported Paul and Silas (Acts 17.4), and in Beroea, 'not a few Greek women of high standing as well as men' joined local Jews in receiving the word (17.12). The governor Felix and his wife Drusilla (Acts 24.24) and the king Agrippa and his wife Bernice (Acts 25.13, 23) personalize this bi-gendered pattern of elite patronage, exercised in the one case against and in the other in favor of Paul. Other references to female householders and benefactors closer to home include: Martha (Lk. 10.38–42); Sapphira (Acts 5.1–12); Tabitha (Acts 9.36–43); Mary the mother of John (Acts 12.12); Lydia (Acts 16.14–15, 40); Priscilla (Acts 18). As Mary Rose D'Angelo points out, Luke's 'treatment of women corresponds to the increasing Roman interest in signaling public meanings through appropriations of the domestic world';[3] this is especially the case as regards his representation of female patrons, we would suggest.[4]

If evidence of elite patronage was in itself a source of symbolic capital for the Christian movement, evidence of elite female patronage had a particular message to convey, in a culture that had invested heavy significance in domestic figures of womanly influence.[5] Where a man's public reputation could be tainted by accusations that he was susceptible to the attractions of a seductress 'bent on

---

2 Schaberg, 'Luke', p. 287.
3 D'Angelo, '(Re)Presentations of Women', p. 188.
4 On female patrons in early Christianity, see Torjesen, *When Women Were Priests*, pp. 89–109.
5 Kate Cooper, 'Insinuations of Womanly Influence: An Aspect of the Christianization of the Roman Aristocracy', *Journal of Roman Studies* 82 (1992), pp. 150–64; see also *idem*, *The Virgin and the Bride: Idealized Womanhood in Late Antiquity* (Cambridge, MA: Harvard University Press, 1996), pp. 1–19.

tempting a man by private allurements to a betrayal of public duty', it could also be buttressed by demonstrations that he acquiesced to the influence of a woman 'whose soothing charm would ideally restore him to order when he had strayed, and persuade him to hear the voice of reason'.[6] The exercise of influence, essentially familial in its idealization, exceeded the bounds of the family as soon as it became a public image. Women with *resources* were women with potentially widespread influence as patrons: as rhetorical figures appearing in ancient texts, they are therefore highly charged emblems of social power, exercised either positively or negatively on the public *acts of men*. Thus, in emphasizing the role of female patrons, Luke is able both to honor and (somewhat heavy-handedly) to instruct the women in his audience,[7] while also serving his (undeniably androcentric) interests in buttressing the reputation of Christianity by enabling its men to go public under the influence of the right kind of women.

If women are figures of influence, they can also represent an excessive gullibility. As Margaret MacDonald has remarked, 'the dual image of the hysterical woman as both deluded female and influential evangelist' constituted a potent rhetorical scare figure not infrequently invoked in pagan attacks on Christianity.[8] Luke's own, equally potent doubling of figures of female patronage with figures of female healing or exorcism subtly engages the complexity and volatility of women's traditional rhetorical representations. To speak of 'women cured of evil spirits and diseases' is to invoke and defend against women's seducibility and vulnerability to negative influence, while at the same time bringing them closer to figures of positive female influence. This precarious rhetorical balance is sustained throughout Luke–Acts. It apparently plays a role not only in securing the public reputation of Christian communities, not only in instructing its women in appropriate behavior, but also in redefining roles of leadership-as-*diakonia* for men.[9]

None of this is simply good news for women. Nor does Luke–Acts' representation of female patrons give us a *direct* window onto women's historical agency— although it may tell us much indirectly not only about the discursive regimes to which women were subjected but also about the ways in which they may have constituted their subjectivity and exercised their power. We miss valuable opportunities, however, if the zeal to critique the relatively recent history of reception of the text continues to obscure the *complexity* of its female figures. Schaberg, for example, leans heavily on a 'gratitude' easily imaginable but crucially *not mentioned* in Lk. 8.1–3, in order to conflate the figures of healing and patronage, thereby translating the image of the female benefactress into the image of an indebted woman. Loading rather more tit-for-tat reciprocity onto the text than it needs to carry, she nonetheless worries that there is still not enough, as measured by current standards

---

6 Cooper, 'Insinuations of Womanly Influence', p. 153. Although Cooper is referring to the rhetorical representation of the positive influence of a wife or family member, we suggest that the trope is flexible enough to embrace other instances of female persuasiveness on behalf of the common good.

7 On the catechetical or pedagogical function of Luke's representation of women, with concern for its disciplinary aspect, see, e.g., D'Angelo, 'Women in Luke–Acts', pp. 447–48.

8 Margaret Y. MacDonald, *Early Christian Women and Pagan Opinion: The Power of the Hysterical Woman* (Cambridge: Cambridge University Press, 1996), p. 5.

9 See Seim, *Double Message*, p. 85.

of mutuality: 'The women'—presumably acting out of gratitude to Jesus—'are cast in a nonreciprocated role of service or support of the males of the movement.' We might, however, respond that lack of reciprocity at the level of 'resources' (whether material or social)—the ostentatiously generous volunteering of 'service'—is precisely what imbues the ancient patron with power, inscribing the client in turn with social debt. 'Luke's depiction of a female-supported, male-led organization has been mirrored down the centuries by many Christian organizations,' notes Schaberg,[10] but we ask whether she has not here intensified an *anachronistic* patriarchal projection of women's 'auxiliaries' by robbing these ancient female patrons of both their rhetorical and social clout.[11]

Let us return again, in closing, to the Lukan 'pair' with which we began the original essay—namely Lydia and Cornelius. 'The story of Paul and Lydia is in many ways the abbreviated counterpart to the story of Peter and Cornelius in Acts 10,' notes Gail O'Day. 'Lydia is the first official European convert in the same way that Cornelius was the first official Gentile convert.' However, a (by now predictable) shadow falls over the figure of Lydia in O'Day's reading, as Lydia is represented as a sign of exploitation of women that pervades Luke–Acts. 'Lydia embodies Luke's ideal of women's contribution to the church: to provide housing and economic resources'; nonetheless, 'Luke does not credit Lydia with any "leadership role"'.[12] True enough. Yet Luke also fails to credit Cornelius with a 'leadership role'. We, in turn, may be in danger of discrediting Lydia's 'and many others' (cf. Lk. 8.3) if we rob her of her resources as householder and patron (a feat that even Luke–Acts itself has not quite accomplished on its own).

At the same time, the sources of these women's resources, as well as their exploitation, must indeed be considered carefully: a critical analysis of both class and colonialism should accompany—and at points interrupt—the feminist critique of Luke–Acts.[13] 'The first official European convert,' as O'Day names her, Lydia, the prosperous provincial of Acts 16, has historically been closely allied with the colonialist ideology of mission—she is, in short, the ideal convert. Building on the

---

10 Schaberg, 'Luke', pp. 287–88.

11 Schaberg's reading of Luke's depiction of women of means is, to varying degrees, shared by other feminist commentators. Thus, D'Angelo, '(Re)Presentations of Women', p. 185: 'The women are said to be with Jesus not as result of a special call but out of gratitude for cures ... and they share in Jesus' ministry by supporting [Jesus and the twelve] ...' Cf. Seim, *Double Message*, pp. 57–58, on Lk. 8.1–3: 'His [Jesus'] benefaction makes them benefactors. This happens in a way that breaks with an ideal of total reciprocity in which the one service is worth the other.' Seim appears more sensitive to the way in which the two rhetorical figures—healing and patronage—work together and less inclined simply to conflate them into the figure of an indebted woman. Nonetheless, her position is not far from Schaberg's. See also Seim, 'The Gospel of Luke', pp. 739–45. A provocative alternative reading is offered by Robert M. Price, *The Widow Traditions in Luke–Acts: A Feminist-Critical Scrutiny* (SBLDS, 155; Atlanta, GA: Scholars Press, 1997), pp. 127–51, who suggests that Joanna and other figures of female patronage constitute veiled references to the controversial ministry of celibate women preserved in early Christian 'widow traditions'.

12 O'Day, 'Acts', p. 310. See also Martin, 'The Acts of the Apostles', p. 784: Lydia's 'own contribution to the Christian mission includes neither public leadership nor proclamations in any way, nor public affirmation by the community of women and men, although Acts 16.40 suggests that her home functioned as a house-church for Christian women and men'.

13 Cf. Clarice Martin's call for a more complex hermeneutic on behalf of a 'womanist' reading ('The Acts of the Apostles', pp. 787–88).

work of Musa W. Dube Shomanah,[14] Jeff Staley sees in Lydia a female personification of the new, foreign, and distinctly 'Roman' territory that Paul sets out to conquer and recolonize through his evangelism. Alluring in her understated power, the silent Lydia is also tantalizingly receptive. The brief account of this quiet convert is, however, noisily interrupted and thereby complicated by the story of a soothsaying slave girl, whose encounter with Paul leads to her ambiguous 'liberation' from the spirit of pythonic prophecy that has both reinscribed her enslavement and conveyed her abrupt and cryptic protest against the multiplied forces of domination. When viewed through the lens of postcolonial theories of hybridity, the 'good' Lydia (willing convert) and the 'bad' slave girl (ambivalent prophetess of a 'native' cult/ure) may convey a productively double message indeed, for the two two-sided figures of womanly seduction and seducibility do not merely contrast but also collude,[15] standing closely on either side of the boundary of 'conversion', combining 'colonized' and enacting multiple crossings and recrossings of ambivalent borderlands.[16] Staley urges that the linked figures of Lydia and the pythonic slave, like Changing Woman of Navajo mythology, be reread as icons of fluid change and exchange, splitting and recombination, creatively reappropriating 'the new and the old in ways that the colonial power cannot imagine', thereby lending 'a lively postcolonial, post-canonical voice to colonialist-engendered border women ... who otherwise remain co-opted, disempowered, or dead'.[17]

We might further note that the figure of Paul reiterates the ambiguity and shiftiness of the doubled women: split (not least in his relationship to the two women) between the subjection of the colonized and the forces of (counter)colonization, he too is positioned as a hybrid subject in Luke's text.[18] Has he stripped the slave girl of her power,[19] or has he freed her from the oppression of demonic possession and/or her masters' exploitation of resources?[20] (If he has robbed the slave girl of her native gift of prophecy, has he also robbed the householder Lydia of her right to leadership? On the other hand, if his exorcism functions effectively as a critique of the exploitation of the slave, does not that counter the possibility that he himself has simply exploited Lydia's hospitality and relative wealth?) Paul's intervention to release the slave girl from the spirit that claims her leads to his own stripping, beating, and imprisonment, from which he too is subsequently released—thereby closely aligning him with the (in contrast, merely spiritually?) 'liberated' slave. Indeed, Paul gains his freedom by distinctly trick-

---

14 Musa W. Dube Shomanah, *Postcolonial Feminist Interpretation of the Bible* (St Louis: Chalice Press, 2000).

15 Cf. Price's suggestion that the prophetess and Lydia are one and the same (*The Widow Traditions in Luke–Acts*, p. 228).

16 Jeffrey L. Staley, 'Changing Woman: Postcolonial Reflections on Acts 16.6–40', *JSNT* 73 (1999), pp. 113–35 (130), reprinted in this volume, pp. 177–92.

17 Staley, 'Changing Woman', p. 133.

18 Here we have profited from the insights of Eric Thurman, 'Paul, Luke's Action-Figure: Reading Colonial Subjectivity in the Acts of the Apostles' (unpublished paper, Drew University, 2001).

19 As argued by O'Day, 'Acts', pp. 310–11: 'Paul could have attempted to convert the slave girl but instead only silences her ... The scene can be read as emblematic of Luke's silencing of women prophets throughout Acts.'

20 A point emphasized by Seim, *Double Message*, p. 173.

sterish means, his clever double-talk (culminating with the invocation of Roman citizenship) resulting in the drama of a public shaming of the very (Roman-backed) magistrates who had initially shamed and injured him. When Luke represents Paul as saucily prolonging this momentary turning of the tables by insisting on going to visit Lydia before finally leaving town, he also tightens the weave of a narrative that leaves missionary, patroness, and prophetess positioned together (albeit differently) in a shared borderland, thereby further complicating (though by no means eliding) gendered positionalities. Oppressions of class and imperial rule—frequently inscribed on resistant female bodies—are perhaps nowhere *directly* criticized in this notoriously culturally and politically 'conservative' text; nonetheless, we should not overlook the subtle subversions conveyed by such complexly interwoven, archly novelistic narratives.

It becomes apparent that Luke–Acts is not *simply* a triumphalist apologetic that unapologetically aligns Christianity with patriarchy and the cultural and political powers of empire and colonization. Even a brief consideration of Acts 16 exposes the complexity and instability of the text and brings to the surface political critiques that have indirect implications for the interpretation of the hybridized, even arguably tricksterish figure of the female patron. Luke does not challenge the class-based authority of Lydia, whose household (likely including slaves) is baptized with her; he certainly does not challenge it on the basis of her gender. He does, however, interlace her tale with sly interrogations of slavery and imperial rule, calling attention to a political context in which the mutually but differently 'oppressed' may turn against each other unpredictably (as with Paul and the slave girl's masters, Paul and the local magistrates) or discover unexpected and inherently ambivalent collations (as with Paul and Rome, Paul and his jailor, Paul and the slave girl, the slave and Lydia). We should not defend Luke from well-deserved feminist critique. We should, however, do our best to exploit the resources of his double messages in such a way as to acknowledge the necessarily ambiguous power of 'some women', as well as the complexity of both domination and resistance.

CHANGING WOMAN: TOWARD A POSTCOLONIAL POSTFEMINIST INTERPRETATION OF ACTS 16.6–40*

JEFFREY L. STALEY

Reading Acts 16 in a Postcolonial, Postfeminist World[1]

Most contemporary interpreters of Acts 16.6–40 describe Paul's journey into Macedonia as a 'missionary journey to Europe'. This essay challenges that designation, arguing that it is a colonialist geographic designation with no actual textual basis, and one that has helped foster the ideology of modern colonialist missionary movements. Yet there is solid textual evidence for arguing Acts 16.6–40 marks a change in Paul's missionary activity, one that comes more and more into contact with Roman colonial power. Building upon Musa Dube Shomanah's brilliant exploration of biblical 'border women',[2] I believe that Lydia and the pythonic slave girl of Acts 16 function as 'border women'—women whose presence evokes a colonialist 'land possession type-scene' similar to those related with Rahab (Josh. 2), the Syrophoenician woman (Mk 7), and the Samaritan woman (Jn 4). Using autobiographical reflections and two books that deal with the territory of my childhood (*Laughing Boy*, by Oliver La Farge, and *Ceremony*, by Leslie Marmon Silko),[3] I will show how three Native American border women either replicate the biblical colonialist land possession type-scene or challenge it, thereby offering helpful postcolonial, postfeminist appropriations of border women. Perhaps, in the end, the Native American figure of Changing Woman can revitalize biblical border women and deconstruct the colonialist ideology permeating their bodies.

Plotting the Geography of Acts

There is little disagreement among Lukan commentators on the general plot divisions of the book of Acts. The story charts the geographic and cultural movement of early Christianity (Acts 1.8), and it can be plotted along these lines: activity in Jerusalem (Acts 1–7), in Judea and Samaria (Acts 8–12), and in areas north-west of

---

* An earlier version of this essay appeared as 'Changing Woman: Postcolonial Reflections on Acts 16.6–40', in *JSNT* 73 (1999), pp. 113–35.

1 I am particularly attracted to the feminism of Linda Hutcheon (*The Politics of Postmodernism* [New York: Routledge, 1989]). Although she does not use the word 'postfeminism' in her writing, I am adding a 'post' to feminism here in order to connect it with what she (and I) strongly believe feminism brought to the 'post' conversations of the 1980s: a distrust of and challenge to metanarratives, and a pervasive critique of the power relations in human discourses. Thus the 'post' in my 'postfeminism' should be read in conjunction with the 'post' of postcolonialism and postmodernism—not as a rejection of or a turning away from the self-critical cultural critiques of earlier feminisms.

2 *Postcolonial Feminist Interpretation of the Bible* (St Louis: Chalice Press, 2000).

3 Published respectively by New York: Houghton Mifflin Company, 1957; and New York: Penguin Books, 1977.

Judea (Acts 13–28). Furthermore, it is obvious even to an uncritical reader that Paul's proclamation to Gentiles in Acts 13–14 is a new development in the plot. Except for the apostles' debate in Acts 15, Paul is clearly the central character for the rest of the book. Thus, the major plot question scholars must decide is whether Paul's 'first missionary journey' in Acts 13–14 is a challenge to and an aberration from the apostles' central mission—a mission that begins in Acts 1 and leads to the authoritative pronouncements of the Jerusalem Council in Acts 15. If Paul's 'first missionary journey' is an aberration, then Acts 15 is the major turning point of the plot. But if, on the other hand, the Jerusalem Council is an aberration—an aberration and a challenge to *Paul's* missionary activity—then Acts 13 must be the turning point of the plot.

Over the years, commentators have put forward a variety of arguments for these two possible turning points of the book.[4] But it is not my purpose to settle for one of these options over the other. Rather, I am interested in the fact that commentators can develop lengthy arguments for preferring one central turning point over the other, and then turn around and write in such a way that Paul's 'second missionary journey' (Acts 16.6ff.) seems somehow to chart a dramatic new course for the spread of Christianity in ways that his 'first missionary journey' did not.

Many commentators have made this latter point by describing Paul's 'second missionary journey' as 'Christianity entering Europe'.[5] And while it is well known that the ancient Greeks divided the world into three parts (Libya, Asia, and Europe),[6]

---

4 See, for example, H. Conzelmann, *Acts of the Apostles: A Commentary on the Acts of the Apostles* (ed. E.J. Epp and C.R. Matthews; trans. J. Limburg, A.T. Kraabel, and D.H. Juel; Hermeneia; Philadelphia: Fortress Press, 1987), p. xlii; M. Hengel, *Between Jesus and Paul: Studies in the Earliest History of Christianity* (trans. J. Bowden; Philadelphia: Fortress Press, 1983), p. 101; R.I. Pervo, *Luke's Story of Paul* (Minneapolis: Fortress Press, 1990), p. 53.

5 For instance, James Dunn argues that 'This section is primarily intended to demonstrate how it was that Paul first brought the gospel to Europe, or at least into the Aegean Basin' (*The Acts of the Apostles* [Valley Forge, PA: Trinity Press International, 1996], p. 215; cf. p. 218; see also L.T. Johnson, *The Acts of the Apostles* [Sacra Pagina; Collegeville, MN: Liturgical Press, 1992], pp. 281, 290, 297; H.C. Kee, *To Every Nation under Heaven: The Acts of the Apostles* [Valley Forge, PA: Trinity Press International, 1997], pp. 188–89, 191; C.H. Talbert, *Reading Acts: A Literary and Theological Commentary on the Acts of the Apostles* [New York: Crossroad Publishing Company, 1997], pp. 147–48); Pervo, *Luke's Story of Paul*, p. 55; G. Krodel, *Acts: Proclamation Commentaries* (Philadelphia: Fortress Press, 1981), p. 59. Interestingly, R.B. Rackham is one of the few commentators in the last century who questioned the identification of Macedonia with 'Europe'. Writing in 1906, he stated: 'Here we have to be on our guard against the influence of modern ideas of geography. The crisis of the work was not, as is popularly supposed, the crossing over from Asia to Europe. The Macedonian did not say "Come over into Europe", but "into Macedonia"' (*The Acts of the Apostles: An Exposition* [London: Methuen & Company, 1906], p. 272).

6 Herodotus states: 'I cannot guess for what reason the earth, which is one, has three names, all women's, and why the boundary lines set for it are the Egyptian Nile river and the Colchian Phasis river (though some say that the Maeetian Tanaïs river and the Cimmerian Ferries are boundaries); and I cannot learn the names of those who divided the world, or where they got the names which they used. For Libya is said by most Greeks to be named after a native woman of that name, and Asia after the wife of Prometheus; yet the Lydians claim a share in the latter name, saying that Asia was not named after Prometheus' wife Asia, but after Asies, the son of Cotys, who was the son of Manes, and that from him the Asiad clan at Sardis also takes its name. But as for Europe, no men have any knowledge whether it is bounded by seas or not, or where it got its name, nor is it clear who gave the name, unless we say that the land took its name from the Tyrian Europa, having been

Acts offers no explicit evidence to suggest that its author had these geographic divisions in mind when writing his narrative. Recently, however, James Scott has taken a different tack and argued that, similarly to the threefold Greek division of the world, Acts could have been structured around the geographical areas assigned to the three sons of Noah as found in ancient Judaism's 'Table of Nations' (Gen. 10).[7] Thus, for Scott, Acts 2.1–8.25 represents the mission to Shem (Asia), Acts 8.26–40 represents the mission to Ham (Libya), and Acts 9.1–28.31 represents the mission to Japheth (Europe).[8] Although I remain unconvinced by Scott's argument regarding the overall structure of the book of Acts, his collection of data does suggest that first-century readers of the book could have understood Paul's journey to Macedonia as part of an important new territorial expansion of the apostolic witness.

But irrespective of Scott's proposal or any hypothetical reconstruction of how first readers may have understood Paul's Macedonian mission, Acts 16.9 has in fact played an important role in the colonizing rhetoric of European empires from the sixteenth century to the present day. By describing Paul's entrance into Macedonia as 'Christianity entering Europe', Western empire-building nations of the last five centuries have found an apostolic, divinely ordained model ready at hand to justify colonizing and 'winning for the Saviour' hitherto 'unknown' and 'unexplored' continents.[9] Thus, explicitly designating Macedonia as the European continent legitimizes the missionizing agendas of modern colonial empires as much as it clarifies any particular geographic notion, plot structure, or hypothetical reader in the mind of Luke–Acts' author. But I do not want to ignore the plot structure of Acts in order to talk about the ideological foundations of modern Christian missions. For in the end I believe that commentators' designation of Acts 16.6 as 'Christianity's entrance into Europe' is, in fact, based upon certain narrative elements that mark out the second journey by Paul as functionally different from his earlier journey in Acts 13.

A Colonialist Meta-autobiography[10]

It is a hot July afternoon on the Navajo Reservation in northern Arizona, the kind of day that flakes off your skin like a fine alkaline dust. My three brothers and two

---

(it would seem) before then nameless like the rest. But it is plain that this woman was of Asiatic birth, and never came to this land which the Greeks now call Europe, but only from Phoenicia to Crete and from Crete to Lycia' (*Histories* 4.45.1–5; cf. 2.33; 3.115.1; cf. P.S. Alexander, 'Notes on the "Imago Mundi" of the *Book of Jubilees*', *JJS* 33 [1982], pp. 197–214 [197–99]).

7 J.M. Scott, *Paul and the Nations: The Old Testament and Jewish Background of Paul's Mission to the Nations with Special Reference to the Destination of Galatians* (Tübingen: J.C.B. Mohr [Paul Siebeck], 1995), pp. 168–76.

8 Scott, *Paul and the Nations*, pp. 179–80; cf. pp. 48–51.

9 J. Townsend, 'Missionary Journeys in Acts and European Missionary Societies', SBLSP, 24 (1985), pp. 433–37. It is not insignificant that Paul crosses an expanse of water in order to reach 'Europe' (Acts 16.9–11), for the new continents colonized by fifteenth- through nineteenth-century Europeans will also lie across the oceans.

10 Robert Maldonado recently coined the term 'meta-autobiographical' to describe 'the available and recognizable autobiographical *plots* [his emphasis] that the culture of the teller determines' ('Reading Malinche Reading Ruth: Toward a Hermeneutics of Betrayal', *Semeia* 72 [1995], pp. 91–109 [91]). The plot of my meta-autobiographical vignette is determined by what Musa Dube Shomanah calls a 'land possession type-scene', an idea she develops from Robert Alter's analysis

sisters along with our father and his wife have met at Immanuel Mission for a family reunion.[11] It is the first time all of us have been together since our mother's death in 1984. Now it is eleven years later. I have not been to this growing-up place of mine since my son was two years old. And now he is ten and asking questions about everything. 'Is this the house where you lived? Did you ever climb that mesa? Do you know that Indian woman?' My son is finally old enough to store this red sandstone valley in his own memory, apart from any stories I might tell of my childhood spent here. So I am careful about what I show him and where I go.

But at this precise moment my son is not with me. I have sent him off to explore the mission compound with his cousins. At this moment I am standing beside my oldest brother, Rob, at the grave of Sarah Tsosie, a Navajo girl with whom we grew up. Thirty years ago we were both in love with Sarah. At the age of fourteen, Rob's had been an open, reciprocated affection. I ought to know. I used to follow Rob and Sarah around after dark to watch them kiss behind the cinder-block dormitory. My love, on the other hand, was that sweet, secret, unrequited type commonly found in the hearts of jealous, pesky little twelve-year-old brothers.

The intervening thirty years have taken us both far away from Sarah and the reservation where we spent our childhood. We have been away longer and driven farther to get here than anyone else in our family—Rob from Alberta; I, from Oregon. But

---

of betrothal scenes in ancient Hebrew narrative (*The Art of Biblical Narrative* [New York: Basic Books, 1981], pp. 51–52). Dube Shomanah argues that in order to 'validate and to veil the violence of imperialism, gender representations [become] a method of presenting victims of imperialism as those who love, need, or desire to be possessed by imperialist traveling heroes and their nations ... Here land is not just a slab of a physical body, but a web of intrinsically woven tales of power and disempowerment ... written on the bodies of people' (*Postcolonial Feminist Interpretation of the Bible*, pp. 118–19).

11 I fret about the stories I tell from my past, especially those that deal with my years on the Navajo Reservation. In my writing I try to portray the multi-positionality of my interpretive choices (see, for example, J.C. Anderson and J.L. Staley, 'Taking It Personally: Introduction', *Semeia* 72 [1995], pp. 7–18; cf. M.A. Tolbert, 'The Politics and Poetics of Location', in F.F. Segovia and M.A. Tolbert [eds.], *Reading from this Place: Social Location and Biblical Interpretation in the United States* [2 vols; Minneapolis: Fortress Press, 1995], I, pp. 305–17), but sometimes I feel as though I am just another Rahila Khan, that 'feminist from the Indian subcontinent whose work purported to describe the life and experiences of young Asian women in Margaret Thatcher's Britain' who turned out to be a 'male, middle-class, white vicar from Brighton named Toby Forward' (D. Callaghan, 'The Vicar and Virago: Feminism and the Problem of Identity', in J. Roof and R. Wiegman [eds.], *Who Can Speak? Authority and Critical Identity* [Urbana: University of Illinois Press, 1995], pp. 195–207 [195–96]). I know that 'native stuff' is 'in', both in popular culture and in the academic world, and that every white, scholarly kind of guy wishes he could invent a fascinating ethnic heritage for himself. We white guys want to write personally, sympathetically about our radical feminism or about some close friend's ethnicity to show that we are 'au courant' and 'sensitive to issues of gender and race'. And so I worry that my Navajo 'other [may be] adopted merely to provide an opportunity for [me] to masquerade as [a] savior of marginality' (S. Sawhney, 'The Joke and the Hoax: (Not) Speaking as the Other', in J. Roof and R. Wiegman [eds.], *Who Can Speak? Authority and Critical Identity*, pp. 208–20 [216]); see also Greg Salyer's critical remarks in his 'Review of *Reading with a Passion: Rhetoric, Autobiography, and the American West in the Gospel of John*, by Jeffrey L. Staley (New York: Continuum, 1995)', *Literature and Theology* 11 (1997), pp. 320–23, esp. 322–23. Or perhaps I keep 'telling stories with the hope that ultimately [I'll] be able to live [my] way into them [or out of them]' (B.C. Lane, *The Solace of Fierce Landscapes: Exploring Desert and Mountain Spirituality* [New York: Oxford University Press, 1998], p. 144).

now we are side by side at Sarah's hard-packed adobe grave, trying to say goodbye to someone—something—that was once simple, passionate, and young; full of grace and beauty.

Rob and I are here, in the mission cemetery, just a stone's throw from the three-room mission school where our father taught for thirty years. We are standing here without speaking. We are standing here because of one of those generic conversations you start with siblings whom you haven't seen in eight years. It was a conversation I initiated a few hours ago.

I had just sat down at the lunch table next to Greg, my other older brother. 'So,' I began, 'do you ever see any of the Navajo kids we used to go to school with?' I try to make conversation with the most laconic of my brothers, who, after thirty years on the Navajo Reservation, acts more Navajo than half of the Indians in the area.

'Do you ever see William Scott? Or Sam Benally? What about Anna Horse or Bessie Begay? Then there was Sarah Tsosie. No other girl came close to her. I haven't seen her since college when I would occasionally come home from Wheaton. Remember how Mother used to say that Sarah had a "cute figure"? It took me twenty years to figure out that was her Christian way of saying "Sarah is really sexy".'

Greg pauses in the midst of eating a tuna sandwich and smoothes his mustache with his thumb and forefinger. 'Yeah, we were probably all in love with Sarah at one time or another. I used to see her quite a bit. You know, her kids were in school here for a while. She was living over near Red Mesa Trading Post when we got word that she had died. She had had a drinking problem for a number of years. No one knows whether she drank herself to death or committed suicide. Maybe there isn't a lot of difference between the two. I know she died alone. Her body wasn't found for a few days. We buried her up there at the mission cemetery, just east of mother's grave.'

Towering white cumulus clouds rise over the purple Lukachukai Mountains to the south, shrouding Sheepskin Mesa in greys and blues. A breeze suddenly stirs the afternoon air, raising northern Arizona's version of Middle Eastern whirling dervishes. The dust-colored pythonic spirits gather up the remnants of faded flowers and spin them across the cluttered mounds in the mission cemetery. Rob and I stand, silent, both caught up in the twists and turns of our own private memories.

I never kissed her. I never held her close and smelled the scent of mountain cedar in her jet-black hair. I never felt her blue jeans pressed hard against my body. To her I was just a pal, a silly, laughing boy who kept her mind off of Rob while he was far away at a boarding school in New York. After all, I was just twelve, and Sarah was nearly fourteen. So I spent afternoons playing Ping-Pong and badminton with her, teasing her incessantly. Then at night I would dream about her. I would sing every song on the radio for her, and drift off to sleep by counting how many times that day her laughing eyes had fixed on mine. I would hold on to that delicious yearning with a tortured, pubescent heart, and wake in the morning with my pillow stained with tears.

Sarah was baptized at our mission when she was thirteen. Then she beat out my brother Greg by a tenth of a point for the highest honors in her eighth-grade class at the little mission school. But we all lost track of Sarah after graduation. We found out later that she stayed on the reservation, living at home near Mexican Water and taking the bus forty miles to high school in Kayenta. By that time my two brothers and I were attending high school in California, boarding with an uncle and his family. But in the fall of 1966 Sarah Tsosie showed up as a junior at Shiprock High School, where my brothers and I had just transferred. Rob confided in me a few weeks later that he was beginning to get interested in her again. And I felt a strange stirring in my chest, a twinge of jealousy that I thought had died long before. But then we began to hear rumors. Sarah was 'easy'. 'Better drunk than sober.' Crude etchings on bathroom walls outlined her physical attributes and advertised her phone number. We began to watch her guardedly, from a distance. She was different; not the same Sarah we had known in grade school. She didn't study anymore. She skipped classes. She had a look about her that said 'I know things that you haven't even dreamed of yet'. And it was not a happy look.

Rob never did date Sarah. He said he couldn't stomach the kind of girl she had become. And I barely spoke to her those last two years of high school. She was a senior, and I was a junior. She was Navajo. I was white. Things were different in Shiprock, a reservation border town of 1,500 people. Sarah was pregnant before she finished school and married a few months later. It was the first of four or five marriages, some more cruel than others.

Recently I have begun to think of Sarah Tsosie as Slim Girl, a central character in Oliver La Farge's classic novel about Navajo Indians. My brother Rob had a copy of La Farge's book, *Laughing Boy*, in his bedroom when he was in high school, and I know he had read it, because he told me that he liked it a lot. I suspect that Slim Girl reminded him of Sarah Tsosie, too. I wish I had read the book back then, but I didn't. I didn't know then that Oliver Hazard Perry La Farge became a well-respected anthropologist and spokesperson for Native Americans,[12] or that he had won the 1930 Pulitzer Prize in literature for *Laughing Boy* (Hemingway's *A Farewell to Arms* was a distant runner-up that year).[13]

For years after Rob left home the book collected powdery red dust on a shelf in his old bedroom in our home on the Navajo Reservation. I shook the dust off of it a few times over the years and thought about reading it. But I never did. Then when I married, I came into possession of a copy, a required text for a course in Native American Studies that my wife had taken at the University of California at Berkeley. Eventually, without her knowledge, I traded it, along with a number of other books

---

12 Oliver La Farge became one of the strongest opponents of Dillon S. Myer, the controversial commissioner of the Bureau of Indian Affairs (BIA) from 1950 to 1953. Myer was best known for his role as the director of the War Relocation Authority (WRA) which was responsible for incarcerating thousands of Japanese-Americans during World War II (R. Drinnon, *Keeper of the Concentration Camps: Dillon S. Myer and American Racism* [Berkeley: University of California Press, 1987], pp. xxiii–xxciv, 39, 226–27). Dillon Myer saw a natural connection in the US domestic policy of Japanese-American 'relocation' and Native American 'relocations' and hoped to exploit this close association in the postwar years by dissolving all American Indian reservations. Interestingly, Leslie Marmon Silko alludes to the similarity between US/Japanese-American policy and US/Native American policy in her novel *Ceremony* (pp. 6, 17–18, 124, 246), but lays it open to a postcolonial critique (cf. J. Brice, 'Earth as Mother, Earth as Other in Novels by Silko and Hogan', *Critique* 39 [1998], pp. 132–33; and T.E. Benediktsson, 'The Reawakening of the Gods: Realism and the Supernatural in Silko and Hulme', *Critique* 33 [1992], pp. 121–31).

13 D'Arcy McNickle, *Indian Man: A Life of Oliver La Farge* (Bloomington: Indiana University Press, 1971), p. 58.

I had never read, for a stack of books on literary theory at Powell's Bookstore in Portland, Oregon.

Not long ago, on a rainy Thanksgiving weekend in Washington's San Juan Islands, I found myself in a used bookstore, having forgotten to bring along something to read during the long Northwest evenings. I saw a copy of *Laughing Boy* on a shelf and checked the inside cover, half expecting to find my wife's name written there. Instead I found the word 'Erbstoeszer' scrawled across the yellowed page, below a penciled $1.50. I bought the book, despite my wife's insisting that she had a copy around the house somewhere, and read it over the weekend.

If La Farge has shown me that Sarah is a contemporary version of Slim Girl, my reading in postcolonial and feminist criticism has convinced me that Sarah is also much more than that. She is also a variation of Native American border women like Pocahontas and Doña Marina (Malinche).[14] And as I shall argue below, she shares an identity with Lydia and the pythonic slave girl of Acts 16. To my way of thinking, Sarah is all these women spun into one.

As a person related to the borderland characters Lydia and the pythonic slave girl, Sarah Tsosie's death causes me to reevaluate these two biblical women from postcolonial and postfeminist perspectives. I am hoping that I might find in these perspectives a way to critique the colonialist ideology that created both them and Sarah. But to do this I will have to go back and take a closer look at the way in which the author of Luke–Acts constructs Macedonian otherness and territory. Only then can I begin to move on to a creative, self-critical reappropriation of the biblical text and my own colonialist past.

Evidence of Colonialist Borders in Macedonia

For well over a hundred years now, biblical commentators have been content to call Acts 15.36–18.22 Paul's 'second missionary journey'.[15] But unlike any of Paul's preceding or subsequent journeys, this one begins with a vision.[16] Some commentators have read the vision as a mirror of the book's author—Luke, himself, the Macedonian—calling to Paul for help.[17] But few commentators today would be convinced by so naive a view of authorial allusion.[18] And not just today: Origen argued centuries ago for a much different and more ideologically plausible identification. It is an identification that Walter Wink elaborates in his trilogy of books on the language of power in the New Testament. For Origen, and for Wink following in his interpretive footsteps, the Macedonian man in the vision represents the 'angel' of

---

14 C.S. Kidwell, 'Indian Women as Cultural Mediators', *Ethnohistory* 39 (1992), pp. 97–107.
15 Townsend, 'Missionary Journeys in Acts and European Missionary Societies', pp. 433–37; cf. Rackham, *The Acts of the Apostles*, p. 271.
16 Other programmatic visionary experiences in Luke–Acts are found in Lk. 1.11–22; 24.4–11, 23; and Acts 9.10–16; 10.3–20; 22.17–21; 26.19; 27.23–25.
17 This is an attempt to connect the subsequent 'we' text (Acts 16.11–13) with Paul's Macedonian mission (E. Haenchen, *The Acts of the Apostles: A Commentary* [trans. B. Noble and C. Shinn; rev. R.M. Wilson; Philadelphia: Westminster Press, 1971], p. 489).
18 See, for example, Susan Praeder's essay, 'Luke–Acts and the Ancient Novel', SBLSP, 20 (1981), pp. 269–92.

the region,[19] whose power could be challenged or assuaged by Jesus' ambassadors. For them, this angel of Macedonia is comparable to the 'prince of the kingdom of Persia' with whom an unnamed angel and Michael had fought centuries earlier (Dan. 10.5–6, 10–14, 20–21; cf. Rev. 2.1–3.22).

In his commentary on this section of Acts, Charles Talbert collects a number of historical references to the dreams of Roman conquering heroes which provide an ideological context for Wink's and Origen's thesis. For example, Talbert notes how Suetonius (*Julius Caesar* 32) had 'a dream before leaving Spain for Rome that he [would] have sovereignty over the whole world' and that 'Drusus, the father of Claudius, [saw] an apparition of a barbarian woman, speaking in Latin, forbidding him to pursue the defeated Germanic tribes further' (Suetonius, *Claudius* 1).[20] Although Paul is no military leader, his vision in Acts appears to be programmatic like those quoted above, and is consistent with the imperial ideology that underlies those visions.[21] That is to say, the visions provide the divine authorization for a transfer of power. Furthermore, if Origen's and Wink's angelic identification is appropriate, then it makes perfect sense that one of Paul's first acts in the new territory is to perform an exorcism (Acts 16.16–18). As John Dominic Crossan, following the lead of cultural anthropologists, has argued, the physical body is a microcosm of the macrocosmic political system.[22] In the symbolic universe of the Greco-Roman world, exorcisms in 'foreign' territory become explicit political acts connecting political oppression with demonic possession (cf. Mk 5.1–17; 7.24–31). Surely, then, Luke Johnson has sensed the importance of the Acts scene when he says 'we find ... [Paul] doing battle with demonic forces and besting them, *establishing in still another turf-war a further territorial gain* for the "kingdom of God"' (my emphasis).[23]

Perhaps even the often-discussed 'we sections' which begin in Acts 16.11 could be understood at least in part as a rhetorical evocation of Macedonia as new and foreign territory. While the issue is too complex to do justice to here, from a text pragmatics standpoint one must account for why the 'we sections' begin at this particular point in the narrative. On a pragmatic level, the juxtapositioning of first-person pronouns and verbal forms with third-person pronouns and verbal forms (16.10–17) constructs a grammatical, linguistic distinction between Paul and the Macedonians, a distinction that is paralleled by the ethnic differences and the attending plot developments.

---

19 Origen, *Homily on Luke* 12, quoted approvingly in W. Wink, *Naming the Powers: The Language of Power in the New Testament* (Philadelphia: Fortress Press, 1984), p. 32.

20 Talbert, *Reading Acts*, p. 149; cf. Pervo, *Luke's Story of Paul*, p. 55.

21 Interestingly, Rackham rejects the word 'journey' when describing Paul's activity in Macedonia, preferring the more militaristic term 'campaign' (*The Acts of the Apostles*, p. 271 n. 2).

22 J.D. Crossan, *Jesus: A Revolutionary Biography* (San Francisco: HarperSanFrancisco, 1994), pp. 76–77, 88–91, quoting Mary Douglas and other cultural anthropologists. Robert Tannehill notes the literary connections between Acts 16.16–18 and the story of the Gerasene demoniac (Lk. 8.26–39; cf. Acts 19.12–15), but without mentioning the political implications of the stories (*The Narrative Unity of Luke–Acts: A Literary Interpretation*. II. *The Acts of the Apostles* [Minneapolis: Fortress Press, 1990], p. 197).

23 Johnson, *Acts of the Apostles*, p. 297.

Finally, the designation of the demon-possessed girl as 'pythonic' (16.16) evokes the Greek hieropolis of Delphi (still to the west), the omphalos (navel) of the ancient Greek world.[24] This pythonic spirit of Delphi stands in marked contrast to Jerusalem (to the east), the omphalos of the Jewish and early Christian world,[25] and the center of the book of Acts up to this point in the narrative: a place where God's holy spirit had earlier filled an entire house with amazing displays of power (Acts 2.1–13).

But not only is Macedonia marked out as *foreign* territory: it is also the *most explicitly Roman* territory that Paul has yet entered. The narrator in this section of Acts uses numerous terms for Roman power (κολωνία [16.11], στρατηγοί [16.20, 22, 35, 36, 38], ῥαβδοῦχος [Latin, *lictor*; 16.35, 38], Ῥωμαῖος ὑπάρχοντας [16.37, 38]),[26] along with the less explicit listing of such cities as Neapolis ('New City') and Philippi ('the leading city of Macedonia'),[27] which were important Roman settlements in the area. As Talbert notes, there are also three 'charges leveled against the missionaries', which help to reinforce in political language the foreign character of Paul and his entourage: first, they are called Ἰουδαῖοι (16.20), which evokes their ethnic identity;[28] second, 'they are charged with disturbing the peace [which] is an appeal to the Roman obsession with public order' (16.20a); and third, they are 'charged with advocating customs that are not lawful for Romans to adopt or practice' (16.20b).[29] Significantly, this is the first time in Paul's journeys that Gentiles rather than Jews have been the instigators of opposition to his missionary activity.[30]

---

24 Scott, *Paul and the Nations*, p. 20; cf. Alexander, 'Notes on the "Imago Mundi"', p. 198.

25 Alexander, 'Notes on the "Imago Mundi"', p. 204.

26 Kee, *To Every Nation*, pp. 197–200; F.F. Bruce, *Commentary on the Book of the Acts* (New ICC; Grand Rapids: Eerdmans, 1954), pp. 335–36; J.H. Neyrey, 'Luke's Social Location of Paul: Cultural Anthropology and the Status of Paul in Acts', in B. Witherington III (ed.), *History, Literature and Society in the Book of Acts* (Cambridge: Cambridge University Press, 1996), pp. 251–79, esp. 263–64.

27 Richard Ascough has recently argued that πρώτης τῆς Μακεδονίας πόλις should be the preferred reading of the textual variant in Acts 16.12, based upon a cultural assessment of civic pride in ancient Philippi rather than upon the city's actual political significance ('Civic Pride at Philippi: The Text-Critical Problem of Acts 16.12', *NTS* 44 [1998], pp. 93–103; cf. Neyrey, 'Luke's Social Location of Paul', pp. 268–70).

28 Talbert calls this 'an appeal to nationalism and racial prejudice' (*Reading Acts*, p. 152), but is using the terms 'nationalism' and 'racial prejudice' in anachronistic ways (cf. Neyrey, 'Luke's Social Location of Paul', pp. 255–60, 276–79).

29 Talbert, *Reading Acts*, p. 152. Talbert goes on to argue that on another level 'there are [five] ... points this section makes regarding the relation of believers to the state ... [I]t shows the legitimacy of disciples' appealing to their legal rights as protection against unjust treatment by nonbelievers ... it says believers must be prepared to suffer unjustly because Roman officials are sometimes swayed by mob hysteria ... it claims that the state is usually reasonable and will correct mistakes when these are made clear ... it makes very clear that the disciples are not the troublemakers but are the victims of those with questionable motives ... [and] such unjust suffering at the hands of the state lends credence to one's claims' (pp. 153–54; cf. Conzelmann, *Acts of the Apostles*, p. 133; R.J. Cassidy, *Society and Politics in the Acts of the Apostles* [Maryknoll, NY: Orbis Press, 1987], pp. 87–89, 150–53, 162).

30 Cf. Acts 13.6–8, 48–51; 14.1–7, 19–20. See also Acts 17.4–5, 12–13; 18.12–13. The only other case of Gentile-instigated opposition occurs much later in Ephesus, when Demetrius the silversmith starts a riot (18.23–28).

These six elements—Paul's vision, the exorcism, the political and legal language of Roman hegemony, the we/them language, the lack of Jewish opposition, and the evocation of the omphalic Delphic oracle—all mark Macedonia as important, new, and foreign territory for Paul's missionary activity. But it is primarily Paul's encounter with the two women that marks the territory as a major bordercrossing in the book of Acts. And it is the author's juxtapositioning of Lydia the 'good' woman with the pythonic 'bad' girl that offers the contemporary reader the most fruitful grounds for a postcolonial, postfeminist critique of that particular border.

In her important book entitled *Postcolonial Feminist Interpretation of the Bible*, Musa Dube Shomanah focuses her attention on those texts in the biblical tradition where there seems to be a connection between 'bad' women and new (soon to be conquered) territory.[31] And although her primary attention centers on the story of Rahab (Josh. 1) as the model for what she calls an ancient Hebrew 'land possession typescene', she also discusses the Canaanite or Syrophoenician woman (Mt. 15; par. Mk 7) and the Samaritan woman (Jn 4) as figures who fit into the same stereotypical pattern.[32] The elements that Dube Shomanah isolates in the typescene are: (1) a traveling hero journeys to a foreign land, (2) meets a woman, (3) and bonds with her.[33] Although Dube Shomanah does not mention Lydia and the 'spirit-possessed' girl in Acts 16 in her assemblage of biblical examples, I believe that these two women function in the same way as do the other three women—as a means to legitimize the ideological and territorial conquests of a nascent Christianity. But what is unique about the Acts text is the fact that it is the only biblical account where the reader finds *two* women on the border—one who is clearly a more positive character than the other.[34]

Halvor Moxnes's study of patron–client relations in Luke–Acts quite nicely describes the first woman, Lydia, as a representative of feminine propriety.[35] She is

---

31 *Postcolonial Feminist Interpretation of the Bible*, pp. 57–80.

32 Musa Dube Shomanah borrows the term 'type-scene' (*Postcolonial Feminist Interpretation of the Bible*, pp. 118–21) from Robert Alter's analysis of betrothal scenes in ancient Hebrew narrative (*The Art of Biblical Narrative*, pp. 51–52). However, Dube Shomanah's appropriation of the term is somewhat problematical, since in Alter's view biblical type-scenes isolate 'a series of recurrent narrative episodes *attached to the careers of biblical heroes* ... [which] catch [the] protagonists *only at the crucial junctures in [their] lives*' (Alter, *The Art of Biblical Narrative*, p. 51; my emphasis). Thus, by attending to the author's manipulation of the type-scene's motifs the interpreter gains insight into the art of biblical characterization (Alter, *The Art of Biblical Narrative*, p. 52). But Dube Shomanah's analysis does not focus on hero or heroine figures of the stature of Jacob, Moses, or Saul, as much as on the secondary characters in the scenes. Nor does she attempt to show how the *manipulation* of the motifs subtly affects a particular author's ideological strategy. Nevertheless, I do believe that Dube Shomanah has clearly identified an important colonization *motif* in biblical narrative, one which she goes on to deconstruct in an important, decolonizing manner (*Postcolonial Feminist Interpretation of the Bible*, pp. 157–95).

33 Dube Shomanah, *Postcolonial Feminist Interpretation of the Bible*, p. 120.

34 The exorcism of a demon from the Syrophoenician woman's daughter (Mk 7.24–30) is another 'land possession typescene' which mentions two women, but the daughter in the story does not function as a character. However, it is perhaps significant that this Markan story is missing from Luke. Could it be that Acts 16.11–21 is the author's oblique response to Mk 7.24–30?

35 H. Moxnes, 'Patron–Client Relations and the New Community', in Neyrey (ed.), *The Social World of Luke–Acts* (Peabody, MA: Hendrickson, 1991), pp. 241–68 (262–63); see also J.H. Neyrey, 'Luke's Social Location of Paul', pp. 264–65, 275. Cf. M.R. D'Angelo, 'Women in Luke–Acts: A Redactional View', *JBL* 109 (1990), pp. 441–61 (453, 455, 458–59).

'a patron who considers her benefactions as an act of reciprocity for the far greater spiritual benefits that she has received. Moreover, her patronage is offered very humbly; if her gift is accepted, she in fact receives the larger gift of recognition of her faith.'[36] On the other hand, the second female character, the prophetic 'bad girl', is typically described by commentators as one who has 'prostituted her divinatory capacity for the benefit of her owners'.[37] Yet the 'bad girl's' annoying proclamation, 'These men are slaves of the Most High God' (Acts 16.17), probably reflects a localized rumor, the colonized people's 'manic vehicle of fear' and 'an uncontrolled, yet strategic affect of political revolt',[38] as much as it reflects any (misguided) theological revelation.

In his recent study of the widow traditions in Luke–Acts, Robert Price argues on historical-critical grounds that Lydia and the pythonic slave girl were originally one person: Lydia, the dealer in purple cloth, a woman with a significant prophetic gift.[39] From Price's perspective, the author has cloned the 'positive' figure Lydia into 'the Pythoness, her own "evil twin"'.[40] Although I am not particularly convinced by Price's imaginative historical reconstruction or by his hypothetical redaction history of the Philippian women traditions, I do think that his desire to yoke the two women of Acts 16 reflects a genuine insight into the colonialist underpinnings of the Lukan bordercrossing story. But at this point the perspective of recent postcolonial theory addresses the text's problematics more sharply than any dubious historical or redactional reconstruction could.

---

36 Moxnes, 'Patron–Client Relations and the New Community', p. 262; cf. F.M. Gillman, 'Early Christian Women at Philippi', *Journal of Gender in World Religions* 1 (1990), pp. 59–79.

37 Kee, *To Every Nation*, p. 197. Cf. Dunn's aside to the effect that 'one can well imagine, for example, a dim-witted slave girl, who had picked up phrases used offhand by missionaries, following them around and calling them out in the way Luke records' (*Acts of the Apostles*, p. 221). Johnson calls the slave girl and her masters 'the equivalent of an urban dog and pony show', *Acts of the Apostles*, p. 298). But surely in that patriarchal world it is her masters (κύριοι, Acts 16.16, 19) who are the manipulators of her mantic gift. Nevertheless, the fact that Paul exorcises the spirit from the girl is evidence that the author views it as an oppositional and deceptive power (see, for example, P.R. Trebilco, 'Paul and Silas—"Servants of the Most High God" (Acts 16.16–18)', *JSNT* 36 [1989], pp. 51–73). For a different point of view, see R.M. Price who argues that the prophetic voice being stifled in Acts 16 is that of the authentic Christian prophetess (*The Widow Traditions in Luke–Acts: A Feminist-Critical Scrutiny* [SBLDS, 155; Atlanta, GA: Scholars Press, 1997], pp. 225–34; esp. 228–29).

38 H.K. Bhabha, *The Location of Culture* (New York: Routledge, 1994), p. 199, as quoted in J. Perkinson, 'A Canaanite Word in the Logos of Christ; or The Difference the Syro-Phoenician Woman Makes to Jesus', *Semeia* 75 (1996), pp. 61–85 (70); cf. p. 66; see also R. Boer, 'Green Ants and Gibeonites: B. Wongar, Joshua 9, and Some Problems of Postcolonialism', *Semeia* 75 (1996), pp. 129–52 (144).

39 Price, *The Widow Traditions in Luke–Acts*, pp. 225–34; esp. 228–29. Price cites as supporting evidence his interpretation of the Joanna vignette (Lk. 8.2–3; pp. 127–51, esp. 129–30, 138–40). More recently, Kathy Chambers has argued for connecting the slave girl and Lydia because of their common comic effect ('At the Expense of Women: Humor (?) in Acts 16.14–40', in Athalya Brenner [ed.], *Are We Amused? Humour about Women in the Biblical Worlds* [BTC, 2; New York: Continuum, 2003]), pp. 79–89, esp. 87–89.

40 Price, *The Widow Traditions in Luke–Acts*, p. 229. Price goes on to argue—following the suggestion of William M. Ramsay—that the epithet 'Jezebel' in Rev. 3.20 might also refer to the demonizing of the prophetess Lydia in much the same manner as the Acts 16 text does (*The Widow Traditions in Luke–Acts*, pp. 233–34).

Toward a Postcolonial, Postfeminist Reappropriation of Acts 16.6–40

Lydia is from Thyatira, a city in the Roman province of Asia long noted for its purple dye industry.[41] Similarly, the three border women who precede her in the Christian canon are associated with blue-red colors: Rahab the Canaanite places a crimson thread in her window (τό σπαρτίον το κόκκινον, Josh. 2.18, 21); the Canaanite, or Syrophoenician woman lives in a land called reddish-purple (the proper noun 'Phoenicia' is derived from φοινίκεος, Mk 7.26); and the Samaritan woman, whose witness is associated with a harvest of white-headed grain (λευκαί, Jn 4.35–36), prefigures the harvest among non-Jews (Jn 12.20–23)—a harvest that comes only through the death of the scarlet-hued seed (κόκκος, Jn 12.24; cf. 19.2, 5).

Spider Woman, a feminine deity in Pueblo mythology, plays a central role in Leslie Marmon Silko's novel *Ceremony* and is likewise a character full of color. In Navajo mythology she is called Changing Woman, and like Spider Woman she is known by the colors she wears: black, white, red, and blue. These four colors in her rainbow are captured in the mother-earth substances of jet, shell, abalone, and turquoise. Together they blend into a rich, dark purple—Lydia's hue. It is the same mix of colors Slim Girl wears when Laughing Boy first sees her.[42] The color purple thus binds together these six border women—the four ancient Eastern Mediterranean women, and the two Western twentieth-century Native American women—in a postmodern, postcolonial, postfeminist weave of intertextual allusions.

Oliver La Farge's novel, *Laughing Boy*, takes place on the Navajo Indian Reservation in 1915, seven years prior to the founding of the mission where I spent my childhood. At least once the author mentions Sweetwater, the old trading post four miles north-west of where I grew up.[43] La Farge recalls in the foreword to the 1962 edition of his book that he chose the year 1915 because 'romanticism made him feel that he should cast back in time to a less corrupted, purer era'.[44] 'In the space of thirty years, however, the wholeness has gone ...'[45] That loss of wholeness is represented in the book by the character Slim Girl, who marries Laughing Boy, the story's protagonist.

Slim Girl is a border woman who participates in the same colonialist ideology that gives life to Lydia and the pythonic slave girl of Acts 16. Like my childhood friend Sarah Tsosie, and like Lydia and the pythonic slave girl, Slim Girl is a person who *embodies* the ambiguous relationship of the colonized to the colonizer. Like Malinche in the conquistadores' legends of Central America and like Pocahontas in the story of the founding of the British colonies in America, Slim Girl is a complex character.[46] But there is a twist in La Farge's appropriation of the ideology of the

---

41 Hans Conzelmann notes that a damaged inscription found at Philippi has the word 'PVRPVPARI, "purple" still visible' (*Acts of the Apostles*, p. 130).

42 La Farge, *Laughing Boy*, pp. 15–16; cf. 35, 50, 177.

43 T'o Tlikahn' is La Farge's spelling of the Navajo word for 'Sweetwater'. It was the closest trading post to our mission, and my brothers and I would go there every couple of weeks to spend our hard-earned allowances (*Laughing Boy*, p. 13).

44 La Farge, *Laughing Boy*, p. 5.

45 La Farge, *Laughing Boy*, p. 6.

46 For an analysis of Native American border women in colonial literature, see V. Stolcke, 'Invaded Women: Gender, Race, and Class in the Formation of Colonial Society', in M. Hendricks and P. Parker (eds.), *Women, 'Race' and Writing in the Early Modern Period* (London: Routledge,

colonized border woman. For in his novel, told from the perspective of Laughing Boy, a traditional Navajo, the secondary character Slim Girl is the reader's main contact with the white world. As the story develops, the reader learns that Slim Girl has been educated in a boarding school where she was converted to Christianity. After her schooling she lived in a reservation border town where she worked as a prostitute. When she meets Laughing Boy, several years later, she is living on the edge of the border town in a house built by a Mexican man. From there she regularly travels to the town to meet with a white rancher who pays her for her sexual services. When Laughing Boy inquires about her activities in the town and the source of her money, she lies to him and tells him that she does housecleaning for a missionary family. Laughing Boy and Slim Girl soon marry, on the edge of the border town, far away from their own clans. With no family members present, Slim Girl procures a drunken medicine man to perform a traditional Navajo wedding ceremony.

Slim Girl, the border woman, is like the pythonic slave girl of Acts 16. Slim Girl represents all things new and evil, and although she is not the subject of an exorcism, the tension in the novel revolves around the issue of what holds more power—traditional Navajo ways (embodied by Laughing Boy) or American colonialist ways (embodied by Slim Girl). Slim Girl represents change. The colors of her jewelry and clothing also show that she represents the rainbow-hued Changing Woman of Navajo mythology. And if the reader somehow should miss this symbolic connection, La Farge has her say to Laughing Boy as she lies dying, '... you have changed because of me; in you I shall live'.[47] But for La Farge, Slim Girl's (or Changing Woman's) adaptation to American culture can only be seen as negative; a part of imperial American colonialism that will ultimately destroy even those who, like her, think they are powerful enough to twist American culture to their own ends.

By way of contrast, the male character Laughing Boy represents what is traditional, good, and pure in Navajo ways. Still, he desires the border woman and marries her against the advice of his relatives. But Slim Girl grows to love Laughing Boy and does not merely use him for her own ends. Like Lydia, she is wealthy, and with her money she procures the necessities with which to begin 'traditional' life as a Navajo. She also willingly learns from her husband about the Navajo ways she had lost when she attended the Christian boarding school.[48] But in the end Slim Girl, or Changing Woman, becomes one more victim sacrificed to American colonialism. Ultimately she embodies the colonial ideology that underlies most of the novel. For Oliver La Farge's colonialist ideology effectively disempowers any native voice that would attempt to deconstruct that colonial power by requiring Slim Girl to die at the end of the book. Thus the female, bordercrossing character gives up her life to 'save' Slim Boy from the white man's ways. Fittingly for the era in which the book was written, she is murdered by a traditional Navajo man. Like the Lydia/slave girl

---

1994), pp. 272–89; and K. Robertson, 'Pocahontas at the Masque', *Signs* 21 (1996), pp. 551–83. Border women of the Bible are discussed by Maldonado, 'Reading Malinche Reading Ruth', pp. 97–100; I.R. Kitzberger, 'Border Crossing and Meeting Jesus at the Well: An Autobiographical Re-reading of the Samaritan Woman's Story in John 4.1–44', in *idem* (ed.), *The Personal Voice in Biblical Scholarship* (London: Routledge, 1999), pp. 111–27; and by Dube Shomanah (*Postcolonial Feminist Interpretation of the Bible*).

47 La Farge, *Laughing Boy*, p. 177.
48 La Farge, *Laughing Boy*, pp. 45–47.

double, Slim Girl/Changing Woman is the symbolic sacrificial victim that unwittingly allows American imperial power to continue to exert its control over the colonized Navajo.

For all the good the author of *Laughing Boy* hoped to accomplish in his novel (or that the author of Luke–Acts hoped to accomplish in narrating Paul's journey into Macedonia), La Farge was unable to break free from the colonialist ideology that created the reservation borders in the first place. That task is left to the blue-bodied characters in Leslie Marmon Silko's novel *Ceremony*, who find ways to appropriate their colonial, borderland past and transform it into a viable, postcolonial, postfeminist life-way.

Ceremony reflects an important postcolonial shift in the metaphorical status of the border woman. Like Acts 16 and the novel *Laughing Boy*, *Ceremony* is set near a border town: Gallup, New Mexico, a few years after the end of World War II. Tayo, the main character, is half-white, half-Laguna; a veteran who suffers from post-traumatic stress syndrome and returns to the reservation after he supposedly has been cured by white doctors. It is obvious to his family and friends that he is not well, and so his grandmother obtains the names of two native medicine men who might be able to help him. But it is not Ku'oosh, a medicine man from his own Laguna tribe, who cures him.[49] Instead an old Navajo medicine man named Betonie sets Tayo on the path toward healing and wholeness. Because Betonie lives on the outskirts of Gallup, a reservation border town, he is able to find traces of truth in the cultures of both the colonizer and the colonized. So he performs for the half-breed Tayo a healing ceremony that incorporates Tayo's two divergent worlds. It is a mixed-up, topsy-turvy ritual that sets Tayo on the road to wholeness.[50] And throughout Tayo's journey toward wholeness, the color blue dominates.[51]

The novel's female characters, although many, are symbolized as one person: the ever-mutating Spider Woman of Laguna mythology (known as Changing Woman in Navajo mythology). Spider Woman, or Changing Woman, is in the turquoise blue of the satin dress of Black Swan, a Mexican prostitute;[52] Spider Woman/Changing Woman is in the blue of Mount Taylor;[53] the blue swimsuit of the model in a Coca-Cola calendar;[54] the blue of old Betonie's shirt;[55] and in the blue of the Ute woman's tight Western pants.[56] Spider Woman/Changing Woman's color is found in the most incongruous places. It functions as a kind of cultural hypertext, linking the reader to new postcolonial, postfeminist perspectives and possibilities. In all these contexts the color blue reflects Silko's critical appropriation of the woman of the 'borderland typescene',[57] a personage whom we first saw in the biblical tradition. But unlike La

49 Silko, *Ceremony*, pp. 33–39.
50 Silko, *Ceremony*, pp. 116–45.
51 Kathleen Manley makes the argument that '[t]he color blue provides ... links among the ceremonies with Night Swan, Betonie, and Ts'eh' ('Leslie Marmon Silko's Use of Color in *Ceremony*', *Southern Folklore* 46 [1989], p. 138, cf. 137, 139).
52 Silko, *Ceremony*, pp. 84, 98.
53 Silko, *Ceremony*, p. 100.
54 Silko, *Ceremony*, p. 153.
55 Silko, *Ceremony*, p. 119.
56 Silko, *Ceremony*, p. 155.
57 Significantly, Tayo recalls a previous meeting with a mysterious woman (Spider Woman) precisely at the moment he is cutting through the barbed-wire fence that separates the reservation from a white man's ranch (*Ceremony*, p. 194; cf. 176–77, 183).

Farge or the author of Luke–Acts, Silko seems to be arguing that the colonizer's own stories can be used to benefit and heal the colonized if those stories' power can be critically appropriated into the tradition of the colonized.[58] Thus, in Silko's reading of the border woman, the colonized are empowered—even called—to engage their wits and creatively reappropriate the new and old in ways that the colonial power cannot imagine. Here, finally, the voice of the colonized is engaged: it talks back, it argues, it challenges. That voice is critically involved in active dialogue with the colonizer's ideology. *Ceremony* offers a lively, postcolonial, postfeminist, post-canonical voice to colonialist-engendered border women like Sarah Tsosie, Slim Girl, and Lydia and the pythonic slave girl who otherwise remain co-opted, disempowered, or dead.

Conclusion

A postcolonial, postfeminist reading of Acts 16.6–40 allows one to understand Lydia and the pythonic slave girl in a new way. Where other commentators and missionizing folk write about the women separately, with Lydia being the positive role model and the slave girl being the negative role model for 'native' responses to the gospel, a postcolonial, postfeminist reading resists viewing them independently. Instead, the focus of postcolonialist, postfeminist attention is on their paired geographical status as border women.

At this point, my particular reading of Acts 16, conceived and nurtured in memories of a colonialist childhood on the Navajo Reservation and confirmed by my recent reading of *Laughing Boy*, gains insight from Dube Shomanah's creative work. For as her analysis makes evident, there is a series of biblical stories where border women embody the doubled identity of helper and betrayer. Since Lydia and the pythonic slave girl are the first people Paul meets in explicitly defined Roman territory, they also reflect the conflicted status of colonized peoples. But the author of Acts carefully disguises the gospel's colonialist effects. For in describing Paul's encounter with *two* border women, the author effectively deflects the reader's attention from Paul's role as ideological colonizer and instead tries to force the reader to choose between the two opposing responses to Paul's message. There is, therefore, no middle ground in this text: Lydia, the good woman, welcomes Paul the conqueror, and the evil slave girl who challenges Paul is forever silenced. There is no place in this author's narrative repertoire for more complex border women like Rahab, the Canaanite/Syrophoenician woman, or the Samaritan woman. And certainly there is no place in Acts for a borderland character like Silko's half-breed Tayo, who struggles for survival on the edges of two different worlds.

In conclusion, I do not think that we have to find a decolonizing strategy in Acts to save the biblical text from imperialist, patriarchal ideologies. If we are honest

---

58 This perspective is seen most clearly in characters like Tayo's grandmother who is able to mingle 'all of creation [with] two names: an Indian name and a white name' and still see the underlying unity (*Ceremony*, pp. 68–69; cf. 259–60); and in Betonie, the Navajo medicine man who can say, 'You see, in many ways, the ceremonies have always been changing' (Silko, *Ceremony*, p. 126; cf. 132, 150, 153–54; cf. B.A. St Andrews, 'Healing the Witchery: Medicine in Silko's *Ceremony*', *Arizona Quarterly* 14 [1988], pp. 86–94; and N.R. Rand, 'Surviving What Haunts You: The Art of Invisibility in *Ceremony*, *The Ghost Writer*, and *Beloved*', *MELUS* 20 [1995], pp. 21–32).

about our ideological and ethical commitments from the outset, then perhaps Leslie Marmon Silko's contrapuntal voice in *Ceremony* will be enough to challenge our colonialist readings of Acts 16. Perhaps Spider Woman/Changing Woman can function as an important intertextual supplement to Acts 16, a supplement that creates space for an invigorating postcolonial, postfeminist conversation with traditional biblical texts. In this new environment, experiments in postcolonial, postfeminist, post-canonical exegesis will empower colonized minds, hearts, and voices to speak and act in fresh, enlivening ways.

GENDERING VIOLENCE: PATTERNS OF POWER AND CONSTRUCTS OF MASCULINITY IN THE ACTS OF THE APOSTLES*

TODD PENNER AND CAROLINE VANDER STICHELE

The book of Acts generally plays a critical role for scholars of early Christianity, since, apart from providing a historical background for the letters of Paul, it represents the only coherent, sustained, and substantive account of Christian origins we possess. As a result, modern constructions of Christian origins dovetail well with Acts' significant focus on geographical movement (from Jerusalem, outward to Judea and Samaria, through Asia Minor, and on to Rome), as well as with its various narratives of heroic feats performed first by the Jerusalem apostles and then, in the latter half of the book, by Paul. The situation is little different with respect to the ideology of the text: scholars readily replicate and reinscribe the perspective of the text understood as the 'real' and 'authoritative' version of the narrated events. Little consideration is given to ways in which the narrative might be alternatively construed. Although some scholars have challenged the dominant paradigm provided by Acts,[1] the stories of the subaltern other on the whole tend to remain submerged behind the dominant textual voice. Critics all too readily and frequently capitulate to the persuasive strategies of the writer of the text, the result being that complexity and ambiguity in interpretation are easily passed over for the simplicity offered by tradition.[2] In light of these tendencies in and patterns of interpretation it is important to pay careful attention to the discursive practices that inform the literary processes and products of early Christianity. This current essay explores

---

* This essay was originally presented to the 'Violence and Representations of Violence among Jews and Christians Consultation' at the Society of Biblical Literature Annual Meeting in Atlanta, 22 November, 2003. Special thanks go to Shelly Matthews and Leigh Gibson for their invitation to participate in this engaging panel discussion. We are also grateful for the feedback provided by David Frankfurter on that occasion. Finally, A.-J. Levine's comments on an earlier draft of this piece were most helpful. Research support for Todd Penner was provided by the National Endowment for the Humanities (NEH) Summer Stipend.

1 See, e.g., Ron Cameron, 'Alternate Beginnings—Different Ends: Eusebius, Thomas, and the Construction of Christian Origins', in L. Borman, K. Del Tredici, and A. Standhartinger (eds.), *Religious Propaganda and Missionary Competition in the New Testament World: Essays Honoring Dieter Georgi* (NovTSup, 74; Leiden: Brill, 1994), pp. 501–25; and the brief comments by Clarice J. Martin, 'The Acts of the Apostles', in E. Schüssler Fiorenza (ed.), *Searching the Scriptures* (2 vols.; New York: Crossroad, 1994), II, pp. 763–99 (773–76).

2 The ease with which the ideology of the text is replicated in modern scholarly discourse is aptly illustrated in the following comment by François Bovon related to violence in early Christian narratives: 'With a high degree of realism these early Christians knew that evil and violence were universal, present in every society, in the church, and in the soul. The triumph of violence seemed inescapable. But they also knew that zones of peace could be established, that models of nonretaliation could be created, and that victory over demonic bestiality could be hoped for, not only through the victory of the cross ... but also through the power of human love' ('The Child and the Beast: Fighting Violence in Ancient Christianity', *HTR* 92 [1999], pp. 369–92 [371]).

these larger issues with respect to violence in Acts, using a gender-critical prism to address Lukan ideology in its relationship to the broader sociocultural world. This approach can be considered important to feminist biblical studies, since feminist scholars are in no way immune from the rhetorical power of the text. Without critical engagement of these issues, feminist analysis of Acts runs the risk of reaffirming the oppressive structures that in principle it is committed to reassessing and challenging.

Contextualizing Violence in Acts

In light of the preceding observations, it may come as no surprise that only a few scholars have been interested in examining critically the patterns of violence that appear throughout the Lukan narrative. Although it is not unusual for interpreters to note the killing of Stephen or the threats on the life of Paul, there is something about the violence, something about the 'matter of factness' of it in the narrative, that convinces many readers simply to note the 'horrors' to which early Christians were subjected and to move on, as the 'realities' of the violent acts described in the text are wedded to the interpretive lens provided by the same text. François Bovon's comments are rather typical in this respect: 'As we can see from the Book of Acts, Jesus' attitude, when confronted with suffering and death, became emblematic, even paradigmatic for his followers: Luke describes the first Christian martyr, Stephen, with the traits of an agonizing "Jesus".'[3] Yet it is likely we miss something if we merely note the 'fact' of Stephen's martyrdom,[4] if we only examine the historical contexts for how it was that trials were conducted[5] or the nature of mob-violence in the Roman empire,[6] or if we only explore the ways in which the pattern of the rejected prophet (like Jesus) is played out repeatedly with respect to the apostles and Paul.[7] In all of this, few scholars have made a sustained effort to conceptualize 'violence' as both a Lukan theme and narrative strategy.

Violence, however, is not just something that 'happened' to early Christians or something that is only framed in particular theological ways; rather, it becomes enacted again (before the reader) every time a reading of Acts is undertaken. The dramatic narratives in Acts project graphic images of violence done to early Christians in various centers around the empire and it is precisely this feature that the

---

3 Bovon, 'The Child and the "Beast"', p. 379.

4 For the most recent assessments affirming this 'factness', see François Bovon, 'The Dossier on Stephen, the First Martyr', *HTR* 96 (2003), pp. 279–315; and Nicholas H. Taylor, 'Stephen, the Temple, and Early Christian Eschatology', *RB* 110 (2003), pp. 62–85.

5 Brian Rapske, *The Book of Acts and Paul in Roman Custody* (Grand Rapids: Eerdmans, 1993); and esp. Heike Omerzu, *Der Prozess des Paulus: Eine exegetische und rechtshistorische Untersuchung der Apostelgeschichte* (BZNW, 115; Berlin: de Gruyter, 2002).

6 On Jewish vigilante action in the text, see Torrey Seland, *Establishment Violence in Philo and Luke: A Study of Non-Conformity to the Torah and Jewish Vigilante Reactions* (BibInt Series, 15; Leiden: Brill, 1995); and *idem*, 'Once More—The Hellenists, Hebrews, and Stephen: Conflicts and Conflict Management in Acts 6–7', in P. Borgen, V.K. Robbins, and D.B. Gowler (eds.), *Recruitment, Conquest, and Conflict: Strategies in Judaism, Early Christianity and the Greco-Roman World* (ESEC, 6; Atlanta: Scholars Press, 1998), pp. 169–207.

7 David P. Moessner, '"The Christ Must Suffer": New Light on the Jesus–Peter, Stephen, Paul Parallels in Luke–Acts', repr. in D.E. Orton (ed.), *The Composition of Luke's Gospel* (Leiden: Brill, 1999), pp. 117–53.

narrative focalizes as a spectacle paraded before the eyes of the reader.[8] The Christian movement does not merely originate in a violent world; it is, from a Lukan perspective, the feature subject acted upon in violence. The ideology critic, however, must question the nature and extent of this representation of Christians as hapless victims of aggression, as well as the narrative justification that serves to sanction this view. In short, violence is as much on the page as behind it.[9]

As one turns to the images of violence in Acts, the picture that most readily emerges is that Christians are the ones who fall victim to violence. There is, for instance, the heroic response of the apostles to the violence inflicted upon them.[10] In Acts 5.40–41, when the council has the apostles flogged, the apostles appear filled with joy because they are deemed worthy to be dishonored on account of Jesus' name. However, the apostles are not the only ones to face persecution. In Acts 8.1 the perspective is broadened to the whole church in Jerusalem, and in Acts 9.1–2 Paul goes after all 'disciples of the Lord', both men and women. The figure of Paul is in this respect instructive because his role changes in the course of the narrative. Prior to his conversion he is situated outside of the community and represented as a persecutor. He is complicit in the death of Stephen, holding the cloaks of those stoning him, and is presented as vehemently seeking out and persecuting 'those belonging to the way' (8.3). However, from the moment he himself becomes a disciple his own life is said to be in danger (9.23, 29). In a reconfiguration of the earlier stoning of Stephen, Paul, after being stoned in Lystra (14.19), declares that 'it is through many persecutions that we must enter the kingdom of God' (14.22). This affirmation clearly demonstrates that the pivotal point with respect to violence in the narrative revolves around one's position within or without the community. Violence thus demarcates as righteous the insiders, who remain faithful in the face of threats to their lives, while depicting those outside of the community as lacking such virtue.[11]

---

8 Andrew Feldherr, *Spectacle and Society in Livy's* History (Berkeley: University of California Press, 1998), provides a good treatment of *energeia* in ancient historiography, particularly the graphic description of events that enacts the past before the reader in a vivid and dramatic manner so as to create the most impact.

9 This issue is also important because of the 'effective history' of the biblical text, wherein the text actually serves to recreate and legitimate similar patterns of behavior in subsequent readers (i.e., there is violence 'in front' of the text as well). See further, Heikki Räisänen, 'The Effective "History" of the Bible: A Challenge to Biblical Scholarship', *SJT* 45 (1992), pp. 303–24. For a critical engagement of the issue of violence in the New Testament, see Michel Desjardins, *Peace, Violence and the New Testament* (BS, 46; Sheffield: Sheffield Academic Press, 1997).

10 Richard I. Pervo, *Profit with Delight: The Literary Genre of the Acts of the Apostles* (Philadelphia: Fortress Press, 1987), p. 27, notes the *theologia gloriae* that permeates the narrative in Acts, so that 'suffering' becomes the occasion to demonstrate heroic qualities, rather than reflecting 'real' experience as such.

11 Scott Cunningham, *'Through Many Tribulations': Theology of Persecution in Luke–Acts* (JSNTSup, 142; Sheffield: Sheffield Academic Press, 1997), develops the various components that fuel the meta-framework involved in the Lukan persecution motif: (1) persecution is part of the divine plan; (2) it involves the rejection of 'God's prophets'; (3) the persecuted followers stand in line with God's prophets from the past; (4) it is a result of being a follower of Jesus; (5) it provides the opportunity for perseverance by the believer; and (6) God triumphs in situations of persecution (pp. 337–38). The ideological texture here aims at shoring up the believer's own commitment to remaining steadfast in persecution, which is supported by the reassurance that God is ultimately in control.

The flip side of such 'unjustified' violence performed by outsiders is the 'just' violence displayed elsewhere in the text. This violence can take on different forms. First of all, the narrative firmly establishes that the transcendent figure behind the early Christian movement has the power and authority to enact physical violence on particular individuals within the community and without. The story of Ananias and Sapphira (Acts 5.1–11) illustrates a violent response of the deity to individuals inside of the community,[12] while Herod (Acts 12.20–23), who is depicted as a tyrant vying for power with Acts' transcendent deity, is dispatched via a most horrible death.[13] A trajectory of divinely—and narratively!—sanctioned violence can be detected here, one that targets individuals for punishment or retaliation for particular 'wrong-doings' understood as challenges to divine or divinely instituted authority.[14] Established in the narrative as legitimate, this violence also comes with an 'otherizing' effect with respect to the community sanctioned as righteous, and in fact plays a critical role in demarcating the boundaries of the community.[15] Further, in the case

---

12 Given the narrative structure of the account, it is not surprising to find that most interpretations focus on deciphering the precise reason for the punishment. See esp. Daniel Marguerat, 'Ananias and Sapphira (Acts 5. 1–11): The Original Sin', repr. in K. McKinney (ed.), *The First Christian Historian: Writing the 'Acts of the Apostles'* (trans. K. McKinney, G.J. Laughery, and R. Bauckham; SNTSMS, 121; Cambridge: Cambridge University Press, 2002), pp. 155–78; and Richard S. Ascough, 'Benefaction Gone Wrong: The "Sin" of Ananias and Sapphira in Context', in S.G. Wilson and M. Desjardins (eds.), *Text and Artifact in the Religions of Mediterranean Antiquity: Essays in Honour of Peter Richardson* (SCJ, 9; Waterloo, Ont.: Wilfrid Laurier University Press, 2000), pp. 91–110. This interpretation is imposed by the text on its readers and is also reproduced by scholars when they present the death of Ananias and Sapphira as something they brought upon themselves. Feminist scholars often discuss Sapphira's role with respect to the blame without questioning this larger framework. Turid Karlsen Seim, for example, stresses the couple's function as a negative example: 'Both wife and husband agree in keeping the money back, both attempt to lie, and both are punished for their lack of honesty and for their breach of loyalty' (*The Double Message: Patterns of Gender in Luke–Acts* [Studies of the New Testament and its World; Edinburgh; T. & T. Clark; Nashville: Abingdon, 1994], p. 78). An even stronger statement is made by Ivoni Richter Reimer, as she presents their deaths as the consequence of their own individual sin: both are guilty, even if for different reasons—Ananias because he took the initiative; Sapphira because she failed to resist (*Women in the Acts of the Apostles: A Feminist Liberation Perspective* [trans. L.M. Maloney; Minneapolis: Fortress Press, 1995], pp. 11–23). So also Martin, 'Sapphira dies as a result of her own perfidy' ('The Acts of the Apostles', p. 780).

13 O. Wesley Allen, *The Death of Herod: The Narrative and Theological Function of Retribution in Luke–Acts* (SBLDS, 158; Atlanta: Scholars Press, 1997), provides a good assessment of the 'death of the tyrant' type scene that Luke utilizes for the narrative, which hinges on the embedded cultural value (i.e., tyrants deserve death) for the effectiveness of the image.

14 The fundamental difference between Herod's death and that of Jesus in Acts is that the former is interpreted in terms of divine punishment, while the latter is presented as sanctioned by God through the resurrection of Jesus (Acts 2.24–32). Although death may ultimately be linked up in both cases with the deity, the narrative motivation is entirely different. That said, at a core level there may also lie a similarity in that both serve to characterize the deity as holding absolute power over life and death.

15 As in a wide range of literature from the Dead Sea Scrolls to the Wisdom of Solomon, the 'mark' of the community's righteousness is the violence enacted upon it by the 'sons of darkness'. Violence in this sense is a stock topos, one that literally marks the righteous as 'elect' on account of their willingness to suffer. Thus, violence against the community or individual is necessitated narratively as well. It is no surprise, then, that in Acts first the apostles suffer violence, then the whole community, and finally Paul and his companions. To be 'in' is to be 'acted against' by outsiders (Pervo, *Profit with Delight*, p. 28, however, views the theme of persecution almost entirely as a narrative device to initiate the 'traveling' of the heroes).

of Ananias and Sapphira, insiders are just as easily turned into (dead) outsiders through violence.[16]

Within this framework of so-called legitimate and illegitimate violence, however, lies another often unnoted feature of the Lukan narrative: Christians are not just the object of—mostly physical—violence as they are beaten, flogged, imprisoned or killed, they also appear as perpetrators of violence, albeit in a more disguised way, since the rhetoric of the text does not characterize them or the deity in a negative manner. Although the narrative heroes generally do not respond with physical violence, they retaliate with different, but equally violent, means. As the protagonists are in a minority position in the narrative, physical violence is often not really an option, and, more to the point, from the discursive portrayal of violence in Acts it is 'in the character' of the outsiders to be physically brutal.[17] Thus, a reader is easily enticed into reading 'with' the text in terms of its rather simplistic portrayal of insiders versus outsiders.

There is, however, more violence than meets the eye, if one does not restrict violence to just physical action, but also includes what Michel Desjardins describes as non-physical forms of violence,[18] such as verbal aggression or structural violence. A different picture of the interaction between insiders and outsiders emerges as a result, as the Christian response now appears as far from peaceful. First, there is violence inherent in the oppositional rhetoric used by the protagonists themselves as they respond with verbal aggression in directly condemning their opponents. Not only Stephen in his speech (esp. in Acts 7.51–53), but also Paul (18.6) clearly display what Desjardins identifies as an 'insider-outsider mentality', wherein the outsiders are linked up with Satan and the insiders with God (cf. 5.3; 13.10).[19] The narrative victims thus retaliate with verbal violence, affirming their own moral superiority over and against the enemy, while at the same time confirming the essentially evil nature of their opponents. This understanding of the situation, expressed by the characters on a narrative level, basically reflects the view of Luke, who uses the speeches of the characters to legitimate/substantiate his own understanding of the situation. There is, therefore, a direct authorial voice present behind the verbal violence displayed in the text.

A further level of violence perpetuated against outsiders can be found in physically aggressive acts of insiders enacted in the narrative. The story of Paul and

---

16 The deaths in Acts are all violent insofar as they are not 'natural' but bring about a premature ending to someone's life either directly through physical action, or, as is the case here, indirectly through divine intervention.

17 The images of 'opponents' in Acts represent stock features of characterization in antiquity. See further, Luke T. Johnson, 'The New Testament's Anti-Jewish Slander and the Conventions of Ancient Polemic', *JBL* 108 (1989), pp. 419–41.

18 Desjardins, *Peace, Violence*, p. 12. Desjardins adopts the definition of Robert McAfee Brown, who describes violence as that which 'violates the personhood of another in ways that are psychologically destructive rather than physically harmful' (Robert McAfee Brown, *Religion and Violence* [Philadelphia: Westminster, 2nd edn, 1987], p. 8). Although clearly a modern and Western understanding of violence, it is nevertheless heuristically helpful in order to acquire a fuller grasp of the ideology of the Lukan text.

19 Desjardins, *Peace, Violence*, pp. 100–101. Although he does not elaborate upon this issue for Acts, his observation that 'the Jews in the New Testament, with varying degrees of intensity and passion, are treated as outsiders' (p. 101), is particularly relevant for the second part of Acts.

Elymas before the proconsul in Acts 13 represents a primary example of this phenomenon, wherein the outsider is physically blinded in his struggle for power with Paul. In a reversal of Paul's contest with Jesus on the road to Damascus, where Paul is blinded but then released, Elymas wanders off the scene in darkness (13.11). Violence here consists of the mutilation of Elymas's body, while simultaneously marking the authority and power of Paul.[20] This and similar episodes attest to a disturbing pattern of violence in Acts in which the 'innocent' insiders, who frequently meet with physical violence, enact their own retaliatory measures against their opponents. Through word and deed, then, Acts reflects a subtle yet powerful insider view of violence, that is, when 'we' do it, it is 'justice'; when 'they' do it, it is 'violence'. In other words, the negative characterization of the violent outsider not only creates a foil to heighten the virtue of the insider, but also endorses as 'fair' and 'just' any action of violence taken against the outsiders by those on the inside. The narrative discursive structures are critical here for establishing and maintaining these lines of 'legitimate' and 'illegitimate' action.

Gender, Geography, and Authorial Voice

Violence is never perpetuated in a vacuum, and insofar as it intersects with characters in Acts, it does so in a highly gendered manner. Mary Rose D'Angelo has significantly advanced this area of investigation, most recently highlighting the ways in which male characters circumscribe female identity in the text, developing the 'domestic' characterization of women whereby premium Roman imperial values are demonstrated for the readership.[21] Most significant for this study is D'Angelo's insight into the relationship of gender to imperial Roman discourse as part of a larger rhetorical strategy of both verbal and physical comportment, moving from the body of the individual upward through the body of the family/house, and finally to the empire itself. Women in many respects exist in imperial narration as a critical component of masculine discourse—as the body of empire is inscribed in and through the manipulation and sometimes even disfigurement of female characters.[22]

---

20 This mutilation of the flesh represents the 'ownership' and 'agency' of the one inflicting the wound on the body of the victim. For a discussion of this element in its broader cultural environment, see Maud Gleason, 'Mutilated Messengers: Body Language in Josephus', in S. Goldhill (ed.), *Being Greek under Rome: Cultural Identity, the Second Sophistic and the Development of Empire* (Cambridge: Cambridge University Press, 2001), pp. 50–85 (79–80, 84).

21 Mary Rose D'Angelo, 'The *ANHP* Question in Luke–Acts: Imperial Masculinity and the Deployment of Women in the Early Second Century', in A.-J. Levine with Marianne Blickenstaff (eds.), *A Feminist Companion to Luke* (FCNTECW, 3; London: Sheffield Academic Press, 2002), pp. 44–69; and *idem*, ' "Knowing How to Preside over his Own Household": Imperial Masculinity and Christian Asceticism in the Pastorals, *Hermas*, and Luke–Acts', in S.D. Moore and J. Capel Anderson (eds.), *New Testament Masculinities* (SBLSS, 45; Atlanta: SBL, 2003), pp. 265–95 (284–93).

22 For a discussion of this feature in Roman literature, see Sandra R. Joshel, 'The Body Female and the Body Politic: Livy's Lucretia and Verginia', in A. Richlin (ed.), *Pornography and Representation in Greece and Rome* (New York: Oxford University Press, 1992), pp. 112–30; and *idem*, 'Female Desire and the Discourse of Empire: Tacitus's Messalina', in J.P. Hallett and M.B. Skinner (eds.), *Roman Sexualities* (Princeton, NJ: Princeton University Press, 1997), pp. 221–54.

Given that the broader context of Acts is the Roman empire, attention to the relationship of violence to gender in Acts is paramount. The connection between gender and violence established here is more specifically based on the conviction that violence in the narrative of Acts arises from the same discursive structures that also underlie the narrative's display of women. Violence is not just something that happens to men and women in the text; it is in fact a gendered act, and the domestication of female identity that D'Angelo notes finds its counterpart in the violence associated mainly with male characters in the narrative. In other words, the domestication of women finds a complement in the outward display of power and violence in the public forum enacted by male characters.[23]

In Acts both the perpetrators and victims of physical violence are in most cases males. In Jerusalem, for instance, the perpetrators are the Jewish leaders and their victims are the leaders of the newly formed messianic community. With the onslaught of Paul's persecution of the community, however, not just the leaders but all disciples now face persecution. Another scenario can be found in the travel narratives where Paul and his companions are the victims and their persecutors are often crowds instigated by 'the Jews' (e.g., in Lystra [Acts 14.19] and Thessalonica [17.5]), while in other places so-called 'pagan' interests are more directly at stake and hence the violence shifts to non-Jewish instigation (e.g., the cult of Artemis in Ephesus, with Demetrius as leader of the opposition against Paul [19.23–25]). At times, violent responses seem to be informed by social- and economic-class issues as well. This is the case for instance in Acts 13.50, where opposition to Paul and Barnabas comes from both the leading women and men of Pisidian Antioch. In this case women seem to operate in the public sphere first and foremost as members of their social class.

When space ('public' or 'private') appears as a critical component of the action of violence in Acts it encapsulates particular sociocultural configurations and intersections of social class and gender.[24] This broader notion allows one to conceptualize 'space' more fully in the narrative, moving from literal 'space' (in a house; in the temple) to spatiality in empire (in terms of imagined geography) to the 'space' occupied by the authorial voice itself. The configuration we want to explore further

---

23 As the portrayal of Bernice and Drusilla at the end of Acts demonstrates, the presence of women in the public sphere does not essentially change this picture. See Seim, *Double Message*, pp. 134–35; and Caroline Vander Stichele, 'Gender and Genre: Acts in/of Interpretation', in T. Penner and C. Vander Stichele (eds.), *Contextualizing Acts: Lukan Narrative and Greco-Roman Discourse* (SBLSymS, 20; Atlanta: Scholars Press, 2003), pp. 311–29 (311–18).

24 The distinction between private and public sphere used by Seim (*Double Message*, pp. 118–47) has its limitations since the idea of 'privacy' is a largely modern concept. It makes more sense to distinguish between the house and the public forum or arena as gendered spaces, especially in prescriptive texts. As Seim rightly observes, men operated and dominated in both, while women's mobility and public presence were more restricted and regulated. See also the criticisms of the binary opposition between both spaces by Marianne Sawicki, *Crossing Galilee: Architectures of Contact in the Occupied Land of Jesus* (Harrisburg, PA: Trinity Press International, 2000), pp. 78–79; and Shelly Matthews, *First Converts: Rich Pagan Women and the Rhetoric of Mission in Early Judaism and Christianity* (Contraversions: Jews and Other Differences; Stanford: Stanford University Press, 2001), p. 84. A more complex discussion of the gendered features related to public and private spaces is found in Jorunn Økland, 'Women in their Place: Paul and the Corinthian Discourse of Gender and Sanctuary Space' (PhD diss., University of Oslo, 2000), pp. 109–31.

here is this relationship of gender to geography and authorial voice, particularly the interplay among the three in Luke's narrative.

Given this framework of analysis, then, it is critical to begin by paying attention to the precise location of violence in the narrative—and, by contrast, where violence does not take place. It is, for instance, striking that there is no violence in Athens (17.16-34). Here, both proponents and opponents engage Paul with words, and Paul responds with (unusually) conciliatory rhetoric. The center of Greek life and culture is honored in a way that the margins from the perspective of the Roman empire— reflected in Asia Minor and Jerusalem—are not. Athens is not unruly or out of control, and in this respect it centers the travel narrative.[25] Athens is, in turn, framed by the scenes in Thessalonica and Corinth, where in the case of the latter, even with a proconsul present, mob violence runs amok (18.12-17). The scene in Ephesus is perhaps most extreme in this sense, as the entire city is whipped into a frenzy (19.28-41). Again, violence is perpetrated by crowds that run wild, thus symbolizing the out-of-control situation on the 'edge' of empire. Moreover, the violence in Jerusalem taking place both at the beginning and end of Acts, first against the apostles and then against Paul, further situates such action in particular locales. It is perhaps not surprising that, given the narrative status of Athens as the center of civic virtue and culture, Asia Minor and Jerusalem appear reduced to 'exotic' outposts of civilization.[26] Both presence and absence of violence can therefore be considered essential to the Lukan narrative framework in reflecting sociocultural values embedded in a gendered geographical horizon. In other words, places and spaces are neither value nor gender neutral, but relate to the broad sociocultural configuration of Lukan ideology, particularly the replication of imperial discursive practices in the construction of early Christian symbolic imagination.

Luke thus appears keenly interested in establishing spatial relationships and boundaries in his narrative. These symbolic movements are essential for assessing the power relations that he seeks to establish and in which violence is played out. Moreover, the relationship of center to margins is a gendered phenomenon, that is, the orderly nature of ideal public masculine comportment in Athens is contrasted with the more ignoble characterizing of those consumed by their passions on the

---

25 On the idealized portrait of Athens reflected in Acts 17, see Hans-Josef Klauck, *Magic and Paganism in Early Christianity: The World of the Acts of the Apostles* (trans. B. McNeil; Edinburgh: T. & T. Clark, 2000), p. 81. From the perspective of the Greek East (and the Second Sophistic), Athens represents the cultural centre of empire. Graham Anderson, *The Second Sophistic: A Cultural Phenomenon in the Roman Empire* (New York: Routledge, 1993), pp. 119-26, notes both the reverence for Athens as the cultural center and the Hellenization/Athenization of Rome, reflecting diverse strategies for creating a sustainable past for present Greek identity in the Roman imperial period. See also Simon Swain, *Hellenism and Empire: Language, Classicism, and Power in the Greek World, AD 50-250* (Oxford: Clarendon Press, 1996), pp. 74-79, 91-93; and Tim Whitmarsh, ' "Greece is the World": Exile and Identity in the Second Sophistic', in Goldhill (ed.), *Being Greek under Rome*, pp. 269-305 (271-73).

26 Although Jerusalem is frequently understood to be the symbolic geographical and theological centre of the Lukan narrative, in Acts it is the place of 'founding', from where expansion starts rather than its culmination point (see Mikeal C. Parsons, 'The Place of Jerusalem on the Lukan Landscape: An Exercise in Symbolic Cartography', in R.P. Thompson and T.E. Phillips (eds.), *Literary Studies in Luke–Acts: Essays in Honor of Joseph B. Tyson* (Macon, GA: Mercer University Press, 1998), pp. 155-71 (167-71).

outer edges. In this discursive portrayal an implicit effeminization takes place, insofar as the narrative opponents display the opposite quality—excess—by appearing out of control.[27]

Alongside Athens, Rome also performs a crucial role in Luke's imaginary cartography of empire: it is both present in terms of its legions (and ruling proconsuls) stationed throughout its territory—as omnipresent as the transcendent deity—as well as relatively marginal as a location of action and violence, with only a closing reference to Paul's imprisonment in the actual city (Acts 28.16). Much less violence is associated with the Romans, who are mostly concerned with maintaining order (and seem relatively indifferent to the fate of the Christians). Here the trial scenes predominate and the discourse is mostly judicial. Still, even if Rome is presented as the (distant) political center of the empire, the Romans cannot prevent violence from happening. Indeed, in the final narrative of Paul's trial in Jerusalem the Romans fear for his life (23.29–30), with Jews plotting to kill him in transport (23.12, 20–21). On the one hand, this seems to demonstrate their inability to maintain peace and harmony; on the other, it creates the impression that the burgeoning evil threat by the largely Jewish opponents cannot be contained.

This broader framework is instructive: empire is everywhere, but in some sense nowhere. Saundra Schwartz aptly notes the place of Rome in Acts as follows: '... Rome [is] a vanishing point outside the frame of the narrative. Although invisible, it is the center point that organizes the actions and verdicts within provincial courtrooms on the peripheries of the empire.'[28] Yet, while Rome is in principle in control, its power to impose order seems unsustainable. It is here that we also catch a glimpse of the colonial nature of the Roman empire, since military power is used to colonize other people and violence to suppress conflicts where Roman control is perceived to be threatened in the occupied territories.[29] Moreover, in these images of imperial Rome, especially at the intersection of geography and violence in Acts, a gendered picture can be observed, as traditional Greek and Roman images of empire are subverted, and a relocation of ideal masculine comportment in the male heroes of Acts takes place. *Imperium* and *virtus* are now found in figures like Paul, who not only occupy, but in some sense also displace, Athens as a space of cultural sophistication and Rome as a locus of colonial power in the narrative.

Finally, in line with the focus on geography and gender one also needs to recognize a third 'space' that relates the author to the spatiality engendered in the text, insofar as the identity constructed in the text relates not just to the Christian

---

27 Craig A. Williams, *Roman Sexuality: Ideologies of Masculinity in Classical Antiquity* (New York: Oxford University Press, 1999), pp. 138–42, notes that if the ideal male is the 'controlled' male, then the binary opposite holds true for those who are vilified: they are out of control, excessive, lazy, and sexually licentious (see also Stephen D. Moore and Janice Capel Anderson, 'Taking It Like a Man: Masculinity in 4 Maccabees', *JBL* 117 [1998], pp. 249–73 [254–58]). Since masculinity is the culturally defined center, the one vilified is also being effeminized (at least implicitly) as a result (Catharine Edwards, *The Politics of Immorality in Ancient Rome* [Cambridge: Cambridge University Press, 1993], pp. 92–96, provides a brief but interesting discussion of this phenomenon with respect to the Roman depiction of the Greeks).

28 Saundra Schwartz, 'The Trial Scene in the Greek Novels and in Acts', in Penner and Vander Stichele (eds.), *Contextualizing Acts*, pp. 105–33 (132).

29 The actions of the tribune to quell the mob violence in Jerusalem would seem to suggest this interpretation (21.31–35; 23.10; cf. 19.40; but notice the response of Gallio in 18.12–17).

movement itself, but perhaps even more so to Luke, the writer of the account. The imperial atmosphere of masculine comportment and display, quintessential in the formation of the narrative flow, also reflects on Luke's own manly performance.[30] Frequently scholars have been interested in reconstructing the theology of Luke or the Lukan community, but few have in fact pushed the discussion in the direction taken here: that is, what does the narrative reveal about the *ethos* of Luke himself? Violence in the Lukan narrative is not just something that 'frames' or 'happens' in the narrative, and the gender relations reflected in the violence are not accidental or circumstantial. Rather, they are fundamental features of the story itself, and the relationship of the early Christian narrative heroes to that violence is precisely the nexus for analyzing the broader context of Lukan ideology, not only the image that is thereby projected of the early Christian community, but perhaps, even more so, the image that Luke projects of himself.

Seneca reminds his readers of the Greek proverb: 'a man's speech is just like his life'.[31] In this cultural discursive environment it comes as no surprise, then, to find largely silent women and speaking men in the book of Acts.[32] The 'speaking voice' in Acts is clearly a powerful male-gendered voice, which, finally, says something about Luke and the masculine image he projects through inscribing it on the narrative Christian community and especially its leaders, with whom Luke seems to identify the most, given the role they play in proclaiming *his* gospel.[33] The resultant picture is one of a strong public—particularly verbal—presence and performance,

---

30 For discussion of these and related matters with respect to the public persona of the orator, see Erik Gunderson, *Staging Masculinity: The Rhetoric of Performance in the Roman World* (Ann Arbor: University of Michigan Press, 2000); Amy Richlin, 'Gender and Rhetoric: Producing Manhood in the Schools', in W.J. Dominik (ed.), *Roman Eloquence: Rhetoric in Society and Literature* (London: Routledge, 1997), pp. 90–110; and Joy Connolly, 'Mastering Corruption: Constructions of Identity in Roman Oratory', in S.R. Joshel and S. Murnaghan (eds.), *Women and Slaves in Greco-Roman Culture* (London: Routledge, 1998), pp. 130–51.

31 Seneca contextualizes the proverb as follows: 'Wantonness in speech is proof of public luxury ... A man's ability cannot possibly be of one sort and his soul of another. If his soul be wholesome, well-ordered, serious, and restrained, his ability also is sound and sober. Conversely, when one degenerates, the other is also contaminated' (LCL; *Epistle* 114.2–3; cf. Dionysius, *Antiquitates romanae* 1.1.3). For further development of the *ethos* theory only touched on here, see Todd Penner and Caroline Vander Stichele, 'Unveiling Paul: Gendering Ethos in 1 Corinthians 11.2–16', in T.H. Olbricht and A. Eriksson (eds.), *Rhetoric, Ethic, and Moral Persuasion in Biblical Discourse* (ESEC; T&T Clark International, forthcoming).

32 Cf. Seim, *Double Message*, pp. 253–56.

33 The Christian leaders are presented as endowed with power (*dunamis*) from above. Thus, the apostles receive power from the Holy Spirit (1.8) just as Jesus received power from God (10.38). Power and grace are also attributed to Stephen (6.8) and patterned on Moses' own power (7.22), and powerful deeds also are enacted by God through Paul (19.11). In conjunction with this dynamic power from 'above', also stressed throughout Acts is that especially the leaders of the Christian community speak with boldness (*parresia*)—i.e., power in word. The characterizations of Peter in Acts 2.29 and of Peter and John in 4.13 and 4.29 are in line with this focus, as is the portrayal of the believers gathered together to pray to God to 'grant to your servants to speak your word with all boldness'. Their prayer is heard as 'all were filled with the Holy Spirit and spoke the word of God with boldness' (4.31). In the same vein Paul is pictured as 'speaking boldly' (*parresiazomai*; 9.27, 28; [with Barnabas] 13.46 and 14.3; 19.8; 26.26). It is even the last thing we hear about him in the closing verse of Acts, where he is presented as teaching about the Lord Jesus Christ in Rome 'with all boldness' (28.31). See S.C. Winter, 'Παρρησία in Acts', in J. Fitzgerald (ed.), *Friendship,*

which ultimately finds its source in God. Even more to the point, this public display of the characters matches the implicit construction of Luke's own *ethos*, as these figures demonstrate the best values of the *polis*, creating a locus of high value and culture for the Christian community they represent.[34] In so doing Luke has inscribed his own character in narrative—holding up for the reader cardinal virtues of imperial male comportment, which the early Christian figures embody in dramatic ways, a framework that values speaking and acting well. Moreover, in this respect the gendered and spatial/geographical nature of the Lukan images coalesce: the Greek civic values of the *polis* (denoted here by the center, Athens) are represented most forcefully by those characters who not only exhibit such values, but who also embody the fullest possible expression of masculine power and control as a result.[35]

With respect to violence in the narrative, then, its multi-textured gendered nature arises precisely from this broader sociocultural value of masculine comportment—manifested in *imperium* and *virtus*—which ultimately finds its source in the writer of the text.[36] Not only does this framework help one appreciate more fully the Lukan depiction of women, it also enables one to assess better the relationship of gender and violence in the text. The gendered acts of violence and spaces of enactment seem to be correlated with the masculine performance of Luke himself, whose own construction of identity in the text is written against the foils of female and male characters, insiders and outsiders, and spaces and places of empire. Thus, as much as Luke may appear to resist empire, there is at the center of his narrative project an embracing of its fundamental value-system.

Imperial Geography and Gendered Violence

In several insightful articles, Gary Gilbert has drawn attention to the relationship between the list of nations in Acts 2 and imperial geography, highlighting the Christian appropriation of Roman propaganda.[37] This emphasis is significant, since the violence enacted in the narrative is brought about precisely as a result of its expansion outwards from Jerusalem. In this sense the narrative of Luke–Acts reflects the colonial politics of imperial Rome. In particular, the notion of the conquering of

---

Flattery, and Frankness of Speech: Studies on Friendship in the New Testament World (NovTSup, 82; Leiden: Brill, 1996), pp. 185–202; and Loveday Alexander, ' "Foolishness to the Greeks": Jews and Christians in the Public Life of the Empire', in G. Clark and T. Rajak (eds.), *Philosophy and Power in the Graeco-Roman World: Essays in Honour of Miriam Griffin* (New York: Oxford University Press, 2002), pp. 229–49 (243–49).

34 See further, Todd Penner, 'Civilizing Discourse: Acts, Declamation, and the Rhetoric of the *Polis*', in Penner and Vander Stichele (eds.), *Contextualizing Acts*, pp. 65–104 (esp. pp. 89–100).

35 The connection between civic virtue and masculine comportment is aptly demonstrated by Epictetus's comments on hair in his *Discourses* (3.1.27–35), where he argues that men who 'cut' and 'pluck' the hair on their body undermine their masculine identity and are therefore not suitable for political service in the *polis*.

36 The reader also plays a critical role as spectator in this dynamic of 'display'. Chris Frilingos, 'Sexing the Lamb', in Moore and Anderson (eds.), *New Testament Masculinities*, pp. 309–17 (297–317), develops this element with respect to the violence on display in the book of Revelation.

37 Gary Gilbert, 'Roman Propaganda and Christian Identity in the Worldview of Luke–Acts', in Penner and Vander Stichele (eds.), *Contextualizing Acts*, pp. 233–56; and *idem*, 'The List of Nations in Acts 2: Roman Propaganda and the Lukan Response', *JBL* 121 (2002), pp. 497–529.

territory both through violent acts and benevolence, as reflected in the *Res Gestae* of Augustus,[38] may have had a significant bearing on the persuasive narrative strategies adopted in Acts.[39] And yet, as with the Augustan rhetoric, there is an extreme disjunction between the *pax* that is proclaimed and the 'history' that unfolds. The Lukan travel narratives highlight the tragic irony that the story that so resolutely proclaims the bringing of peace (10.36) should display so much (seemingly) inevitable violence.

The travel narratives of Paul open with the aforementioned confrontation between Bar-Jesus or Elymas and Paul in Cyprus (Acts 13.4–12). Often engaged in terms of its import for the conflict between Christianity and ancient magical practice, more significant for the issues under discussion here is the manner in which Elymas leaves the stage: he has lost the 'show-down' with Paul and must now 'grope' around in order to find someone to help him (13.11). In direct contrast to the scene where Paul himself plays/assumes the role of the weak individual as a result of being blinded on the road to Damascus and having to rely on others in the city (9.8–9, 17–18), Paul, now fully situated within the Christian community, displays his masculine power.[40] Social status is primarily at stake in this contest: Paul rises in status, as the proconsul sides with him; Elymas is lowered in status, as he now loses the support of his benefactor—indeed, he loses his 'territory' as such. The triumphalism of the narrative deceptively overshadows the violent structure that gives meaning to the whole scenario and that may even have provided pleasure for its early Christian readers. Moreover, apart from the explicit act of violence against the body of Elymas, two implicit aspects can be noted: the Greco-Roman sociocultural context makes the combat form of masculine interaction significant in the first place, and the Christian narrative structure endorses this intervention as an act brought on by the 'hand of the Lord'. At the beginning of Paul's travel narrative one thus observes a Christian reconfiguration of dominant discursive practices of male comportment. Interpreters such as Susan Garrett, who seek to move this engagement to a meta-narrative level of a battle between Jesus and the Devil, in this respect simply follow the narrative script, which justifies the action against Elymas because he is declared to be 'a son of the devil' (13.10).[41] Although any ancient reader could be expected to anticipate the rhetorical description of the opponent in such terms, the final cultural topics of 'lord' and 'devil' ultimately imbue the Greco-Roman combat scene

---

38 For a discussion of the imperial geography meshed with Augustan colonial aims in the *Res Gestae*, see Claude Nicolet, *Space, Geography, and Politics in the Early Roman Empire* (trans. H. Leclerc; Ann Arbor: University of Michigan Press, 1991), pp. 15–27.

39 On the connections between Luke–Acts and the propaganda of the *Pax Romana*, see esp. Allen Brent, 'Luke–Acts and the Imperial Cult in Asia Minor', *JTS* 48 (1997), pp. 111–38; idem, *The Imperial Cult and the Development of Church Order: Concepts and Images of Authority in Paganism and Early Christianity before the Age of Cyprian* (VCSup, 45; Leiden: Brill, 1999), pp. 91–95, 113–18; and Anna Janzen, *Der Friede im lukanischen Doppelwerk vor dem Hintergrund der Pax Romana* (EH, 752; Frankfurt: Lang, 2002).

40 Klauck, *Magic and Paganism*, pp. 54–55, is right to see here the 'mirror' image of the former incident with Paul on the road to Damascus, but probably goes too far by turning this simply into Paul's confrontation with his 'alter-ego' (a shadow of his former self), since in the latter scenario the real violence done to Elymas is neglected as a result.

41 Susan Garrett, *The Demise of the Devil: Magic and the Demonic in Luke's Writings* (Minneapolis: Fortress Press, 1989), pp. 83–86.

with particular meaning and importance for the early Christian reader. Such a description has power only in a cultural discursive context that fully legitimates and values the violent structure of the text. It thus represents the 'givens' shared by elite males in this culture, which do not have to be promoted or defended, because they are assumed.

A further tradent of the broader cultural norm of masculinity is reflected particularly in the paired stories related to women—Lydia and the slave girl in Acts 16. The story of the possessed slave girl in Acts 16.16–18 represents a counter-narrative to the one just told about Lydia in Acts 16.13–15, and in many respects they function in tandem.[42] In the first instance, the prominent Lydia is in some sense domesticated through her conversion, as this simultaneously relocates her *in* the community and *under* Paul.[43] In her only dialogue in the story, Lydia invites Paul into her house—eliciting the value of hospitality and thus demonstrating cardinal domestic virtues, while also clearly acknowledging his (apostolic) authority (11.15).[44] This feature represents the critical flip side of the public display of masculine identity evident throughout the travel narrative. As the ordering of the imperial household is understood to signal something significant about the male head of household—in this case the emperor—regarding his ability to govern and rule,[45] so here we see Paul performing that function in the narrative as founding 'father' of a particular emergent Christian community. In a similar vein the official representatives of the Roman empire at the end of the book—Felix and Agrippa—are portrayed as dominant males in the company of prominent females (Drusilla and Bernice, respectively), thus demonstrating social control and imperial 'family values'.[46]

While the encounter with Lydia takes place at a place of prayer outside the gate with only women present (16.13), the second encounter with a female, immediately following the Lydia episode, is fully situated in the public forum. In a scenario

---

42 This feature is noted by F. Scott Spencer, 'Out of Mind, Out of Voice: Slave-Girls and Prophetic Daughters in Luke–Acts', *BibInt* 7 (1999), pp. 132–53 (147).

43 Matthews, *First Converts*, pp. 85–89 (cf. 54–55, 62, 70–71), presses for the apologetic function of Lydia as a prominent Gentile female adherent to the missionary movement. The view of Lydia as high-standing and wealthy is also advocated by Gail O'Day, 'Acts', in C.A. Newsom and S.H. Ringe (eds.), *The Woman's Bible Commentary* (Louisville, KY: Westminster/John Knox, 1992), pp. 305–12 (310); and Martin, 'Acts of the Apostles', p. 784. That Lydia should rather be regarded as a member of the lower classes is argued by Richter Reimer, *Women in the Acts of the Apostles*, p. 267; and Luise Schottroff, 'Lydia: A New Quality of Power', in *idem*, *Let the Oppressed Go Free: Feminist Perspectives on the New Testament* (trans. A.S. Kidder; Louisville, KY: Westminster/John Knox Press, 1993), pp. 131–37.

44 As D'Angelo points out, hospitality is a major characteristic of the women whom Luke presents as patrons of the early Christian communities (e.g. Mary in Acts 12, Priscilla in Acts 18, as well as Tabitha in Acts 9). 'To men, Luke–Acts assigns the ministry of the word; to women, the ministry of benefactions and hospitality' ('*ANHP* Question', p. 68).

45 Susan Fischler notes, 'As male authority figures, the emperors and their heirs were displayed as revealing the prowess of the heroes and the stately attributes of the first citizens of the empire. But to complete the image of the patriarch, the emperors also needed to display control over their household. They needed a wife or other female authority figure who was restrained and maternal, whose body was seen as fertile and thus symbolic of the continuity of the dynasty' ('Imperial Cult: Engendering the Cosmos', in L. Foxhall and J. Salmon [eds.], *When Men Were Men: Masculinity, Power and Identity in Classical Antiquity* [New York: Routledge, 1998], pp. 165–83 [179]).

46 D'Angelo, '*ANHP* Question', pp. 65–66.

similar to the one involving Elymas and the proconsul, here the slave girl represents the battleground between Paul and her male owners. Her fate is entirely beside the point; there is no real sense of 'healing' or 'liberation' in this narrative. At stake, rather, is the demonstration of power, and, even more to the point, Paul's superiority over other males (and his God over theirs).[47] Interpretations that focus on the 'demonic' element again miss the point—this is a battle between men for control over her spirit, which is a source of profit for her owners. For Paul, however, she is an annoyance and a nuisance.[48]

In this contest, the superiority and power of the Christian heroes are located in the verbal and spiritual realm, as Paul orders the spirit in the 'name of Jesus Christ' to leave the girl and this immediately happens (Acts 16.18). Ironically, the spirit in question proclaims the truth about Paul and Silas (16.17), presenting them as servants of the most high God, while her owners, to the contrary, are depicted as greedy and slanderous, misrepresenting Paul and Silas as troublemakers (16.19–21), which results in physical violence against Paul and Silas (16.21–24).[49] Nevertheless, the heroes again prevail, because their prayer and hymns to God are heard, an earthquake takes place, the power of their word (cf. 4.31) is thus affirmed, and their control over the situation is restored. The character of Paul is everywhere being established and affirmed in the narrative. His words and deeds cannot be matched in the civic forum, where the opponents become jealous, trying to dispatch him by violent means (cf. Stephen in Acts 6.8–15). The configuration is consonant with the manly civic comportment that Luke is establishing over and against the portrayal of the opponents. As the Christian territory expands, the violent scenes increase, but Paul remains steadfast. The contrasting comportment of figures is striking: true virtue rests in those exhibiting persuasive words and powerful deeds, none of which are displayed in the opponents. These features of the characterization of Paul can be related to his portrayal as an ideal philosopher. In this respect, the framing of the public performance by references to the 'house' of Lydia into which Paul enters (16.15, 40) dovetails the public life of the philosopher with his private sphere of influence in the homes of elite members of society.[50] In both instances the

---

47 As Matthews (*First Converts*, p. 90) notes, the expression *pneuma pythona* in Acts 16.16 can be translated as 'pythonian spirit', thus evoking associations with the oracle of Apollo in Delphi. Rather than being possessed by evil spirits then the slave girl should rather be understood as a Pythian prophet and the confrontation with Paul should be viewed in terms of a competition in which the 'most high God' (16.17) triumphs over Apollo (cf. Klauck, *Magic and Paganism*, pp. 65–67).

48 The suggestion by Richter Reimer, *Women in the Acts of the Apostles*, pp. 182–83, that the slave girl could have been relocated (using a manumission framework) into the Christian community clearly goes beyond the evidence and in some sense 'mutes' the girl's experience in the text even further. Luke has no interest in the girl after she is 'freed' from her bondage; there is no sense of commitment to her in the narrative. Pervo is probably correct to note that such absolute (and ambivalent?) uses of power as found here suggest that the canonical Acts in this respect partakes of the same ethos as the apocryphal Acts (*Profit with Delight*, p. 63).

49 See further the recent treatment by Kathy Chambers, 'At the Expense of Women: Humor(?) in Acts 16.14–40', in A. Brenner (ed.), *Are We Amused? Humour about Women in the Biblical Worlds* (BTC, 2; New York: Continuum, 2003), pp. 79–89, who notes that the truthfulness of the slave girl's statement is completely disregarded in the commentaries on the passage.

50 Seim, *Double Message*, p. 133; and Alexander, ' "Foolishness to the Greeks"', pp. 233–43.

comportment of Paul is at stake and in both cases, albeit in different ways, his influence is the primary focus.[51]

In light of the gender-critical reading developed here, two aspects can be noted. On the one hand there is concern to demonstrate that through their conversion even high-standing women such as Lydia enter within the sphere of authoritative male control in an emergent Christian community and that Greco-Roman social values are fully manifested in the same. On the other hand, those same values have a counter display outside of the community in male combat, centered here in the female body of the slave girl. The respective social status of the two women in these narratives demonstrates that, while Luke is intent on displaying the interaction of Paul with powerful women, he is much less concerned to have this erstwhile Christian hero interact with a slave girl. In other words, the gendered nature of the implicit and explicit violence in these dual episodes also has a socioeconomic bias, as elite women are given prominence but simultaneously kept in check, while the lower-class character is quite literally considered an annoyance.[52] The social structures that underlie the narrative are also essential for sustaining the image of Paul throughout—the violence in the public forum is a natural outgrowth of the embedded and expected social masculine norms evidenced throughout the entire scenario. Violence is inherently connected to the social-cultural value-system that Luke here accepts as conventional and normative.

The travel narrative is illuminating precisely for what is at stake in Luke's presentation: Paul's *ethos* or character is established decisively in the narrative through powerful words and deeds. A further illustration of this feature is the parallel to the Elymas and slave-girl stories found towards the end of the travel narrative, involving the seven sons of the high priest Sceva, who are itinerant exorcists. The agonistic nature of this scenario is made obvious in that just before the exorcists are mentioned in the narrative reference is made to manifold healings by Paul in Ephesus (19.11–12). God's power is manifested through Paul in remarkable ways, but when the sons of Sceva enter the ring in the contest for power they immediately lose control. Indeed, their story, quite possibly told for Christian amusement, displays a marked degree of violence enacted on their bodies. When they try to invoke the spirit in the name of Jesus and by association also Paul (19.13), the spirit acknowledges the power of Jesus and Paul, but not the power of these exorcists (19.15). In what is

---

51 Like his epic counterpart Odysseus, who was a model for 'wandering' philosophers in the Second Sophistic, Paul too represents a source of cultural authority and dominance (Whitmarsh, 'Greece is the World', pp. 292–93). On the image of Paul as *Kulturbringer* (in line with heroes such as Osiris or Hercules), see Doron Mendels, 'Pagan or Jewish? The Presentation of Paul's Mission in the Book of Acts', in H. Cancik, H. Lichtenberger, and P. Schäfer (eds.), *Geschichte—Tradition—Reflexion: Festschrift für Martin Hengel zum 70. Geburtstag* (3 vols.; Tübingen: Mohr Siebeck, 1996), I, pp. 431–52.

52 For an earlier assessment of Luke's fundamental ambivalence with respect to his female characters, see Jacob Jervell, 'The Daughters of Abraham: Women in Acts', repr. in *idem*, *The Unknown Paul: Essays on Luke–Acts and Early Christian History* (Minneapolis: Augsburg, 1984), pp. 146–57. More recently, Ann Graham Brock has argued that the oft-noted feature of women's subordination in the D-text of Acts is firmly entrenched in the Lukan narrative dynamic ('Appeasement, Authority, and the Role of Women in the D-Text of Acts', in T. Nicklas and M. Tilly (eds.), *The Book of Acts as Church History/Apostelgeschichte als Kirchengeschichte* [BZNW, 120; Berlin: de Gruyter, 2003], pp. 205–24).

a short but graphic description, the spirit 'dominates' and 'overthrows' the men, completely humiliating them: they are stripped naked and mutilated, thereby suffering a further loss of status (19.16). Not only are they depicted as impotent exorcists, they are, moreover, beaten by the very demon they sought to eradicate. In the end, however, the battle is not between them and the demon, but between the powerful and potent image of Paul established in the narrative and all others who try to claim similar power. As with Elymas, there is a domesticating edge to the fate of the sons of Sceva—their demise is not narratively neutral or merely descriptive. The cultural implications are clear: just as Lydia is brought under male control by Paul, Elymas and the sons of Sceva suffer a similar fate—but it is worse for them: as males, they lose not only social status, but also their masculine standing before the reading audience, as they are humiliated, left impotent, and, quite literally in the case of the sons of Sceva, exhibited as a laughing stock. In line with the model of masculine comportment delineated above, these figures thus appear effeminized for the reading audience. In this sense the Christian reconfiguration of the broader Greco-Roman sociocultural discourse involves a significant degree of emasculation of the 'other' in the public forum.

In summary, then, a dual function can be noted with respect to gender in the Acts narrative. Those inside the community undergo a particular form of domestication, as they are inscribed within the sphere of male control and displayed for the reading audience as reflecting ideal imperial virtues. But those same imperial values have an outward display, which results in conquest and combat in the public forum. The violence directed at the Christian communities from outside meets a strangely quiet, domesticated household within, which is matched by the disorder and chaos of those situated outside. At the same time, the heroes of the Lukan narrative mark their territory through words and deeds, on the one hand building a domestic community space, but matching that with public comportment in displays of rhetorical and numinous power, which affirms them to be the locus of masculine identity in the text. Paul as the cultural hero—the ideal Jew, the astute Greek, and the legally adept Roman[53]—embodies this masculine paradigm in each of these specific contexts. Paul is the *Übermensch* of the narrative—he is the one who is not just 'all things to all men', but the one who is 'everyman to all men'. In the end, Paul represents not just the ideal Christian in the story; he is the ideal male. In light of the comments made earlier with respect to Luke's own *ethos* on display in this narrative and given the powerful contours of his portrayal of Paul, one cannot help but wonder if Luke's own identity is not embodied in his literary portrait of Paul. As an elite cultured male, Paul may well represent Luke's narrative alter ego.

Ordering the Household

By way of conclusion the following points can be made. First, violence functions on multiple levels in Acts—there is both legitimate and illegitimate violence, with the nature of what is 'legitimate' depending first and foremost on one's status as an insider or outsider, including one's relationship to the ultimate, transcendent Power

---

53 See further, John C. Lentz, *Luke's Portrait of Paul* (SNTSMS, 77; Cambridge: Cambridge University Press, 1993), pp. 23–61.

(holder/broker) in the narrative. The reversal of the imperial order in Acts is not so radical as one at first may be inclined to believe. Allegiances/alliances may shift, but the fundamental power structure stays in place. As a result, the sociocultural and economic features of imperial violence continue to function both inside and outside the early Christian communities in the story. Moreover, Luke seems to share and promote broad sociocultural commitments and values about places and their importance in the imperial imagination, insofar as locations of/in empire affect the portrayal of violence in Acts.

Second, violence is a gendered phenomenon in Acts and functions in a variety of ways. In light of ancient views of male comportment and control, violence should be seen on one level as perpetuating the status of the social and cultural male elite (Roman, Greek, and/or Jewish). Masculine comportment displayed in *virtus* and *imperium* represents a sociocultural value-system embedded and embodied in the Christian community throughout the narrative by means of either domestication or violence (physical acts, verbal aggression, or vilifying characterizations of outsiders), denoting more disturbing and pervasive patterns of the masculine cultural norm, ultimately identified with the transcendent deity, who narratively and normatively sustains and legitimates them. As such, both serene scenes of domestication, as well as public arenas wherein males combat for winner or loser status, reflect a broad emphasis on control. Yet the implication of the argument here is that beneath this display of violence in the public forum and domestic space lies the more systematic and systemic aggression of colonial power, which is also reinscribed thoroughly and completely in the Acts narrative.

Third, if one takes seriously that ancient narratives also reflect the projected *ethos* or character of their writers, then the broad and multi-layered patterns of violence in the book of Acts say something, finally, about Luke himself. The act of writing Acts becomes at one level a demonstration of Luke's own self-comportment as elite male in empire—his own demonstration of *virtus* and *imperium* for (and over) the reader. His radical story may provide an alternative plot, but the social and cultural substructure fundamentally resonates with models readily identifiable elsewhere in the Greco-Roman culture. Not only in the composition, but indeed through it, Luke battles for control over his readers—to win their trust through the trustworthiness of his representation. But this is more than just the 'facts'; this representation is in essence an acceptance of Luke as the normative cultural elite male and a fundamental endorsement of the value-system and logic of empire. Luke may proclaim that Jesus has brought peace, but the peace of Christ is like the peace of Caesar: both establish it wielding a double-edged sword.

BIBLIOGRAPHY

Abrahamsen, V., 'Women at Philippi: The Pagan and Christian Evidence', *JFSR* 3.2 (1987), pp. 17–30.
——'Women at Philippi and Paul's Philippian Correspondence' (paper delivered at the SBL Annual Meeting, 1987), cited in Reimer, *Women in the Acts of the Apostles*, p. 128.
Alcoff, L., 'Cultural Feminism versus Post-Structuralism: The Identity Crisis in Feminist Theory', *Signs* 13 (1988), pp. 405–36.
Alexander, L., ' "Foolishness to the Greeks": Jews and Christians in the Public Life of the Empire', in G. Clark and T. Rajak (eds.), *Philosophy and Power in the Graeco-Roman World: Essays in Honour of Miriam Griffin* (New York: Oxford University Press, 2002), pp. 229–49.
Alexander, P.S., 'Notes on the "Imago Mundi" of the *Book of Jubilees*', *JJS* 33 (1982), pp. 197–214.
Allen, O.W., *The Death of Herod: The Narrative and Theological Function of Retribution in Luke–Acts* (SBLDS, 158; Atlanta: Scholars Press, 1997).
Alter, R., *The Art of Biblical Narrative* (New York: Basic Books, 1981).
Amandry, P., *La mantique apollinienne à Delphes: Essai sur le fonctionnement de l'oracle, Bibliothèque des écoles français d'Athènes et de Rome* (Paris: Boccard, 1950).
Anderson, G., *The Second Sophistic: A Cultural Phenomenon in the Roman Empire* (New York: Routledge, 1993).
Anderson, J.C., 'Reading Tabitha: A Feminist Reception History', in E.S. Malbon and E.V. McKnight (eds.), *The New Literary Criticism and the New Testament* (JSNTSup, 109; Sheffield: Sheffield Academic Press, 1994), pp. 108–44.
Anderson, J.C., and J.L. Staley, 'Taking It Personally: Introduction', *Semeia* 72 (1995), pp. 7–18.
Andrews, W.L. (ed.), *Sisters of the Spirit: Three Black Women's Autobiographies of the Nineteenth Century* (Bloomington: Indiana University Press, 1986).
Archer, L.J., *Her Price is Beyond Rubies: The Jewish Woman in Graeco-Roman Palestine* (JSOTSup, 60; Sheffield: Sheffield Academic Press, 1990).
Arlandson, J.M., *Women, Class, and Society in Early Christianity: Models from Luke–Acts* (Peabody, MA: Hendrickson, 1996, 1997).
Ascough, R.S., 'Benefaction Gone Wrong: The "Sin" of Ananias and Sapphira in Context', in S.G. Wilson and M. Desjardins (eds.), *Text and Artifact in the Religions of Mediterranean Antiquity: Essays in Honour of Peter Richardson* (SCJ, 9; Waterloo, Ont.: Wilfrid Laurier University Press, 2000), pp. 91–110.
——'Civic Pride at Philippi: The Text-Critical Problem of Acts 16.12', *NTS* 44 (1998), pp. 93–103.
Atwood, R., *Mary Magdalene in the New Testament Gospels and Early Tradition* (European University Studies. Series 23. 457; Bern: Peter Lang, 1993).

Baker-Fletcher, Karen, 'Anna Julia Cooper and Sojourner Truth: Two Nineteenth-Century Black Feminist Interpreters of Scripture', in Schüssler Fiorenza (ed.), *Searching the Scriptures*, I, pp. 41–51.

Balch, D.L., 'ἀκριβῶς.... γράψαι (Luke 1.3): To Write the *Full* History of God's Receiving All Nations', in Moessner (ed.), *Jesus and the Heritage of Israel*, pp. 229–50.

—— *Let Wives Be Submissive: The Domestic Code in I Peter* (SBLMS, 26; Atlanta: Scholars Press, 1981).

Barber, E.W., *Women's Work: The First 20,000 Years. Women, Cloth, and Society in Early Times* (New York/London: Norton, 1994).

Barrett, C.K., *A Critical and Exegetical Commentary on the Acts of the Apostles* (ICC; 2 vols.; Edinburgh: T. & T. Clark, 1994).

Basil, *Saint Basil: Ascetical Works* (Fathers of the Church, 9; trans. M. Monica Wagner; New York: Fathers of the Church, Inc., 1950).

Bassler, J.M., 'The Widows' Tale: A Fresh Look at 1 Tim. 5.3–16', *JBL* 103.1 (1984) pp. 23–41.

Bauernfeind, O., *Kommentar und Studien zur Apostelgeschichte* (WUNT, 22; Tübingen: Mohr, 1980).

Benediktsson, T.E., 'The Reawakening of the Gods: Realism and the Supernatural in Silko and Hulme', *Critique* 33 (1992), pp. 121–31.

Benjamin, D.C., 'The Persistant Widow', *TBT* 28 (1990), pp. 213–19.

Bettelheim, B., *The Uses of Enchantment: The Meaning and Importance of Fairy Tales* (New York: Random House Vintage Books, 1977).

Beyer, H.W., 'διακονέω', *TDNT*, II, pp. 81–94.

Bhabha, H.K., *The Location of Culture* (New York: Routledge, 1994).

Birch, B.C., 'The First and Second Books of Samuel', *NIB*, II, pp. 949–1383

Bird, P.A., *Missing Persons and Mistaken Identities: Women and Gender in Ancient Israel* (OBT; Minneapolis: Fortress Press, 1997).

Blue, B., 'Acts and the House Church', in D.W.J. Gill and C. Gempf (eds.), *The Book of Acts in its First Century Setting.* II. *The Book of Acts in its Graeco-Roman Setting* (2 vols.; Grand Rapids: Eerdmans; Carlisle: Paternoster, 1994), II, pp. 184–86.

Bobrick, E., 'The Tyranny of Roles: Playacting and Privilege in Aristophanes' Thesmophoriazusae', in Dobrov (ed.), *The City as Comedy*, p. 94.

Boer, R., 'Green Ants and Gibeonites: B. Wongar, Joshua 9, and Some Problems of Postcolonialism', *Semeia* 75 (1996), pp. 129–52.

Bonz, M.P., *The Past as Legacy: Luke–Acts and Ancient Epic* (Minneapolis: Fortress Press, 2000).

Boor, W. de, *Die Apostelgeschichte* (Wuppertaler Studienbibel; Wuppertal: Brockhaus, 1965).

Borret, M., *Sources chrétiennes* (5 vols.; Paris: Editions du Cerf, 1967–76).

Bovon, F., 'The Child and the Beast: Fighting Violence in Ancient Christianity', *HTR* 92 (1999), pp. 369–92.

—— 'The Dossier on Stephen, the First Martyr', *HTR* 96 (2003), pp. 279–315.

—— 'Der Heilige Geist, die Kirche und die menschlichen Beziehungen nach Apostelgeschichte 20, 36–21, 16', in *idem*, *Lukas in neuer Sicht* (Biblisch-

Theologische Studien, 8; Neukirchen–Vluyn: Neukirchener Verlag, 1985), pp. 181–204.

Boyarin, D., *A Radical Jew: Paul and the Politics of Identity* (Contraversions, 1; Berkeley: University of California Press, 1994).

—— 'Paul and the Genealogy of Gender', in A.-J. Levine (ed.) *A Feminist Companion to Paul* (FCNT 6; London: T. & T. Clark, 2004), pp. 13–41.

Bremen, R. van, *The Limits of Participation: Women and Civic Life in the Greek East in the Hellenistic and Roman Periods* (Amsterdam: Gieben, 1996).

—— 'Women and Wealth', in A. Cameron and A. Kuhrt (eds.), *Images of Women in Antiquity* (Detroit, MI: Wayne State University Press, 1983), pp. 223–41.

Brenner, A. (ed.) *Are We Amused? Humour about Women in the Biblical Worlds* (BTC, 2; London: T. & T. Clark; New York: Continuum, 2003).

Brent, A., *The Imperial Cult and the Development of Church Order: Concepts and Images of Authority in Paganism and Early Christianity before the Age of Cyprian* (VCSup, 45; Leiden: Brill, 1999).

——'Luke–Acts and the Imperial Cult in Asia Minor', *JTS* 48 (1997), pp. 111–38.

Brice, J., 'Earth as Mother, Earth as Other in Novels by Silko and Hogan', *Critique* 39 (1998), pp. 132–33.

Brock, A.G., 'Appeasement, Authority, and the Role of Women in the D-Text of Acts', in T. Nicklas and M. Tilly (eds.), *The Book of Acts as Church History/Apostelgeschichte als Kirchengeschichte* (BZNW, 120; Berlin: de Gruyter, 2003), pp. 205–24.

Brodie, T.L., 'The Accusing and Stoning of Naboth (1 Kgs 21.8–13) as One Component of the Stephen Text (Acts 6.9–14; 7.58a)', *CBQ* 45 (1983), pp. 417–43.

—— 'Luke 7, 36–50 as an Internalization of 2 Kings 4.1–37: A Study in Luke's Use of Rhetorical Imitation', *Biblica* 64 (1983), pp. 457–85.

—— 'Luke the Literary Interpreter: Luke–Acts as a Systematic Rewriting and Updating of the Elijah–Elisha Narrative in 1 and 2 Kings' (PhD diss., Pontifical University of St Thomas Aquinas, 1981).

—— 'Luke–Acts as an Imitation and Emulation of the Elijah–Elisha Narrative', in E. Richard (ed.), *New Views of Luke and Acts* (Collegeville, MN: Liturgical Press, 1990), pp. 78–85.

—— 'Reopening the Quest for Proto-Luke: The Systematic Use of Judges 6–12 in Luke 16.1–18.8', *Journal of Higher Criticism* 2.1 (Spring 1995), pp. 68–101.

—— 'Towards Unravelling Luke's Use of the Old Testament: Luke 7.11–17 as an Imitatio of 1 Kings 17.17–24', *NTS* 32 (1986), pp. 247–67.

Brooten, B., 'Early Christian Women and their Cultural Context: Issues of Method in Historical Reconstruction', in Collins (ed.), *Feminist Perspectives*, pp. 65–92.

—— 'Junia ... Outstanding among the Apostles', in L. Swidler and A. Swidler (eds.), *Women Priests: A Catholic Commentary on the Vatican Declaration* (New York: Paulist Press, 1977), pp. 141–44.

—— *Women Leaders in the Ancient Synagogue: Inscriptional Evidence and Background Issues* (BJS, 36; Atlanta and Chico, CA: Scholars Press, 1982).

Broughton, T.R.S., 'Roman Asia Minor' in T. Frank (ed.), *An Economic Survey of Ancient Rome* (6 vols.; Patterson, NJ: Pageant Books, 1959), IV, pp. 499–918.

Broughton, V.W., 'Twenty Year's Experience of a Missionary', in Gates (ed.), *Spiritual Narratives*, pp. 1–140.
Brown, R.E., 'Jesus and Elisha', *Perspective* 12 (1971), pp. 84–104.
Brown, R.M., *Religion and Violence* (Philadelphia: Westminster, 2nd edn, 1987).
Bruce, F.F., *Commentary on the Book of the Acts* (Grand Rapids: Eerdmans, 1954; New ICC; rev. edn 1992).
—— *The Pauline Circle* (Grand Rapids: Eerdmans; Exeter: Paternoster, 1985).
Burrus, V. and K. Torjesen, 'Household Management and Women's Authority', in K. Torjesen, *When Women Were Priests,* pp. 53–87.
Callaghan, D., 'The Vicar and Virago: Feminism and the Problem of Identity', in J. Roof and R. Wiegman (eds.), *Who Can Speak? Authority and Critical Identity* (Urbana: University of Illinois Press, 1995), pp. 195–207.
Calvin, J., *The Acts of the Apostles* (Calvin's New Testament Commentaries; trans. J.W. Fraser and W.J.G. MacDonald; Grand Rapids: Eerdmans, 1965).
Cameron, R., 'Alternate Beginnings—Different Ends: Eusebius, Thomas, and the Construction of Christian Origins', in L. Borman, K. Del Tredici, and A. Standhartinger (eds.), *Religious Propaganda and Missionary Competition in the New Testament World: Essays Honoring Dieter Georgi* (NovTSup, 74; Leiden: Brill, 1994), pp. 501–25.
Camp, C.V., and C.R. Fontaine, 'Proverbs', in Wayne A. Meeks (ed.), *The HarperCollins Study Bible: New Revised Standard Version* (New York: HarperCollins, 1993), pp. 984–85.
Carter, W.,'Getting Martha out of the Kitchen: Luke 10.38–42', *CBQ* 58 (1996), pp. 264–80.
Cassidy, R.J., *Society and Politics in the Acts of the Apostles* (Maryknoll, NY: Orbis Press, 1987).
Chambers, K., 'At the Expense of Women: Humor(?) in Acts 16.14–40', in A. Brenner (ed.), *Are We Amused? Humour about Women in the Biblical Worlds* (BTC, 2; London: T. & T.Clark, 2003), pp. 79–89.
Chariton, 'Chaereas and Callirhoe', in B.P. Reardon (ed. and trans.), *Collected Ancient Greek Novels* (Los Angeles: University of California Press, 1989).
Chrysostom, J., *Homilies on the Acts of the Apostles and the Epistle to the Romans* (Nicene and Post-Nicene Fathers, 11; ed. P. Schaff; trans. J. Walker, J. Sheppard, and H. Browne; Grand Rapids: Eerdmans, 1956).
——'Homilies on the Epistles of Paul to the Corinthians', in P. Schaff (trans. and ed.), *A Select Library of the Nicene and Post-Nicene Fathers of the Christian Church* (14 vols.; Grand Rapids: Eerdmans, 1982).
Collins, A.Y. (ed.), *Feminist Perspectives on Biblical Scholarship* (SBL Biblical Scholarship in North America, 10; Chico, CA: Scholars Press, 1985).
Collins, J.N., *DIAKONIA: Re-interpreting the Ancient Sources* (New York: Oxford University Press, 1990).
Collins, M.S., 'Money, Sex, and Power: An Examination of the Role of Women as Patrons of the Ancient Synagogue', in P.J. Haas (ed.), *Recovering the Role of Women: Power and Authority in Rabbinic Jewish Society* (South Florida Studies in the History of Judaism, 59; Atlanta: Scholars Press, 1992), pp. 5–22.

Collins, P.H., *Black Feminist Thought* (New York: Routledge & Kegan Paul, 1990).
Connolly, J., 'Mastering Corruption: Constructions of Identity in Roman Oratory', in S.R. Joshel and S. Murnaghan (eds.), *Women and Slaves in Greco-Roman Culture* (London: Routledge, 1998), pp. 130–51.
Connolly, R.H. (ed.), *Didascalia Apostolorum* (Oxford: Clarendon Press, 1929).
Conzelmann, H., *Acts of the Apostles: A Commentary on the Acts of the Apostles* (ed. E.J. Epp and C.R. Matthews; trans. J. Limburg, A.T. Kraabel, and D.H. Juel; Hermeneia; Philadelphia: Fortress Press, 1987).
Cook, A.B., *Zeus: A Study in Ancient Religion* (1914–40; reprint, 3 vols. in 2; New York: Biblo & Tannen, 1965).
Cooper, K., 'Insinuations of Womanly Influence: An Aspect of the Christianization of the Roman Aristocracy', *Journal of Roman Studies* 82 (1992), pp. 150–64.
—— *The Virgin and the Bride: Idealized Womanhood in Late Antiquity* (Cambridge, MA: Harvard University Press, 1996).
Corley, K.E., *Private Women, Public Meals: Social Conflict in the Synoptic Tradition* (Peabody, MA: Hendrickson, 1993).
Cross, F.L., and E.A. Livingston (eds.), *Oxford Dictionary of the Christian Church* (Oxford: Oxford University Press, 2nd edn., 1983).
Crossan, J.D., *Jesus: A Revolutionary Biography* (San Francisco: HarperSanFrancisco, 1994).
Culler, J., *On Deconstruction* (Ithaca, NY: Cornell University Press, 1982).
Cunningham, S., *'Through Many Tribulations': Theology of Persecution in Luke–Acts* (JSNTSup, 142; Sheffield: Sheffield Academic Press, 1997).
Daly, M., *Gyn/Ecology: The Metaethics of Radical Feminism* (Boston: Beacon Press, 1978).
D'Angelo, M.R., 'The *ANHP* Question in Luke–Acts: Imperial Masculinity and the Deployment of Women in the Early Second Century', in A.-J. Levine (ed.), *A Feminist Companion to Luke*, pp. 44–69.
—— '"Knowing How to Preside over his Own Household": Imperial Masculinity and Christian Asceticism in the Pastorals, *Hermas*, and Luke–Acts', in S.D. Moore and J. Capel Anderson (eds.), *New Testament Masculinities* (SBLSS, 45; Atlanta: Society of Biblical Literature, 2003), pp. 265–95.
—— '(Re)Presentations of Women in the Gospel of Matthew and Luke–Acts', in R.S. Kraemer and M.R. D'Angelo (eds.), *Women and Christian Origins* (Oxford: Oxford University Press, 1999), pp. 171–95.
—— 'Women in Luke–Acts: A Redactional View', *JBL* 109 (1990), pp. 441–61.
Dareste, R., B. Haussoulier, and T. Reinach (eds. and trans.), *Recueil des inscriptions juridiques grecques* (Rome: 'L'Erma' di Bretschneider, 1965).
D'Arms, J.H., *Commerce and Social Standing in Ancient Rome* (Cambridge, MA: Harvard Univeristy Press, 1981).
Darr, J., *On Character Building: The Reader and the Rhetoric of Characterization in Luke–Acts* (Louisville, KY: Westminster/John Knox, 1992).
Davies, S.L., *The Revolt of the Widows: The Social World of the Apocryphal Acts* (Carbondale: Southern Illinois University Press, 1980).
deBoer, E., 'The Lukan Mary Magdalene and the Other Women Following Jesus', in A.-J. Levine (ed.) *A Feminist Companion to Luke,* pp. 140–60.

de Lauretis, T., 'Upping the Anti in Feminist Theory', in Hirsch and Keller (eds.), *Conflicts in Feminism,* pp. 255–70.

Desjardins, M., *Peace, Violence and the New Testament* (BS, 46; Sheffield: Sheffield Academic Press, 1997).

Dewey, J., '1 Timothy', in Newsom and Ringe (eds.), *The Women's Bible Commentary* (exp edn 1998), pp. 444–49.

Dibelius, M., 'Style Criticism of the Book of Acts', in *idem, Studies in the Acts of the Apostles* (ed. H. Greeven; trans. M. Ling; London: SCM Press; New York: Charles Scribner's Sons, 1956).

Dodds, E.R., *Euripides' Bacchae* (Oxford: Oxford University Press and Clarendon Press, 2nd edn, 1960).

Donovan, J., *Feminist Theory: The Intellectual Traditions of American Feminism* (New York: F. Ungar, 1985; New York: Continuum, 1990).

Douglass, J.D., *Women, Freedom, and Calvin* (Philadelphia: Westminster Press, 1985).

Drinnon, R., *Keeper of the Concentration Camps: Dillon S. Myer and American Racism* (Berkeley: University of California Press, 1987).

Dube Shomanah, M.W., *Postcolonial Feminist Interpretation of the Bible* (St Louis: Chalice Press, 2000).

DuBois, E.C., 'Comment on Karen Offen's "Defining Feminism: A Comparative Historical Approach"', *Signs* 15 (1989), pp. 195–97.

Dunn, J.D.G., *The Acts of the Apostles* (Valley Forge, PA: Trinity Press International, 1996).

Easterling, P.E., 'From Repertoire to Canon', in *idem* (ed.), *The Cambridge Companion to Greek Tragedy* (Cambridge: Cambridge University Press, 1997).

Edwards, C., *The Politics of Immorality in Ancient Rome* (Cambridge: Cambridge University Press, 1993).

Eisen, U., *Women Officeholders in Early Christianity: Epigraphical and Literary Studies* (Collegeville, MN: Liturgical Press, 2000).

Elliott, J.H., 'Temple versus Household in Luke–Acts: A Contrast in Social Institutions', in J.H. Neyrey (ed.), *The Social World of Luke–Acts: Models for Interpretation* (Peabody, MA: Hendrickson, 1991), pp. 211–40.

Esler, P.F., *Community and Gospel in Luke–Acts* (SNTSMS, 57; Cambridge: Cambridge University Press, 1987).

Fauth, W., 'Pythia', *PW*, XXIV, pp. 515–48.

Felder, C.H. (ed.), *Stony the Road We Trod: African American Biblical Interpretation* (Minneapolis: Fortress Press, 1991).

Feldherr, A., *Spectacle and Society in Livy's History* (Berkeley: University of California Press, 1998).

Feldman, L.H., *Josephus's Interpretation of the Bible* (Hellenistic Culture and Society, 27; Berkeley: University of California Press, 1998).

Fetterley, J., *The Resisting Reader: A Feminist Approach to American Fiction* (Bloomington: Indiana University Press, 1978).

Fiensy, D., *The Social History of Palestine in the Herodian Period: The Land Is Mine* (Studies in the Bible and Early Christianity, 20; Lewiston, NY: Edwin Mellen Press, 1991).

Fischler, S., 'Imperial Cult: Engendering the Cosmos', in L. Foxhall and J. Salmon (eds.), *When Men Were Men: Masculinity, Power and Identity in Classical Antiquity* (New York: Routledge, 1998), pp. 165–83.

Fitzmyer, J.A., *The Acts of the Apostles: A New Translation with Introduction and Commentary* (AB, 31; New York: Doubleday, 1998).

—— *The Gospel According to Luke* (2 vols. AB, 28: New York: Doubleday, 1981).

Foerster, W., 'πύθων', *TDNT*, VI, pp. 917–20.

Foley, H.P., 'The Conception of Women in Athenian Drama', in *idem* (ed.), *Reflections of Women in Antiquity* (New York: Gordon & Breach, 1981) pp. 127–68.

—— 'The Female "Intruder" Reconsidered: Women in Aristophanes' *Lysistrata* and *Ecclesiazusae*', *CP* 77.1 (1982), pp. 1–21.

—— 'Penelope as Moral Agent', in Beth Cohen (ed.), *The Distaff Side: Representing the Female in Homer's* Odyssey (Oxford: Oxford University Press, 1995), pp. 94–97.

Foote, J.A.J., 'A Brand Plucked from the Fire: An Autobiographical Sketch by Mrs. Julia A.J. Foote,' in Andrews (ed.), *Sisters of the Spirit*, pp. 161–234.

Fowler, R.M., *Let the Reader Understand: Reader-Response Criticism and the Gospel of Mark* (Minneapolis: Fortress Press, 1991).

Frilingos, C., 'Sexing the Lamb', in S.D. Moore and J.C. Anderson (eds.), *New Testament Masculinities* (SBLSS, 45; Atlanta: SBL, 2003), pp. 309–17.

Frost, K.B., *Exits and Entrances in Menander* (Oxford: Clarendon Press, 1988).

Fulkerson, M.M., 'Contesting Feminist Canons: Discourse and the Problem of Sexist Texts', *JFSR* 7 (1991), pp. 53–74.

Fuss, D., 'Reading Like a Feminist', *Differences* 1 (1989), pp. 77–92.

Garrett, S., *The Demise of the Devil: Magic and the Demonic in Luke's Writings* (Minneapolis: Fortress Press, 1989).

Gasque, W.W., *A History of the Interpretation of the Acts of the Apostles* (Peabody, MA: Hendrickson, 1989).

Gates, H.L. (ed.), *Spiritual Narratives: M.W. Stewart; J. Lee; J.A.J. Foote; V.W. Broughton* (The Schomburg Library of Nineteenth-Century Black Women Writers; New York: Oxford University Press, 1988; facsimile of 1886 edn; Chicago: The Pony Press, 1907).

Gaventa, B.R., *Acts* (Abingdon New Testament Commentaries; Nashville: Abingdon, 2003).

—— *From Darkness to Light: Aspects of Conversion in the New Testament* (OBT; Philadelphia: Fortress Press, 1986).

Georgi, D., *The Opponents of Paul in Second Corinthians* (Philadelphia, Fortress Press, 1986).

Gifford, C.D., 'American Women and the Bible: The Nature of Woman as a Hermeneutical Issue', in Collins (ed.), *Feminist Perspectives*, pp. 11–34.

Gilbert, G., 'The List of Nations in Acts 2: Roman Propaganda and the Lukan Response', *JBL* 121 (2002), pp. 497–529.

—— 'Roman Propaganda and Christian Identity in the Worldview of Luke–Acts', in T. Penner and C. Vander Stichele (eds.), *Contextualizing Acts: Lukan Narrative and Greco-Roman Discourse* (SBLSS, 20; Atlanta: Scholars Press, 2003), pp. 233–56.

Gill, D.W.J., 'Acts and the Urban Elites', in D.W.J. Gill and C. Gempf (eds.), *The Book of Acts in its First Century Setting*. II. *The Book of Acts in its Graeco-Roman Setting* (2 vols.; Grand Rapids: Eerdmans; Carlisle: Paternoster, 1994), pp. 105–18.

Gillman, F.M., 'Early Christian Women at Philippi', *Journal of Gender in World Religions* 1 (1990), pp. 59–79.

—— *Women Who Knew Paul* (Zacchaeus Studies; Collegeville, MN: Liturgical Press, 1992).

Gillman, J., 'Hospitality in Acts 16', *LS* 17 (1992), pp. 189–91.

—— *Possessions and the Life of Faith: A Reading of Luke–Acts* (Zacchaeus Studies: New Testament; Collegeville, MN: Liturgical Press, 1991).

Gilmore, D.D., 'Introduction: The Shame of Dishonor', in *idem* (ed.), *Honor and Shame and the Unity of the Mediterranean* (Washington, DC: American Anthropological Association, 1987), pp. 2–21.

Glancy, J.A., *Slavery in Early Christianity* (Oxford: Oxford University Press, 2002).

Gleason, M.W., *Making Men: Sophists and Self-Presentation in Ancient Rome* (Princeton, NJ: Princeton University Press, 1995).

—— 'Mutilated Messengers: Body Language in Josephus', in S. Goldhill (ed.), *Being Greek under Rome: Cultural Identity, the Second Sophistic and the Development of Empire* (Cambridge: Cambridge University Press, 2001), pp. 50–85.

Gold, B.K., 'εὐκοσμία in Euripides' Bacchae', *AJP* 98 (1977), pp. 3–15.

Goldhill, S. (ed.) *Being Greek under Rome: Cultural Identity, the Second Sophistic and the Development of Empire* (Cambridge: Cambridge University Press, 2001).

Grant, R.M., *A Short History of the Interpretation of the Bible* (Philadelphia: Fortress Press, 2nd edn, 1984).

Greeven, H., 'εὐσχήμων,' *TDNT*, II, p. 770.

Greeven, H. (ed.), *Martin Dibelius: Studies in the Acts of the Apostles* (Mifflintown: Sigler Press, 1999).

Gunderson, E., *Staging Masculinity: The Rhetoric of Performance in the Roman World* (Ann Arbor: University of Michigan Press, 2000).

Gunn, D.M., and D.N. Fewell, *Narrative in the Hebrew Bible* (Oxford: Oxford University Press, 1993).

Haenchen, E., *The Acts of the Apostles: A Commentary* (trans. B. Noble and G. Shinn; rev. R.McL. Wilson; Philadelphia: Westminster Press, 1971).

Hallett, J.P., 'Women's Lives in the Ancient Mediterranean,' in R.S. Kraemer and M.R. D'Angelo (eds.), *Women and Christian Origins* (Oxford: Oxford University Press, 1999), pp. 13–34.

Hands, A.R., *Charities and Social Aid in Greece and Rome* (Ithaca, NY: Cornell University Press, 1968).

Harding, S., 'Conclusion: Epistemological Questions', in S. Harding (ed.), *Feminism and Methodology* (Bloomington: Indiana University Press, 1987), pp. 181–90.

Harnack, A. von, *Luke the Physician: The Author of the Third Gospel and the Acts of the Apostles* (trans. J.R. Wilkinson; London: Williams & Norgate; New York: G.P. Putnam, 2nd edn, 1909).

—— *Mission and Expansion of Christianity in the First Three Centuries* (trans. and ed. James Moffatt; 2 vols.; London: Williams & Norgate; New York: G.P. Putnam's sons, 2nd edn enl. and rev., 1908).

Harrill, J.A., 'The Dramatic Function of the Running Slave Rhoda (Acts 12.15–16): A Piece of Greco-Roman Comedy', *NTS* 46 (2000), pp. 151–57.

Hay, D.M., 'Things Philo Did and Did Not Say about the Therapeutae', SBLSP (1992), pp. 673–93.

Hedges, E., 'The Needle or the Pen: The Literary Rediscovery of Women's Textile Work', in F. Howe (ed.), *Tradition and the Talents of Women* (Urbana: University of Illinois Press, 1991), pp. 338–64.

Hemer, C.J., *The Book of Acts in the Setting of Hellenistic History* (ed. Conrad H. Gempf; Winona Lake, IN: Eisenbrauns, 1990).

Henderson, J., '*Lysistrate*: The Play and its Themes', *Yale Classical Studies* 26 (1980), pp. 153–218.

Hengel, M., *Between Jesus and Paul: Studies in the Earliest History of Christianity* (trans. J. Bowden; Philadelphia: Fortress Press, 1983).

—— 'The Dionysian Messiah', in *idem*, *Studies in Early Christology* (Edinburgh: T. & T. Clark, 1995), pp. 293–331.

Hennecke, E., *New Testament Apocrypha* (ed. Wilhelm Schneemelcher; 2 vols.; Philadelphia: Westminster Press, 1964).

Henrichs, A., 'Changing Dionysiac Identities', in B.F. Meyer and E.P. Sanders (eds.), *Jewish and Christian Self-Definition* (3 vols., Philadelphia: Fortress Press, 1982), III, pp. 137–60.

—— 'Greek Maenadism from Olympias to Messalina', *HSCP* 82 (1978), pp. 121–60.

Henry, M., *Matthew Henry's Commentary in One Volume* (ed. L.F. Church; Grand Rapids: Zondervan, 1961).

Hirsch, M., and E.F. Keller (eds.), *Conflicts in Feminism* (New York: Routledge & Kegan Paul, 1990).

Hock, R.F., *The Social Context of Paul's Ministry: Tentmaking and Apostleship* (Philadelphia: Fortress Press, 1980).

Homer, *The Odyssey* (trans. E.V. Rieu; Baltimore, MD: Penguin, 1961).

—— *The Odyssey* (trans. R. Fagles; introduction and notes B. Knox; New York: Viking Penguin, 1996).

hooks, b., *Ain't I a Woman: Black Women and Feminism* (Boston: South End Press, 1981).

Horsley, G.H.R., *New Documents Illustrating Early Christianity* (7 vols.; North Ryde, New South Wales, Australia: Ancient History Documentary Research Centre, Macquarie University, 1981–94).

Hutcheon, L., *The Politics of Postmodernism* (New York: Routledge, 1989).

Ilan, T., *Jewish Women in Greco-Roman Palestine* (Peabody, MA: Hendrickson, 1996).

Jackson, F.J. Foakes, and K. Lake, *The Acts of the Apostles* (5 vols.; The Beginnings of Christianity, part 1; ed. H.J. Cadbury and K. Lake; London: Macmillan, 1933; Grand Rapids: Baker Book House, 1979).

Janzen, A., *Der Friede im lukanischen Doppelwerk vor dem Hintergrund der Pax Romana* (EH, 752; Frankfurt: Lang, 2002).

Jervell, J., 'The Daughters of Abraham: Women in Acts', in *idem*, *The Unknown Paul*.
—— *The Unknown Paul. Essays on Luke–Acts and Early Christian History* (Minneapolis: Augsburg, 1984).
Jervell, J., and W.A. Meeks (eds.), *God's Christ and his People: Studies in Honor of Nils Alstrup Dahl* (Oslo: Universitetsforlaget, 1977).
Johnson, E.A., *She Who Is: The Mystery of God in Feminist Theological Discourse* (New York: Crossroad, 1992).
Johnson, L.T., *The Acts of the Apostles* (Collegeville, MN: Liturgical Press, 1992).
—— *The Literary Function of Possessions in Luke–Acts* (SBLDS, 39; Chico, CA: Scholars Press, 1977).
—— 'The New Testament's Anti-Jewish Slander and the Conventions of Ancient Polemic', *JBL* 108 (1989), pp. 419–41.
Johnson, S.E., 'Acts', in H.G. May and B.M. Metzger (eds.), *The New Oxford Annotated Bible, Revised Standard Version* (New York: Oxford University Press, 1977), pp. 1319–60.
Jones, A.R., 'Dematerializations: Textile and Textual Properties in Ovid, Sandys, and Spenser', in M. de Grazia, M. Quilligan, and P. Stallybrass (eds.), *Subject and Object in Renaissance Culture* (Cambridge: Cambridge University Press, 1996), pp. 189–209.
Josephus, *The Life* (trans. H.St.J. Thackeray; LCL; Cambridge, MA: Harvard University Press, 1926).
Joshel, S.R., 'The Body Female and the Body Politic: Livy's Lucretia and Verginia', in A. Richlin (ed.), *Pornography and Representation in Greece and Rome* (New York: Oxford University Press, 1992), pp. 112–30.
—— 'Female Desire and the Discourse of Empire: Tacitus's Messalina', *Signs* 21.1 (1995), pp. 50–82; repr. in J.P. Hallett and M.B. Skinner (eds.), *Roman Sexualities* (Princeton, NJ: Princeton University Press, 1997), pp. 221–54.
Kahl, B., 'Toward a Materialist-Feminist Reading', in Schüssler Fiorenza (ed.), *Searching the Scriptures*, I, pp. 225–40.
Kee, H.C., *To Every Nation under Heaven: The Acts of the Apostles* (Valley Forge, PA: Trinity Press International, 1997).
Kidwell, C.S., 'Indian Women as Cultural Mediators', *Ethnohistory* 39 (1992), pp. 97–107.
Kittredge, C.B., *Community and Authority: The Rhetoric of Obedience in the Pauline Tradition* (HTS, 45; Harrisburg, PA: Trinity Press International, 1998).
Kitzberger, I.R., 'Border Crossing and Meeting Jesus at the Well: An Autobiographical Re-reading of the Samaritan Woman's Story in John 4.1–44', in *idem* (ed.), *The Personal Voice in Biblical Scholarship* (London: Routledge, 1999), pp. 111–27.
Klauck, H.-J., *Magic and Paganism in Early Christianity: The World of the Acts of the Apostles* (trans. B. McNeil; Edinburgh: T. & T. Clark, 2000).
Kleinknecht, H., 'πνεῦμα, πνευματικός', *TDNT*, VI (1968), pp. 332–451.
Knox, J., *Marcion and the New Testament: An Essay in the Early History of the Canon* (Chicago: University of Chicago Press, 1942).
Koenig, J., *New Testament Hospitality: Partnership with Strangers as Promise and Mission* (OBT, 17; Philadelphia: Fortress Press, 1985).

Koester, H., *Introduction to the New Testament* (2 vols.; New York and Berlin: de Gruyter, 1982).

Konstan, D., *Greek Comedy and Ideology* (New York: Oxford University Press, 1995).

Kraemer, R.S., 'Ecstasy and Possession: The Attraction of Women to the Cult of Dionysus', *HTR* 72 (1979), pp. 55–80.

—— *Her Share of the Blessings: Women's Religions among Pagans, Jews, and Christians in the Greco-Roman World* (Oxford: Oxford University Press, 1992).

—— *Maenads, Martyrs, Matrons, Monastics: A Sourcebook on Women's Religions in the Greco-Roman World* (Philadelphia: Fortress Press, 1988).

—— 'Monastic Jewish Women in Greco-Roman Egypt: Philo on the Therapeutrides', *Signs* 14.1 (1989), pp. 342–70.

Krodel, G., *Acts: Proclamation Commentaries* (Philadelphia: Fortress Press, 1981).

Krueger, C., *The Reader's Repentance: Women Preachers, Women Writers, and Nineteenth-Century Social Discourse* (Chicago: University of Chicago Press, 1992).

Kuefler, M., *The Manly Eunuch: Masculinity, Gender Ambiguity, and Christian Identity in Late Antiquity* (Chicago: University of Chicago Press, 2001).

Kümmel, W.G., *Introduction to the New Testament* (trans. Howard Clark Kee; Nashville and New York: Abingdon Press, 17th edn, 1975).

La Farge, O., *Laughing Boy* (New York: Houghton Mifflin Co., 1957).

Lane, B.C., *The Solace of Fierce Landscapes: Exploring Desert and Mountain Spirituality* (New York: Oxford University Press, 1998).

LaVerdiere, E., *Dining in the Kingdom of God: The Origins of the Eucharist according to Luke* (Chicago: LTP, 1994).

—— 'The Widow's Mite', *Emmanuel* 92 (1986), pp. 316–21, 341.

Lefkowitz, M.R., and M.B. Fant (trans. and eds.), *Women's Life in Greece and Rome: A Sourcebook in Translation* (Baltimore, MD: Johns Hopkins University Press, 2nd edn, 1992).

Lentz, J.C., *Luke's Portrait of Paul* (SNTSMS, 77; Cambridge: Cambridge University Press, 1993), pp. 23–61.

Lerner, G., *The Creation of Feminist Consciousness: From the Middle Ages to Eighteen-Seventy* (Women and History, 2; New York: Oxford University Press, 1993).

—— *The Female Experience: An American Documentary* (Indianapolis: Bobbs–Merrill, 1977).

Levine, A.-J., 'Sacrifice and Salvation: Otherness and Domestication in the Book of Judith', in J.C. Vanderkam (ed.), *'No One Spoke Ill of Her': Essays on Judith* (SBLEJL, 2: Atlanta: Scholars Press, 1992), pp. 17–30.

—— 'Tobit: Teaching Jews How to Live in the Diaspora', *BR* 8 (1992), pp. 42–51, 64.

—— (ed.) *A Feminist Companion to John* (2 vols; FCNT, 4–5; London: Sheffield Academic Press, 1992).

—— (ed.) *A Feminist Companion to Luke* (FCNT, 3; London: Sheffield Academic Press, 2003).

—— 'Womens Humor and Other Creative Juices', in A. Brenner (ed.), *Are We*

Amused? Humour about Women in the Biblical Worlds (London: T. & T. Clark, 2003), pp. 120–26.

Lewis, N., Y. Yadin, and J. Greenfield (eds.), *The Documents from the Bar Kokhba Period in the Cave of Letters* (Jerusalem: Israel Exploration Society, 1989).

Lewy, H., *Sobria Ebrietas: Untersuchungen zur Geschichte der Antiken Mystik* (Geissen: Töpelmann, 1929).

Linforth, I.M., 'The Corybantic Rites in Plato', *University of California Publications in Classical Philology* 13.5 (1946), pp. 121–62.

—— 'Telestic Madness in Plato, *Phaedrus* 244DE', *University of California Publications in Classical Philology* 13.6 (1946), pp. 163–72.

MacDonald, D.R., *Christianizing Homer:* The Odyssey, *Plato, and* The Acts of Andrew (New York: Oxford University Press, 1994).

—— *There Is No Male and Female: The Fate of a Dominical Saying in Paul and Gnosticism* (HDR, 20; Philadelphia: Fortress Press, 1987).

—— 'Virgins, Widows, and Paul in Second Century Asia Minor', in P.J. Achtemeier (ed.), *SBL Seminar Papers* (Missoula, MT: Scholars Press, 1979), pp. 169–84.

MacDonald, M.Y., *Early Christian Women and Pagan Opinion: The Power of the Hysterical Woman* (Cambridge: Cambridge University Press, 1996).

Malbon, E.S., 'The Poor Widow in Mark and her Poor Rich Readers', *CBQ* 53 (1991), pp. 589–604.

Malbon, E.S., and J.C. Anderson, 'Literary-Critical Methods', in Schüssler Fiorenza (ed.), *Searching the Scriptures*, I, pp. 241–54.

Maldonado, R., 'Reading Malinche Reading Ruth: Toward a Hermeneutics of Betrayal', *Semeia* 72 (1995), pp. 91–109.

Malherbe, A.J., ' "Gentle as a Nurse", the Cynic Background to I Thessalonians 2', *NovT* 12 (1970), pp. 203–17, reprinted in *idem, Paul and the Pagan Philosophers* (Minneapolis: Fortress Press, 1989), pp. 35–48.

—— 'Hospitality and Inhospitality in the Church', in *idem, Social Aspects of Early Christianity* (Philadelphia: Fortress Press, 2nd edn, 1983), pp. 92–112.

—— *Paul and the Popular Philosophers* (Minneapolis: Fortress Press, 1989).

Malina, B.J., *The New Testament World: Insights from Cultural Anthropology* (Louisville, KY: Westminster/John Knox, rev. edn, 1993).

Manley, K., 'Leslie Marmon Silko's Use of Color in *Ceremony*', *Southern Folklore* 46 (1989), pp. 137–39.

Marguerat, D., 'Ananias and Sapphira (Acts 5. 1–11): The Original Sin', in K. McKinney, G.J. Laughery, and R. Bauckham (trans.), *The First Christian Historian: Writing the 'Acts of the Apostles'* (SNTSMS, 121; Cambridge: Cambridge University Press, 2002), pp. 155–78.

—— 'Le mort d'Ananias et Sapphira (Acts 5. 1–11) dans la stratégie narrative de Luc', *NTS* 39 (1993), pp. 209–26.

Marshall, I.H., 'Acts and the "Former Treatise" ', in B.W. Winter and A.D. Clarke (eds.), *The Book of Acts in its First Century Setting. I: The Book of Acts in its Ancient Literary Setting* (6 vols.; Grand Rapids, MI: Eerdmans, 1993), pp. 163–82).

Martin, C.J., 'The Acts of the Apostles', in Schüssler Fiorenza (ed.), *Searching the Scriptures*, II, pp. 763–99.

—— 'A Chamberlain's Journey and the Challenge of Interpretation for Liberation', *Semeia* 47 (1989), pp. 105–36.

—— 'The *Haustafeln* (Household Codes) in African American Biblical Interpretation: "Free Slaves" and "Subordinate Women"', in Felder (ed.), *Stony the Road We Trod*, pp. 206–31.

Matthews, S., *First Converts: Rich Pagan Women and the Rhetoric of Mission in Early Judaism and Christianity* (Contraversions: Jews and Other Differences; Stanford, CA: Stanford University Press, 2001).

—— 'The Need for the Stoning of Stephen', in Matthews and Gibson (eds.), *Violence in the New Testament*.

Matthews, S., and E.L. Gibson (eds.), *Violence in the New Testament* (forthcoming).

McCarter, P.K., *II Samuel* (AB, 9; Garden City, NY: Doubleday, 1984).

McCreesh, T.P., 'Wisdom as Wife: Proverbs 31:10–31', *RB* 92 (1985), pp. 25–46.

McNickle, D., *Indian Man: A Life of Oliver La Farge* (Bloomington: Indiana University Press, 1971).

McRay, J., *Archaeology and the New Testament* (Grand Rapids: Baker Book House, 1991).

Meeks, W.A., *The First Urban Christians: The Social World of the Apostle Paul* (New Haven, CT: Yale University Press, 1983).

Meiselman, M., *Jewish Woman in Jewish Law* (New York: Ktav, 1978).

Mendels, D., 'Pagan or Jewish? The Presentation of Paul's Mission in the Book of Acts', in H. Cancik, H. Lichtenberger, and P. Schäfer (eds.), *Geschichte— Tradition—Reflexion: Festschrift für Martin Hengel zum 70. Geburtstag* (3 vols.; Tübingen: Mohr Siebeck, 1996), I, pp. 431–52.

Metzger, B.M., *A Textual Commentary on the Greek New Testament* (New York: United Bible Societies, 1971).

Meyers, C., *Discovering Eve: Ancient Israelite Women in Context* (New York/Oxford: Oxford University Press, 1988).

Michaelis, W., 'πρῶτος', *TDNT*, VI, p. 866.

Michel, O., 'οἰκονόμος', *TDNT*, V, pp.. 149–51.

Miller, N.K., 'Arachnologies: The Woman, The Text, and the Critic', in *idem* (ed.), *The Poetics of Gender* (New York: Columbia University Press, 1986), pp. 270–95.

Moessner, D.P. (ed.) *Jesus and the Heritage of Israel: Luke's Narrative Claim upon Isreal's Legacy* (Philadelphia: Trinity Press International, 1999).

—— '"The Christ Must Suffer": New Light on the Jesus–Peter, Stephen, Paul Parallels in Luke–Acts', repr. in D.E. Orton (ed.), *The Composition of Luke's Gospel* (Leiden: Brill, 1999), pp. 117–53.

Mohanty, C.T., 'Cartographies of Struggle: Third World Women and the Politics of Feminism', in C.T. Mohanty, A. Russo, and L. Torres (eds.), *Third World Women and the Politics of Feminism* (Bloomington: Indiana University Press, 1991), pp. 1–47.

Moore, C.A., *Tobit: A New Translation with Introduction and Commentary* (AB, 40A; New York: Doubleday, 1996).

Moore, S.D., and J.C. Anderson, (eds.), *New Testament Masculinities* (SBLSS, 45; Atlanta: SBL, 2003).

—— 'Taking It Like a Man: Masculinity in 4 Maccabees', *JBL* 117 (1998), pp. 249–73.
Mount, C., *Pauline Christianity: Luke–Acts and the Legacy of Paul* (NovTSup, 54; Leiden: Brill, 2002).
Moxnes, H., 'Patron–Client Relations and the New Community', in J.H. Neyrey (ed.), *The Social World of Luke–Acts* (Peabody, MA: Hendrickson, 1991), pp. 262–63.
Munck, J., *The Acts of the Apostles* (AB, 31; Garden City, NY: Doubleday, 1967).
Murphy-O'Connor, J., *Paul: A Critical Life* (Oxford: Oxford University Press, 1997).
—— 'Prisca and Aquila: Traveling Tentmakers and Church Builders', *BR* 8 (1992), pp. 40–51, 62.
Nasrallah, L., *An Ecstasy of Folly: Prophecy and Authority in Early Christianity* (HTS, 52; Cambridge, MA: Harvard University Press, 2003).
Nestle, W., 'Anklänge an Euripides in der Apostelgeschichte', *Philologus* 13 (1900), pp. 46–57; idem, *Griechische Studien: Untersuchungen zur Religion, Ditchtung und Philosophie der Griechen* (Aalen: Scientia Verlag, 1968).
Newsom, C.A., and S.H. Ringe (eds.), *The Women's Bible Commentary* (London: SPCK; Louisville, KY: Westminster/John Knox, 1992).
Neyrey, J., 'Ceremonies in Luke–Acts: The Case of Meals and Table Fellowship', in *idem* (ed.), *The Social World of Luke–Acts* (Peabody, MA: Hendrickson, 1991), pp. 361–87.
—— 'Luke's Social Location of Paul: Cultural Anthropology and the Status of Paul in Acts', in B. Witherington III (ed.), *History, Literature and Society in the Book of Acts* (Cambridge: Cambridge University Press, 1996), pp. 251–79.
—— 'What's Wrong with this Picture? John 4, Cultural Stereotypes of Women, and Public and Private Space', *BTB* 24.2 (1994), pp. 77–91, repr. in A.-J. Levine (ed.), *A Feminist Companion to John,* I, pp. 98–125.
Nicolet, C., *Space, Geography, and Politics in the Early Roman Empire* (trans. H. Leclerc; Ann Arbor: University of Michigan Press, 1991).
Norris, F.W., 'Basil of Caearea' (*sic*) in E. Ferguson (ed.), *Encyclopedia of Early Christianity* (New York: Garland, 1990), p. 141.
O'Day, G.R., 'Acts', in Newsom and Ringe (eds.), *The Women's Bible Commentary* (1992), pp. 305–12; (exp. edn, 1998), pp. 394–402.
Offen, K., 'Defining Feminism: A Comparative Historical Approach', *Signs* 14 (1988), pp. 119–57.
Økland, J., 'Women in their Place: Paul and the Corinthian Discourse of Gender and Sanctuary Space' (PhD diss., University of Oslo, 2000).
Omerzu, H., *Der Prozess des Paulus: Eine exegetische und rechtshistorische Untersuchung der Apostelgeschichte* (BZNW, 115; Berlin: de Gruyter, 2002).
Osiek, C., 'The Family in Early Christianity: "Family Values" Revisited', *CBQ* 58.1 (1996), pp. 1–24.
—— 'The Widow as Altar: The Rise and Fall of a Symbol', *Second Century* 3 (1983), pp. 159–69.
Osiek, C., and D.L. Balch, *Families in the New Testament World: Households and Churches* (The Family, Religion, and Culture Series; Louisville, KY: Westminster/John Knox Press, 1997).

Ostriker, A.S., *Feminist Revision and the Bible* (Bucknell Lectures in Literary History; Oxford: Basil Blackwell, 1993).
O'Toole, R., 'The Parallels between Jesus and Moses', *BTB* 20 (1990), pp. 22–29.
Pack, R.A., *Greek and Latin Literary Texts from Greco-Roman Egypt* (Ann Arbor: University of Michigan Press, 2nd edn, 1965).
Packer, J.W., *The Acts of the Apostles* (The Cambridge Bible Commentary on the New English Bible; Cambridge: Cambridge University Press, 1966).
Page, D.L. (ed.) *Select Papyri* (3 vols; LCL; Cambridge, MA: Harvard University Press, 1970–).
Pallas, D.I., and S. Charitonides, 'Inscriptions Lyciennes trouvées à Solômos près deCorinthe', *Bulletin de correspondence hellénique* 83.2 (1959), pp. 496–508.
Parsons, M.C., 'The Place of Jerusalem on the Lukan Landscape: An Exercise in Symbolic Cartography', in R.P. Thompson and T.E. Phillips (eds.), *Literary Studies in Luke–Acts: Essays in Honor of Joseph B. Tyson* (Macon, GA: Mercer University Press, 1998), pp. 155–71.
Parsons, M.C., and R.I. Pervo, *Rethinking the Unity of Luke and Acts* (Minneapolis: Fortress Press, 1993).
Parvey, C.F., 'The Theology and Leadership of Women in the New Testament', in R.R. Ruether (ed.), *Religion and Sexism: Images of Woman in the Jewish and Christian Traditions* (New York: Simon & Schuster, 1974), pp. 117–49.
Penner, T., 'Civilizing Discourse: Acts, Declamation, and the Rhetoric of the *Polis*', in T. Penner and C. Vander Stichele (eds.), *Contextualizing Acts: Lukan Narrative and Greco-Roman Discourse* (SBLSS, 20; Atlanta: Scholars Press, 2003), pp. 65–104.
Penner, T., and C. Vander Stichele, 'Unveiling Paul: Gendering Ethos in 1 Corinthians 11.2–16', in T.H. Olbricht and A. Eriksson (eds.), *Rhetoric, Ethic, and Moral Persuasion in Biblical Discourse* (ESEC; T. & T. Clark International, forthcoming).
Perkinson, J., 'A Canaanite Word in the Logos of Christ; or The Difference the Syro-Phoenician Woman Makes to Jesus', *Semeia* 75 (1996), pp. 61–85.
Pervo, R.I., *Luke's Story of Paul* (Minneapolis: Fortress Press, 1990).
—— *Profit with Delight: The Literary Genre of the Acts of the Apostles* (Philadelphia: Fortress Press, 1987).
—— 'Wisdom and Power', *ATR* 67 (1985), pp. 307–25.
Peskowitz, M., '"Family/ies" in Antiquity: Evidence from Tannaitic Literature and Roman Galilean Architecture', in S.J.D. Cohen (ed.), *The Jewish Family in Antiquity* (BJS, 289; Atlanta: Scholars Press, 1993), pp. 9–36.
—— *Spinning Fantasies: Rabbis, Gender, and History* (Berkeley: University of California Press, 1997).
Pilgrim, W., *Good News to the Poor: Wealth and Poverty in Luke–Acts* (Minneapolis: Augsburg, 1981).
Plaskow, J., 'Christian Feminism and Anti-Judaism', *Crosscurrents* 28 (1978), pp. 306–309.
—— 'Anti-Judaism in Feminist Christian Interpretation', in Schüssler Fiorenza (ed.), *Searching the Scriptures,* I, pp. 117–29.
Pleket, H.W. (ed.), *Epigraphica* II. *Texts on the Social History of the Greek World* (Leiden: Brill, 1969).

—— 'Urban Elites and Business in the Greek Part of the Roman Empire', in P. Garnsey *et al.* (eds.), *Trade in the Ancient Economy* (London: Chatto & Windus, 1983), pp. 131–44.

Plümacher, E., 'The Mission Speeches in Acts and Dionysius of Halicarnassus', in D.P. Moessner (ed.), *Jesus and the Heritage of Israel,* pp. 251–66.

Plutarch, *Moralia* (trans. F.C. Babbitt *et al.*; LCL; Cambridge, MA: Harvard University Press, 1927–69).

Polhill, J.B., 'The Hellenist Breakthrough: Acts 6–12', *Review and Expositor* 71 (1974), pp. 475–86.

Pomeroy, S.B. (ed.), *Plutarch's* Advice to the Bride and Groom *and* A Consolation to his Wife (Oxford: Oxford University Press, 1999).

—— 'Reflections on Plutarch, *Advice to the Bride and Groom*', in *idem* (ed.), *Plutarch's* Advice, pp. 33–42.

Portefaix, L., *Sisters Rejoice: Paul's Letter to the Philippians and Luke–Acts as Seen by First-Century Philippian Women* (ConBNT, 20; Stockholm: Almqvist & Wiksell, 1988).

Praeder, S., 'Luke–Acts and the Ancient Novel', SBLSP, 20 (1981), pp. 269–92.

Price, R.M., *The Widow Traditions in Luke–Acts: A Feminist-Critical Scrutiny* (SBLDS, 155; Atlanta, GA: Scholars Press, 1997).

Rackham, R.B., *The Acts of the Apostles: An Exposition* (London: Methuen & Company, 1906).

Radet, G., and P. Paris, 'Inscriptions de Syllion en Pamphylie', *Bulletin de correspondence hellénique* 13 (1889), pp. 486–97.

Räisänen, H., 'The Effective "History" of the Bible: A Challenge to Biblical Scholarship', *SJT* 45 (1992), pp. 303–24.

Ramsay, W.M., *The Cities and Bishoprics of Phrygia* (New York: Arno Press, 1975 [1895–97]).

Rand, N.R.,'Surviving What Haunts You: The Art of Invisibility in *Ceremony*, *The Ghost Writer*, and *Beloved*', *MELUS* 20 (1995), pp. 21–32.

Rapske, B., *The Book of Acts and Paul in Roman Custody* (Grand Rapids: Eerdmans, 1993).

Redalié, Y., 'Conversion ou libération? Notes sur Actes 16, 11–40', *Bulletin du centre protestant d'études* 26.7 (1974), pp. 6–17.

Reid, B., 'Beyond Petty Pursuits, and Wearisome Widows', *Int* 56 (2002), pp. 284–94.

—— *Choosing the Better Part? Women in the Gospel of Luke* (Collegeville, MN: Liturgical Press, 1996).

—— ' "Do You See This Woman?": A Liberative Look at Luke 7.36–50 and Strategies for Reading Other Lukan Stories Against the Grain', in A.-J. Levine (ed.) *A Feminist Companion to Luke* (FCNTECW, 3; London: Sheffield Academic Press, 2002), pp. 206–20.

Reimer, I.R., *Women in the Acts of the Apostles: A Feminist Liberation Perspective* (trans. L.M. Maloney; Minneapolis: Fortress Press, 1995).

Richlin, A., 'Gender and Rhetoric: Producing Manhood in the Schools', in W.J. Dominik (ed.), *Roman Eloquence: Rhetoric in Society and Literature* (London: Routledge, 1997), pp. 90–110.

Robert, L., 'Recherches épigraphiques', *Revue des études anciennes* 62 (1960), p. 330.

Robertson, K., 'Pocahontas at the Masque', *Signs* 21 (1996), pp. 551–83.

Rohrbaugh, R.L., 'The Pre-Industrial City in Luke–Acts: Urban Social Relations', in J.H. Neyrey (ed.), *The Social World of Luke–Acts: Models for Interpretation* (Peabody, MA: Hendrickson, 1991), pp. 125–49.

Roof, J., and R. Wiegman (eds.), *Who Can Speak? Authority and Critical Identity* (Urbana: University of Illinois Press, 1995).

Rutherford, W.G. (ed.), *The New Phrynicus* (Hildesheim: Georg Olms, 1968 [1881]).

Ryan, R., 'Lydia, A Dealer in Purple Goods', *Bible Today* 2 (1984), pp. 287–89.

St Andrews, B.A., 'Healing the Witchery: Medicine in Silko's *Ceremony*', *Arizona Quarterly* 14 (1988), pp. 86–94.

Salyer, G., 'Review of *Reading with a Passion: Rhetoric, Autobiography, and the American West in the Gospel of John*, by Jeffrey L. Staley (New York: Continuum, 1995)', *Literature and Theology* 11 (1997), pp. 320–23.

Sandbach, F.H., *The Comic Theatre of Greece and Rome* (New York: W.W. Norton & Company, Inc., 1977).

Sanders, E.P., *Judaism: Practice and Belief, 63 BCE–66 CE* (Philadelphia: Trinity Press International, 1992).

Sanders, J.T., *The Jews in Luke–Acts* (Philadelphia: Fortress Press, 1987).

Sangster, M.E., *From My Youth Up* (Signal Lives: Autobiographies of American Women; New York: Arno Press, 1980; repr. of the 1909 edn [New York: Revell Company, under the title *An Autobiography: From My Youth Up: Personal Reminiscences*]).

—— *The Women of the Bible: A Portrait Gallery* (New York: The Christian Herald, 1911.)

Sawhney, S., 'The Joke and the Hoax: (Not) Speaking as the Other', in J. Roof and R.Wiegman (eds.), *Who Can Speak? Authority and Critical Identity*, pp. 208–20.

Sawicki, M., *Crossing Galilee: Architectures of Contact in the Occupied Land of Jesus* (Harrisburg, PA: Trinity Press International, 2000).

Sawyer, D.F., *Women and Religion in the First Christian Centuries* (London: Routledge, 1996).

Schaberg, J., 'Luke', in Newsom and Ringe (eds.), *The Women's Bible Commentary* (1992), pp. 275–92 (exp. edn, 1998), pp. 363–80.

Schille, G., *Die Apostelgeschichte des Lukas* (THNT, 5; Berlin: Evangelische Verlagsanstalt, 1983).

Schneider, G., *Die Apostelgeschichte* (2 vols.; HTKNT, 5; Freiburg: Herder, 1982).

Scholes, R., 'Reading Like a Man', in A. Jardine and P. Smith (eds.), *Men in Feminism* (New York: Methuen, 1987).

Schottroff, L., *Let the Oppressed Go Free: Feminist Perspectives on the New Testament* (trans. A.S. Kidder; Louisville, KY: Westminster/John Knox Press, 1993).

—— 'Lydia: A New Quality of Power', in *idem*, *Let the Oppressed Go Free* pp. 131–37.

—— *Lydia's Impatient Sisters: A Feminist Social History of Early Christianity* (trans. B. and M. Rumscheidt; Louisville, KY: Westminster/John Knox Press, 1995).

—— 'Women as Followers of Jesus in New Testament Times', in N.K. Gottwald and R.A. Horsley (eds.), *The Bible and Liberation: Political and Social Hermeneutics* (Maryknoll, NY: Orbis; London: SPCK, rev. edn, 1993), pp. 458–59.

Schottroff, L., S. Shroer, and M.-T. Wacker (eds.), *Feminist Interpretation: The Bible in Women's Perspective* (Minneapolis: Fortress Press, 1998).

Schüssler Fiorenza, E., *But She Said: Feminist Practices of Biblical Interpretation* (Boston: Beacon Press, 1992).

—— 'A Feminist Critical Interpretation for Liberation: Martha and Mary (Luke 10.38–42)', *Religion and Intellectual Life* 3 (1986), pp. 16–36.

—— *In Memory of Her: A Feminist Theological Reconstruction of Christian Origins* (New York: Crossroad, 1983; 10th anniversary edn., 1994).

—— 'Introduction: Transforming the Legacy of the Women's Bible', in idem (ed.), *Searching for the Scriptures*, I. pp. 1–28.

—— 'Luke 13.10–17: Interpretation for Liberation and Transformation', *Theology Digest* 36 (1989), pp. 303–19.

—— 'The "Quilting" of Women's History: Phoebe of Cenchreae', in P.M. Cooey, S.A. Farmer, and M.E. Ross (eds.), *Embodied Love: Sensuality and Relationship as Feminist Values* (San Francisco: Harper & Row, 1987), pp. 35–49.

—— *Revelation: Vision of a Just World* (Proclamation Commentaries; Minneapolis: Fortress Press, 1991).

Schüssler Fiorenza, E. (ed.), *Searching the Scriptures* (2 vols.; New York: Crossroad, 1993, 1994).

Schwartz, S., 'The Trial Scene in the Greek Novels and in Acts', in T. Penner and C. Vander Stichele (eds.), *Contextualizing Acts: Lukan Narrative and Greco-Roman Discourse* (SBLSS, 20; Atlanta: Scholars Press, 2003), pp. 105–33.

Schweickart, P.P., 'Reading Ourselves: Toward a Feminist Theory of Reading', in E.A. Flynn and P.P. Schweickart (eds.), *Gender and Reading: Essays on Readers, Texts, and Contexts* (Baltimore: Johns Hopkins University Press, 1986), pp. 31–62.

Schwöbel, C., 'Calvin', in R.J. Coggins and J.L. Houlden (eds.), *A Dictionary of Biblical Interpretation* (Philadelphia: Trinity Press International; London: SCM Press, 1990), pp. 98–101.

Scott, J.M., *Paul and the Nations: The Old Testament and Jewish Background of Paul's Mission to the Nations with Special Reference to the Destination of Galatians* (Tübingen: J.C.B. Mohr [Paul Siebeck], 1995).

Secombe, D.P., *Possessions and the Poor in Luke–Acts* (Linz: Studien zum Neuen Testament und seiner Umwelt, 1983).

Segal, E., *Roman Laughter: The Comedy of Plautus* (New York: Oxford University Press, 1987).

Seim, T.K., *The Double Message: Patterns of Gender in Luke–Acts* (Studies of the New Testament and its World; Edinburgh: T. & T. Clark; Nashville: Abingdon, 1994).

—— 'The Gospel of Luke', in Schüssler Fiorenza (ed.), *Searching the Scriptures*, II, pp. 728–62.

Seland, T., *Establishment Violence in Philo and Luke: A Study of Non-Conformity to the Torah and Jewish Vigilante Reactions* (*BibInt* Series, 15; Leiden: Brill, 1995).
—— 'Once More—The Hellenists, Hebrews, and Stephen: Conflicts and Conflict Management in Acts 6–7', in P. Borgen, V.K. Robbins, and D.B. Gowler (eds.), *Recruitment, Conquest, and Conflict: Strategies in Judaism, Early Christianity and the Greco-Roman World* (ESEC, 6; Atlanta: Scholars Press, 1998), pp. 169–207.
Showalter, E., 'Critical Cross-Dressing: Male Feminists and the Woman of the Year', *Raritan* 2 (1983), pp. 130–49.
Shrein, S., *Quilting and Braiding: The Feminist Christologies of Sallie McFague and Elizabeth A. Johnson in Conversation* (Collegeville, MN: Liturgical Press, 1998).
Silko, L.M., *Ceremony* (New York: Penguin Books, 1977).
Seim, Turid Karlsen, *The Double Message: Patterns of Gender in Luke–Acts* (Edinburgh: T. & T. Clark, 1994).
—— 'The Gospel of Luke', in Schüssler Fiorenza (ed.), *Searching for The Scriptures,* II, pp. 728–62.
Sim, D., 'The Women Followers of Jesus: The Implications of Luke 8.1–3', *Heythrop Journal* 30 (1989).
Skinner, M., *Locating Paul: Places of Custody as Narrative Settings in Acts 21–28* (SBL Academia Biblica, 13; Atlanta: Society of Biblical Literature; Leiden: Brill Academic Publishers, 2003).
Sly, D., *Philo's Perception of Women* (BJS, 209; Atlanta: Scholars Press, 1990).
Snitow, A., 'A Gender Diary', in Hirsch and Keller (eds.), *Conflicts in Feminism*, pp. 9–43.
Spencer, F.S., *Acts* (Readings: A New Biblical Commentary; Sheffield: Sheffield Academic Press, 1997).
—— 'The Ethiopian Eunuch and his Bible: A Social-Science Analysis', *BTB* 22 (1992), pp. 156–58.
—— 'Neglected Widows in Acts 6.1–7', *CBQ* 56 (1994), pp. 715–33.
—— 'Out of Mind, Out of Voice: Slave-Girls and Prophetic Daughters in Luke–Acts', *BibInt* 7 (1999), pp. 132–53.
—— *The Portrait of Philip in Acts: A Study of Roles and Relations* (JSNTSup, 67; Sheffield: Sheffield Academic Press, 1992).
Stadter, P.A., '*Philosophos kai Philandros*: Plutarch's View of Women in the *Moralia* and the *Lives*', in S.B. Pomeroy (ed.), *Plutarch's Advice*, pp. 173–82.
Stählin, G., 'χήρα', *TDNT*, IX, pp. 440–65.
Staley, J.L., 'Changing Woman: Postcolonial Reflections on Acts 16.6–40', *JSNT* 73 (1999), pp. 113–35.
Stanton, E.C., *The Woman's Bible* (Salem, NH: The Ayer Company; repr. edn; New York: European Publishing Company, 1988).
Staples, A., *From Good Goddesses to Vestal Virgins: Sex and Category in Roman Religion* (London: Routledge, 1998).
Stegemann, W., *Zwischen Synagoge und Obrigkeit: Zur historischen Situation der lukanischen Christen* (FRLANT, 152; Göttingen: Vandenhoeck & Ruprecht, 1991).

Stern, M., *Greek and Latin Authors on Jews and Judaism* (3 vols.; Jerusalem: Academy of Sciences and Humanities, 1974–84).

Stolcke, V., 'Invaded Women: Gender, Race, and Class in the Formation of Colonial Society', in M. Hendricks and P. Parker (eds.), *Women, 'Race' and Writing in the Early Modern Period* (London: Routledge, 1994), pp. 272–89.

Strabo, *Geography* (trans. H. Jones; LCL; Cambridge, MA: Harvard University Press, 1941–55).

Swain, S., *Hellenism and Empire: Language, Classicism, and Power in the Greek World, AD 50–250* (Oxford: Clarendon Press, 1996).

Swidler, L., *Biblical Affirmations of Woman* (Philadelphia: Westminster Press, 1979).

Talbert, C.H., *Reading Acts: A Literary and Theological Commentary on the Acts of the Apostles* (New York: Crossroad Publishing Company, 1997).

Tannehill, R.C., ' "Cornelius" and "Tabitha" Encounter Luke's Jesus', *Int* 48 (1994), pp. 347–56.

—— *The Narrative Unity of Luke–Acts: A Literary Interpretation* (2 vols.; Minneapolis: Fortress Press, 1990).

Taylor, N.H., 'Stephen, the Temple, and Early Christian Eschatology', *RB* 110 (2003), pp. 62–85.

Thesleff, H. (ed.), *The Pythagorean Texts of the Hellenistic Period* (Åbo, Finland: Åbo Akademi, 1965).

Thurman, E., 'Paul, Luke's Action-Figure: Reading Colonial Subjectivity in the Acts of the Apostles (unpublished paper, Drew University, 2001).

Thurston, B.B., *The Widows: A Women's Ministry in the Early Church* (Minneapolis: Fortress Press, 1989).

Tolbert, M.A., 'The Politics and Poetics of Location', in F.F. Segovia and M.A. Tolbert (eds.), *Reading from this Place: Social Location and Biblical Interpretation in the United States* (Minneapolis: Fortress Press, 1995), pp. 305–17.

—— 'Protestant Feminists and the Bible: On the Horns of a Dilemma', in A. Bach (ed.), *The Pleasure of her Text: Feminist Readings of Biblical and Historical Texts* (Philadelphia: Trinity Press International, 1990), pp. 5–23.

Torjesen, K.J., *When Women Were Priests: Women's Leadership in the Early Church and the Scandal of their Subordination in the Rise of Christianity* (San Francisco: HarperSanFrancisco, 1993).

Townsend, J., 'Missionary Journeys in Acts and European Missionary Societies', SBLSP 24 (1985), pp. 433–37.

Trebilco, P.R., 'Paul and Silas—"Servants of the Most High God" (Acts 16.16–18)', *JSNT* 36 (1989), pp. 51–73.

Tyson, J.B., 'Acts 6.1–7 and Dietary Regulations in Early Christianity', *Perspectives in Religious Studies* 10.2 (1983), pp. 145–61.

—— 'The Emerging Church and the Problem of Authority in Acts', *Int* 42 (1988), pp. 132–45.

—— 'The Problem of Food in Acts: A Study of the Literary Patterns with Particular Reference to Acts 6.1-7', in P.J. Achtemeier (ed.), *Society of Biblical*

Literature 1979 Seminar Papers (Missoula, MT: Scholars Press, 1979), pp. 69–85.

Vander Stichele, C., 'Gender and Genre: Acts in/of Interpretation', in T. Penner and C. Vander Stichele (eds.), *Contextualizing Acts,* pp. 311–29.

Versnel, H.S., *Inconsistencies in Greek and Roman Religion* (Studies in Greek and Roman Religion, 6; Leiden: Brill, 1990).

Walcot, P., 'On Widows and their Reputation in Antiquity', *Symbola Osloenses* 66 (1991), pp. 5–26.

Wallace-Hadrill, A., 'Ethics and Trade in the Roman Town', in J. Rich and A. Wallace-Hadrill (eds.), *City and Country in the Ancient World* (London: Routledge, 1991), pp. 241–69.

Wan, S.-K.,'Charismatic Exegesis: Philo and Paul Compared', *Studia Philonica* 6 (1994), pp. 54–82.

Wardman, A., *Religion and Statecraft among the Romans* (Baltimore, MD: Johns Hopkins University Press, 1982).

Washington, M.H., 'Introduction to *A Voice from the South* by Anna Julia Cooper', in Gates (ed.), *Spiritual Narratives,* pp. xxvii–liv.

Weems, R.J., 'Reading *Her Way* through the Struggle: African American Women and the Bible', in Felder (ed.), *Stony the Road We Trod,* pp. 57–80.

Wegner, J.R., *Chattel or Person? The Status of Women in the Mishnah* (New York: Oxford University Press, 1988).

Weinreich, O., 'Gebet und Wunder', in Friedrich Focke, *et al.* (eds.), *Genethliakon: Wilhelm Schmid zum siebzigstend Geburstag* (Tübingen Beiträge zur Altertumswissenschaft, 5; Stuttgart: Kohlhammer, 1929), pp. 200–462.

Whedbee, J.W., *The Bible and The Comic Vision* (Cambridge: Cambridge University Press, 1998).

Whitmarsh, T., ' "Greece is the World": Exile and Identity in the Second Sophistic', in S. Goldhill (ed.), *Being Greek under Rome, Cultural Identity, the Second Sophistic and the Developement of Empire* (Cambridge: Cambridge University Press, 2001), pp. 269–305.

Wicker, K.O., '*Mulierum Virtutes* (*Moralia* 242E–263C)', in H.D. Betz (ed.), *Plutarch's Ethical Writings and Early Christian Literatures* (Leiden: Brill, 1978), pp. 106–34.

Wilken, R., *The Christians as the Romans Saw Them* (New Haven, CT: Yale University Press, 1984).

Willard, F.E., and M. Livermore, *A Woman of the Century* (Detroit: Gale Research, repr., 1967).

Williams, C.A., *Roman Sexuality: Ideologies of Masculinity in Classical Antiquity* (New York: Oxford University Press, 1999).

Wills, L., *The Jewish Novel in the Ancient World* (Myth and Poetics; Ithaca, NY: Cornell University Press, 1995).

Wimbush, V.L., 'Reading Texts through Worlds, Worlds through Texts', *Semeia* 62 (1993), pp. 129–39.

Wink, W., *Naming the Powers: The Language of Power in the New Testament* (Philadelphia: Fortress Press, 1984).

Winkler, J.J., *The Constraints of Desire*: *The Anthropology of Sex and Gender in Ancient Greece* (New Ancient World; New York: Routledge, 1990).

Winter, S.C., 'Παρρησία in Acts', in J. Fitzgerald (ed.), *Friendship, Flattery, and Frankness of Speech: Studies on Friendship in the New Testament World* (NovTSup, 82; Leiden: Brill, 1996), pp. 185–202.

Witherington, Ben, III, *The Acts of the Apostles: A Socio-Rhetorical Commentary* (Grand Rapids, MI: Eerdmans; Carlisle: Paternoster, 1998).

—— 'On the Road with Mary Magdalen, Joanna, Susanna, and Other Disciples—Luke 8.1–3', *ZNW* 70 (1979), pp. 243–48, repr. in A.-J. Levine (ed.) *A Feminist Companion to Luke*, pp. 133–39.

Wright, A.G., 'The Widow's Mites: Praise or Lament? A Matter of Context', *CBQ* 44 (1982), pp. 256–65.

Zagagi, N., *The Comedy of Menander: Convention, Variation and Originality* (Bloomington: Indiana University Press, 1995).

Zeitlin, F.I., 'Cultic Models of the Female: Rites of Dionysos and Demeter', *Arethusa* 15 (1982), pp. 129–57.

—— 'The Dynamics of Misogyny: Myth and Mythmaking in the *Oresteia*', *Arethusa* 11.2 (1978), pp. 149–83.

INDEX OF REFERENCES

BIBLE

OLD TESTAMENT

Genesis
3.7	140
3.16–19	140
3.21	140

Exodus
15.20	75
32.18	100
35–40	140–1, 141
35.23–26	151
36.8	141

Numbers
18	163
27.8	84

Deuteronomy
23.1	57
25.5	80

Joshua
2.18, 21	188

Judges
4–5	75

2 Samuel
3.29	134

1 Kings
18.17–24	27

2 Kings
4.32–37	27
22.14	75
23.7	141

2 Chronicles
34.22	75

Proverbs
31	141, 144, 147

Isaiah
32.15–17	69
56.3–5	57

Joel
2.28	36, 63
3	49

APOCRYPHA

Tobit
1.16	142
2.11–14	141–2
3.1–6	142

NEW TESTAMENT

Matthew
6.21b	89
9.18–26	25, 27
15	186
22.23–33	79
28.18–20	62

Index of References

Mark
5.21–43	25, 27
7.24–30	186, 188
12.18–27	79
15.43	16, 157

Luke
1.8	202
1.38	102
2.36–38	73, 74–6
3.8	202
3.11	145
4.25–26	73, 76, 82
5.36	142
7.11–17	76–7, 82
7.22	202
7.36–50	168
8	17
8.1–3	12, 17137, 155, 159, 162, 167–9, 170, 172, 173–4
8.40–46	25, 27, 81
9.28–36	75
10.38–42	84, 96–7, 137, 172, 202
11.9–13	79
12.27–28, 32	142–3
15.8–10	84
16.3–4	99
16.13	161–2
16.19–31	150
18.1–8	8, 73, 77–9, 82
18.1–15	95
18.4–5	99
19.1–9	162
19.11	202
20.27–40	74, 79–80, 82
20.45–47	73, 81, 82
21.1–4	8, 73, 81–2
22.26–27	82
22.56	97
23.53	102
24	11
24.41	91

John
4	186
12.20–23	188
18.22	102

Acts
1	52
1–7	177
1.4	62–3
1.6	62
1.8	62, 63, 66, 177
1.12–14	63–4
1.13–15	63
1.15–26	135
2	38
2.1–8.25	179
2.1–13	185
2.2	64
2.4	63
2.5	166
2.16–21	36–7, 75
2.21	63
2.24	102, 196
2.41	66
2.45	83
3.22–23	75
4.4	66
4.32–37	83, 163
4.32–5.11	71
5.1–12	58, 172, 196
5.12–42	71
5.38–39	89
5.40–1	195
6	8, 9, 52
6.1	43
6.1–6	27, 71, 73, 82–6, 145
6.4	43, 44, 145
6.5	9
6.7	66
6.8–15	206
6.12–15	66
7	7
7.37	75
7.51–53	197
8	50
8–12	177
8.1–3	7, 66, 195
8.6–13	71
8.14–25	71
8.26–40	38, 125, 179
9.1	57, 195
9.1–28.31	179

9.31–43	28	17.4	16, 125, 147, 155–8, 161, 169, 172
9.32–3	43		
9.32–35	26	17.5	199
9.35	43	17.12	16, 125, 147, 155–8, 161, 169, 172
9.36	30, 43, 143		
9.36–42	22–48, 73, 86–7, 144–5, 172	17.28–29	138
		17.33	125
9.39	30, 36, 143	18.1–4, 18–28	150–3
10	15, 38	18.1–8	152, 172
10.1–48	125, 145	18.3	84
10.34	37, 38	18.23–28	185
10.36	204	19.6–7	75, 197
11.3	127	19.11–20	71
11.15	205	19.23–25	199
11.25	163	20.7–12	25, 27
11.27–30	75	20.18–38	58
12	10, 11, 102–3	21.9	49, 75, 128
12.6–17	89–97, 155	21.10–14	75
12.12–17	16, 17, 162–4, 165, 166, 169–70, 172	21.14	59
12.14	91–3	23.2–4	102
12.20–23	196	23.12, 20–21	201
13–28	178	23.29–30	201
13.1	75	24.17	145
13.4–12	204	24.24	172
13.6	75	25.1–12	7, 66
13.7–12	125	25.13, 23	172
13.10	204	26	7
13.11	204	26.14	106
13.50	16, 17, 147, 156–7, 158, 199	28.3–6	96
14.19	199	28.7	16, 156
14.22	195	28.16	201
15.32	75	28.28–31	137, 202
15.36–18.22	183		
16	12, 20, 21, 174	*Romans*	
16.6–40	177–92	16.1	36
16.9	179	16.7	45
16.10–17	184		
16.11–40	111–33	*1 Corinthians*	
16.13–15	70, 84, 105–10, 146, 147, 148–9, 172, 205, 206	7.8, 25–40	73
		16.15	131
16.14	124–5, 150	*Galatians*	
16.16–18	184, 205, 206	1.11–12	103
16.19–40	111–12, 146, 206	3.27–28	150
16.31	110		
17	17	*Philippians*	
		4.2–3	14, 131

Colossians		2.21	117
4.10	163, 169	2.35–37	115, 117
1 Thessalonians		Dio Chrysostom	
2.9	153	*Discourses*	
		18.6.7	113
1 Timothy			
5.3–16	27, 73, 74	*Homilies on the Acts of the Apostles*	
5.9–10	30, 74	29–30	
5.16	9, 42, 86		
		Homiles on the Epistles of Paul to the Corinthians	
Revelation			
2.20–23	111, 133	29.2	130
3.20	187		
18.7	73	Dionysius of Halicarnassus	
		Roman Antiquities	
ANCIENT AND CLASSICAL REFERENCES		4.29	54
		8.51	54–5
Aristophanes		Epictetus	
Horae	115	*Discourse 3*	
		1.27–35	203
Lysistrata	121	22.38–49	58
Athenaeus		Euripides	
Deipnosophists		*Bacchae*	12–14, 105–10, 111–15, 116
5.20d	110		
5.197e	109	215–25	114–15
5.198c	109–10	256–57	105
		498	113
Augustus		794–95	106
Res Gestae	204		
		Melanippe Captive	121–2
Basil			
Morals		Eusebius	
73	30	*Historia ecclesiastica*	
74	30	3.31	50, 128, 133
75	30		
		Herodotus	
Chaereas and Callirhoe		*Histories*	
1.1	156	4.45.1–5	178–9
1.2	55		
2.4, 5	156	Homer	
2.11	156	*Homeric Hymn 7*	109
Cicero	13	*Iliad*	
De legibus	117–18	63.312–65	121

Odyssey	12, 98–104	10.96.8	132
1.409–14	139		
1.415–16	139	Plutarch	
2.127–30	139	*Conjugalia praecepta*	
		140D	120
Josephus			
Antiquities of the Jews		*Crassus*	
18	13, 111	33.1–4	113
20	114		
		De defectu oraculorum	
Livy	13, 115	414E	129
History of Rome			
26.9.7–8	122	*De Iside de Osiride*	
		364E	120
Lucian			
The Eunuch		*Moralia*	
6	57	309C	157
The Ignorant Book Collector		*Mulierum virtutes*	14, 119–20
19	113	249E–F	120
Origen	19	*Pericles*	
Contra Celsum		1.3–4	148
2.34	113		
3.25	129–30	*Quaestionum convivialum*	120–1
7.3–7	129–30		
		Seneca	
Homily on Luke		*Epistle*	
12	183–4	114.2–3	202
Ovid		*On Providence*	
Metamorphoses		5.4–7	58
6	139–40		
		Strabo	
Philo		*Geography*	
De specialibus legibus		13.3	156
3.169	123		
3.171	123	Suetonius	
3.172–77	123	*Claudius*	
		1	184
De vita contemplativa	13–14, 118–19		
83–85	118	*Julius Caesar*	
88	118	32	184
Pliny the Younger		Tacitus	13
Letters		*Annals*	
4.19.2–4	84	11.31.2	115

Virgil
Aeneid
2.501–15   122
11.477–87   122

INDEX OF AUTHORS

Abrahamsen, V. 131
Addams, J. 33
Alcoff 46
Alexander, L. 185, 203, 206
Allen, O.W. 196
Alter, R. 179–80, 186
Amandry, P. 129
Anderson, G. 200, 201
Anderson, J.C. 2–4, 9, 15, 22–48, 180
Andrews, W. 38
Archer, L.J. 122
Arlandson 5, 10, 16-17, 52, 72, 93–4, 144, 155-70, 160, 162, 163, 165, 168, 171, 172, 173, 174
Ascough, R.S. 185, 196
Atwood, R. 85
Babrick, E. 94
Baker-Fletcher, K. 36, 45
Bal, M. 24
Balch, D.L. 54, 84, 118, 122
Barber, E.W. 135
Barrett, C.K. 93
Bassler, J.M. 86
Bauernfeind, O. 129
Benediktsson, T.E. 182
Benjamin, D.C. 77
Bettelheim, B. 11, 101
Beyer, H.W. 82
Bhabha, H.K. 187
Birch, B.C. 134
Bird, P.A. 135, 141
Blue, B. 146
Bobrick, E. 94
Boer, R. 187
Bonz, M.P. 124, 131
Boor, W. de 129

Bovon, F. 128, 193, 194
Bremen, R. van 122
Brent, A. 204
Brice, J. 182
Brock, A.G. 207
Brodie, T.L. 99
Brooten, B. 40, 45, 85, 112, 149, 152
Broughton, T.R.S. 163, 167
Broughton, V.W. 36
Brown, R.E. 75
Brown, R.M. 197
Bruce, F.F. 150, 185
Burrus, V. 17–18, 171–6
Callaghan, D. 180
Calvin, J. 31–2, 35, 45, 48
Cameron, R. 193
Camp, C.V. 141
Carter, W. 84
Cassidy, R.J. 185
Chambers, K. 9–11, 89–97
Charitonides, S. 166
Clarke, A.D. 138
Collins, J.N. 82
Collins, M.S. 85
Collins, P.H. 47
Connolly, J. 202
Connolly, R.H. 76
Conzelmann, H. 26, 27, 178, 185, 188
Cook, A.B. 130
Cooper, A.J. 33, 34, 36
Cooper, K. 122, 172, 173
Corley, K.E. 84, 122, 127
Cotter, W. 77
Cross, F.L. 29, 30
Crossan, J.D. 184
Cunningham, S. 195

Index of Authors

Daly, M. 136
D'Angelo, M.R. 5, 20, 39, 42–3, 46–7, 51, 52, 72, 74, 75–6, 77, 128, 145, 146, 186, 198, 205
Dareste, R. 165
D'Arms, J.H. 124
Darr, J. 138
Davies, S.L. 87
deBoer, E.A. 17
Desjardins, M. 195, 197
Dewey, J. 86
Dibelius, M. 26, 28
Dodds, E.R. 106, 115
Donovan, J. 33
Douglass, J.D. 32
Drinnon, R. 182
Dube Shomanah, M.W. 174–5, 177, 179–80, 186, 189, 191
DuBois, E.C. 33
Dunn, J. 90, 93, 178, 187
Easterling, P.E. 113
Edwards, C. 201
Eisen, U. 87
Elaw, Z. 36
Elliott, J.H. 145
Esler, P. 72, 127
Fant, M.B. 156, 159, 166, 168
Fauth, W. 129
Feldherr, A. 195
Fetterley, J. 2, 23
Fewell, D.N. 137
Fiensy, D. 163
Fischler, S. 205
Fitzmyer, J.A. 72, 75, 79, 80, 143
Foley, H.P. 116, 121, 139
Fontaine, C.R. 141
Foote 48
Foote, J.A.J. 36–9, 46, 48
Fowler, R.M. 22
Frilingos, C. 203
Frost, K.B. 92
Fulkerson, M.M. 23
Fuller, M. 33
Fuss, D. 23
Garrett, S. 204
Gaventa, B.R. 4–6, 8, 9, 16, 49–60
Georgi, D. 129

Gifford, C.D. 45
Gilbert, G. 203
Gill, D.W.J. 125, 148
Gillman, F.M. 147
Gillman, J. 72, 149, 150
Gilman, C.P. 33
Gilmore, D.D. 134
Glancy, J.A. 90, 125, 128
Gleason, M. 198
Gold, B.K. 116
Grant, R.M. 29
Greenfield, J. 164, 166, 168
Greeven, H. 93, 157
Grimke, S. 33
Gunderson, E. 202
Gunn, D.M. 137
Haenchen, E. 26, 27, 90–1, 163, 183
Hallett, J.P. 134, 135
Hands, A.R. 157, 159
Harill, J.A. 10, 91–2, 98
Harnack, A. von 4, 5
Harnack, A. von 50
Haussoulier, B. 165
Hay, D.M. 118
Hedges, E. 135, 136, 137–8
Hemer, C.J. 147
Henderson, J. 121
Hengel, M. 107, 178
Hennecke, E. 131
Henrichs, A. 114, 115, 117, 120
Henry, M. 32–3, 146
Hock, R.F. 151, 152, 153
hooks, b. 22, 25
Horsley, G.H.R. 125
Hutcheon, L. 177
Ilan, T. 142
Jackson, F.J. Foakes 42
Jervell, J. 26, 72, 207
Johnson, E.A. 136, 154, 184
Johnson, L.T. 72, 178, 197
Johnson, S.E. 26
Jones, A.R. 140
Joshel, S.R. 115, 198
Kahl, B. 137, 143
Kanyoro, M. 6–7, 9, 21, 61–70
Kee, H.C. 178, 185, 187
Kidwell, C.S. 183

Kittredge, C. 131
Kitzberger, I.R. 189
Klauck, H.-J. 200, 204, 206
Knox, J. 102
Koenig, J. 149
Koester, H. 131
Konstan, D. 90
Kraemer, R.S. 87, 114, 115, 118, 121, 141
Krueger, C. 36
Kuefler, M. 56
Kümmel, W.G. 50
La Farge, O. 19, 177–92
Lake, K. 42
Lane, B.C. 180
Lauretis, T. de 46
LaVerdiere, E. 72, 81
Lee, J. 36
Lefkowitz, M.R. 156, 159, 166, 168
Lentz, J.C. 57, 208
Lerner 138
Lerner, G. 45, 138
Levine, A.-J. 1–21
Lewis, N. 164, 166, 168
Livermorem, M. 34
Livingstone, E.A. 29, 30
MacDonald, D.R. 11, 12–13, 105–10
MacDonald, M.Y. 173
Malbon, E.S. 22, 23, 81
Maldonaldo, R. 179
Malherbe, A.J. 101, 129, 132
Malina, B.J. 148
Manley, K. 190
Marguerat, D. 196
Marshall, I.H. 138
Martin, C.J. 38, 82, 145, 171, 174, 193, 196, 205
Matthews, S. 13–14, 60, 85, 111–33, 199, 205, 206
McCarter, P.K. 134
McCreesh, T.P. 141
McNickle, D. 182
McRay, J. 89
Meeks, W.A. 125, 147, 158
Meiselman, M. 85
Mendels, D. 207
Metzger, B.M. 151

Meyers, C. 135
Michaelis, W. 156
Michel, O. 167
Miller, N.K. 136, 137
Moessner, D.P. 194
Mohanty, C.T. 22
Moore, C.A. 142
Moore, S.D. 201
Mount, C. 131
Moxnes, H. 186–7
Munck, J. 26, 28
Murphy-O'Connor, J. 150, 151, 152
Nestle, W. 106, 112
Newsom, C.A. 6
Neyrey, J. 72, 122, 152, 185, 186
Nicolet, C. 204
Norris, F.W. 30
O'Day, G.R. 5, 39, 40, 43–4, 46–7, 94, 143, 145, 174, 175, 205
Offen, K. 33
Okland, J. 199
Omerzu, H. 194
Osiek, C. 84, 87, 122
Ostriker, A.S. 23, 24
Pack, R.A. 113
Packer, J.W. 26
Page, D.L. 122
Pallas, D.I. 166
Parsons, M.C. 26, 138, 200
Parvey, C. 39, 40–1, 46, 47
Penner, T.C. 20–1, 193–209
Pervo, R.I. 9, 26, 28, 91, 96, 97, 99, 101–2, 112, 113–14, 126, 129, 138, 178, 195, 196
Peskowitz, M.B. 122, 138, 139
Plaskow, J. 40
Pleket, H.W. 125, 156, 157, 158, 159, 166, 167, 168
Plümacher, E. 54
Polhill, J.B. 71
Pomeroy, S.B. 120
Portefaix, L. 112, 113, 148
Prader, S. 183
Price, R.M. 5, 11–12, 52, 87, 98–104, 174, 175, 187
Rackham, R.B. 178, 183, 184
Räisänen, H. 195

Ramsay, W.M. 156, 187
Rand, N.R. 191
Rapske, B. 194
Redalie, Y. 126
Reid, B.E. 2, 7–9, 71–88, 150
Reimer, I.R. 5, 51–2, 83, 84, 86, 90, 93, 112, 124, 125, 128, 129, 132, 143, 146, 147, 148, 152, 156, 158, 196, 206
Reinach, T. 165
Rich, A. 136
Richlin, A. 202
Ringe, S.H. 6
Robert, L. 166
Robertson, K. 189
Rohrbaugh, R.L. 124
Rutherford, W.G. 157
Ryan, R. 148
Salyer, G. 180
Sandbach, F.H. 95
Sanders, E.P. 163
Sanders, J.T. 125
Sangster, M.E. 34–6, 40–1, 44, 46
Sawhney, S. 180
Sawicki, M. 199
Sawyer, D.F. 122
Schaberg, J. 5, 53, 72, 171, 172, 174
Schille, G. 127
Schneider, G. 26, 28
Schottroff, L. 124, 125, 132, 135, 147, 148, 149, 151, 152, 205
Schüssler Fiorenza, E. 5, 6, 24, 42–3, 47, 51, 52, 83, 84, 132, 133, 136, 137, 143, 161, 168
Schwartz, S. 201
Schweickart, P.P. 23, 24, 39
Schwöbel, C. 31
Scott, J. 179
Seim, T.K. 1, 5, 52, 74, 83, 128, 133, 143, 152, 171, 173, 174, 175, 196, 199, 202, 206
Seland, T. 194
Shein, S. 136
Showalter, E. 23
Shroer, S. 135
Silko, L.M. 19-20, 177–92
Sim, D. 168
Skinner, M. 58
Sly, D. 123
Snitow, A. 46
Spencer, F.S. 5, 14–16, 46, 49, 52, 60, 85, 90, 94, 134–54, 205
St. Andrews, B.A. 191
Stadter, P.A. 120
Stählin, G. 27–8, 42
Staley, J.L. 18–20, 177–92
Stanton, E.C. 33, 34, 44, 47
Staples, A. 122
Stern, M. 113
Stolcke, V. 188
Stowe, H.B. 138
Swain, S. 200
Swidler, L. 42
Talbert, C.H. 94, 178, 184, 185
Tannehill, R.C. 26, 28, 93, 127, 128, 143, 145, 184
Taylor, N.H. 194
Thesleff, H. 123
Thurman, E. 175
Thurston, B.B. 39, 41–2, 47, 72, 87
Tolbert, M.A. 23, 24, 180
Torjesen, K.J. 17–18, 122–3, 147, 171–6
Townsend, J. 179, 183
Trebilco, P.R. 129, 187
Truth, S. 33
Tyson, J.B. 71, 85
Vander Stichele, C. 20–1, 193–209
Versnel, H.S. 116
Wacjer, M.-T. 135
Wallace-Hadrill, A. 124
Wan, S.-K. 119
Wardman, A. 122
Washington, M.H. 33
Weems, R.J. 23, 24, 37
Wegner, J.R. 165
Weinreich, O. 111–12, 113
Whitmarsh, T. 27, 200, 207
Wicker, K.O. 120
Wilkin, R. 113
Willard, F.E. 34
Williams, C.A. 201
Williams, K. 187
Wills, L. 114

Wimbush, V.L. 38
Wink, W. 19, 183-4
Winkler, J. 56
Winter, B.W. 138
Winter, S.C. 202-3
Witherington III, B. 85, 147
Wright, A.G. 81
Wright, F. 33
Yadin, Y. 164, 166, 168
Zagagi, N. 93, 95
Zeitlin, F.I. 116, 121
Zell, K. 36